China and the Great War

China's role in the First World War has been a curiously neglected topic. This book is the first full-length study of China's involvement in the conflict from perspectives of international history, using largely unknown archival materials from China, France, Germany, the UK, and the USA. It explains why China wanted to join the war and what were its contributions to the war effort and the emerging world order in the postwar period. The book also demonstrates that China's participation in the First World War was not only a defining moment in modern Chinese and world history, but also the beginning of China's long journey toward internationalization.

In this groundbreaking and provocative book, Professor Xu adds a new dimension to our collective memory of the war, its tragedy and its significance, and restores the China war memory to its rightful place.

XU GUOQI is Wen Chao Chen Chair of History at Kalamazoo College. He is a leading scholar in the field of the international history of China, and is currently working on a study of sports and China's internationalization, 1896–2001. He has taught history in both China and the United States.

Studies in the Social and Cultural History of Modern Warfare

General Editor
Jay Winter *Yale University*

Advisory Editors
Omer Bartov *Brown University*
Carol Gluck *Columbia University*
David M. Kennedy *Stanford University*
Paul Kennedy *Yale University*
Antoine Prost *Université de Paris-Sorbonne*
Emmanuel Sivan *Hebrew University of Jerusalem*
Robert Wohl *University of California, Los Angeles*

In recent years the field of modern history has been enriched by the exploration of two parallel histories. These are the social and cultural history of armed conflict, and the impact of military events on social and cultural history.

Studies in the Social and Cultural History of Modern Warfare presents the fruits of this growing area of research, reflecting both the colonization of military history by cultural historians and the reciprocal interest of military historians in social and cultural history, to the benefit of both. The series offers the latest scholarship in European and non-European events from the 1850s to the present day.

For a list of titles in the series, please see end of book.

China and the Great War

*China's pursuit of a new national identity
and internationalization*

Xu Guoqi

CAMBRIDGE
UNIVERSITY PRESS

CAMBRIDGE UNIVERSITY PRESS
Cambridge, New York, Melbourne, Madrid, Cape Town, Singapore, São Paulo

Cambridge University Press
The Edinburgh Building, Cambridge CB2 2RU, UK

Published in the United States of America by Cambridge University Press, New York

www.cambridge.org
Information on this title: www.cambridge.org/9780521842129

© Xu Guoqi 2005

First published 2005

Printed in the United Kingdom at the University Press, Cambridge

A catalogue record for this book is available from the British Library

Library of Congress Cataloguing in Publication data
Xu, Guoqi.
China and the Great War : China's pursuit of a new national identity and
internationalization / Xu Guoqi.
    p.   cm. – (Studies in the social and cultural history of modern warfare)
Includes bibliographical references and index.
ISBN 0-521-84212-3 (alk. paper)
1. China – Foreign relations – 20th century.   2. World War, 1914–1918 – China.
3. National characteristics, Chinese.   I. Title: China's pursuit of a new national identity
and internationalization.   II. Title.   III. Series.
DS775.8X784   2004
940.3'51 – dc22   2004054233

ISBN-13 978-0-521-84212-9 hardback
ISBN-10 0-521-84212-3 hardback

To my parents

Contents

Illustrations

Acknowledgments

My interest in the topic of China and the Great War started in the late 1980s when I was working with others on a book about the history of American foreign relations. I was intrigued by the sea changes in Chinese perceptions of Woodrow Wilson during the short period of the First World War. In the early 1990s when I came to Harvard University to pursue my doctoral degree, I decided to write a dissertation on the topic that had become my intellectual obsession by then. I was extremely fortunate to have Professor Akira Iriye as my academic advisor; he has provided generous and unfaltering support and encouragement through the years. I am also profoundly grateful to two other members of my dissertation committee, William C. Kirby and Ernest R. May. Like Iriye, they have shared their boundless knowledge and penetrating insights whenever I needed them and have provided much expert guidance and encouragement, as well as the example of their outstanding scholarship. Without these three mentors, this book would not have taken the shape it has.

I am indebted to many institutions for making this study possible. Harvard-Yenching Institute provided me with extremely generous funding for my graduate studies, and a grant from the Krupp Foundation greatly facilitated my over-six-month research stint in Germany. A research fellowship from Harvard University's Center for European Studies enabled me to stay in Paris and London for half a year to visit many different archives. The Charles Warren Center for Studies in American History at Harvard generously provided summer research funds that enabled me to use the National Archives in Washington, DC. A research grant from Harvard's Department of History helped me travel to Nanjing and spend a productive summer in the Second National Historical Archives of China. The Weatherhead Center for International affairs at Harvard appointed me a graduate fellow for several years, with an office where I shared, tested, and discussed my ideas with experts from different disciplines. The University of Toronto and York University Joint Centre for Asia Pacific Studies and the Center for Chinese Studies at the University of Michigan (Ann Arbor) both have provided accommodation as well as stimulating, vibrant, and nurturing academic settings when I worked on this study in different stages. My deep gratitude to Ernest P. Young, Martin Powers, Paul M. Evans, and B. Michael Frolic, all four of them directors of the above-mentioned centers, for their kindness in hosting me at their great institutions. A debt of gratitude also goes to Kalamazoo College, which has kindly provided me with generous financial support and granted me academic leave to work on this book.

Many people have helped me in this study. I am particularly indebted to the following individuals: to Yang Shengmao, professor at Nankai University and my lifetime mentor, for his efforts and determination to train me to be a fine historian; to Chen Sanjing and Zhang Li, both at the Institute of Modern History, Academia Sinica, Taipei, who went out of their way to make sure my stay at the institute's Archives was a pleasant experience; and to Calvin Hsu of the Asia Library at the University of Michigan, who has always been helpful whenever I need materials and other support. I also benefited from audience comments following my talks at Harvard University, Stanford University, and the University of Michigan, among others, and from the suggestions and criticisms from the audience and discussants in several conferences where I have presented my work. I would like to express my thanks in particular to the following people as well: to Yeh Wen-hsin for her suggestions and comments when both of us attended a Berlin conference on China's internationalization, to David Strauss and the anonymous reviewers who provided valuable advice on where and how to strengthen the text. I also owe thanks and a deep debt of gratitude to Professor Jay Winter for his confidence in this study and for his support to include this book in his series at Cambridge University Press, and to Elizabeth Howard, a dream editor any author would like to have, whose encouragement and suggestions have improved this work in production. I also would like to express my profound debt of gratitude to Terre Fisher, who has read many different drafts of the book and made comments, corrections, and suggestions that have improved it in both style and content. Without her sharp eyes and superb editing skills, the shape of the final text would have suffered. Thanks also to William Laurent, who has kindly offered his editorial expertise, and to Isabelle Dambricourt of Cambridge University Press, for her help in selecting a picture for the cover and for her thoroughness and speed.

Finally, I want to thank my family. My parents, although they were never able to go to school, understand the importance of what I am doing and have never complained as their elder son has traveled around the world to do research, but rarely has had time to write or visit them. To my wife, Ann, language cannot express properly my appreciation for all the years of love, encouragement, support, and sacrifice. Without her, this work would never have been completed. My children, Margaret, Julia, and Tom, each used his or her own way to sustain me throughout the long and sometimes frustrating process of book writing and provided much-needed inspiration. The patience, understanding, and much comic relief they have provided helped to bring this work to a timely completion. All the above-mentioned institutions and individuals have legitimate claims to any credit this book may win; I am, of course, solely responsible for its shortcomings.

Note on romanization

This book employs the *pinyin* system for the transliteration of Chinese names with the exceptions of names such as Confucius, Wellington Koo, Sun Yat-sen that are familiar in the West with their established spellings. In citing Western-language sources that use the older different spelling systems, however, references to persons and places have been left unchanged.

Introduction

> It was the best of times, it was the worst of times, it was the age of wisdom, it was the age of foolishness, it was the epoch of belief, it was the epoch of incredulity, it was the season of Light, it was the season of Darkness, it was the spring of hope, it was the winter of despair, we had everything before us, we had nothing before us, we were all going direct to Heaven, we were all going direct the other way.
>
> Charles Dickens[1]

Stanley Hoffmann recently noted that France had "two obsessions" for the whole of the twentieth century, namely, Germany and concern for its position in the world.[2] The Chinese, one might argue, have been obsessed with one thing and one thing only since the turn of the twentieth century: how to join the world community as an equal member. One could write Chinese history from many perspectives and approaches, but this single-minded passion is surely key to understanding modern China. This fixation on its status in the world has fundamentally defined China's perception of itself, the world, its foreign relations, and national identity.

We could further argue that the many revolutions and events in twentieth-century China were closely linked to and motivated by China's desire for integration into the world community (what I will call internationalization); in this sense, they can be seen as a natural extension of Voltaire's "century of revolutions."[3] On March 11, 1925, one day before he died, Sun Yat-sen, who has been lionized as a revolutionary pioneer by the Communists, signed his Political Testament, a short but influential document that summarizes his lifelong political actions and his instructions to followers of the Nationalist party. It reads,

---

[1] Charles Dickens, *A Tale of Two Cities* (Oxford: Oxford University Press, 1989), 1.

[2] Stanley Hoffmann, "France: Two Obsessions for One Century," in Robert A. Pastor, ed., *A Century's Journey: How the Great Powers Shape the World* (New York: Basic Books, 1999), 63–89.

[3] François-Marie Arouet (Voltaire) wrote on September 16, 1772 to Jean le Rond d'Alembert, "My dear philosopher, doesn't this appear to you to be the century of revolutions?" Cited from Keith Michael Baker, *Inventing the French Revolution* (Cambridge: Cambridge University Press, 1990), 203.

For forty years, I have devoted myself to the cause of national revolution, the objective of which is to restore to China its liberty and a rank equal [to that of the other nations]. The experience of those forty years has convinced me that if we wish to attain that objective, we must rouse the popular masses and unite with the peoples of the world that treat us on an equal footing, so as to pursue the common fight. Today, the revolution has not yet triumphed. May all our comrades . . . continue the struggle for this victory.[4]

For Sun, the revolution meant not only the overthrow of the Manchu dynasty or the Three Peoples' Principles; more fundamentally, it concerned China's status in the world. Sun's many political foes might disagree with him, but most of them shared a belief in the push to international recognition that underpinned his revolution. Accordingly, if we call the twentieth century "the Chinese century of revolution," the Chinese upheavals, like the French Revolution in 1789 and the Russian Revolution in 1917 – both focusing on domestic politics and exportation of the revolutionary experience to the world – addressed not only internal political contests, but also aimed to thrust China into the world as a new nation and into the family of nation-states.

Many seemingly isolated and non-political events in China today may be understood in light of this obsession with international prestige and Chinese national pride and historical frustrations. Nationwide responses to Beijing's bid to host the Olympics are a most recent case in point. For the Chinese, the Olympics are not simply a sports event, but represent something deep and fundamental. The Chinese see hosting the Olympics as a validation of their nation's long road to international acceptance, a sign that China has overcome its "century of humiliation and shame" and become a full member of the community of nations. It was exactly because of this deep feeling that many Chinese, especially urban youth and intellectuals, felt the West treated it as a third-rate country and had conspired to keep it from taking its rightful place on the world stage when in 1993 Beijing lost its first bid to Sydney for hosting the 2000 Summer Games. Accordingly, when Beijing was successful in its bid for the 2008 Summer Games, people all over China welcomed it as a giant step toward international recognition as an equal. They were overjoyed. The night of July 13, 2001 (the day the selection was announced) was, as a *People's Daily* editorial the next day called it, "a sleepless night for all 1.3 billion Chinese." According to *New York Times* reports the next day, many in Beijing celebrated the happy news with the national anthem,

---

[4] Marie-Claire Bergère, *Sun Yat-Sen*, trans. Janet Lloyd (Stanford: Stanford University Press, 1998), 406.

which revealingly begins, "Qilai, bu yao zuo nuli de renmen" (Rise up, you people who no longer want to be slaves).[5]

Chinese exuberance at hosting the Olympics clearly demonstrates the depth and significance of the Chinese passion for international status and asserting their national pride. But how did this clearly seminal concern take shape historically, and under what circumstances? Can these vital concerns be traced to or identified with a particular historical event that crystallized them in action? Although few scholars have addressed these questions, they are crucial for students of China and world history. I contend that this passion was first clearly articulated and acted upon during China's struggle to play a part in the First World War.

China's Great War: an unwritten chapter in world history

How was it that the First World War triggered Chinese interest in world affairs and compelled China to rethink its perception of itself and the world? This book will consider how the Great War became a defining moment, a turning point in shaping the Chinese worldview, and its further development. This essentially European war would affect the fate of China in many unexpected ways.

One might wonder, if the war was so important to China, why have historians failed to credit the China connection and largely ignored the topic of Chinese interest and participation in it?[6] Why does no book in any language consider Chinese participation in the First World War from the perspective of China's quest to establish its national identity and pursue increased international engagement? The neglect of the Chinese angle is even more obvious given the richness of studies of the First World War and its impact on other countries, in which the war is universally recognized as one of the most significant events in world history.[7] No wonder the Great War has continued to absorb scholars for decades. Historians have studied it from every possible perspective, covering its

---

[5] Craig S. Smith, "Joyous Vindication and a Sleepless Night," *The New York Times*, July 14, 2001.

[6] For existing Chinese studies on the First World War, see Huang Jiamu, "Zhongguo dui Ouzhan de chubu fanying," *Zhongyuan yanjiuyuan jindai shi yanjiusuo jikan* 1 (1969); Chen Sanjing, "Zhongguo pai bing canjia Ouzhan zhi jiaoshe," in *Zhonghua minguo lishi yu wenhua taolunji* (Taipei: 1984); Peng Xiangjin, "Dui Qirui tuidong Zhongguo canjia Ouzhan zhi yanjiu" (M.A. thesis, National Taiwan University, 1969); Huang Jinlin, "Lishi de yi shi xiju: Ouzhan zai Zhongguo," *Xin shi xue* 7, no. 3 (September 1996).

[7] For the most recent survey of the study of the war, see Michael Howard, "The Great War: Mystery or Error?" *The National interest* 64 (2001).

wider significance as well as particular themes and incidents. We can easily find fine works on broad issues such as the war's impact on American society,[8] and the generational issue and the war in Europe.[9] The period of the war symbolized, according to Henry May, the "end of innocence" in the United States[10] and the "end of an era" in Spain, according to a more recent study.[11] The fascination continues.

Given the rich scholarship on the First World War, it is surprising that China's participation passes with little or no notice. No book dealing with the war in general pays much attention to the China factor. For example, John Keegan, a prominent historian of military history, totally ignores China's interest in the war in his otherwise excellent book called simply *The First World War*.[12] Another book on the Great War by Niall Ferguson entitled *The Pity of War* mentions nothing about China, although an account of Chinese involvement would have provided poignant support for his major theme.[13] No wonder William C. Kirby points out that "[o]ne could read widely on the history of the First World War and never know that China took part in it."[14]

We have a legitimate reason to ask why such a gap exists. Where are the studies of Chinese popular responses to the war to counterbalance Robert Wohl's seminal *Generation of 1914*? Where are the systematic analyses of the impact of the war on Chinese society to match the brilliant study of American society by David Kennedy's *Over Here*? Where are the studies like Frederick Dickinson's work on World War I Japan?[15]

The current scholarship in this area leaves many key questions unanswered. Was this period, as is commonly supposed, simply a politically confused warlord era, in which China was too passive in its diplomacy and so got pushed around by other powers? What impact did the war have in China? Did China contribute to it? To what extent was the Chinese interest in world affairs piqued by the war? Finally, how did the war experience help shape China's national identity and push to internationalization? All these issues have yet to be explored through a close examination of Chinese engagement in the First World War.

---

[8] David Kennedy, *Over Here* (New York: Oxford University Press, 1980).

[9] Robert Wohl, *The Generation of 1914* (Cambridge, MA: Harvard University Press, 1979).

[10] Henry F. May, *The End of American Innocence: A Study of the First Years of Our Own Time, 1912–1917* (New York: Columbia University Press, 1992).

[11] Franciso J. Romero Salvado, *Spain 1914–1918: Between War and Revolution* (London: Routledge, 1999), 135–49.

[12] John Keegan, *The First World War* (New York: Alfred A. Knopf, Inc., 1999).

[13] Niall Ferguson, *The Pity of War* (London: The Penguin Group, 1999).

[14] William C. Kirby, "The Internationalization of China: Foreign Relations at Home and Abroad in the Republican Era," *The China Quarterly* 150, no. 2 (June 1997): 442.

[15] Frederick R. Dickinson, *War and National Reinvention: Japan in the Great War, 1914–1919* (Cambridge, MA: The Harvard East Asia Center, 1999).

To be sure, the early Republic of China was weak and its domestic politics chaotic. China had been marginalized in the international system and its internal political structure was unstable. But these facts still do not justify the conventional view that China was not capable of effective diplomacy or lacked the motivation to change its status. This assumption discounts the fact that while stronger powers commonly rely on non-diplomatic means, weaker ones pay special attention to diplomacy because that is perhaps the only way to promote or protect their national interests. Weakness rather than strength sometimes gives rise to a brilliant stroke of diplomacy. Charles Maurice de Talleyrand's France after Napoleon was defeated is an excellent example. Thanks to Talleyrand's skillful negotiations, the recently vanquished France not only kept its territory intact but, more importantly, was even allowed to join the ranks of top world powers.

Another conventional argument, that China really had nothing to do with the essentially European war, is simply not accurate. As a semicolonial country where many European nations such as Germany and Britain had carved out spheres of interest, China was bound to be dragged into the war one way or another. Therefore, it was better to take the initiative. With the First World War China abandoned its traditional isolationist foreign policy and initiated several attempts to get involved. Although China did not succeed in entering the war until August 1917, this response to world affairs reflected new thinking about the country's international role that had begun to emerge in the late nineteenth century.

China's performance during the war period might not have been politically impressive, but diplomatically it did rather well. Kirby was right when he wrote recently, "The story of Chinese diplomacy in the Republican era is one of stunning accomplishments from a position of unbelievable weakness." For Kirby, "The Qing fell, but the empire remained. More accurately, the empire became the basis of the Chinese national state. This was perhaps the greatest accomplishment of Republican diplomacy."[16] Arguably it was the early Republic of China that provided the foundation for this overall achievement. In its first years the Republican government initiated a series of impressive diplomatic actions aimed at protecting Chinese national sovereignty and for this it deserves due credit. But one cannot make full sense of Kirby's argument without appreciating China's new internationalist approach during the First World War era, an extremely important transition period across the entire global community.

---

[16] Kirby, "The Internationalization of China: Foreign Relations at Home and Abroad in the Republican Era," 437.

Although during much of the Great War period the Chinese people suffered from political chaos, economic weakness, and social misery, this was also a time of excitement, hope, high expectation, optimism, and new dreams. It may be compared to the Warring States era in ancient Chinese history and the revolutionary period in Charles Dickens's famous novel, *A Tale of Two Cities*. The clash of ideas, political theories, and the prescription of national identities provided high stimulation to China's ideological, social, cultural, and intellectual creativity and engendered a strong determination for change. New ideologies, explanations of history, and even reactions to developments in the Great War abounded and could be found in new print media across the country. The appearance of new political ideologies (nationalism rather than Confucianism; nation-state instead of culturalism), the return to China of Western-trained students, the activism of a new bourgeois class (rather than the old gentry and traditional mandarins), the emergence of a public sphere and modern print media, and above all, the changing international system itself all pushed China toward self-renewal. At no other time in modern Chinese history has the mobilization of public opinion and its social and intellectual resources played such a crucial role in shaping China's political, cultural, and social directions, at the same time fueling its search for a national identity. At no time previously had the Chinese shown such enormous interest in international affairs and initiated a new diplomacy aimed at renewing the state and preparing its entry onto the world stage. Unfortunately, all this excitement, vitality, and passion have gone missing in traditional treatments of China's foreign relations in the Great War period.

International history in the study of Chinese national identity

An international history perspective on China and the First World War may help us project new light on this subject. The methodology of international history as practiced by master historians Akira Iriye and Michael Hunt, among others, who have brought this relatively new sub-field to a level of excellence, seems more promising than the traditional approach.[17]

---

[17] See, for instance, Akira Iriye, *China and Japan in the Global Setting* (Cambridge, MA: Harvard University Press, 1992); Akira Iriye, *Global Community: The Role of International Organizations in the Making of the Contemporary World* (Berkeley: University of California Press, 2002); Michael Hunt, *Ideology and U.S. Foreign Policy* (New Haven: Yale University Press, 1987); Michael Hunt, *The Making of a Special Relationship: The United States and China to 1914* (New York: Columbia University Press, 1983); Akira Iriye, *Power and Culture: The Japanese–American War, 1941–1945* (Cambridge, MA: Harvard University Press, 1981).

Iriye points out that unlike traditional diplomatic history, international history tries to "go beyond the national level of analysis and to treat the entire world as a framework of study." Moreover, since international relations are essentially "interactions among cultural systems," the study of these extra-systematic relations must consider "the essential features within the given systems and see how they affect their interactions with one another."[18] To put it another way, international history is a methodology that focuses on macro-history, emphasizing culture and society in addition to traditional diplomatic history. It explores the relationship between an international power system and a particular cultural outlook, between nationalism and internationalism, between national ambitions and collective disappointments, and, to cite Iriye again, it examines international affairs "in terms of dreams, aspirations, and other manifestations of human consciousness."[19] This approach emphasizes communication within and among nations and seems a more reliable compass for reaching a new understanding of China's negotiation of two systems of world order: its own official worldview, focused on culture and morality, and the Western world order, primarily based on economic and military power.

Thus we can base our analysis of Chinese interest in the First World War on the neglected intellectual foundations of Chinese diplomacy and come to understand how China was affected by the world order as a whole, even as it contributed to defining that order. The international history approach will also highlight the connections between Chinese domestic politics and international affairs.

If a new methodology can enrich our assessment of China and its European war connection, the perspective of national identity and internationalization may open new vistas for us to consider. Su Dongpo, a famed poet of the eleventh century, once wrote "bushi Lushan zhen mian mu, zhi yuan shen zai ci shan zhong." Loosely put, one cannot appreciate the true face of Mt. Lu if he or she stays within the boundary of the mountain. In other words, we have to go beyond the subject in order to get at the truth. The problems of national identity and internationalization present an excellent angle from which to examine the place of China in the world of the early twentieth century. The desire for internal renewal and full membership in the world community is key to understanding the

---

[18] Akira Iriye, "Culture and Power: International Relations as Intercultural Relations," *Diplomatic History* 3, no. 3 (1979): 115. Akira Iriye, "The Internationalization of History," *American Historical Review* 94, no. 1 (1989): 4.

[19] Akira Iriye, "Culture and International History," in Michael J. Hogan and Thomas G. Paterson, eds., *Explaining the History of American Foreign Relations* (Cambridge: Cambridge University Press, 1991), 214–25.

nation's mood, its domestic and foreign policy, its approach to the world affairs, and its perception of itself. The passions aroused by concern with international status, the process of internationalization, and the creation of a new national identity meant that in the wake of humiliations and the fear of spreading colonization, Chinese were determined to forge ahead toward realization of their collective aspirations in the new century.

The idea of "national identity" is a relatively new one for historians, although sociologists and especially psychologists have used the word "identity" widely since the 1950s. Erik Erikson, a psychoanalyst, is perhaps most responsible for making the identity issue popular. He defined identity as "a subjective sense of an invigorating sameness and continuity."[20] Just as the general notion of personal identity is about who one is and how one defines oneself, national identity can mean how a country associates with other nations and the sense of its position in the world. As Anthony Smith points out, the process of "self-definition and location is in many ways the key to national identity."[21]

But like the identity issue in general, national identity is multidimensional, vague, and often difficult to pin down. Its precise content may differ from time to time and from region to region, and there is still no agreement among scholars on how best to define the term. Most students of the subject agree that national identity is, to a certain extent, a cultural identity, consisting of a shared tradition and history, as well as identification with the state.[22] Culture, tradition, and a nation's self-perception of its status in the world, among other things, are the fundamental features of national identity.[23] If a country has problems with these issues, it will certainly face a crisis.

With this working definition, we can observe that China after 1895 had extremely serious problems with its existing identity. Prior to the First World War, China had gone through a tremendous cultural upheaval and

---

[20] Erik Erikson, *Identity: Youth and Crisis* (New York: W. W. Norton & Company, 1968), 19.

[21] Anthony D. Smith, *National Identity* (Reno: University of Nevada Press, 1991), 17.

[22] About different definitions, see William Bloom, *Personal Identity, National Identity, and International Relations* (Cambridge: Cambridge University Press, 1990); Smith, *National Identity;* Lowell Dittmer and Samuel S. Kim, *China's Quest for National Identity* (Ithaca: Cornell University Press, 1993), 1–31, 237–40; Sidney Verba, "Sequences and Development," in Leonard Binder, ed., *Crises and Sequences in Political Development* (Princeton: Princeton University Press, 1971); Lucian Pye, "Identity and the Political Culture," in Leonard Binder, ed., *Crises and Sequences in Political Development* (Princeton: Princeton University Press, 1971), 110–11.

[23] Smith, *National Identity*, 14–16; Edward Friedman, *National Identity and Democratic Prospects in Socialist China* (Armonk, NY: M. E. Sharpe, 1995); G. Hoston, *The State, Identity, and the National Question in China and Japan* (Princeton: Princeton University Press, 1994); Peter Boerner, ed., *Concepts of National Identity: An Interdisciplinary Dialogue* (Baden-Baden: Nomos, 1986).

social transformation that had significantly changed and destabilized its political system as well as its understanding of itself and the world. The New China was determined to develop a new national identity, shake off its sorry recent past, and rethink its traditional view of the world order. It wanted to join the new international system, now dominated by the West, which was itself experiencing historic changes. Reflecting upon their country's status in the world after its defeat in the Sino-Japanese War in 1895, many Chinese began to seriously doubt the value of their traditional culture, history, language, and even civilization. China's foreign policy and thinking about the outside world also came under critical scrutiny. In many ways, the Chinese lost their sense of sameness and historical continuity with pre-1895 China. To understand the country after 1895, and especially its foreign relations, this identity crisis is key.

Sorting out a new national identity was crucial for several reasons. First, there were the painful humiliations and diplomatic isolation China had experienced in the late eighteenth and nineteenth centuries. The hope for a new China provided the impetus for a broad consideration of just what it meant to be Chinese and what China could become. Moreover, the desire for internationalization was closely linked to this internal renewal. From the perspective of international history, then, the concept of national identity can serve as a bridge linking China's internal and external orders.

The Great War in Chinese history

If national identity and internationalization are useful concepts for understanding China, the First World War seems to be a particularly appropriate time frame for examining the identity issue. China's social transformation and cultural revolution coincided with the war, and moreover, the First World War compelled China to associate with other countries whether it wished to or not. The war provided the momentum and opportunity for China to redefine its relations with the world through its efforts to inject itself into the war and thus position itself within the family of nations. Finally, the era of the First World War not only coincided with a period of tremendous change in China; it also came to stand for, as James Joll has noted, "the end of an age and beginning of the new one" in the international arena.[24] The war signaled the collapse of the existing international system and the coming of a new world order, an obvious development that fed the desires of the Chinese to change their country's international status. In consequence, the First World War was profoundly

---

[24] James Joll, *The Origins of the First World War* (London: Longman, 1984), 1.

significant in shaping Chinese society, politics, diplomacy, foreign relations, and popular perceptions about what it meant to be Chinese. If the First World War was a watershed event in China's search for national identity and efforts to enhance its position in the world, it also left a lasting legacy by shaping Chinese perceptions of the world order and the West. Chinese bitterness at the injustice of the postwar peace conference would be rekindled whenever China was wronged by the powers. The war and its aftermath, therefore, should be considered pivotal in shaping modern Chinese historical consciousness and national mooring.

China's very weakness and domestic political chaos proved strong motivations to enter and alter the international system. The implications of the 1911 Revolution also forced the Chinese to shift their attention to changes in the world system. The opening of the First World War was the first major world event to engage the imagination of the Chinese social and political elite, generating great fascination and excitement. Changes in the Chinese worldview and the destabilizing forces loosed by the war set the stage for China to play a role in world affairs, even though the war seemed to have no immediate impact on China itself. Using the war as a window on building national identity, I will go on to analyze China's internationalization in its wake; this will shed new light on Chinese diplomatic strategies and goals in the First World War.

In the course of examining how China used the occasion of the First World War to reinsert itself into the international system, I will also try to identify the roots of Chinese idealism or romanticism about the West, the origins of its new diplomacy, and the consequences of its quest to enter and alter the world system.

My focus is not on the war itself, but the war as a vehicle for China's regeneration, renewal, and transformation. I argue that because the Chinese were eager to move away from their old isolationist world outlook, the European war was considered an excellent opportunity for joining the emerging world order. In strong contrast to the conventional view that China was pulled into the war by outside forces, my view establishes that the Chinese leadership deliberately manipulated circumstances in its effort to join the war.

Unlike a traditional diplomatic history, this project includes the study of the mood, emotions, inspirations, ambitions, and frustrations of the Chinese people. When the war broke out in Europe, Chinese counterparts to Wohl's "generation of 1914" in Europe were clearly a new force in the struggling nation. They shared with the Europeans a sense of destiny and crisis and responsibility. Unlike the European generation, however, the Chinese elite were not "wanderers between two worlds"; they were determined to make a new China out of the old. They declared a cultural war against the hegemony of the "old" – old culture, old tradition, and old identity. They collectively behaved as the vanguard of cultural and political change and initiated a great transformation. For these Chinese, China was no "wasteland," but a land of experimentation, hope, and a new sense of self.

The tragedy and paradoxes of the war in China and the world

The story of the First World War is one of tragedy, paradoxes, and contradictions. John Keegan bluntly points out that "the First World War is a mystery. Its origins are mysterious. So is its course." The powers went to war in the name of national sovereignty, to defend national territory, and supposedly for principles. "Principle perhaps was at stake," Keegan writes, "but the principle of the sanctity of international treaty, which brought Britain into the war, scarcely merited the price eventually paid for its protection." For principle, "France fought at almost unbearable damage to its national well-being." Defense of the principles of the mutual security agreements, as Keegan demonstrates, "was pursued [by Germany and Russia] to a point where security lost all meaning in the dissolution of state structures. Simple state interest, Austria's impulse and the oldest of all reasons for war making, proved, as the pillars of imperialism collapsed about the Habsburgs, no interest at all."[25] Niall Ferguson goes even further, simply stating that the First World War was a terrible mistake. "The victors of the First World War had paid a price far in excess of the value of all their gains; a price so high, indeed, that they would very shortly find themselves quite unable to hold on to most of them."[26] In this sense, "it was something worse than a tragedy, which is something we are taught by the theatre to regard as ultimately unavoidable. It was nothing less than the greatest *error* of modern history [italics original]."[27]

Nor did the United States escape the war's paradoxes and contradictions. America joined the conflict in the name of fighting a "war to end all wars," a naive position that was to bitterly disappoint in light of the horrors of the battlefield and tragedy of the Second World War that followed. Although the American president Woodrow Wilson was a driving force behind the idea of a new world order and the League of Nations, in a twist of fate, the United States refused to join the League because Congress did not share Wilson's determination and vetoed the peace treaty.

---

[25] Keegan, *The First World War*, 426.   [26] Ferguson, *The Pity of War*, 436.
[27] Ibid., 462.

If the Great War generated paradoxes and contradictions among its main protagonists, China's engagement in it was no different. Chinese interest in the war developed out of a sense of victimization. Yet the very imperialist forces that had humiliated and oppressed China also served as inspiration. The Chinese sought to defeat imperialism by adopting the imperialists' motivation and ideology. The new ideology of nationalism fueling China's revolution, internal renewal, and transformation was based in the Chinese desire to join the world, to become a modern nation-state, and a strong and powerful country. This same nationalism, however, suppressed the traditional values that had formerly marked Chinese civilization and undermined its unique character. In a sense, the dynamism of the era is reflected in its combination of political nationalism, cultural iconoclasm, and diplomatic internationalism in the Chinese approach to world affairs.

China's diplomacy during the Great War transcended the normally polarized boundary between nationalism and internationalism. In the Chinese case, the goals of both were compatible, and in fact, both were important elements of the Chinese conception of a new world order. Chinese internationalism, however, conflicted with global reality. While China tried wholeheartedly to learn from the West and to reform and transform itself, its efforts to consolidate into a new, modern nation were crippled by financial rot to a certain extent created by the Great Powers, which had inflicted huge burdens on the Chinese through indemnities, harmful loans, and many unequal treaties that constrained the country's growth and development. The Great Powers also rejected China's repeated bids to become an equal member of the international system; they refused to allow it to regain control of its territory in Shandong and treated the Chinese high-handedly at the postwar Paris Peace Conference.

One reason for Chinese eagerness to join the war was the problem of the Japanese invasion. Japan was China's most threatening and determined enemy. Why then did China enter the war on the same side as Japan? The reason was strategic – China had to be part of the winning team to attend the postwar peace conference on the best possible footing to represent its interests. The Chinese obsession with international status is the key to understanding this seemingly contradictory move. In this sense, the "declared" war between China and Germany was phony because there had been no fighting and Germany was not the intended enemy. Germany became a victim – or vehicle – in China's big-picture strategy. Germany was in fact a friend in disguise since it helped China springboard into the world arena.

Once China decided to join the war, it was both determined and creative in achieving its goal. The Chinese government sent laborers to France to help boost British and French human resources, for example. As early as 1915, a "laborers as soldiers" scheme had been worked out to link China with the Allied cause when its official entry into the war was uncertain. Huge numbers of Chinese laborers worked side by side with the Allies in Europe during the war. Large numbers of them died near the battlefield. In this light it was illiterate Chinese peasants who served in the vanguard of China's efforts to establish a new national identity. Their labor, their sacrifices, and their lives provided Chinese diplomats in Paris with a critical tool in their battle for recognition, inclusion on the world stage, and internationalization.

Given this background, China understandably had a handful of war aims when it finally officially joined the war: short-term financial benefits and the recovery of Shandong and other German and Austrian spheres of interests, as well as the long-term goal of becoming an equal partner among the world powers. But by the time China was allowed to join the war, the powers had concluded a series of secret treaties with Japan that would fundamentally undermine Chinese plans and aspirations. In other words, by the time China finally acquired the means (entering the war) to realize its goals, those goals had been largely sacrificed.

Many Chinese war aims went unfulfilled not only because of the hostile international system, but more importantly, because of the messy domestic politics associated with its war participation plan. Key players such as Prime Minister Duan Qirui, who pushed the war policy, eventually became a liability to Chinese progress toward participation. Joining the war was supposed to be an opportunity for China, but the bungling of the Duan Qirui cabinet turned that prospect into political farce. The dispute over the Beijing government's war policy had grave consequences: it led to the dissolution of the parliament, the resignations of President Li Yuanhong and Duan himself, and even a civil war.

Other leaders such as Kang Youwei and Sun Yat-sen also played contradictory roles in the story of Chinese engagement in the Great War. Kang's former student Liang Qichao was a great advocate for entering the war, but Kang opposed the move in 1917. Yet it also was Kang who, after China had entered the war, became so excited at the prospect of the war's bringing about a new world order, especially through the proposed League of Nations, that he spent much time and energy rewriting his early essay on *datong* (great unity); he now argued that China and the world would benefit from this new development. Sun Yat-sen's case is even more ironic. It was Sun who played a crucial role in China's internationalization and strengthened the Chinese passion for full membership in the community of nations. But in 1917 he strongly opposed Duan's war entry policy and argued that it was a wrong move. Interestingly enough, as soon as the Beijing government declared war on Germany, Sun's government in Guangzhou followed suit. Why such inconsistency, so many contradictions?

The reversals did not stop with Chinese politicians. Wilson's image in China, for instance, changed dramatically from the "world's number one good man" in the 1917–18 period to "Wilson the empty talker" (*Wei da pao*) after the so-called Paris betrayal. His famous fourteen-point blueprint for a new world order was turned into the scathingly sarcastic equation "fourteen equals zero" in the Chinese press.

The Beijing government war policy was intensely damaging to Chinese domestic politics, yet to a certain extent China still benefited from it in both the short and the long term. If we accept Keegan's and Ferguson's thesis that the First World War was a tragedy or a great error that nobody gained from, we might see, ironically, that poor weak China gained decently from it. Through its participation in the war, China recovered a portion of its national sovereignty and rid itself of certain national humiliations such as the Boxer indemnity payments due Germany and Austria. Although the gains were not as great as Chinese leaders had hoped, China was at least able to attend the postwar peace conference, making its fate a world issue and giving it a platform from which to inject its own ideas into the creation of a new world order. Furthermore, China's war policy won the partial destruction of the old unequal treaty system: Germany, the false enemy, signed the first equal treaty with China immediately after the war. None of these developments would have been possible had China not taken the initiative to join the war effort. Thus, China might have been better off domestically had Duan not rushed into the war; still, the war policy was a brilliant diplomatic move, though it would have many unintended and sometimes damaging consequences.

During the Great War, for the first time in its modern history, China articulated a desire to join the world community as an equal and took action to do so. By this effort it tried to correct the near-fatal mistakes made in the eighteenth and nineteenth centuries when it refused to accommodate the new international system and failed to acknowledge the power of the West. This time it was the West that refused to accept China, but at the Paris Peace Conference, the Chinese fought back. Their refusal to sign the Treaty of Versailles marked the first time since the Opium War that China had stood up to the West. This was also the first time Chinese public opinion played an important role in shaping both foreign policy and the nascent national identity. At no other time in China's modern history were its policies so deeply embedded in, and based on, foreign affairs and public opinion. This episode has, without doubt, colored the country's thinking and behavior in its dealings with the West. In Paris, the Chinese people felt bitterly betrayed, and so this period is also a tale of broken hopes, frustrated dreams, and "defeat-in-victory." To an extent, some Chinese bitterness toward the West after the Paris Peace Conference has continued to color perceptions about peace, development, security, and certainly the West itself.

During the period of the First World War, the Chinese elite tried to build a nation-state without the old ingredients of Chinese culture and tradition. They tried to redefine China's national identity in terms that had nothing to do with its own civilization and experience. The coexistence of liberalism and warlordism was a strange mix that made China seem a monster with two heads, each facing a different direction. In fact, a dual policy making process existed during this period: on one side were modern, outward-looking bureaucrats and social elite groups who tried hard to push China into the international system, and on the other were ultra-conservatives who wished only to stop the clock, effectively mortgaging China's future for their own benefit. The tensions generated by this process created an acute dilemma that put in jeopardy the creation of a new national identity and made China's entry into the international system difficult and circuitous.

More importantly, for China the era of the First World War was an age of innocence. The very search for identity is itself symbolic of this. According to Erikson, identity is a slogan for the end of childhood, for the crucible of adolescence, for the success of socialization.[28] The same can be said at the national level. China's cry for recognition, for association with other countries, its anger at the exploitation of its weakness, its pleas for help and its eagerness to emulate are all aspects of immaturity and innocence. To put it another way, national identity is not only about what we are, but more importantly, about what we seek to be. In the Chinese case, the gap between desire and reality was considerable. The quest for a national identity was a kind of romance: its advocates idealized what China should be and what to emulate.

The innocence of the new China coincided with, and was reinforced by, the fate of the generation brought up from 1890 to 1920. China's response to world affairs in general and to the First World War in particular must

---

[28] For details on this point, see Erikson, *Identity: Youth and Crisis*.

be understood in light of the aspirations of the Chinese who grew up during this period.[29] The May Fourth Movement in 1919 signaled the end of this age of innocence since it grew from many Chinese elite groups' disillusionment with the Western powers and their better understanding of themselves and world problems.

China in the year 1919, in the wake of the European war, was fundamentally different from the China of 1914 – socially, intellectually, culturally, and ideologically. The sea changes that had taken place had occurred to a great extent because of what happened during the war and at the Paris Peace Conference. Now, as China has entered another century, it does so in the wake of more unprecedented changes in its social, economic, and diplomatic arenas, stimulated by economic reform and the opening-up policy initiated in 1978 by Deng Xiaoping.

The revolution Sun Yat-sen wrote of in his will has still not succeeded. The Chinese still struggle to assert themselves and remain passionate about their nation's place in the world. It has been a long journey. The following is an account of the beginning of that journey; it is a complex story with many twists and a strange ending. What will happen to China's current effort is another story to be told another time.

---

[29] For a better understanding on this point, see Jon L. Saari, *Legacies of Childhood: Growing up Chinese in a Time of Crisis, 1890–1920* (Cambridge, MA: Harvard University Press, 1990).

Part I

The stage is set

1 China's preparation for entry into the international system

> Never before had the entire political education of a great nation been the work of its men of letters, and it was this peculiarity that perhaps did most to give the French Revolution its exceptional character and the régime that followed it the form we are familiar with. Our men of letters did not merely import their revolutionary ideas to the French nation; they also shaped the national temperament and outlook on life. In the long process of molding minds to their ideal pattern their task was all the easier since the French had no training in the field of politics, and they thus had a clear field. The result was that our writers ended up by giving the Frenchman the instincts, the turn of mind, the tastes, and even the eccentricities of a literary man. And when the time came for action, these literary propensities were imported into the political arena.
>
> Alexis de Tocqueville[1]

To understand the relationship between China and the Great War, we must start with the times. Chinese political and intellectual culture from 1895 to 1914 was shaped by a dual process, namely, intensive internationalization and internalization. By internationalization I mean the ways Chinese actively engaged in and were engaged by the international system, ideas, forces, and trends; it was a process that compelled China to associate with the outside world and the international system. Internationalization was driven by shifts in the flow of social, intellectual, economic, ideological, and cultural resources between China and the wider world, as well as by new Chinese interest in foreign affairs and their position in the world. Two kinds of internationalization were at play: a passive process and a progressive one. The first responded to intensified foreign encroachment on Chinese territory, to strong foreign influence on Chinese port cities, the Chinese economy, finances, markets, and overall development. Progressive internationalization involved actions initiated by the Chinese themselves and included their embracing Western education, political theories, and foreign political models, as

---

[1] Alexis de Tocqueville, *The Old Regime and the French Revolution* (New York: Doubleday, 1955), 274–75.

well as actively promoting Chinese interests in the world arena. Internalization here refers to the process and conditions whereby China renewed itself and prepared for internationalization, the process by which China adopted and modified external impulses and made them its own. These processes, then, bridged China's domestic reforms and agendas and its foreign policy. Internationalization and internalization would eventually turn China upside down and transform it in many unprecedented ways, in both its internal politics and its foreign relations.

The clash of two world orders

China was in the throes of a great transformation as the international system moved to the brink of the First World War. This transformation was closely linked to the dangerous situation the country faced after its defeat in the Sino-Japanese War in 1895. Although China had suffered one defeat after another at Western hands since the Opium War, only the Sino-Japanese War of 1894–95 really compelled the Chinese to think seriously about their destiny and the value of their civilization; more importantly, it caused them to question their traditional identity.[2]

The Chinese sense of frustration, humiliation, and impotence in the face of Western incursions and a Westernized Japan proved powerful motivations for change. The Sino-Japanese War meant many things for China. It subjected the country to a much greater degree of foreign control than before. Japan imposed a huge indemnity subsequent to the war and along with penalties such as the Boxer Indemnity levied by other foreign powers, the burden of foreign debt effectively crushed almost every opportunity for self-directed modernization and nation building. But the psychological impact of the war was even greater. As Liang Qichao (1873–1929), the influential author and thinker of late Qing and early Republican China, noted, the war "awakened China from the great dream of four thousand years."[3] Yan Fu (1853–1921), Liang's contemporary and the famous translator of many influential foreign works by authors such as Adam Smith, Thomas Huxley, Herbert Spencer, John Stuart Mill, and Charles de Secondat de Montesquieu, wrote in 1895 that the impact of the Sino-Japanese War on China "will be so serious and significant that

---

[2] For a recent study on the Sino-Japanese War, see Qi Qizhang and Wang Yuhui, eds., *Jia Wu zhan zheng yu jin dai Zhongguo he shi jie* (Beijing: Renmin chubanshe, 1995). S. C. M. Paine, *The Sino-Japanese War of 1894–1895: Perceptions, Power, and Primacy* (New York: Cambridge University Press, 2003).

[3] Liang Qichao, "Gai ge qi yuan," *Yin bing shi he ji* (Beijing: Zhonghua shuju, 1989), VI: 113.

one might argue China has not experienced an equivalent upheaval since the Qin dynasty [221–206 BC]."[4] Yan was perhaps the first to use the phrase "national salvation" to awaken fellow Chinese to the seriousness of the situation.[5] Japan's devastating victory was both a turning point and a shared point of reference for Chinese perceptions of themselves and the world.

The Chinese defeat and ensuing self-doubt may be charged to the clash of two different conceptions of the world order. Although its foreign relations from the Han to Yuan dynasties were based in practice on parity to achieve concrete foreign policy objectives, and worldviews of official China across those thousand years were not fixed but adaptable, during the period of the Ming and Qing dynasties the Chinese state to a great extent sustained a sense of a cultural centrality and political and moral superiority. Furthermore, although China had for long periods been divided into two or more states, the ideal or myth of a centralized, united China where Confucian ideology prevailed was the only desirable and legitimate model.[6]

In this idealized scheme, China was the Middle Kingdom, the core and heart of the world order. This view not only rejected a world of formally equal states, but also represented a system not based on national territory. It downplayed the role of military and economic power in determining and maintaining the world order. Many Chinese literati believed that China maintained world order and its superior position by emphasizing the harmony between humanity and nature and between China and other countries. Its superiority in culture and morality was instrumental to *hua* (benevolently transforming) barbarian people. When foreigners could not be sinicized, or when the Chinese sense of cultural superiority was threatened, the Chinese elite appealed to categorical differences between peoples and moved to expel the outsiders and seal the country off from outside influences. They justified this isolationist policy by quoting a Confucian classic, the *Zuozhuan*, which claimed that if foreigners were not the same race as "us" (which meant they could not be sinicized), their minds must be different ("fei wo zu lei, qi xin bi yi"). In these cases, as Frank Dikötter observes, "The foreigner was never faced: the myth

---

[4] For a detailed and excellent study on Yan Fu, see Benjamin Schwartz, *In Search of Wealth and Power: Yen Fu and the West* (Cambridge, MA: Harvard University Press, 1964).

[5] Wang Shi, ed., *Yan Fu ji* (Beijing: Zhonghua shuju, 1986), III: 521.

[6] For details on this point, see Morris Rossabi, *China among Equals: The Middle Kingdom and Its Neighbors, 10th–14th Centuries* (Berkeley: The University of California Press, 1983); Jin-Shen Tao, *Two Sons of Heaven: Studies in Sung–Liao Relations* (Tucson: The University of Arizona Press, 1988).

of his inferiority could be preserved, absorbed or expelled; he remained a nonentity."[7] By understanding world affairs this way, the Chinese had lived in self-imposed isolation for centuries. The Sinocentric perspective in the minds of many Chinese elite groups during the Qing period prevented China from engaging in world affairs. The Chinese lived in a dream of their country being the eternal center of world civilization, the only place where everything was in harmony.

In fact China's traditional notion of world order in the modern period actually pivoted on the idea of isolation. Closed-mindedness and isolation might be called the main characteristics of late Qing official foreign policy. The attitude to the outside world was simple non-engagement. In the mindset of the die-hard traditionalists, civilization rather than the nation-state, traditional rites rather than the law of nations, defined the Chinese world order. They argued that foreigners should come to China only to pay tribute and homage. If they did not, China was not obliged to reach out. After all, as the Qianglong emperor told King George III in 1793, the Celestial Empire was too great and too rich to engage in normal diplomacy and trade relations with foreigners. Foreign countries need only approach China as tributary powers.[8]

Therefore, the official worldview in late imperial China was clearly based on a hierarchical system rooted in the idea of Chinese superiority rather than on equal status among nation-states. It offered no distinction between state and society, between civilization and state, or between tribute and diplomacy. Morality rather than legality was most important in China's affairs of state. Until the late nineteenth century "Middle Kingdom syndrome" made it difficult for China to adapt psychologically to the new reality of international affairs. Long convinced of its own superiority, China had refused to join the family of nations even after the West had compelled it to turn over its resources and open its markets to the world in the wake of the Opium War.

But the Opium War did introduce important changes. The war shook the Chinese belief in their centrality and diplomatic autonomy. Yet, even "the most devastating diplomatic consequence of the Opium War," to use William C. Kirby's phrase, could not entirely shake the Chinese isolationist worldview.[9] Die-hard conservatives and the Qing court still refused to

---

[7] Frank Dikötter, *The Discourse of Race in Modern China* (London: Hurst & Company, 1992), 29.

[8] Ssu-Yü Teng and John King Fairbank, eds., *China's Response to the West: A Documentary Survey, 1839–1923* (Cambridge, MA: Harvard University Press, 1954), 19.

[9] William C. Kirby, "Traditions of Centrality, Authority, and Management in Modern China's Foreign Relations," in Thomas W. Robinson and David L. Shambaugh, eds., *Chinese Foreign Policy: Theory and Practice* (Oxford: Oxford University Press, 1994), 17.

accept the new reality, and Middle Kingdom syndrome persisted until the turn of the twentieth century. In other words, not until the early twentieth century was China willing to embrace a new foreign policy and assume a new attitude toward foreign affairs. The First World War marked the beginning of the Chinese struggle for diplomatic freedom of maneuver in foreign policy.

In sharp contrast to the traditional Chinese notion of world order based on soft power – culture, morality, and human harmony – the European-dominated international system from the eighteenth century on focused more on hard power – military and economic strength and competition. This was more a political system than a cultural one, characterized by aggression and territorial expansion. In the European system the idea of nation-state rather than civilization had become the main focus, and the main advocates of this new system were expansionists. The industrial revolution, capitalist ambitions, and Enlightenment ideology made the Western system more dynamic and outward-looking than the traditional Chinese one.

By the late nineteenth century, clashes between these two different world orders had demonstrated just how obsolete the official Chinese worldview had become. Many Chinese recognized this and the fact that in the new world system, hard power, not culture or morality, ruled. They found that their country had fallen into a peripheral and semi-colonial status, and the West had become the center of the world.

This new realism marked a profound, even revolutionary change in the attitude of the Chinese toward world affairs and their country at the turn of the twentieth century. Chinese elite groups, no matter what their attitude to Chinese tradition and civilization, agreed that if China was to survive, it must change. Change therefore became a buzzword. The famous reformer Kang Youwei observed that China "would not have been willing to reform so wholeheartedly if it had not experienced the 1895 war, which hurt it so badly and caused such devastating pain."[10] To a certain extent, one can argue that the 1898 reforms of Kang Youwei and Liang Qichao reflected their burning desire for change. As Kang told the Guangxu emperor, "My understanding of the international situation is that only a nation which can adapt itself to changing conditions can maintain itself." He went on to encourage the emperor to reform the government. If China could "change completely, it could become strong; a limited change no longer serves any purpose." Kang argued, "What China suffers from is enslavement by its old ways and its refusal to see that change is necessary." China had to undertake political and

---

[10] Tang Zhijun, ed., *Kang Youwei zhenglunji* (Beijing: Zhonghua shuju, 1981), I: 239.

constitutional reforms, similar to those of the Meiji era in Japan, in order to survive.[11]

A possibility that terrified many Chinese was the potential breakup of the country as a geopolitical entity. With the new wave of foreign encroachment initiated by the Sino-Japanese War, almost every literate Chinese had become aware of this threat. There was widespread fear among Chinese elites that China could disappear as a country and the Chinese could disappear as a people. Finally even the Qing court understood the seriousness of the situation and began introducing a series of "New Policies" aimed at better fitting China into the new world order. These policies mainly focused on administrative and constitutional reforms, including the establishment of a series of new government agencies – the Ministry of Foreign Affairs in 1901, the Ministry of Commerce in 1903, and the Ministry of Education in 1905.[12] The New Policies showed that the Qing court had become serious about renewing the country and preparing it to become part of the larger world.

Unfortunately, the majority Han Chinese had lost patience with this Manchu dynasty and counted the Qing reforms as too little too late. Many radical Chinese believed that the Qing itself was a major obstacle to change and China's survival as a nation, and they blamed the Qing for every problem the country faced. To many social elites, the government seemed simply incompetent. Wu Tingfang, once a high official in the Qing government but later a major player in the revolution, explained this point well in his open letter to foreigners dated November 1911. In it he wrote that the Qing government had demonstrated an incapacity to rule its people or conduct the affairs of the nation in a manner compatible with modern history and the development of the civilized world. This rotten dynasty had brought China to a position of degradation; it was scorned, and its institutions and generally retrogressive policies were the objects of contempt. "The minds of the [Chinese] people are made up for change," argued Wu.[13]

Wu was not alone. Many Chinese in the early twentieth century even questioned the Chineseness of the Manchus. They argued that, whatever their degree and profession of "Chineseness," the Manchus were a

[11] Kang Youwei, "Shang Qingdi di liu shu," in *Kang Youwei zheng lun ji*, I: 211–12.
[12] Prior to 1901, the central administration in China consisted primarily of the six ministries or boards, which had formed the heart of the bureaucracy for more than one thousand years. These were the Ministries of Civil Appointments, Revenue, Ceremonies, War, Punishments, and Public Works.
[13] For the French version, see Quai d'Orsay, Chine, Politique intérieure, Dossier Général, NS, XXX: 129; for a slightly different Chinese version, see Wu Tingfang, "Zhi geyou bang chengren Zhonghua minguo dian," November 12, 1911, in Ding Xianjun and Yu Zuofeng, eds., *Wu Tingfang ji* (Beijing: Zhonghua shuju, 1993), I: 367–68.

different race. They were willing to collaborate with Western foreigners and imperialists against the interests of the Chinese as a people in order to protect their own interests. Interestingly, these arguments are supported by recent scholarship on the Manchus. Pamela Crossley, a leading authority on Manchu government, points out that Manchu imperial ideology departed in many ways from the inherited Chinese one. Their emperors had never pretended to be Han Chinese.[14]

For many fair-minded Chinese elite groups, however, the Qing was only part of the problem, not its root. They began to doubt the traditional Chinese conception of the world order. If China wanted to survive, its people had to fundamentally change their way of life and undergo a series of transformations. Sun Yat-sen stressed that China had to catch up with the main tide of the world: "Being in accordance with the billowing world tide will bring [China] prosperity, opposing it will bring doom."[15] The evolving Chinese attitude toward the world provided an intellectual basis for the country's quest for renewal and a new identity. The 1911 Revolution could not have been sustained merely by a few hot-headed soldiers and their elite patrons; the widespread outcry for change was critical to its success.

As a consequence of the Sino-Japanese War of 1894–95, many Chinese became convinced that only by becoming a nation-state could China successfully ride the world tide. And more importantly, only by joining this new world order did China have any hope for survival and the possible recovery of its past glory.

From China as Middle Kingdom to China as nation-state

At the turn of the twentieth century, China had not yet embraced such concepts as the nation-state or the world system as political reality.[16] As a matter of fact, despite its long history and civilization, China did not even have an official name. Surveying the histories of the twenty-five major dynasties, one can find 2,259 paragraphs using the term *zhong guo* or "middle kingdom." This same term is used 613 times in the Confucian

[14] Pamela Crossley, *A Translucent Mirror: History and Identity in Qing Imperial Ideology* (Berkeley: University of California Press, 1999).
[15] Julie Lee Wei et al., eds., *Prescriptions for Saving China: Selected Writings of Sun Yat-Sen* (Stanford: Hoover Institution Press, 1994), 58.
[16] For recent studies on the development of nationhood and nationalism in China, see Henrietta Harrison, *The Making of the Republican Citizen: Political Ceremonies and Symbols in China, 1911–1929* (Oxford: Oxford University Press, 2000); Harrison, *China* (London: Arnold, 2001); Philip A. Kuhn, *Origins of the Modern Chinese State* (Stanford: Stanford University Press, 2002).

Thirteen Classics. Yet in both sources *zhong guo* was used either in a geographical or cultural sense. The name *zhong guo* as a political entity in the modern sense had never been formally adopted. Liang Qichao wrote, "Nothing makes me more ashamed than the fact that our nation has no name [save for dynastic names], which defies the principle of respecting the people."[17]

If the Confucian tradition had a concept of nation, it was purely in a cultural sense. China was a civilization, and this assumption was fully reflected in Qing foreign policy. Although the idea of the nation-state was new for China, it had enjoyed currency in Europe since the Westphalian system was established there in the middle of the seventeenth century. Having reached maturity in the eighteenth and nineteenth centuries, especially after the French revolution, the nation-state was understood to have dual functions: externally, it claimed sovereignty within its territorial boundaries; internally, it claimed to represent the people of the nation. The concept of the nation-state in association with national sovereignty and territorial integration took hold in China only after its defeat in the Sino-Japanese War. As Liang Qichao wrote at the turn of the twentieth century, "We Chinese had no idea of the nation-state."[18] As was the case in imperial France, where the autocratic state was embodied in the monarch – "l'état, c'est moi" – in China "all the lands within the six directions belong to the emperor" and "wherever there is a sign of human presence, all are subjects of the emperor."[19] The state's legitimacy was founded on divine right (the emperor was known as the "son of heaven"), by bloodline, or by a moral-political formulation known as "the mandate of heaven." Prior to the Republican era China had no national flag except dynastic or royal banners and no constitution that defined citizens' rights.

As the Chinese gradually came to terms with the new international reality, they were inspired to create a new identity for China. Culturalism as the ideal of Chinese identity had to be replaced by the concept of a nation-state based on a non-Chinese world order and by the norms of the international system. As the sociologist Immanuel Wallerstein recently argued, the formation of a nation-state provides a means of mobility enabling some social formations on the periphery to attain "core" status.[20] With

[17] Liang Qichao, "Zhongguo shi xulun," *Yin bing shi he ji*, I: 3.
[18] Liang Qichao, *Xin min shuo* (Taipei: Zhonghua shuju, 1959), 20.
[19] Sima Qian, "Qin Shihuang benji" (Annals of the Qin Shihuang), in *Shiji* (Hong Kong: Zhonghua shuju, 1969), 245.
[20] Immanuel Wallerstein, "The Construction of Peoplehood: Racism, Nationalism, Ethnicity," in Etienne Balibar and Immanuel Wallerstein, eds., *Race, Nation, Class: Ambiguous Identities* (London: Verso Press, 1991), 81–82.

the collapse of their sense of cultural superiority, the Chinese elite wanted China to become "a country in the world," to quote Liang Qichao's phrase.[21] After the disgrace of 1895, the Chinese mission to become a nation-state gradually developed into a national obsession.

By the turn of the twentieth century, many Chinese elite members started to challenge the status quo and claimed that the authority of a state was derived from the people. They argued that the state (i.e., China) should be a legal and political organization, with the power to require obedience and loyalty from its citizens. It should be a community of people, whose members were bound together by a sense of solidarity, a common culture, and a national consciousness. The advocacy for a new conception of Chinese identity represented a profound change in Chinese thinking and presented an enormous challenge to the existing order. To a certain extent, one can argue that the root of the Kang–Liang reforms of 1898 was the idea of a nation-state. The conflict between this emerging concept and dynastic interests led the Manchu conservatives to crack down on reforms with the charge that the reformers' capital crime was their effort "to protect China, not the Great Qing" (*bao Zhongguo, bu bao Da Qing*).[22]

In the late nineteenth century, an enlarged sphere of public opinion and political discussion had begun to take shape. This public sphere would assume two fundamental functions: communication and criticism. I will address this issue in later pages, but here I would like to indicate that these functions further served to dissolve claims of royal absolutism and privilege. Chinese nationalist discourse was dominated by discussions of nation-state, national unity, nationalism, internationalism, the new world order, and even the meaning of *zhong guo*. Several influential Chinese wrestled with and eventually embraced a new national consciousness. Liang Qichao's writings, for example, are full of these discussions. According to Chang Hao, an expert on Liang,

The focus of Liang's social-political thought on the idea of *Ch'un* [*qun*], his zealous search for power and wealth for China, and his strong consciousness of the world as an arena of struggle among many nation-groups, may have seemed to signal his commitment to the ideal of the Western nation-state.

Liang drew a clear distinction between the modern nation and traditional China. By converting to the concept of nation-state, Liang rejected the traditional worldview and exalted a nation-state as "the ultimate focus of loyalty." For Liang, it could be a sign of barbarism for human

---

[21] Liang Qichao, *Yin bing shi he ji*, IV: 39–78.
[22] Liang Qichao, "Wu Xu zhengbianji," *Yin bing shi he ji*, VI: 76.

loyalty either to stop short of or go beyond this focus. Chang claims that Liang's "unqualified commitment to the ideal of a nation-state was accompanied and buttressed by a new view of world order dominated by Social Darwinism."[23] Social Darwinism was, of course, a popular political theory in late nineteenth- and early twentieth-century Europe and the United States, according to which persons, groups, and races are subject to the same laws of natural selection that Charles Darwin had perceived in plants and animals. It emphasized change, struggle, and progress to ensure survival.

Liang was not the only one to embrace the idea of the nation-state in China. Prior to the outbreak of the First World War, almost every member of the Chinese intelligentsia dreamed of China becoming a modern-style nation. In 1905 Wang Jingwei published an important essay on Chinese nationalism entitled "Minzudi guomin" (Citizens of a nation). In it Wang defined a nation in terms of common blood, language, territory, customs, religion, spiritual and physical nature, and history. For Wang it was necessary to conceive of the nation as both a legal entity and a state formed by its citizens.[24] In 1914 Zhang Shizhao further elaborated on the concept of nation-state in an article entitled "Guojia yu zherong" (The nation-state and responsibility). He called on every Chinese to work hard to make true statehood a reality in China.[25] Chinese social elites, especially intellectuals, saw nation building as their responsibility. "The Chinese intelligentsia," writes Michael Gasster, "posed for itself nothing less than the task of defining China's role in the modern world and remodeling her whole intellectual, political, social, and economic fabric to fit that role."[26] The idea of the nation-state was so widespread among the Chinese social elite that "save the nation" and "don't forget your country!" became the cry across China in the early twentieth century.

To create a new national identity, China needed citizens; a nation-state had to be composed of citizens. Therefore, the Chinese creation of a new nation-state necessarily coincided with the formation of a Chinese expression of citizenship. Citizenship means participation in public life, and a citizen is an individual who governs and is governed.[27] With the

---

[23] Hao Chang, *Liang Chi-Ch'ao and Intellectual Transition in China, 1890–1907* (Cambridge, MA: Harvard University Press, 1971), 55–57, 109.

[24] Wang Jingwei, "Minzhu de guomin" (The nation's citizens), in Zhang Nan and Wang Rongzhi, eds., *Xinhai geming qian shinian jian shilun xuanji* (Collection of issues discussed in the ten years before the 1911 Revolution) (Beijing: Sanlian shudian, 1960), Part I, II: 97.

[25] Zhang Shizhao, "Guojia yu zerong," "Jiari Ouzhan zhi yijian," in *Jiayin zazhi cungao* (Taipei: Wenhai chubanshe, 1977), I: 26–61.

[26] Michael Gasster, *Chinese Intellectuals and the Revolution of 1911: The Birth of Modern Chinese Radicalism* (Seattle: University of Washington Press, 1969), 248.

[27] Bart van Steenbergen, "The Condition of Citizenship: An Introduction," in Bart van Steenbergen, ed., *The Condition of Citizenship* (Thousand Oaks, CA: Sage, 1994), 2.

introduction of the nation-state and the appearance of the new citizen, "The individual person was enfranchised in order to participate . . . in a revitalized political order."[28] The idea of citizenship, also a Western idea, had been introduced to China at the same time as the nation-state. Liu Zehua and Liu Jianqing argue, "The consciousness of citizenship in China did not develop naturally out of the history of Chinese society and intellectual culture. It came as fully formed theory and institutions from the West."[29] Liang Qichao and others in the beginning of the twentieth century argued that China needed "new citizens" to participate in the political life of their country. Liang, in an article published on October 15, 1899, lamented the fact that "we Chinese had no idea of citizenship for thousands of years," and late in 1901 he argued that the lack of institutions of citizenship was one reason for China's weakness.[30] His *Xinmin congbao* (New Citizen's Miscellany, 1902–03) and a book on the new Chinese citizen strongly argued the importance of citizens in nation building.

According to Liang and other progressive elite members, China's group-oriented parochialism had inhibited it from becoming a nation-state, so the focus of "new citizens" had to be the national interest and a sense of solidarity with the nation-state. The duties of citizens were to love and be concerned about the nation and the national interest. Once the fate of each individual was identified with that of the state, patriotism would flourish and the nation would survive.[31]

Liang's idea of new citizenship reached maturity in 1902 with publication of his *Xinmin congbao*. The popularity of his writings made "new citizenship" almost a household term in China. A thorough study of the political press in the late Qing leads Joan Judge to conclude that the new citizen of China "did begin to emerge in the final years of the Qing dynasty, an individual with a heightened political consciousness and a deepened commitment to the nation."[32] After the establishment of the Republic of China, the first Chinese citizenship law was passed on November 18, 1912.

New citizenship was not simply a theoretical concern in the minds of progressive elite. By the first decade of the last century it had been put

---

[28] Roger R. Thompson, *China's Local Councils in the Age of Constitutional Reform, 1898–1911* (Cambridge, MA: Harvard University Press, 1995), 6.

[29] Liu Zehua and Liu Jianqing, "Civic Associations, Political Parties, and the Cultivation of Citizenship Consciousness in Modern China," in Joshua A. Fogel and Peter G. Zarrow, eds., *Imagining the People: Chinese Intellectuals and the Concept of Citizenship, 1890–1920* (Armonk, NY: M. E. Sharpe, 1997), 41.

[30] Li Huaxing and Wu Jiayi, eds., *Liang Qichao xuanji* (Shanghai: Shanghai renmin chubanshe, 1984), 40.

[31] For details on this point, see Chang, *Liang Chi-Ch'ao*, 100, 155–56.

[32] Joan Judge, *Print and Politics: 'Shibao' and the Culture of Reform in Late Qing China* (Stanford: Stanford University Press, 1996), 140.

into practice with the introduction of local elections. The Qing court itself participated in China's pursuit of nation-state status by issuing and implementing the regulations of local self-government in 1909. Local elections were held across China in the last years of the Qing, and even Yuan Shikai, a high Qing official at the time, experimented with a Western-style election in Tianjin County in hopes of fostering democracy there. In the opinion of Yuan and his subordinates, local self-government would improve China's relative power in the family of nations, enabling the country to establish sovereignty over its own territory. According to Roger Thompson's recent study, by the fall of 1911, around five thousand local and county councils had been established.[33] The Qing's willingness to participate in this process indicates not only that the trend toward modern statehood was irreversible, but also that Chinese efforts, rather than developing suddenly, represented a gradual process that had begun well before the 1911 Revolution.

With the emergence of citizenship as an issue in Chinese political life, the closed-mindedness and sense of isolation engendered by the traditional worldview was replaced, at least among progressive Chinese elite groups, by openness and a cosmopolitan mentality. As Chen Duxiu told his fellow Chinese, "We must no longer think in terms of isolation and exclusiveness, but of world politics. Today, the world has become a community in which many families live together; in such an arena China cannot live in isolation . . . It is time that we joined the community of nations."[34] Thus, in addition to the emergence of the new citizenship, a new understanding of world order also took hold among the Chinese. According to Chang Hao, "The significance of the formulation of the ideal of [Liang's] new citizen in 1902 is not confined to the emergence of a full-fledged notion of a nation-state; it also signified a new view of the world order which imported some meaning and coherence to a political reality which the Chinese people had long known but with which they had never come to terms. This new world order as conceived by Liang was the opposite of the traditional view."[35]

To become new citizens, the Chinese had to reconstruct their national history, a project the new Chinese elite was eager to take on.

National identity and reshaping Chinese memory

Michel Foucault has argued, "If one controls people's memory, one controls their dynamism . . . it is vital to have possession of this memory, to

---

[33] Thompson, *China's Local Councils in the Age of Constitutional Reform*, 39–40, 110.
[34] Chen Duxiu, "Jinggao qingnian," *Xin qingnian* 1, no. 1 (1915).
[35] Chang, *Liang Chi-ch'ao*, 158.

control it, administer it, tell it what it must contain."[36] The importance of national memory explains why, during the French Revolution, theorists of national sovereignty "opted to transform the *fact* of revolution, in the passive sense dear to classical Republicans, into an *act* of revolution in the active modern sense. The time had come to reorder French history on behalf of the nation."[37] There is a clear link between historical representation and political identity. Matthew Arnold stated as early as 1867 that "culture suggests the idea of the state."[38] This applies to a nation's quest for an identity; when people try to change their national identity, they must reconstruct their historical memory because it contains the attitude toward culture and tradition that defines the identity of a state. Some scholars even make a direct and clear connection between historical memory or "pastness" and national identity.[39]

Human memory, however, is full of distortions, malfunctions, and wishful thinking, and it contains "seven sins" (transience, absent-mindedness, blocking, misattribution, suggestibility, bias, and persistence), as one Harvard psychologist recently wrote.[40] Historical memory is even worse. It is subject to even more "sins" because of political, intellectual, and ideological intervention, and intentional distortions. There are primarily two kinds of "pastness": real and imaginary. Historical memory's main focus was to interpret reality and connect the past with the present. To put it another way, although memory is a body of beliefs and ideas about the past, the main focus of this communicative and cognitive process is not the past, but a serious concern for present national identity. Memory helps a public or society understand both its past and its present and, by implication, its future. As Wallerstein concludes, "Pastness therefore is preeminently a moral phenomenon, therefore a political phenomenon, always a contemporary phenomenon."[41]

---

[36] Keith Michael Baker, *Inventing the French Revolution* (Cambridge: Cambridge University Press, 1990).

[37] Ibid., 58.

[38] Matthew Arnold, *Culture and Anarchy: With Friendship's Garland and Some Literary Essays*, ed. Robert. H. Super (Ann Arbor: University of Michigan Press, 1965), 135.

[39] For instance, political scientist Lucian Pye claims that "how people share their collective memories forms much of the content of their nationalistic identity." See Lucian Pye, "How China's Nationalism was Shanghaied," in Jonathan Unger and Geremie Barmé, eds., *Chinese Nationalism* (Armonk, NY: M. E. Sharpe, 1996), 88. John R. Gillis agrees. He argues that "memory and identity support one another," in John R. Gillis, *Commemorations : The Politics of National Identity* (Princeton: Princeton University Press, 1994), 4.

[40] Daniel L. Schacter, *The Seven Sins of Memory: How the Mind Forgets and Remembers* (Boston: Houghton Mifflin Company, 2001).

[41] Wallerstein, "The Construction of Peoplehood," in Balibar and Wallerstein, eds., *Race, Nation, Class: Ambiguous Identities*, 78.

Like the French revolution, the battle for change in China was also fought in the field of historical memory, real and imaginary. By the turn of the twentieth century, the Qing and traditionalists across China had lost the battle to control Chinese history, and then lost the imperial political system and the culture of old China.

When Chinese progressive elite advocated a radical break with the past in the early twentieth century, they were actually working to reshape the Chinese national memory. The driving force behind this new appraisal of Chinese history was the harsh lesson of the Sino-Japanese War and the desire for a new national identity.[42] This new historical memory was produced through political discussions about Chinese identity that took place in a public sphere in which various parts of the social structure exchanged views. The debates involved several approaches to the problem. One way involved totally rejecting the received past and creating history afresh. Wu Tingfang attributed the 1911 Revolution to a wholesale rejection of the Qing. In his appeal for foreign understanding of the 1911 uprising, Wu explained that the Chinese were fighting to put the past behind them and look forward. He described the Qing government as the epitome of that past, with its arrogance, missteps, and humiliations.

"The China of tomorrow can never be as the China of yesterday," Wu declared. "We are fighting to be men in the world; we are fighting to cast off an oppressive, vicious, and tyrannical rule that has beggared and disgraced China, obstructed and defied the foreign nations, and set back the hands of the clock of the world." In his appeal to the outside world, Wu argued that China should not be judged by its past. What the Chinese were trying to do now was bring their country into its own, "to elevate it to the standard that the people of the Occident have [always] ever been urging [it] to attain."[43]

Wu's view was carried further by others who later argued that not only was the Manchu dynasty bad, but the whole of China's past was a terrible legacy. They even argued that China *had* no national history. Liang Qichao provides a good example of this thinking. In his opinion, history "is simply the story of racial development and racial strife. Aside from race, there is no history." This understanding was obviously influenced by Social Darwinism, and Liang did not try to mask this influence. He declared, "History is the story of the evolution of the human group," and understanding history from this new perspective meant that a "new historiography" was needed in China, since without it there could be no

---

[42] For a recent study on this issue, see Q. Edward Wang, *Inventing China through History* (Albany: State University of New York Press, 2001).

[43] Quai d'Orsay, Chine, Politique intérieure, Dossier General, NS, XXX: 129.

Chinese nationalism. For Liang, China possessed only dynastic histories, "the genealogies" of different families. They had been written for individual rather than collective purposes, and the main focus of this type of history was how to rule people. The dynastic histories should be discarded because reading them was "a waste of brain power," and because they taught the Chinese people a slavish mentality. Chinese of the modern world could hardly derive any sense of national identity from this past. Liang further complained, "The Chinese still have not developed the idea of the nation, for which historians of the past thousands of years can never be excused." Liang thus informed his readers, "If we want to advocate nationalism so that our four hundred million compatriots may stand firm in this world where the fit survive and unfit perish, then every man, woman, and child among us, whether young or old, good or bad, must study our nation's history." Since China did not yet possess a "national" history, Liang strongly argued that the Chinese reexamine their past and cast it in a new light. "If there is no historiographical revolution," he warned, "our country cannot be saved."[44] By the 1910s, almost all Chinese intellectuals were engaged either directly or indirectly in an intense debate on historical memory and had raised their voices on the issue of national identity. After all, "modern memory was born not just from the sense of a break with the past, but from an intense awareness of the conflicting representations of the past and the effort of each group to make its version the basis of national identity."[45]

Ironically, the Qing court itself unwittingly took part in reshaping Chinese historical memory. One important change that the court adopted was the abolition of the traditional civil service examination in 1905. This policy arguably represented a break from a cultural, ideological, and administrative past.[46] The Confucian tradition, on which the old Chinese world order was based, was carried on mainly through the examination system and the supporting educational traditions through which officials were trained. More importantly, the civil service system had been the mainstay of the gentry, and "the gentry were the incarnation of traditional Chinese civilization."[47] With the examination system's abolition, the gentry as a class gradually disappeared, and traditional society lost its magic glue. But the abolition of the civil service examination and the

[44] Liang Qichao, "Xin shi xue," *Yin bing shi he ji*, I: 3–11.
[45] Gillis, "Commemorations: The Politics of National Identity," 8.
[46] For a short analysis of the background of the reform, see Wolfgang Franke, *The Reform and Abolition of the Traditional Chinese Examination System* (Cambridge, MA: Harvard University Press, 1963).
[47] Chuzo Ichiko, "The Role of the Gentry," in Mary Wright, ed., *China in Revolution: The First Phase, 1900–1913* (New Haven: Yale University Press, 1968), 299.

disappearance of the old gentry provided opportunities for new people, a new education system, and a new ideology to fill the vacuum. As historian Mary Wright reminded us, "The abolition of the examination system in 1905 and the simultaneous creation of a Ministry of Education altered with one stroke the basis of the gentry power and of the recruitment of the bureaucracy."[48]

After the establishment of the Republic, the Chinese found several radical ways to indicate their Republic's newness and its divergence from the past political practice. One major change was the adoption of a new calendar. Just as the French Republic embarked on the extraordinary project of altering the time consciousness of the entire Christian world by declaring 1792 to be year 1, the new Republican government chose to give up the traditional lunar calendar and adopt the Western Gregorian calendar. By changing calendars, both the French and the Chinese republics aimed to radically reorient their historical memory.

Indeed the adoption of the Gregorian calendar was the very first law passed by the new Republic of China.[49] On December 31, 1911, the national senate, provisionally formed by delegates from the provinces, passed a resolution to adopt the solar calendar immediately, regarding the next day as the first day of the first month of the first year of the Republic of China. Thus the establishment of the new government marked the commencement of a new era in Chinese history. This mood was captured in an editorial in *Shen Bao*, an influential newspaper based in Shanghai. The editorial declared on January 1, 1912, "We 400 million fellow Chinese all are newborn babies fresh out of our mother's womb. From now on we are new citizens. It is our new responsibility . . . to embrace new morality, new scholarship, new clothing."[50]

Before the introduction of the new calendar, Chinese had officially reckoned time by the reign of an emperor and the lunar calendar. For example, the year 1911 was recorded as the third year of Xuantong according to the old method. After the rebellion that would lead to the new government began, some provinces started to use the legendary Yellow emperor's reign to show their break with the old regime. Under that calendar the year 1911 became the year 4609. But the Yellow emperor calendar was not easy to use and when the Gregorian calendar became law, many provinces in the south immediately switched, and the whole country soon adopted it.[51]

---

[48] Wright, *China in Revolution: The First Phase*, 24.
[49] In 1910, Liang Qichao had suggested that China adopt a solar calendar, but nothing happened then. See his "Gaiyong taiyang lifa yi," *Yin bing shi he ji*, I: 1–3.
[50] "Xinnian zhuci" (New Year's Wishes), in *Shenbao* (The Shanghai Times), January 1, 1912.
[51] *North China Daily News*, January 1, 1912.

The symbolism of the new calendar was especially important because the change had a great impact on people's activities and expectations.[52] The new structure of time, with a seven-day week and Sundays observed as days of rest, was a thing unknown in China before. The British consul's report to his government touched on the symbolism well: "The first of January was specially chosen for the inauguration of the president, so that the date of the commencement of the republic should coincide with that of the foreign year and provide the government with a valid excuse for adopting the Gregorian calendar."[53] Thus Republican China, by adopting the Western calendar, declared its determination to break with the past and to join the greater world system.[54]

If the switch to a new calendar was a break with the temporal past, then relocating the national capital away from Beijing, China's political center for more than five hundred years, was an effort to cut China's link with its spatial past. Many Chinese, especially Republicans in the south, were eager for the capital to be moved. They argued that there were many sufficient reasons for the relocation, from both a material and a sentimental standpoint. According to one newspaper report, in the opinion of millions of Chinese, Beijing stood for oppression and humiliation and was a symbol of the isolation and closed-mindedness of old China. For the last five hundred years Chinese prestige and creativity had lain captive behind the great physical walls of the Forbidden City and behind a metaphorical wall of old identities: poverty, weakness, and isolation. During the 1911 Revolution, the younger Republican leaders argued that Beijing as a capital city, with its long-held traditions, seemed to hold China's past and future in its spell. It seemed to many reform-minded Chinese that one of the pressing necessities of the new republic was to shake itself clear of this insidious influence. This could be done, they argued, only by moving the capital to another place. As one high official in Sun's government explained, "The idea of locating national capitals in inaccessible places belongs to the dark ages." The same official maintained that if the Republic of China "wish[es] to have intercourse with the world, [it] will have no reason" to stay in the old Qing capital.[55] Even Liang Qichao, who

---

[52] On adoption of new calendars and other changes more generally, see Harrison, *The Making of the Republican Citizen.*

[53] Consul Wilkinson to Jordan, January 5, 1912, Bonn, Germany, Archiv des Auswärtigen Amts, R177311.

[54] The idea of Republican China's adopting a new calendar, according to a memoir of Huang Yinbai's wife, came from a staff member (Shen Yunxiang) who worked in the Shanghai military government. He first suggested it to his boss, the Chief of Staff Huan Yinbai. Chen Qimei agreed with the idea and asked Huang to contact Nanjing about the new calendar. See Shen Yunlong, ed., *Xiandai zhengzhi renwu shupin* (Taipei: Wenhai chubanshe, 1966), II: 118.

[55] *The China Press*, January 13, 1912.

was by no means revolutionary, looked at Beijing as a symbol of the past and of evil as well. "The capital, Beijing," Liang claimed, "has become the hotbed of all evils. Not only has the land lost its pleasing features and the water its sweet taste, but a thousand crimes, a myriad of scandals, and all the weird carbuncles and chronic diseases of this sinful world are concentrated there. If the political center stays in Beijing, China will never see a single day of clean government."[56] Nanjing seemed to be a good choice for the new capital in its forthcoming, glorious rejuvenation, and a move there was embraced.[57]

The Chinese also demonstrated their break from the past by changing their dress and cutting off their queues, a symbol of Manchu rule. The traditional official dress – long gown and mandarin jacket – was especially annoying to the Republican government. The Ministry of Foreign Affairs (Waijiaobu) wired its diplomats abroad on February 12, 1912, to inform them that "official dress will be changed temporarily to the usual dress of American civil officials."[58] Not only did official attire change, but average Chinese dress underwent great changes as well. George E. Anderson, the American consul-general in Hong Kong, witnessed this change first hand. In his report regarding the cotton trade he wrote, "Change in the Chinese dress is much more extensive than had been anticipated. Thousands of Chinese in the open ports have not only done away with their queues, but have turned to foreign dress altogether. Foreign-dress tailors in Hong Kong had orders booked for all they can do for several months." People in the interior, especially businessmen and local elite members, were not far behind. They modified characteristic Chinese clothing to appear semi-foreign in style.[59]

In short, for the Chinese, the recasting of their national history was to help free them from the past and make them a new people, focusing on their future rather than their past.

The rise of a new public

One of the most important changes in China at the turn of the twentieth century was the emergence of a new public. According to John Fincher,

---

[56] Liang Qichao, *Yin bing shi he ji*, XXV: 196.

[57] Although Beijing would eventually regain its position as the national capital, the symbolism of breaking away from the spatial past is too important for scholars to ignore. President Yuan Shikai's hesitation about moving south and many Chinese social elite' fear of foreign intervention contributed to the failure of the permanent relocation of the capital.

[58] Waijiaobu to Chinese diplomats abroad, February 12, 1912, Germany, Archiv des Auswärtigen Amts, R17731, 131.

[59] *The Republican Advocates*, May 18, 1912; the original document can be found in Germany, Archiv des Auswärtigen Amts, R18073.

the emergence of a public that replaced the traditional gentry "explains the large size of the registered electorate in 1912, the response to the 1913 'second revolution,' the reaction to the Twenty-one Demands of 1915, opposition to the restoration of 1916, and finally, the background of the May Fourth Movement of 1919."[60] Among many factors that affected the development of this new public, educational reform was crucial. The Qing court initiated education reforms and the Republican government pushed them forward. The main thrust of these reforms was the promotion of Western-style learning. In April of 1912, Sun Yat-sen declared that he was "in favor of the adoption of Western education and ideas."[61] Yuan Shikai shared Sun's idea, expressing hope that "the citizens of this country will introduce among themselves the enlightened education [system] from foreign countries."[62]

Thus, the new education was to transform Chinese attitudes and habits of thinking and help China integrate itself into the world. Yuan Shikai noted, "When I considered the problem of giving this nation a place in the world, I became aware of the absolute necessity of outfitting the people with entirely new equipment of knowledge and ideas, and of eradicating their fundamental lack of independence and initiative as indispensable antecedents to equal intercourse between China and the nations of the world."[63] "It is hoped that the deep change in the national mind will receive the sympathetic notice and consideration of the world powers."[64]

Although politicians like Yuan might only pay lip service to this change, new-style schools did appear everywhere in China. Eagerness for a new kind of knowledge was also reflected in the large number of Chinese students who went abroad to study after the Sino-Japanese War – especially to Japan. To be sure, a few Chinese had studied abroad before 1895. For instance, during the years 1872–75, at the suggestion of Zeng Guofan and Li Hongzhang, 120 teenagers were sent in four groups to study in the United States. From 1877 to 1897, 85 cadets from the Fuzhou Shipyard School traveled to England and France to study. Yan Fu, the famous translator of Western works, was one of the students from Fuzhou who studied in Europe.[65] But the number was limited and the trend did not become fashionable and clear until 1895. The flood of Chinese students going to Japan and other countries was spurred on by the cries

[60] John Fincher, "Provincialism and National Revolution," in Wright, ed., *China in Revolution: The First Phase*, 220.
[61] *Hong Kong Telegraph*, April 29, 1912.   [62] *The Peking Gazette*, October 11, 1913.
[63] *The China Press*, October 10, 1912.   [64] *The Peking Daily News*, October 10, 1912.
[65] Chen Jiang, "Western Learning and Social Transformation in the Late Qing," in Frederic Wakeman and Wang Xi, eds., *China's Quest for Modernization: A Historical Perspective* (Berkeley: University of California Press, 1997), 154.

for "national salvation." From 1895 to 1905, fifteen thousand Chinese students went to Japan alone. There they found access to a world of new ideas, and discussed and debated the future of their homeland in the new world order.[66]

On their return home in the early years of the twentieth century these Chinese introduced ideas from the West to their fellow Chinese. By so doing they helped create new attitudes and a broader cultural horizon for other Chinese. China's "newness" owed much to the experience and contributions of these returned students. Their importance was noticed even before the abolition of the civil service examination. In 1903 and again in 1905 the Qing government recognized their achievements with special examinations in Beijing. Successful candidates were given a *jinshi* degree and government preferences. These degrees in new areas of study, such as law or economics, could be won only by individuals who had studied overseas. By the end of the dynasty, 161 such *jinshi* degrees and 1,213 *juren* degrees in new fields had been awarded.[67]

Returned students were especially active in national politics.[68] For example, among the eighteen cabinet members in Sun Yat-sen's provisional government in Nanjing, fifteen had trained abroad. The first prime minister, Tang Shaoyi, was a member of the first group sent to the United States for study; he was educated at Yale University. Wang Chonghui (1881–1958) became the first foreign minister of Republican China when he was only thirty-two years old.[69] He held a doctoral degree in civil law from Yale University and had been a Barrister at Law of the Middle Temple in London. He is known to the world as the famous author of an English-language annotated translation of the German civil code, which includes an excellent introduction and appendices. *The North China Herald* called him "one of the most brilliant men in China."[70] Chen Jingtao, the minister of finance, was also a returned student. According to the London *Times*' Beijing correspondent George E. Morrison,[71] Chen had "certainly the best knowledge of finance of any living Chinaman." Wu Tingfang, who served as the first minister of justice and later minister

---

[66] For details, see Paula Harrell, *Sowing the Seeds of Change: Chinese Students, Japanese Teachers, 1895–1905* (Stanford: Stanford University Press, 1992), 209–16.

[67] Thompson, *China's Local Councils in the Age of Constitutional Reform*, 44.

[68] For details on this point, see Appendix 1.

[69] For a complete list of foreign ministers during the First World War period, see Appendix 2.

[70] *The North China Herald*, June 15, 1912.

[71] Morrison was born in Australia in 1862 and died in 1920 in London. He served as correspondent for *The Times* of London from 1897 to 1912 and became Political Advisor to the Chinese government from 1912 till his death. For a detailed study on him, see Cyril Pearl, *Morrison of Peking* (Sydney: Angus and Robertson, 1967).

of foreign affairs, studied law in England and was a Barrister at Law of Lincoln's Inn. Cai Yuanpei, the first minister of education, was a Hanlin graduate before he studied the educational systems of Germany and other foreign countries for several years. Song Jiaoren was only thirty-one when he was chosen to be minister of agriculture and forestry. He had worked as a journalist in Shanghai and studied in Japan. Even Vice-president Li Yuanhong had some foreign experience; he had studied military subjects in Tokyo when he was young. Sun Yat-sen, of course, spent many years abroad before the revolution. Although President Yuan Shikai had not been abroad to study, as Sun once pointed out to the media, he had many returned students on his staff, and they kept him informed on international affairs.[72] Before the outbreak of the war in Europe, the president's staff consisted of at least forty men who had trained in England or North America, and sixty or more who had been trained in Japan. Wellington Koo, who later played a key role for China at the Paris Peace Conference, was one of the former.[73] Koo had studied international law under John Bassett Moore (1860–1947) and received his doctoral degree from Columbia University.

Students who received a modern education in China were also active in parliamentary politics. According to Zhang Yufa, the average age among senators in 1912 was 36.8; 65.6 percent of all senators were educated in schools modeled after Western-style schools; among those educated in modern schools, 37.5 percent received their higher education abroad. The average age among congressmen was 36.1 years old; 65.5 percent of them had been educated in modern schools. Among those educated in modern schools, 43.1 percent studied abroad.[74] According to a survey of the 340 US-trained returned students in 1916, 110 worked for the government. Another survey conducted in the same year indicates that of the 1,655 returned students who lived in Beijing in 1916, 1,024 of them worked for the government.[75] In addition to politics, returned students had an impact on every aspect of Chinese life.

With the rise of a new public in politics came the emergence of non-bureaucratic elite, especially the politicized bourgeoisie and professional academicians. Comparadors, merchants, entrepreneurs, and the new intelligentsia were the main representatives of this class. Unlike the old gentry, which based its status and power on Confucianism and land-holding, the new class rose on a new set of values: internationalization,

---

[72] *Hong Kong Telegraph*, April 29, 1912.   [73] *The Times* (London), June 25, 1914.
[74] Zhang Yufa, *Min guo chu nian de zheng dang* (Taibei: Zhong yang yan jiu yuan jin dai shi yan jiu suo, 1985), 291–93, 531, 542.
[75] Wang Qisheng, *Zhongguo liuxuesheng de lishi guiji* (Wu Han: Hubei jiaoyu chubanshe, 1992), 208–09.

nationalism, and modernism. Members of this class were conscious of both national and foreign affairs. Their rise coincided with the appearance of a large urban working class and modern cities.[76] Ironically, the Treaty of Shimonoseki of 1895, which China was compelled to sign after the Sino-Japanese War, played an important role in the rise of these elites and the working class because it allowed foreigners to establish factories in China. Both the entrepreneurial and academic elite and urban workers became deeply involved and invested in creating a new Chinese national identity.[77]

The expansion of modern education proceeded hand in hand with the development and spread of a series of ideologies antagonistic to the status quo. To be sure, the new public was not a coherent body. Some of its members were radical, some rational, some liked republicanism, some preferred a constitutional monarchy. Yet they collectively undermined the existing authority and planted seeds of revolution. The new public in early twentieth-century China, coming from a non-traditional educational background, believing in non-traditional values, and determined to bring about change, immediately caused a crisis of confidence in the existing system at the Qing court. This new public fed the erosion of traditional authority and undermined old ways of life and hierarchies with its spread of skepticism. The lack of harmony between this new public and the old system, and the erosion of the Qing power, eventually led to what Lawrence Stone called in his study of the causes of the English Revolution "the emergence of an obsessive revolutionary mentality."[78] In China, recognition of the dysfunction of society with its alienated new elite bred frustration among intellectuals and political opposition and even radicalism among non-elite. What held this political opposition movement together was the new idea of *guojia* or nation-state. The emergence of a new public and new ideas eventually led China into revolution and an era of political disruption.

The 1911 Revolution and the sense of a new China

The concept of modern revolution was foreign to China. To be sure, the word *geming* (revolution) appears in the Chinese classics and

---

[76] For a detailed study on new merchants and Chinese society, see Zhu Ying, "Qing mo xinxing shangren ji minjian shehui," *Ershi yishiji* (The twenty-first century), (Hong Kong, 1991), III: 37–44.

[77] For an excellent analysis of the rise of non-bureaucratic elite, see Marie-Claire Bergère, *The Golden Age of the Chinese Bourgeoisie, 1911–1937*, trans. Janet Lloyd (Cambridge: Cambridge University Press, 1986), 13–60.

[78] Ibid., 12.

dynastic histories.[79] However, the meaning of *geming* is quite different from our modern sense of revolution. It literally means "to change the mandate [of heaven]," but *geming* did not usually bring political, institutional, and social change. This explains why systemic or revolutionary change is largely absent from China's more than two-thousand-year history, even though this change of mandate had taken place many times. To a great extent, in imperial China *geming* followed just a few patterns: it could involve peasant rebellion, a military takeover, or a *coup d'état* at court. Once the rebels had succeeded, a new dynasty would be established using the traditional political justifications as the new regime did its best to assert its legitimacy through the old ideology, and political and social structures. There are only a few exceptions to this, such as the Taiping Rebellion. Therefore, traditional *geming* was not revolution in the modern sense, it was actually a more straightforward power struggle.

Interestingly, as in the Chinese case, the original meaning of the term "revolution" in the West was fundamentally different from what we understand today. According to Hannah Arendt, revolution originally referred to either the lawfulness of an astronomic movement, described in Nicolaus Copernicus's famous book *De revolutionibus orbium coelestium libri VI*, or the change effected by the so-called Glorious Revolution of Britain when kingly power was transferred to William and Mary in 1688.[80] The modern sense of revolution comes from the short but famous and revealing dialogue between Louis XVI and the Duc de La Rochefoucauld-Liancourt on July 14, 1789, when the latter informed the king of the fall of the Bastille. Louis XVI exclaimed, "C'est une révolte." Liancourt, the messenger, corrected him by saying, "Non, Sire, c'est une révolution." From this dialogue, Arendt concludes that a sense of irresistibility was attached to revolution. After the events in France in 1789, Arendt points out, "Suddenly an entirely new imagery begins to cluster around the old metaphor and an entirely new vocabulary is introduced into political language."[81]

The 1911 Revolution in China was this kind of modern revolution. It went well beyond a change of mandate: it was inspired by new ideas, driven by a new public, and it drew on widespread motivation to set up a brand new political system. The goal of the revolution was not to change the mandate of heaven, but to create the sense of irresistibility

---

[79] For instance, in the official history of the twenty-five major dynasties, the phrase *geming* was used at least 220 times, 25 times in the thirteen classics.

[80] Copernicus's complete works in English translation is entitled *On the Revolutions*, ed. and trans. Edward Rosen (Baltimore: Johns Hopkins University Press, 1978).

[81] Hannah Arendt, *On Revolution* (New York: The Viking Press, 1963), 40–42.

about fundamental changes to be made to Chinese politics, society, and the national identity. The revolution was motivated not by traditional values, but by adapted foreign ideologies and political theories such as national sovereignty, citizenship, nation-state, nationalism, Republicanism, and Social Darwinism. We can argue that the revolution itself focused on China's internationalization, since its goal was to bring China into the world and because it was motivated by new and internationalized political language that fundamentally reshaped Chinese thinking. China's internationalization was also reflected in the revolution's participants. Its leader Sun Yat-sen was primarily based overseas before he came to power in 1912. His many supporters were either foreigners or overseas Chinese. Chinese who had either trained abroad or were educated at home in modern schools became the driving force of the revolution. In this sense, the revolution in China was a distant outgrowth of the European Enlightenment, the same intellectual movement that had inspired the French and American revolutions.

With the appearance of a new public, a "new China" was born. To be sure, this newness did not emerge suddenly; rather, its development was a gradual process. If the Sino-Japanese War had jolted China into a nationwide quest for change and fresh thinking about world affairs, the 1911 Revolution finally achieved China's social, cultural, and political transformation.

Revolution needs revolutionary ideas, and every revolution is an outgrowth of certain political ideas. Daniel Mornet in his famed *Intellectual History of the French Revolution* concludes that "it was, in part, ideas that determined the French revolution."[82] Lawrence Stone also reminds us, "A true revolution needs ideas to fuel it – without them there is only a rebellion or a *coup d'état* – and the intellectual and ideological underpinnings of the opposition to the government are therefore of the first importance."[83] Since all of its political ideas were imported from abroad, the 1911 Revolution itself is a product of China's internationalization. As New Chinese internalized those foreign concepts, they wanted to reproduce them in China. If Thomas Paine's *Common Sense* and other writings played a crucial role in making the American Revolution, the collective cry for a new China in the writings of Liang Qichao, Zou Rong, and others mobilized Chinese to action. The Chinese people had become fed up with the status quo and this meant revolution was inevitable.

One of the most important legacies of the revolution was the overthrow of a two-thousand-year-old dynastic system and the adoption of a new

---

[82] Quote from Roger Chartier, *The Cultural Origins of the French Revolution* (Durham, NC: Duke University Press, 1991), 3.
[83] Stone, *The Causes of the English Revolution 1529–1642*, 98.

polity: republicanism. In 1912 republicanism was still a radical political form; worldwide there were few republics then, among them the United States, France, and Switzerland. But for many Chinese, especially southerners, republicanism represented a form of government that would best help China renew itself and facilitate its integration into the new world order. By late 1911 most Chinese elite groups favored the establishment of a republic. The spirit of republicanism and hatred for despotism was so strong that John Jordan (1852–1925), the veteran British minister to China, observed that even Tang Shaoyi, the delegate representing the Qing government in its negotiations with the South, "appears to have been so influenced by his surroundings as to have expressed his sympathy with the Republican ideal." Jordan's observation is supported by Tang's telegram to Yuan Shikai on December 27, 1911, in which Tang wrote that the chief aim and object of the revolutionary army was to establish a republican form of government. If he would not accept this as a basis for proceeding, then the South was unwilling to continue the negotiations. He told Yuan that his private investigations showed popular feeling in the eastern and southern provinces firmly established in favor of a republic, and nothing could prevent the advance of this feeling.[84]

The fever of revolution was not limited to the South. Even in northern provinces and within Beijing itself, people responded enthusiastically to news of the revolution. According to G. E. Morrison in his letters from Beijing, "Every man I meet here is in favour of the revolution. Even the more enlightened Manchus in the junior ranks are adverse [sic] to their Government."[85] He further stated that he could "meet no one among the intelligent Chinese who is not anti-dynastic."[86] Moreover in Manchuria, the homeland of the Qing regime, revolution also had a strong appeal. "Everyone I have spoken to amongst the Chinese is in favour of the rebels, but they are afraid to say so openly," reported one foreign witness in the area.[87] Chinese enthusiasm for the revolution indicated that the 1911 uprising in central China was not a simply military *coup d'état*, but reflected the collective desire of the Chinese people for change. In this sense, Sun Yat-sen was right when he argued, "This revolution was not brought about by fighting; it was brought about by the

---

[84] Jordan's report to Edward Grey on January 6, 1912, PRO, FO405/229.

[85] Morrison to Braham, Beijing, October 27, 1911, *The Correspondence of G. E. Morrison*, ed. Lo Hui-min (Cambridge: Cambridge University Press, 1976), I: 641.

[86] Morrison to Braham, Beijing, November 17, 1911, *The Correspondence of G. E. Morrison*, I: 661.

[87] W. R. Hughes to Morrison, Fengtien, November 5, 1911, *The Correspondence of G. E. Morrison*, I: 646.

ready response of the people to republicanism."[88] Morrison supported Sun by claiming, "The revolution was the work of reason rather than force."[89]

Under this extremity, the Qing court declared its abdication on February 12, 1912, by publishing an edict from Lung Yu, the Empress Dowager. This edict recognized that most people across the country favored republicanism. Such being the public inclination, the Dowager sadly continued, "How could I bear to disregard the desires of the millions for the sake of the glory of one family? Judging, therefore, the general aspect from without and public opinion within, I specially direct the emperor to bestow the administrative power in common to the whole country, and adopt a constitutional republican government."[90]

Even Yuan Shikai, prime minister for the Qing court, who had played a key role in the Qing's abdication and did not really understand the meaning of republicanism, nonetheless had to pay lip service to it and duly declared himself to be a republican in 1912. In his telegram of February 12, 1912, to the new republican leaders in the South, he declared that he believed a republic was the best form of government. "That in one leap we have passed from autocracy to republicanism," he said, "is really the outcome of the many years of strenuous effort exerted" by Sun and his comrades.[91] In a short time Chinese enthusiasm for republicanism had grown strong, and in early Republican China using the term as a touchstone in conversation became fashionable, although some people like Yuan did not understand the concept at all. In a letter to Yuan Shikai in 1913, even the abdicated emperor Pu Yi hoped that, "henceforward the Republic of China will be governed by a constitutional government in the strict sense of the word, so as to place China on an equal footing among the nations of the world and lay the foundations of the republic on a firm basis to the advantage of the five races."[92]

Some foreign observers also had a high opinion of republicanism in China. They claimed that the comparatively peaceful revolution of China was a remarkable culmination of the wave of republicanism that had girded the world with a chain of republics in less than a century and a half. China added Asia to the list and completed the chain, but it did more than that. "She has brought the republican territory of the world to one

---

[88] *Hong Kong Telegraph*, April 29, 1912, see Quai d'Orsay, Chine, Politique intérieure, Dossier Général, NS, XL: 270.

[89] *Pall Mall Gazette*, London, September 16, 1912.

[90] "Xuantong sannian shieryue ershiwu ri yizhi" (Empress Lungyu decree), in Chinese Historical Association, ed., *Xinhai Geming* (The 1911 Revolution) (Shanghai: Shanghai renmin chubanshe, 1961), VIII: 183.

[91] For the original documents, see ibid.   [92] *The Peking Gazette*, October 11, 1913.

third of its area and by trebling the previous republican population has made every third man in the world a republican citizen," as one Western witness observed.[93] Even Thomas A. Edison noted the importance of the Chinese revolution. At the beginning of 1912 he was asked by the Hearst press to name the major events of the previous year. Most of his list was taken up by concrete improvements such as the discovery of the salvarsan cure or current developments in "aerial navigation," but at the head of his list in the field of politics, he named the 1911 Chinese Revolution.[94]

The rise of republicanism in China was strongly connected with the expectations of a newly energized Chinese public that gradually took shape after 1895. The Chinese cry for nation-state status, as well as the obsession with international position and new citizenship paved the way for China's leap to republicanism.[95] In his confidential memorandum to Dudley D. Braham, editor of the London *Times*, on November 16, 1911, George E. Morrison observed that republicanism in China was closely linked with the Chinese desire to join the world and imitate the West. He wrote that the revolutionaries in the South believed China needed a republic modeled partly on that of America and partly on that of France, with some modifications derived from Switzerland.[96] It was true that the Western experience, especially the American experience, understandably had a strong impact on China's choice to be a republic. For instance, just after the 1911 Revolution, the governor of Jiangsu Province, Chen Dequan, and the governor of Zhejiang Province, Tang Shouqian, telegraphed the governor of Shanghai, Chen Qimei, to propose joint sponsorship of a provincial convention in Shanghai to discuss China's future. This convention would be based on the example of the US Continental Congress during the American War of Independence. Their telegram pointed out that since the Wuchang [1911] Rebellion, every province had followed Wuchang's example, and the republican system had been approved by national public opinion. Now, to guarantee the success of the cause, "China should follow the example of the American system," and hold a provincial conference like the American Continental Conference. Jianxi governor Tan Yankai also suggested that the independent provinces be united into a new state. Chen agreed with them. Li

[93] *The China Press*, October 10, 1912.

[94] *San Francisco Examiner*, January 3, 1912, quote from Henry F. May, *The End of American Innocence: A Study of the First Years of Our Own Time, 1912–1917* (New York: Columbia University Press, 1992), 14–15.

[95] As Peter Zarrow recently pointed out, "Citizenship has proved to be a key concept in the rise of republicanism." Peter G. Zarrow, "Citizenship in China and the West," in Fogel and Zarrow, eds., *Imagining the People*, 3.

[96] Morrison to Braham, *The Correspondence of G. E. Morrison*, 1: 663.

Yuanhong, the selected leader of the Wuchang Revolution, was especially thrilled with the idea of following the American example. He called the suggestion "a definite and permanent solution."[97] Thus the governors' delegation came into being. It was to serve as midwife to the republic and played an important role in its early history. When Yuan Shikai was chosen as president by the delegates, he was hailed as "China's Washington." Yuan himself welcomed this comparison. In his inauguration speech on October 10, 1913, George Washington was the only foreign name he mentioned. Yuan called Washington his model[98] and said that he had accepted the American as his "guide and preceptor."[99] Many Chinese hoped that under Yuan's leadership China would enjoy unity, happiness, and membership in the family of nations.[100]

Like all revolutions in the world, the 1911 Revolution is ambiguous, complex, subversive, and full of contradictions. It is as tempting to define it by what it destroyed as by what it established. Along with some degree of superficiality in thought and cynical expediency in action, one can find faults and shortcomings with the revolution from every perspective. Yet is it fair to do so? Consider Lawrence Stone's description of the English Revolution:

What was important about the English Revolution was not its success in permanently changing the face of England – for this was slight – but the intellectual content of the various opposition programmes and achievements after 1640. For the first time in history an anointed king was brought to trial for breach of faith with his subjects, his head was publicly cut off, and his office was declared abolished. An established church was abolished, its property was seized, and fairly wide religious toleration for all forms of Protestantism was proclaimed and even enforced. For a short time, and perhaps for the first time, there came on to the stage of history a group of men proclaiming ideas of liberty not liberties, equality not privileges, fraternity not deference. These were ideas that were to live on, and to revive again in other societies in other ages . . . Although the Revolution ostensibly failed, although reforms of the electoral system, the law, the administration, were blocked, although the social structure became a good deal more hierarchical and immobile after the Revolution than it was before, something nevertheless survived. There survived ideas about religious toleration, about limitations on the power of the central executive to interfere with the personal liberty of the propertied classes, and about a polity based on the consent of a broad spectrum of society . . . It is this legacy of ideas which makes it reasonable to claim that the crisis in England in the seventeenth century is the first "Great Revolution"

---

[97] Sun Yao, ed., *Zhonghua minguo shiliao* (Taibei: Wen hai chubanshe, 1966), Part I, I: 24–26, 66.

[98] *The Peking Gazette*, October 11, 1913.   [99] *The China Press*, October 10, 1912.

[100] "Canyi Yuan zhi Yuan Shikai baogao xuanju wei linshi dazongtong dian" (Senate telegram to Yuan Shikai reporting he had been elected Provisional President), in Sun Yao, ed., *Zhonghua minguo shiliao*, Part I, I: 53.

in the history of the world, and therefore an event of fundamental importance in the evolution of Western civilization.[101]

Stone's brilliant appraisal of the English Revolution should serve as a model when we assess the Chinese 1911 Revolution. Many of the features Stone sees in the English Revolution can also be found in its Chinese counterpart in the early twentieth century. Despite its many defects, the 1911 Revolution achieved astonishing successes and brought profound changes to China. The choice of republicanism itself indicated that the 1911 Revolution would not be just another turn of the mandate of heaven, which had so often brought about the fall of dynasties. In the opinion of Joseph Levenson, "By its mere existence after thousands of years of monarchy," the republic "offered license to new thought, the solvent of Chinese pieties."[102] With the revolution, no one could legitimately make himself emperor. As Wright reminds us, "Even at the height of the reaction [against the republicanism] around 1915, China was a vastly different country from what it had been fifteen years earlier."[103] So when Yuan Shikai did try to declare himself emperor in 1916, he suffered the biggest defeat of his life and died humiliated. Zhang Xun, a strong enemy of the republican system and a warlord in central China, insisted that the 1911 Revolution had been the result of agitation by intellectuals who were "deeply engrossed in Westernization"; it was not the people's choice.[104] Zhang went on to try and restore the Qing dynasty, but the rapid failure of his scheme proved the widespread presence of republican thinking, the real source of the revolution.

The 1911 Revolution can be better appreciated from the perspective of revolutions having two functions: destruction and construction. Ignoring or emphasizing either part makes a fair evaluation impossible. The revolution's destructive power is undeniable. It totally demolished the legitimacy of the imperial and dynastic system. It also drastically undercut the power of Confucianism and the gentry. Both radical Chinese and ideologically straitjacketed historians claim that the 1911 Revolution accomplished nothing. For example, Lu Xun commented sarcastically that the only difference it made was the exchange of a cotton gown for a fur one by *yamen* officials or the dragon flag of the Qing dynasty for the five-color flag of the Republic.[105] One article in *Dong fang za zhi* claimed that the 1911 Revolution "only overthrew the autocracy in name." The same despotic

---

[101] Stone, *The Causes of the English Revolution 1529–1642*, 146–47.
[102] Levenson, *Confucian China and its Modern Fate*, II: 4.
[103] Wright, *China in Revolution*, 51.
[104] Sun Yao, ed., *Zhonghua minguo shiliao*, Part IV, II: 3.
[105] Lu Xun, *Lu Xun quanji*, II: 310–17.

spirit persisted afterward.[106] Advocates of these views ignore the fact that the Chinese revolution was a process initiated as early as 1895. They overemphasize its failure by pointing to the ultimate failure of republicanism and constitutionalism in China. They do not recognize the renewal or transformation driven forward by the revolution and discount the fact that the new China was still in its infancy. Even though republicanism did not completely live up to expectations after the establishment of the Republic, China did not turn back from its larger goals. The major problem with the view that the 1911 Revolution accomplished nothing is that it does not recognize the many things the revolution's destructive force in fact accomplished. The energy and enthusiasm with which the revolution was pressed in effect legitimized profound changes already under way and allowed them to come to fruition. Even the Qing government had directly, even perhaps unwittingly, participated in the early process of transformation with its so-called New Policies.

The significance of the 1911 Revolution can be further examined from the perspective of the new Chinese attitude toward world affairs. After the revolution, nationalism became a dominant force in Chinese policies. Nationalism demanded a national identity. The quest for a new identity continued unabated. More importantly, the old traditional worldview was buried once and for all.

One feature of the revolution rarely mentioned by scholars is that while it aimed to destroy the old China, it also meant to challenge the legitimacy of the existing world order. Although the revolution did not achieve its full potential, the direction it pointed to would deeply influence China's future development. One can argue that after the 1911 Revolution, China had become a "revolutionary state" within the international system. This phenomenon is unprecedented in Chinese history. This revolutionary state existed not in Lenin's or Mao's ideological sense but in Henry Kissinger's *realpolitik* sense: that is, a state determined to destabilize and reshape the international order of the day. This definition applies to China because it not only worked toward joining the international system, but also aimed at changing the status quo by winning full membership in the family of nations. The 1911 Revolution set the stage for China to make its move.

[106] *Dong fang za zhi* 16, 12: 179–80.

2 The rise of Chinese internationalism and the new diplomacy

> He who gives no thought to what is distant is sure to find grief close at hand.[1]
>
> Confucius

After the 1911 Revolution, nationalism became a defining and most powerful political force in China. While scholars are still debating the precise meaning of nationalism and its role in shaping the reconstruction of nations,[2] Hans Kohn's definition fits most closely with the Chinese situation at the turn of the century. For Kohn, nationalism is "a state of mind, permeating the large majority of a people and claiming to permeate all its members . . . [It] recognizes the nation-state as the ideal form of political organization and the nationality as the source of creative cultural energy and of economic well-being."[3]

Until the turn of the twentieth century, the Chinese sense of identity had turned on a tradition of culturalism.[4] If China's defeat in the

---

[1] The Analects, xv: 11.

[2] How nationalism shaped the reconstruction of nations is still a subject of serious debate. See Anthony D. Smith, "Gastronomy or Geology? The Role of Nationalism in the Reconstruction of Nations," *Nations and Nationalism* (Journal of the Association for the Study of Ethnicity and Nationalism), 1, no. 1 (March 1995): 3–23. For the best book to explain the development of the modern state in China, see Philip A. Kuhn, *Origins of the Modern Chinese State* (Stanford: Stanford University Press, 2002). For a recent study on the development of nationhood and nationalism, see Henrietta Harrison, *China* (London: Arnold, 2001); Arthur Waldron, *From War to Nationalism: China's Turning Point, 1924–1925* (Cambridge: Cambridge University Press, 1995).

[3] Hans Kohn, *The Idea of Nationalism: A Study in its Origins and Political Background* (New York: The Macmillan Company, 1944), 16.

[4] Culturalism, according to Joseph Levenson, was a different mode of national consciousness identified with the moral goals and values of a universalizing civilization. Levenson argues that the Chinese transition from culturalism to nationalism, the awareness of the nation-state as the ultimate goal of political reform, took place at the turn of the century; see Joseph Richmond Levenson, *Confucian China and its Modern Fate; A Trilogy* (Berkeley: University of California Press), I: 98–108. James Townsend also suggests that the history of modern China after the Sino-Japanese War was "one in which nationalism replaces culturalism as the dominant Chinese view of their identity and place in the world"; see James Townsend, "Chinese Nationalism," in Jonathan Unger and Geremie Barmé, eds., *Chinese Nationalism* (Armonik, NY: M. E. Sharpe, 1996), 1.

Sino-Japanese War provided a strong incentive for the Chinese to pay attention to national and international affairs, the concurrent spread of modern education, the emergence of a bourgeois class, and the appearance of a public sphere in the political realm now created a nurturing environment for Chinese nationalism. The exercise of public opinion, public debate, and the creation of a public sphere by private individuals or organizations represented another break from China's past. It created space for discussion and exchanges on political issues, unregulated by the state or political authority.

Nationalism and the blossoming of Chinese public opinion

The emergence of modern nationalism in China has a direct link to the rise of Chinese public opinion. Public opinion in China was a political invention. The development of a political press fundamentally redefined the conditions of the exercise of power. The appearance of political and independent newspapers and discussion groups after the 1895 defeat by Japan was critical to this development. To be sure, newspapers had existed in China prior to 1895. There were seventy-six newspapers and periodicals published in Chinese between 1815 and 1890, about half of which were run by churches or missionaries.[5] These publications did not have much to do with national affairs and only served the interests of their particular groups, whether commercial or religion-related. Government gazetteers, which had been produced for centuries, had nothing to do with public opinion.[6] There had been no independent nongovernmental Chinese political press prior to 1895.[7] The Sino-Japanese War changed that, presenting new opportunities for Chinese journalism. Stephen MacKinnon points out, "It was then that activists like Liang Qichao and others established a bona fide new political press."[8] This view about the crucial link between the Sino-Japanese War and the rise of the private Chinese press that expressed political views enjoys a broad consensus among scholars.[9]

---

[5] Chen Jiang, "Western Learning and Social Transformation in the Late Qing," in Frederic Wakeman and Wang Xi, eds., *China's Quest for Modernization: A Historical Perspective*, 157.
[6] For earlier information, see Roswell S. Britton, *The Chinese Periodical Press, 1800–1912* (Shanghai: Kelly & Walsh, Limited, 1933).
[7] For a detailed study on this issue, see Andrew Nathan, *Chinese Democracy* (New York: Alfred A. Knopf, 1985).
[8] Stephen MacKinnon, "Toward a History of the Chinese Press in the Republican Period," *Modern China* 23, no. 1 (January 1997): 6.
[9] Zeng Shubai wrote that the war brought about a new era in the history of Chinese journalism, giving birth to the political newspaper. For details, see Zeng Shubai, *Zhongguo*

The rise of public political opinion started with the so-called *gongche shangshu* (public vehicle petition) organized by Kang Youwei. In April 1895, eight thousand provincial degree holders who had assembled in Beijing for the triennial national civil service examination learned that China had accepted the disastrous Treaty of Shimonoseki with Japan. Shocked, they mobilized to submit petitions to the Qing court demanding reforms, and further broke with tradition by organizing study societies and independent political newspapers that would introduce their voices into national politics. Journals such as *Shibao, Shiwu Bao, Minbao, Su Bao*, among many others, came to be very influential. Study groups such as the Quanxuehui (Self-Strengthening Study Society), Baoguohui (National Preservation Society), and Zhengwenshe (Political Information Society) served as catalysts for the growth of national consciousness.[10] The purpose of these societies was similar to that of the new press: to arouse people's national consciousness, to argue for the necessity of reform, to show the futility of the traditional Chinese worldview, and to advocate diplomatic equality with the West. Around the time of the 1898 reforms, there were 668 study societies of all kinds in China, most of them dedicated to the topic of China's renewal and transformation.[11] The growth of the press was even more phenomenal; by the turn of the century, China had hundreds of daily newspapers. From 1895 to 1898, according to one figure, about 120 newspapers and magazines were published in Chinese languages. Of these about 80 percent were Chinese owned.[12] Compared to earlier periods, the Chinese public had much better access to media during the war. In 1915 China had 222 newspapers, 165 of which were published in Chinese. By 1919, there were 362 newspapers published in China, 280 of which in Chinese.[13] The British minister to China, John Jordan, in his 1911 annual report to British foreign minister Edward Grey, noted the rapid growth of the Chinese press and concluded that he was certain "newspapers have taken a firm hold on the public mind."[14] The

xinwen shi (Taipei: Shangwu yinshuguan, 1966), 191. Ge Gongzheng also indicated that prior to 1895 most Chinese were not familiar with newspapers. See Ge Gongzheng, *Zhongguo baoxue shi* (Taipei: Xuesheng shuju, 1960), 115.

[10] For a detailed analysis of the Chinese political press, especially *Shibao*, see Joan Judge, *Print and Politics: "Shibao" and the Culture of Reform in Late Qing China* (Stanford: Stanford University Press, 1996).

[11] For details, see Zhang Yufa, *Qing ji de lixian tuanti* (Taipei: Zhong yang yan jiu yuan jin dai shi yan jiu suo, 1971), 114.

[12] Fang Hanqi, ed., *Zhongguo xinwen shiye tongshi* (Beijing: renmin daxue chubanshe, 1992), I: 539.

[13] Zhang Yufa, "Xin wenhua yundong shiqi de xinwen yu yan lun, 1915–1923," *Zhongyang yanjiuyuan jindai shi yanjiusuo jikan* 23 (1993): 287.

[14] Jordan to Grey, 1911 Annual Report, 54–55, PRO, FO405/229.

rapid rise of the press was completely in tune with the new Chinese mood and the new era.

The rise of the political press also coincided with technological changes that offered possibilities for enlarging audiences and speeding the transmission of news. Millions and millions of Chinese were suddenly lifted out of darkness both with the widespread use of kerosene lamps and electric lights and, more importantly, with ready access to intelligent newspapers and new knowledge. In the meantime, with the use of modern printing machines, the cost of the delivery and production of newspapers had greatly decreased so that they became accessible in most areas and to most people who could read. Moreover, in an extraordinary change for China, Reuters' telegrams were being sent daily to the remotest corners of the land.[15] According to Leo Lee and Andrew Nathan, the number of Chinese newspapers posted in 1908 was 24,645,112; by 1919, that number had almost doubled.[16]

A "public" means a reading public, a literate public, and especially a foreign-policy-savvy public. The rise of the press coincided with the appearance of a ready mass audience. In the late Qing period, the audience for information from print sources numbered two to four million. This figure consisted of only the highly literate minority in a country in which perhaps 30 to 45 percent of males and 2 to 10 percent of females had attained basic literacy.[17] In other words, by the late Qing there was already a large reading public which later played an active role in China's foreign policy making and internationalization.

The appearance of a full-blown Chinese press and the widespread dissemination of news information were crucial to China's transformation. The press reported on events in the world and in China, and brought new ideas, new terminology, and new information to its readers.[18] The role of public opinion was also strengthened through the press. According to MacKinnon, "The creation of a new, politically radical press at the turn of the century created a mediating 'public space' in Habermasian terms

[15] *Pall Mall Gazette*, London, September 16, 1912. According to Morrison, two months before the war began, Reuter's proposed to close down his Pacific service on the grounds that it was losing money. The Chinese government, at Morrison's suggestion, came forward with a guarantee to indemnify it against loss so the service was continued. Morrison to Steed, private, February 17, 1915, in Lo Hui-min, ed., *The Correspondence of G. E. Morrison* (Cambridge: Cambridge University Press, 1976), II: 376.

[16] For more information, see Leo Lee and Andrew Nathan, "The Beginnings of Mass China," in David Johnson et al., eds., *Popular Culture in Late Imperial China* (Berkeley: University of California Press, 1985), 372–73, 376.

[17] For details, see ibid., 376, 372–73.

[18] Joan Judge, "Public Opinion and the New Politics of Contestation in the Late Qing, 1904–1911," *Modern China* 20, no. 1 (1994).

that made possible the 1911 Revolution."[19] Andrew Nathan also emphasizes the importance of the Chinese press, claiming, "The beginning of
Chinese democracy can be dated, as nearly as any such large event can be,
to the year 1895. Until then, Chinese politics had been closed to people
outside the bureaucracy."[20] It is fair to say that the Qing court again
participated in the creation of the public sphere with an edict on constitutional preparation in 1906 declaring that "all affairs of state would be
open to public opinion."[21] Public opinion had clearly become a player in
Chinese political and social realms by the early twentieth century, and this
phenomenon helped shape the Chinese attitude toward foreign affairs.

The most important role the news media played was in its definition
of the national consciousness and modern nationalism; after the Sino-
Japanese War these became a public ideology, not simply an ideal in the
minds of a few intellectuals. As Bao Tianxiao remembered, "Chinese
nationalism had been aroused. Most educated people, who had never
before discussed national affairs, wanted to discuss them: Why are others
stronger than we are, and why are we weaker?"[22] Even Zhang Zhidong,
a conservative famous for his so-called *ti-yong* theory,[23] which was completely discredited in the wake of the war, admitted, "After 1895 literary
men of patriotic spirit began to publish journals . . . As a result, gentry
from the most obscure pockets of the realm and isolated peasants learned
for the first time that there *was* a China. Ignorant petty officials and the
whole multitude of would-be scholars learned for the first time that there
were 'current affairs.' "[24] The new information provided an effective vehicle for helping the Chinese to communicate within large groups and share
their feelings and understanding about China and the world. By doing
so, the Chinese press succeeded in creating an "imagined community,"
a sense of belonging to a nation-state.[25]

[19] MacKinnon, "Toward a History of the Chinese Press in the Republican Period," 3.
[20] Nathan, *Chinese Democracy*, preface, x.
[21] "Xuanshi yu bei li xuan xuan xin li ding guan zhi yu," in *Qingmu chou bei li xuan dangan shiliao* (Beijing, 1979), I: 44.
[22] Bao Tianxiao, *Chuanyinlou huiyi lu* (Hong Kong: Da hua chubanshe, 1971), 145.
[23] The most important Chinese response to its weak position in the late nineteenth century was the so-called "ti-yong" theory. This theory argued that the best way for China to identify itself in the new environment was to adopt "Chinese learning as the fundamental principles [*ti*], Western learning for practical applications [*yong*]." To believers of this theory, although China was backward in technology, its traditional culture and civilization were still superior to the West's. Therefore, China needed only to adopt Western technology without changing its civilization and culture. China's national identity should be a mixture of Chinese cultural essence and Western technology.
[24] Ge Gongzheng, *Zhongguo baoxue shi*, 126.
[25] Benedict Anderson, *Imagined Communities: Reflections on the Origin and Spread of Nation-alism* (London: Verso Press, 1991), 37–46.

This sense of solidarity, which had been missing in China prior to 1895, was critical to evolving Chinese nationalism and China's desire to become a nation. Liang Qichao had once lamented that "on the surface the government seems to be a centralized one. However, the country is actually divided into innumerable small units and groups on the basis of either territory or biological relatedness or occupations." Thanks to the political press and the study groups and societies, a crucial link had been created to unite the otherwise variegated and loosely knit Chinese society into a unified and cohesive entity.[26] Because of the wide popularity of newspapers and magazines, one veteran journalist observed, "For the first time in history the Chinese have discovered a common ground of union which has appealed to men of all classes and trades, of all religions, all sections of the community. Unconsciously the Chinese have welded themselves into a nation."[27] A recent study of the political press also concluded that it had "opened up a space in late Qing China not only for re-conceptualizing the structure of politics but also for renegotiating the structure of society."[28] With the appearance of a national consciousness and nationalism, Chinese society as a whole was for a time unified and politically engaged.

The Chinese now shared a mutual concern about their country's fate and its sovereignty. "[I]nsisting on the recovery of sovereign rights and on the creation of instrumentalities to that end through reform was," according to Ernest Young, "the main ideological content of the politicization of gentry and merchants after 1900."[29] Many movements which developed later were closely linked to these trends toward nationalism and politicization. Bryna Goodman in her recent book skillfully demonstrates that even regional networks in Shanghai worked hard to link their local identity with national interests. Political activists of native-place associations "relied on native-place loyalties to stir up patriotic nationalist activity."[30] Zhang Pengyuan has also showed that provincial assemblies actively participated in national politics and promoted national interests.[31] Perhaps the best example of the rise of national consciousness was the anti-American boycott of 1905 over America's Chinese Exclusion

---

[26] See Chang Hao, *Liang Chi-Ch'ao and Intellectual Transition in China, 1890–1907* (Cambridge, MA: Harvard University Press, 1971), 109.

[27] Douglas Tory, *Tomorrow in the East* (London: Chapman & Hall, 1907), 173.

[28] Judge, *Print and Politics*, 79.

[29] Ernest Young, *The Presidency of Yuan Shih-Kai: Liberalism and Dictatorship in Early Republican China* (Ann Arbor: University of Michigan Press, 1977), 16.

[30] Bryna Goodman, *Native Place, City, and Nation: Regional Networks and Identities in Shanghai, 1853–1937* (Berkeley: University of California Press, 1995), 179.

[31] For details, see Zhang Pengyuan, "Provincial Assemblies: The Emergence of Political Participation," *Zhongyang yanjiuyuan jindai shi yanjiusuo jikan* 22 (1983).

Act.[32] The boycott began early in 1905, in Shanghai, and soon shifted its center to Guangzhou; from there it developed into a national movement. Approximately 160 cities joined the boycott drive.[33] Even Chinese women seeking an independent voice and status used nationalism as their own "authorizing discourse."[34]

The sudden awakening of national consciousness even surprised some members of the Chinese elite, such as Zhang Jiang. He commented that the boycott of American goods by Chinese had "spread to all provinces. Nobody even dared to expect that such national consciousness and such civilized protest would have occurred five years ago."[35] Morrison reported, "The Chinese have awakened to a consciousness of nationality. Outrages on Cantonese who have emigrated to the Pacific coast are no longer resented only by the people of Kwantung. They make *all* China indignant."[36] Historian Marie-Claire Bergère also writes,

The boycott of 1905 shows what a remarkable widening of horizons had taken place. Loyalties were no longer confined to a particular corporation or region; from now on they included national loyalty. For the first time, apparently, the Chinese bourgeoisie had consciously asserted itself as a class and given voice to political aims.[37]

The rise of the Chinese press and the new mentality across society were complementary. Many scholars agree that the modern press has served as an agent for historical change.[38] What Pierre Rétat said about the media's role in the French Revolution applies as well to China: "The birth of the [revolutionary] newspaper coincides with that of a new era; it has the vocation of measuring it and defining its rhythm."[39] In China

---

[32] For a recent study on this subject, see Wang Guanhua, *In Search of Justice: The 1905–1906 Chinese Anti-American Boycott* (Cambridge, MA: The Harvard University Asia Center, 2001).

[33] For a recent study on this subject, see Kim Hee-Gyeo, "Dizhi meihuo yundong shiqi Zhongguo min zhong de jindai xing," *Lishi yanjiu* 4 (1997): 92–107.

[34] Joan Judge, "Talent, Virtue, and the Nation: Chinese Nationalism and Female Subjectivities in the Early Twentieth Century," *The American Historical Review* 106, no. 3 (2001): 765–803.

[35] Xu Dingxin, Qiang Xiaomin, *Shanghai zong shanghui shi* (Shanghai: Shanghai shehui kexueyuan chubanshe, 1991), 78, 87.

[36] Mary Wright, *China In Revolution: The First Phase, 1900–1913* (New Haven: Yale University Press, 1968), introduction, 10.

[37] Marie-Claire Bergère, "The Role of the Bourgeoisie," in Wright, ed., *China in Revolution*, 252.

[38] For details, see Elizabeth Eisenstein, *The Printing Press as an Agent of Change*, 2 vols. (Cambridge: Cambridge University Press, 1979); Roger Chartier, ed., *The Culture of Print* (Princeton: Princeton University Press, 1979); Samuel Popkin, *Media and Revolution: Comparative Perspectives* (Lexington: University of Kentucky Press, 1995).

[39] Rétat, "Forme et discours d'un journal révolutionnaire: les Révolutions de Paris en 1789," quote from Popkin, ed., *Media and Revolution*, 21.

the new public helped to introduce what Lin Yutang called the "golden period" (1895–1911) of the Chinese press, which subsequently nurtured the revolutionary environment.[40] Liang Qichao announced in 1912 that "the establishment of the Republic of China was the result of a revolution of ink, not a revolution of blood."[41] Sun Yat-sen seemed to agree with this, declaring in 1912 that the reason "the [1911] revolution has finally succeeded today is due to the power of the press. The press enjoys this power because it is able to instill ideals in people's minds."[42] The press had "set the stage and defined the aims . . . that toppled the dynasty," and the revolution in turn had "enhanced the connection between the modern press and political power as part of the process of state building."[43]

The new press not only played a crucial role in the making of the revolution, but was also an important factor in the rise of Chinese nationalism, a complicated phenomenon which had several aspects. For Sun Yat-sen and his followers in the period of 1895 to 1911, nationalism is perhaps better described as ethnic nationalism, namely, anti-Manchu nationalism. This kind of nationalism emerged as both an ideology and a movement that created a common sense of identity, mobilizing popular support against an oppressive state structure. Sun Yat-sen's Xingzhonghui (Revive China Society), founded in 1895 and a predecessor of the Nationalist party, clearly had that aspect. For many people such as Liang Qichao and Kang Youwei, nationalism included new ingredients for nation building. Liang regarded it as "a doctrine of the most honest, upright, and just in the world."[44] In early 1902, he wrote to his mentor Kang Youwei, "Today is a crucial time for advancing nationalism, without which no nation-state can be built."[45]

Liang's nationalism was obviously a form of statism; he made this distinction very clear in 1906 by arguing that "today only statism (*guojia zhuyi*) can save China."[46] But for most Chinese, nationalism meant anti-imperialism and making China a full member of the world community. After the republic was founded in 1912, Chinese nationalism became in fact state nationalism or statism. "What is the principle of

[40] Lin Yutang, *A History of the Press and Public Opinion in China* (New York: Greenwood Press, 1968), 94.
[41] Liang Qichao, *Liang Rengong xiansheng yanshuo ji* (Beijing: Zheng meng yin shu ju, 1912), 4.
[42] Sun's speech in Shanghai, April 16, 1912; see Julie Lee Wei et al., eds., *Prescriptions for Saving China*, 70.
[43] MacKinnon, "Toward a History of the Chinese Press in the Republican Period," 4.
[44] Li Huaxing and Wu Jiayi, eds., *Liang Qichao xuanji* (Selected writings of Liang Qichao) (Shanghai: Shanghai renmin chubanshe, 1984), 191, 210.
[45] Ding Wenjiang and Zhao Fengtian, eds., *Liang Qichao nianpu changbian* (Shanghai: Shanghai renmin chubanshe, 1983), 286.
[46] Li Huaxing and Wu Jiayi, eds., *Liang Qichao xuanji*, 527.

nationalism?" asked Sun Yat-sen in 1924. It is "equivalent to the 'doctrine of the state.' "[47] Both new Chinese social elite and the working class were the vanguards of this kind of nationalism, whose sole purpose was to revitalize China and win it equal status. Chinese statism at this time "expresses the inflamed desire of the insufficiently regarded to count for something among the cultures of the world."[48] Indeed, as John Breuilly notes, statism motivated by a strong desire for a national identity "provides people with the means to identify their own position in the world in relation to others."[49]

Moreover, Chinese nationalism was at root political nationalism. Before the outbreak of World War I, British publicist Norman Angell made a striking statement: "Political nationalism has become for the European of our age the most important thing in the world, more important than humanity, decency, kindness, pity, more important than life itself."[50] This also held true in China. Just as the French Revolution meant the coming of age of modern nationalism, the 1911 Revolution meant the coming of age of Chinese political nationalism, a nationalism that would serve as a means for constructing a new political identity.[51] The cause of Chinese nationalism, and the core of its content, according to Levenson, "was intellectual alienation from traditional Chinese culture," and the rejection of the "Chinese way of life." This nationalism "began as a paradox, a doctrine with increasingly obvious internal tensions. The nationalist protected tradition so that he might be a nationalist and be able to attack it."[52] Chinese nationalism thus presented a dilemma because it articulated a forceful and near-total rejection of the traditional cultural sense of identity.

Nationalism as internationalism

The emergence of Chinese nationalism was itself part of the process of China's internationalization, a result of Western economic and military encroachment and cultural and political challenge. The very term

---

[47] Sun Yat-sen, *San Min Chu I*, translated by Frank Price (New York: Da Capo Press, 1975), 4–5.
[48] Quoted from William Pfaff, *The Wrath of Nations: Civilization and the Furies of Nationalism* (New York: Simon & Schuster, 1993), 41.
[49] John Breuilly, *Nationalism and the State* (Chicago: University of Chicago Press, 1994), 381.
[50] Louis L. Snyder, *Encyclopedia of Nationalism* (New York: Paragon House, 1990), vii.
[51] John Breuilly argues that "Nationalism is explicitly political. It appeals to people in terms of their rights and their own identities rather than in terms of their shared beliefs." See Breuilly, *Nationalism and the State*, 80.
[52] Levenson, *Confucian China and its Modern Fate*, I: 95, 108.

minzu (meaning a nation, a people) was imported; it did not exist in the Chinese lexicon until 1899, and the concept of *minzu zhuyi* (nationalism) was first used by Liang Qichao in 1901, then by Sun Yat-sen in 1904.[53] Moreover, as Rebecca E. Karl argues in her recent book, "Crucial to the original formulation of Chinese nationalism" is the "global historical moment of the turn of the [twentieth] century" that was "conceptually linked to China's post-1895 intellectual and social crisis."[54] In this sense, the rise of Chinese nationalism, according to Karl, "marked a Chinese intervention in the world." It directly related to their "redefinitions of themselves and of the world." "[T]he conscious articulation of a global Chinese nationalist discourse and praxis became possible . . . as the world as a structured totality became visible."[55]

An especially interesting aspect of the Chinese experience was the lack of polarization between nationalism and internationalism, at least in the early years. Just as Liang's new citizen was expected to be a member of the world and the nation simultaneously (*xue wei Zhongguo ren, xue wei shijie ren*),[56] nationalism (*minzu zhuyi*) and internationalism (*shijie zhuyi*) were for many years two sides of the same coin. In his *Xinmin shuo*, for instance, Liang mentioned *minzu zhuyi* seven times, and *shijie zhuyi* twice, and he argued that they were closely interconnected. Early Chinese nationalism went beyond statism (*guojia zhuyi*) to embrace internationalism. As Tang Xiaobing has described it, "A global imaginary of identity underlay the discourse of nationalism."[57] Indeed, Yuan Shikai said as much in his inauguration speech as Chinese president on October 10, 1913. Yuan stated that China, as a new republic, "would completely discard all old ideas from her isolation era" and join the family of nations.[58] What Yuan tried to argue here was actually a new approach to nationalism, one that Wilhelm Reich has called "nationalist internationalism" or "internationalist nationalism."[59]

---

[53] For Liang Qichao's article on nationalism, see "Guojia shixian bian qian yi tong lun" in Li Huaxing and Wu Jiayi, eds., *Liang Qichao xuanji*; Michael Yahuda, "The Changing Faces of Chinese Nationalism: The Dimensions of Statehood," in Michael Leifer, ed., *Asian Nationalism* (London: Routledge, 2000), 27.

[54] Rebecca E. Karl, *Staging the World: Chinese Nationalism at the Turn of the Twentieth Century* (Durham, NC: Duke University Press, 2002), x.

[55] Ibid., 196, 201.

[56] Liang's point is important even today since the perspective he mentioned is still controversial. "Nobody," Hannah Arendt says, "can be a citizen of the world as he is a citizen of his country." See Arendt, "Karl Jaspers: Citizen of the World?" in Arendt, ed., *Men in Dark Times* (New York: Harcourt, Brace and World, 1968), 81.

[57] Xiaobing Tang, *Global Space and the Nationalist Discourse of Modernity: The Historical Thinking of Liang Qichao* (Stanford: Stanford University Press, 1996), 22.

[58] Bai Jiao, *Yuan Shikai yu Zhonghua minguo* (Shanghai: Renwen yuekanshe, 1936), 65–66.

[59] Wilhelm Reich has discussed this point well in his *Les hommes dans l'Etat* (Paris: Payot, 1978).

Of course, internationalist nationalism was not unique to this period. Decades later, when dealing with the Soviet Union, Mao argued that internationalism and nationalism remained compatible.[60] Internationalist nationalism was not unique to China either. Mohandas K. Gandhi, Jawaharlal Nehru, and Rabindranath Tagore, three great Indian thinkers and nationalists, all have been described as both nationalist and internationalist.[61] Gandhi is reported to have said that it was impossible for one to be an internationalist without being a nationalist and he always asserted that "my nationalism is intense internationalism." Because "the struggle for India's freedom was thus part of a larger world movement concerning all mankind," Gandhi believed that nationalism was a necessary step on the way to internationalism.[62] According to Indian scholar Mool Chand, "Nehru's internationalism was progressive and political, whereas Gandhi's was humanitarian and religious, and that of Tagore spiritual and cosmopolitan."[63] One could argue that the ancient Chinese ideal of *datong* (great unity) and the unity of Christendom in Medieval Europe had elements of internationalism. The Chinese *datong* ideal and the Holy Roman Empire's Christendom, although in fact more aspirations than realities, were both aimed at the kind of elements of what we now term internationalism.

The Chinese approach to nationalist internationalism, the backbone of Republican China's foreign policy, did not come about suddenly; it had been collectively articulated over a period of decades by both the government and individuals. The old utopian *datong* was developed further in the late nineteenth century by such thinkers as Kang Youwei. Kang's articulation of this concept was new wine in an old bottle. His utopianism was oriented toward the future, rather than the ancient past, as was common in traditional Chinese thinking. As Arif Dirlik claims, "Kang's society of great unity represented the final stage of human progress following states of familism and nationalism, in that order. The utopia drew its name and virtues from a native Chinese utopian tradition, but already its inspiration came from the future," which transcended the Chinese sphere and took global society as its scope.[64] So Kang's idea was different from nationalist internationalism because he focused on an ideal world that was far beyond the existing world order. Where nationalist internationalism was based

---

[60] Steven Goldstein, "Nationalism and Internationalism: Sino-Soviet Relations", in Thomas W. Robinson and David Shambaugh, ed., *Chinese Foreign Policy: Theory and Practice* (Oxford: Oxford University Press, 1994), 224–65.

[61] For this point, see Mool Chand, *Nationalism and Internationalism of Gandhi, Nehru and Tagore* (New Delhi: M. N. Publishers and distributors, 1989).

[62] Ibid., 2, 116–17.   [63] Ibid., 9.

[64] Arif Dirlik, *Anarchism in the Chinese Revolution* (Berkeley: University of California Press, 1991), 50, 55.

on Western political and nationalistic concepts and squarely focused on the present, *datong* emphasized traditional Chinese concepts and concerns.

At the turn of the twentieth century, it was fashionable to talk about *shijie zhuyi* (internationalism). Liang Qichao in late 1899 elaborated on the connection between nationalism and internationalism. He argued that in the Chinese case, "Nationalism can also be called internationalism" because the fate of China was directly linked to world affairs.[65] But Liang's argument is not systematic, and it was perhaps Yang Du who first tried to explain the connection in a systematic and intellectual fashion.

Yang Du (1874–1932) was a political reformer who later became a major figure in Yuan Shikai's monarchical scheme. He was perhaps the first Chinese to coin the term "internationalist nationalism" (*shijie de guojia zhuyi*). Starting in late 1906, Yang published a series of articles entitled "Jintie zhuyi shuo" (The theory of gold-ironism) in the new journal *Zhongguo xinbao*, of which he was editor-in-chief. According to his own definition, the theory of gold-ironism concerned how to make China economically rich and militarily powerful. In this 140,000-character article, he devoted much space to his idea of internationalist nationalism, arguing that the new world order was based on economic and military power. If China wanted to survive in this new environment, it had to play the same game as the Great Powers. Yang claimed that his approach would provide a blueprint for China's joining the new world system successfully. Only by achieving both wealth and power could China become an active member of the world system, and Yang argued that China already had the resources to put his ideas into practice.[66] For Yang and other advocates of the new approach, joining the world and participating in international affairs as an equal member was key to nationalist internationalism.

On January 5, 1912, Republican China published a document entitled "Manifesto from the Republic of China to All Friendly Nations" to publicize its internationalist approach. Signed by Sun Yat-sen, it was the first important foreign policy document of the Republic. The very beginning of the manifesto argued that the Manchu regime had failed to heed the painful lessons learned under the heel of foreign powers, and subsequently the Qing court had placed itself and China beneath the contempt of the world. "To remedy these evils and render possible the entrance of China into the family of nations we fought [the Qing] and formed our [own] government." The document declared that it was Republican China's constant aim and firm determination to build upon

---

[65] Li Huaxing and Wu Jiayi, eds., *Liang Qichao xuanji*, 101.
[66] Yang Du, "Jingtie zhuyi shuo," *Zhongguo xinbao*, 1–6 (1906, 1907).

"a stable and enduring foundation for a national structure compatible with the potentialities of our long-neglected country." It was a message of "peace and good will" indicated by "hope of being admitted into the family of nations not merely to share their rights and privileges but also to co-operate with them in the great and noble task called for in the uplifting of the civilization of the world."[67] Sun, in his inauguration speech as provisional president, also promised the world that Republican China "will assume responsibility as a civilized country to enjoy the benefits that a civilized nation should have." China would rid itself of all policies that had dishonored it under the Qing, and especially all isolationist policies. It would pursue peaceful diplomacy to "develop friendship and harmony" with foreign countries, and the government would work hard "to rejoin China with the international community" and promote world peace.[68]

To make China's new approach clear to the world and to pave its way into the family of nations, early Republican leaders took full advantage of the muscle of the media – a practice unprecedented in China's foreign affairs. Sun maintained that China "must appeal to the people of the civilized world in general," and the peoples of the United States and France in particular, for their sympathy and support. In his pleas to both countries, Sun expressed his hope that China might find many Lafayettes among the Americans and French in its quest for a new national identity.[69] Wu Tingfang used the media especially skillfully. When the new republic had yet to be officially founded, he appealed through William Randolph Hearst for recognition of the new China by the West. Professing "friendly greetings to the whole world" from the Chinese nation which had been "born anew in travail of revolution," Wu directly asked the powers to recognize this new nation and uphold friendly trade and intercourse with it. With their successful revolution, Wu argued, the Chinese people had written the "most glorious page in Chinese history with a bloodless pen." China was now ready to be welcomed into the family of nations.[70]

China's public opinion campaign had positive results. On December 13, 1911, *The New York American*, a Hearst journal, directly asked the US Congress to send a message of sympathy to China. It claimed, "It

---

[67] Sun Yao, ed., *Zhonghua minguo shiliao* (Historical records of Republican China) (Taipei: Wenhai chubanshe, 1966), I, Part I, 28–32; see also *The China Press*, January 6, 1912.

[68] Sun Yao, *Zhonghua minguo shiliao*, I, Part I, 27–28.

[69] Sun Yat-sen, "Zhongguo wenti de zheng jieju", in *Sun Zhongshan ji* (Beijing: Zhonghua shuju, 1981), I: 248–55; see also Quai d'Orsay, Chine, Politique intérieure, Dossier Général, NS, DCXXXVI.

[70] Wu Tingfang to Hearst from Shanghai, November 15, 1911, *The New York American*, November 16, 1911.

would be both in harmony with the traditions of the United States and in conformity with international law if the Congress in Washington should extend the sympathy of this great nation to the patriots of China now battling to establish a popular government in that vast empire." The journal further argued that "Chinese lovers of liberty and free institutions" were engaged in a great struggle to overthrow the ancient despotism that had stood like a great wall barring the introduction of modern ideas into China. The United States should not withhold its encouragement since the Chinese cause was just and ought to succeed. Its success would result in the progress and happiness of China's people and be a historic step in the progress of the world toward a higher and more enlightened civilization.[71] Under the influence of people such as Hearst, the US Congress passed a resolution in early 1912 to congratulate "the people of China on their assumption of the powers, duties, and responsibilities of self-government."[72] The Wilson Administration soon followed suit by recognizing the Republic of China; the United States was the first major country to do so.[73]

China's desire to join the world was clearly reflected in its many domestic agendas. At the opening of the National Assembly on April 8, 1913, the members and visitors were handed a circular headed "A Few Words to the Members." The circular read as follows:

The people of our country were despised by the world for a long time. Since the establishment of the Republic, our citizens have shown the world their good qualities, and foreigners have gradually treated us with respect. Now that the National Assembly has been formed, taking place for the first time in China after thousands of years, it is the best opportunity for our citizens to make a worldwide reputation. We have heard that there are several hundred foreigners in Beijing who will come to the assembly today, and that they will observe the [good] order of our people and the purport of our discussions, as to decide the question of our recognition. We hope, therefore, that our most respect[ed] and [beloved] members will maintain a dignified and graceful demeanor when representing the citizens of our whole nation, so that we may command the respect and win the friendship of foreigners.[74]

China was prepared to embrace the West and no longer pretended to ignore its economic and political inferiority; it was determined to learn from the West. Liu Kuiyi, minister of commerce and industry, declared that what China was anxiously striving for was to establish good

---

[71] The 62nd Congress, 2nd session, House of Representatives, Report No. 368, 2.
[72] United States Congressional Record, February 29, 1912.
[73] *The Peking Daily News*, May 3, 1913.
[74] This booklet is found in Quai d'Orsay, Chine, Politique intérieure, Dossier Général, NS, XLIX: 64.

government. "I hope foreign nations will give us advice on how to do this."[75] The young nation, with all earnestness, enthusiasm, openness, and perhaps a bit of naiveté, was working hard to join the international system and present its concerns to other countries. From the turn of the twentieth century to the outbreak of World War I, China attended a number of universal forums, among them the Hague Convention (1899–1907), the Geneva Convention (1906), the convention relating to hospital ships (1904), the convention for the creation of an international agricultural institute (held in Rome) (1905), the Hague Opium Convention (1912–14), and the Convention for the Publication of Customs Tariffs (1890).

China assumed a major role in the crusade to stop the opium trade, since many Chinese believed opium addiction was a sign of national weakness. Of course, it also carried the humiliation of the Opium War. Kathleen Lodwick has concluded that those who wanted China to be a modern nation realized that the success of the crusade "meant all Chinese had to be involved in creating the new state."[76] Under pressure from Chinese nationalists, the Qing court in 1906 had issued an imperial edict banning the use of opium. China signed an opium agreement with Great Britain in 1911, and attended the first, second, and third international opium conferences (at the Hague in 1912, 1913, and 1914, respectively). China was one of the few countries that wanted to eradicate opium and other drug trades once and for all; many other countries involved only paid lip service to this cause. China used every occasion to lobby for eradication of the opium trade. As World War I drew to a close, Yan Huiqing, who had represented China at two opium conferences, wrote to US Secretary of State Robert Lansing suggesting that the signing and ratification of the Opium Convention of 1913 be included as one of the conditions in the peace treaty. This idea was not adopted, however, and subsequent conferences on opium under the auspices of the League of Nations failed to produce serious results.[77] Nevertheless, the Chinese campaign to end the use of opium after 1906 was, according to Lodwick, perhaps "the largest and most vigorous effort in world history to stamp out an established social evil."[78]

The new Chinese approach to world affairs was strongly conditioned by *neiluan waihuan* (troubles within and threats from without) and

---

[75] *The China Press*, October 10, 1912.
[76] Kathleen L. Lodwick, *Crusaders against Opium: Protestant Missionaries in China, 1874–1917* (Lexington, KY: The University Press of Kentucky, 1996), 6.
[77] Yan Huiqing, *East–West Kaleidoscope, 1877–1944: An Autobiography* (New York: St. John's University Press, 1974), 87.
[78] Wright, *China in Revolution*, 14.

the fact that since the turn of the century, foreign powers had almost completely dominated China, with Chinese domestic politics becoming closely linked to the foreign presence.[79] The Great Powers' friendly attitude toward China would have a strong impact on the effectiveness of the new Chinese efforts.

Unfortunately, foreign powers had not been friendly toward the Qing, and perhaps with the exception of the United States, this same attitude persisted once the Republic of China was founded. The powers cared little about China's dream of entering the international system as an equal; they refused to recognize the new republic until they got what they wanted from it. Yuan Shikai, whom the powers claimed to support, openly aired his resentment. He told his political advisor G. E. Morrison that every time the British minister to China discussed affairs with him, whether it was a question of Yunnan or of opium, he threatened that unless his claims were granted, England would not recognize the Republic.[80] Japanese and French ministers were even worse: three days after the outbreak of the 1911 Revolution, the Japanese War Ministry's Military Affairs Bureau prepared a memorandum suggesting various alternatives. "Should we be satisfied with south Manchuria, occupy parts of Chihli and Shangsi provinces to take possession of resources in central China, control the mouth of the Yangtze so as to occupy the rivers resources as well as the mines of Tayeh, or seek the concession of Kwangtung or Fukien Province?" Historian Akira Iriye remarks, "It was as if the Chinese revolution was giving Japan an excellent opportunity to expand its territory."[81] From the very beginning, then, China's drive for internationalism was jeopardized by non-cooperation from the Great Powers.

China's foreign policy public

Both China and the world in the period between 1895 and 1914 had experienced profound changes. Although these changes necessarily riddled Chinese efforts to join the world with contradictions and ambiguities, it set the stage for China to participate within the new world order and led to the rise of a new group in China – the foreign policy public – on the eve of the First World War. China's obsession with its world status, the currency of modern nationalism, and the emergence

[79] Zhang Yilin, *Xin Taiping shi ji* (Taipei: Wenhai chubanshe, 1966), 64.
[80] Morrison to C. W. Campbell, Beijing, October 24, 1912, *The Correspondence of Morrison*, II: 41.
[81] Akira Iriye, *Japan in the Wider World* (London: Longman, 1997), 41.

of a new press certainly augmented the growing strength of public opinion. Bernard Cohen argues that the media inescapably bring the world of foreign policy to the public, to outsiders of all kinds, shaping their knowledge as well as their incentives and opportunities for participation in the policy-making process. He also contends that since members of the media are among the most articulate and informed outside the actual foreign-policy-making process, they unavoidably affect the environment in which foreign policy decisions are made by insiders.[82] This was exactly the case in China during the war. By the vehicles of newspapers, magazines, circulars, and speeches, among other media forums, Chinese elite groups broadcast their opinions, ideas, and appeals to their fellow Chinese. With expanded access to new information on national and foreign affairs, some Chinese began to demonstrate a greater than average interest in foreign policy; they became what we can consider a true foreign policy public.

A thorough study of this foreign policy public is crucial in discerning the web of connections between China and the world in general and between the Chinese and the First World War in particular. Unfortunately, the data are either lacking or disorganized because the debate on the war among the Chinese social elite was dispersed and unstructured. Here I can only attempt a preliminary analysis, with certain constraints. I have to assume that the debate among the elite is substantially representative of public debate on foreign policy in general. This top-down process seems to have generally been the case in China: mass public opinion followed elite opinion.

According to Gabriel A. Almond, the foreign policy public consists of a four-stage hierarchy, with the general public at the base, official leadership at the apex, and the public opinion elite below the leadership but above an "attentive public."[83] Its structure is pyramidal, with a large base of the disinterested and the ignorant, a small layer of interested and informed observers (the attentive public) above that, and at the top, a very thin layer of active participants (including both foreign policy makers and the public opinion elite) who engage in foreign-policy debate, discussion, and decision making both in and outside government. The dividing lines between these layers are blurred and permeable. It is difficult to determine who qualifies as the top elites and who qualifies as the attentive public by virtue of interest, information, and activity. Differing responses to the

---

[82] For details, see Bernard C. Cohen, *The Press and Foreign Policy* (Princeton: Princeton University Press, 1963).

[83] G. A. Almond, *The American People and Foreign Policy* (New York: Frederick Praeger, 1960), v: 137–38.

same foreign policy issues by the same individuals at different times make classifications more difficult. The foreign policy public, as Ernest May points out, "consists of many publics, each made up of men and women with other interests."[84]

Given all these complexities, we can indulge in only very rough estimates of the size of the foreign policy public in China. Very few qualify for the top, but almost every literate Chinese of this period qualifies for the attentive public.[85] The mass or general public consisted of people who usually pay no attention to foreign policy yet who may become briefly interested from time to time by virtue of their profession (e.g., laborers who went to Europe and people whose lives were affected by the war because of their career as industrialists, workers in particular factories, and so on); their locations (people who lived in Shandong were greatly affected by the war); or particular public events such as publication of the Japanese Twenty-one Demands, the Laoxikai Incident, and the May Fourth Movement.

Chinese society during World War I was especially suited for the formation of a foreign policy public. China had traditionally been an elite-dominated society; it looked to the elite to rule and guide, a reliance that continued even after Republican China was founded. Sun Yat-sen, although he vowed to fight for a democratic China, was really an elitist. To build up the state, he made it clear, elite had to be given even greater power. The average Chinese had to surrender to "men of ability." He once openly declared that the four hundred million Chinese were "A Dous" (A Dou was an emperor in the Three Kingdoms period notorious for his dim-wittedness) having authority but lacking ability, simple and stupid without a spark of talent. They should allow wise and knowledgeable people – Zhuge Liang (a brilliant and loyal prime minister of the same

---

[84] Ernest R. May, *American Imperialism* (New York: Atheneum, 1968), 41–42.

[85] It is difficult to measure the size of this attentive public. One way is to look at numbers of literate Chinese. According to Leo Ou-fan Lee and Andrew Nathan, elementary and middle school enrollments in selected years are as follows:

Year	Elementary	Middle
1907	918,586	31,682
1909	1,532,746	85,689
1912	2,795,475	103,045
1916	3,843,454	111,078
1918–20	5,031,687	132,432

For details, see Leo Ou-fan Lee and Andrew Nathan, "The Beginnings of Mass Culture: Journalism and Fiction in the Late Ch'ing and Beyond," in Johnson et al., eds., *Popular Culture in Late Imperial China*, 375.

period) – to rule them.[86] Such ideas clearly derived from the philosopher Mencius' idea that men who labor with their minds should rule, and men who labor with their hands should be governed. Liang Qichao, an extremely influential voice, was also strikingly elitist. He once declared that as a clear-headed member of the elite, he was prepared to challenge the four hundred million ignorant people (of China) by educating and awakening them.[87] So the tradition of a top-down infusion of information and framing of public discussion may have strongly informed the shape and interests of the emerging Chinese foreign policy public.

By the First World War, the environment in China was ripe for broader elite participation in the formation of foreign policy. From the turn of the twentieth century, the growing importance of public opinion in foreign affairs had become obvious, and many Chinese elite members were determined to take advantage of it. The Chinese public's new interest in foreign affairs came to engage international events, as in the response to recognition of the Republic of China by the United States. After news of the recognition spread, the general chamber of commerce in Guangdong Province held an extraordinary meeting to discuss it and decided to send the following telegraph to the president of the United States: "Our country is indebted to you for your recognition. We feel exceedingly joyful and happy. Henceforth the relations of our two countries will become more friendly and our commerce will prosper all the more. We respectfully express our thankfulness."[88] After almost two decades of preparation, expanding their knowledge base, changing their attitudes and social structure, the Chinese public had begun to lend its voice to the foreign policy making process. The outbreak of World War I provided the final catalyst for this new public; with the start of the Great War social elites began to really focus on foreign policy making and organized themselves into a true foreign policy public.

On another front, with the advent of modern nationalism, even non-elite Chinese (or in historian Thomas Bailey's phrase, "the man in the street") began to take foreign affairs into their own hands;[89] their weapons were boycotts and strikes against foreign goods and companies. An editorial that appeared around 1916 in the foreign press speaks volumes about

---

[86] A Dou and Zhuge Liang are popular figures in *Romance of the Three Kingdoms*, a novel written by Luo Guangzhong (1330–1400). For Sun's comments, see Hu Hanmin, ed., *Zongli quanji*, 165–66; Sun Yat-sen, *Sun Zhongshan xuanji* (Selected writings of Sun Yat-Sen) (Beijing: Renmin chubanshe, 1981), 767.

[87] Liang Qichao, "Ju guo jie wo di," in *Yin bing shi he ji* (Collected Writings of Liang Qichao) (Beijing: Zhonghua shuju, 1989), v: 16–17.

[88] *South China Morning Post*, May 15, 1913.

[89] Thomas Bailey, *The Man in the Street* (New York: Macmillan Company, 1948).

the effects of this new tool. Entitled "Plain talk to the Chinese," it reads as follows:

Boycotts and strikes, in lieu of diplomatic action, are becoming somewhat of a fad with the Chinese. They have been practised with impunity and considerable success for the past fifteen or twenty years . . . We wish to impress upon the Chinese people and Government that these anti-foreign agitations are becoming somewhat of a nuisance, and it is high time the foreign powers stepped in and put a stop to them.

The same editorial warned that boycotts against the foreigners can be carried out "once too often, and it looks to us that they have just now reached this once-too-often stage. It may be just as well to remind the Chinese Government, in case they conclude that the Allies are too busy in Europe to pay serious attention to Chinese affairs, that the Japanese are one of the allies, and their hands are not particularly tied at present."[90] From this opinion piece, one gets a clear impression that China's foreign policy public during the Great War period not only took vigorous action but was also successful in engaging the attention of the foreign powers.

No matter how naive China's foreign policy public may have been, its existence greatly influenced the Chinese government's attitude and policy regarding the First World War. During the war, mobilization of public opinion was a widespread and sometimes a shared activity for social elites and the government. The emergence of a foreign policy public made opinion leaders such as Liang Qichao and Chen Duxiu into part of a nationwide "power elite," to borrow C. Wright Mills's famous phrase.[91] They, along with government officials, set the tone and stage for China's response to the war in Europe and paid close attention to its development.

The advent of the new diplomacy

With the emergence of a foreign policy public, Chinese diplomacy was radically readjusted. Here I define "new diplomacy" in a purely Chinese context. The ideas of nation-state, laws of nations, and national sovereignty were not new in European diplomacy but their emergence in China engendered a sense of "newness" and enthusiastic interest. Even the idea of diplomacy in the Western sense was new to China. Below I will show how the new diplomacy was fundamentally different from "traditional" Chinese interaction with other countries. The Qing government only instituted a formal foreign ministry in 1901 under pressure from the West and had not deigned to involve itself in foreign affairs.

[90] Ellen N. LaMotte, *Peking Dust* (New York: The Century Co., 1919), 106–07.
[91] C. Wright Mills, *The Power Elite* (New York: Oxford University Press, 1956).

There are several revealing examples of this attitude. In the 1860s, after a series of defeats at the hands of the West, the Qing court decided to establish a school to train students in foreign languages and foreign affairs. But conservatives, including many high officials, were strongly opposed to this. The sentiment of such die-hard isolationists was circulated by the following verse as a way to voice their criticism:

> The foreign devils are so tricky
> They have forced the Qing court to set up a foreign language school;
> Qing high officials have no long-term strategy
> And are stupid enough to seduce good Chinese youth into learning from those who are different from our race.[92]

The general attitude toward foreign affairs was based on ignorance, and when the Qing court organized the first contingent of government-sponsored students to be sent to the United States in 1872, it ran into trouble recruiting them. Many parents hesitated to accept the offer. As one of those prospective Chinese students put it later, "We had the chance of a lifetime then, but we were afraid to take the risks. We heard that the Great Mei Kuo (Great America) was a land of cannibals, and we did not like the idea of being sent over and having our skins scalped."[93] For many conservative literati, willingness to learn anything about foreign affairs, let alone go abroad, was nothing short of a dishonor. Some went so far as to consider a job at the Zongli Yamen humiliating and shameful.[94] Wo Ren, a high official at the Qing court, was said to have wept with shame upon hearing of his appointment to this office. He allegedly planned to resign from all posts and even deliberately injured himself to avoid accepting the appointment.[95]

If setting up a foreign language school and selecting students to study abroad posed problems, establishing permanent Chinese diplomatic missions abroad was simply unthinkable. While the Convention of Beijing (1860) recognized the presence of Western diplomatic representation in China, the Qing government did not send its own representatives to the West until sixteen years later. To many conservative Chinese, a permanent foreign mission was a terrible idea. As Li Ciming claimed in a diary

---

[92] For a further discussion regarding the foreign language school dispute, see Weng Tonghe, *Weng Tonghe riji* (Beijing: Zhonghua shuju, 1989). Entries of March 18, 20, 29, 1867, I: 519–21.

[93] Tyau Min-Chien, *China Awakened* (New York: The Macmillan Company, 1922), 20.

[94] Zongli Yamen is the Chinese name of a temporary office in charge of foreign affairs. The office was created in 1861 after foreign troops invaded Beijing and set up their permanent diplomatic residences there.

[95] Weng Tonghe, *Weng Tonghe riji*. Entries of April 29, May 3, 4, June 9, 13, July 13, 1867, I: 529–44.

entry in 1876, a Chinese mission to foreign countries "looks parasitic and is similar to being held hostage. It will be controlled and laughed at by foreigners at will. [Therefore,] such a mission would only humiliate its country."[96] The first Chinese foreign mission to the United States and European countries (1868) was perhaps understandably headed by a retired American diplomat, Anson Burlingame, since no Chinese high officials wanted or were qualified to lead it. As late as the late nineteenth century, few Chinese were willing to bear the humiliation of being sent abroad; it was considered a fate worse than banishment.

The first Chinese resident minister to a foreign country, Guo Songtao, was not assigned until 1876.[97] Unlike most of his contemporaries, Guo was interested in foreign affairs and believed in diplomacy, but his acceptance of a mission to England made him a hated man among the literati. A fellow Hunanese, Wang Kaiyung, wrote in his diary that "we Hunanese feel ashamed to be associated with Guo." Some people even considered Guo's willingness to go abroad an act of treason, and they threatened to end his life and to destroy his ancestral temple. A verse similar to one elicited by the foreign language school project was composed to ridicule him:

> He stands out among his contemporaries,
> He is raised above his peers,
> Yet the nation of Yao and Shun
> Cold-shoulders him.
> He cannot serve human beings,
> So how can he serve devils?
> What is the point of leaving
> The land of his parents?[98]

But as Chinese society underwent its great transformation after 1895, the mentality toward foreign affairs experienced a sea change as well. Study abroad became the dream of many Chinese students, and the field of foreign affairs gradually came to be viewed as a glorious career. Many of the best and brightest students turned their interest to foreign affairs and chose to be diplomats; among them, Wellington Koo, Yan Huiqing, and Wu Chaoshu are good examples. This development made it possible to organize a strong professional team in foreign affairs after the founding of the Republic of China. Change in this area had several dimensions:

---

[96] Li Ciming, *Yuemantang riji* (Taipei: Wenhai chubanshe, 1963), IX: 4824.

[97] For details on Guo's mission, see J. D. Frodsham (translator and annotator), ed., *The First Chinese Embassy to the West: The Journals of Kuo Sung-T'ao, Liu Hsi-Hung and Chang Tê-Yi* (Oxford: Clarendon Press, 1974).

[98] Wang Kaiyun, *Xiangyilou riji* (Taipei: Xuesheng shuju, 1964), I: 144.

besides the change of mentality I have already discussed, there was also institutional change. The first foreign minister of the new republic, Lu Zhengxiang, undertook a series of reforms including the introduction of a foreign service examination – an important step in selecting qualified diplomats.[99] The third change was the government's handling of foreign affairs. During the early years of the republic, high officials in the Beijing government generally chose to leave most foreign policy issues to professionals in the Foreign Ministry owing to their complexity and the quick turnaround of personnel in the cabinets.[100] More importantly, these professional diplomats – Koo and others – shared similar educational backgrounds and a strong motivation to help China join the international system. They held "an identical outlook on the importance of foreign relations for China's eventual destiny as a major factor in the world."[101]

Although the role of professional diplomats in foreign policy making was not always clearly defined and the changes in attitude took place gradually, these developments in Chinese diplomacy would have been unthinkable before the First World War. The new diplomacy responded to public opinion in shaping foreign policy.

To be sure, public opinion is vital, yet it is also elusive and subjective. The public can be manipulated and misled. Some members of the public are well informed and rational, some may be less informed and emotional. Public opinion on foreign policy is even more difficult to study. The very concept of public opinion for this period may be somewhat misleading since the majority of Chinese were illiterate farmers who had no idea of what was going on either domestically or externally. Still, one thing is certain and clear. Like the foreign policy public analyzed earlier, public opinion in foreign affairs had become an important instrument of foreign policy-making in China during the period under discussion.

There were at least three different voices of public opinion: the government, the press, and citizens' groups (elite and non-elite). The role of government in China at this time is difficult to categorize. The offices of the president and cabinet did not always take the same positions and in foreign affairs there were fundamental differences between them. An exchange between Liang Qichao and President Li Yuanhong on public opinion is an excellent case in point: Both men used "public opinion" to justify their position for or against China's entry into war, but what

---

[99] Cao Rulin, *Yi Sheng zhi huiyi* (Hong Kong: Chun Qiu chubanshe, 1966), 108; see also Luo Guang, *Lu Zhengxiang zhuan* (The biography of Lu Zhengxian) (Taipei: Shangwu yinshuguan, 1966), 83–85.
[100] V. K. Wellington Koo, *Gu Weijun huiyi lu* (Beijing: Zhonghua shuju, 1983), I: 392–93.
[101] See Koo's preface for Yan Huiqing, *East–West Kaleidoscope: 1877–1944*, vii.

constituted public opinion for each was different.[102] The foreign policy public that emerged during this period worked hard to have an impact in policy-making, and many elite members in that foreign policy public encouraged the government's use, and even manipulation, of public opinion to better serve policy-making. Liang Qichao insisted, "Skillful politicians will secretly direct public opinion but publicly declare that they themselves are subject to it."[103] Still, with the domestic situation in flux and the government's low prestige abroad, Chinese public opinion was one of the most powerful tools the government commanded in its attempts to shape foreign affairs.

The Chinese government's handling of Japan's Twenty-one Demands is one good case in point. As noted earlier, Chinese public opinion was aroused to an unprecedented level when news of Japan's demands broke, and the government tried, in a number of ways, to turn that into a bargaining chip. Since no diplomatic support was forthcoming from other countries, Chinese officials from the very beginning closely monitored public opinion as they engaged in negotiations with Japan. Japan worried about opposition to its plan from the other powers and insisted that the Chinese keep the demands a secret, but the Chinese Foreign Ministry was aware of the impact of foreign public opinion, and its members secretly kept the Great Powers' representatives in Beijing fully informed. Wellington Koo met with the American minister to Beijing, Paul Reinsch, almost every night during the period of negotiations. According to one account, it was Koo who leaked the Japanese demands to the American media, which soon reported on the issue. *The Washington Post* published the complete list of the demands in early February.[104] As Lu Zhengxiang, Minister for Foreign Affairs and a chief negotiator with the Japanese, told Reinsch, "[a]ll that China hopes is that America and the world may know and judge."[105] Chinese officials did everything they could to leak the demands, hoping to solicit support from world opinion. At the same time, Chinese diplomats abroad closely followed their host countries' media coverage of the Sino-Japanese negotiations.[106] On the domestic

[102] Xu Tian (Zhang Guogan), "Dui De-Ou canzhan (China's declaration of war on Germany and Austria)," *Jindai shi ziliao* 2 (1954).

[103] Liang to Yuan Shikai, February 23, 1913, in Ding Wenjiang, ed., *Liang Rengong xiansheng nianpu changbian chugao* (Taipei: Shijie shuju, 1959), II: 381.

[104] Wang Gangling, *Ouzhan shiqi de Meiguo dui Hua zhengce* (Taipei: Xuesheng shuju, 1988), 44.

[105] Paul Samuel Reinsch, *An American Diplomat in China* (Garden City, NY: Doubleday, Page & Company, 1922), 141.

[106] Skimming the numerous reports from Chinese legations abroad during this negotiation period, one finds many Chinese diplomats focused on foreign public opinion. For details, see Zhongyang yanjiuyuan jindai shi yanjiusuo, ed., *Zhong Ri guanxi shiliao: ershiyi tiao jiaoshe*, 2 vols. (Taipei: Zhongyang yanjiuyuan jindai shi yanjiusuo, 1985).

front, elite members of the foreign policy public such as Liang Qichao remained close to the policy-making process and could keep the public informed in addition to pressuring the Chinese government not to capitulate to Japan.

While the appeal to public opinion on both the domestic and foreign fronts may not have produced a significant diplomatic result and China still received no real diplomatic support from the Great Powers, the publicity at least compelled Japan to modify its demands, and put the Japanese on the moral defensive. The support gained through the public opinion campaign aided Chinese diplomats who skillfully exploited it in their negotiations. Jordan was impressed with Chinese negotiation skills during roughly 100 days and twenty-four sessions of official negotiations. He declared that "[i]f it was merely a question of dialectical gymnastics, I should be inclined to back the Chinese."[107] The Chinese government did not give in until Japan presented an ultimatum and China faced a possible military showdown. As Jordan emphasized in his official report to the British Foreign Office, "It is common knowledge that the demands were forced through the point of the bayonet, Japan having actually landed between 20,000 and 30,000 men in Manchuria and at Tsingtao."[108]

Even its defeat in the diplomatic battle did not dissuade China from further engaging in a campaign to influence public opinion. On May 12, three days after it accepted the Japanese ultimatum but two weeks before the final agreements were signed, the Chinese Foreign Ministry openly published detailed documents showing the history of its negotiations. At the same time, the Chinese Foreign Ministry told its diplomats abroad to let their host countries know the real story of the negotiations and arranged to get that account published in foreign newspapers.[109] Beijing also sent copies of the official views about the negotiations to local Chinese officials nationwide.[110] During the First World War era, China repeatedly resorted to public opinion, asking the world to judge how sorely China had been wronged by other powers. Another case, the Zhengjiatun Incident, was reported in detail by the Chinese government to the world in both Chinese and English.

The so-called Zhengjiatun Incident took place in the summer of 1916. Zhengjiatun is a small town in China's northeast. When Chinese and Japanese soldiers there clashed over a minor issue, the Japanese government blamed China and used the incident to press China into crucial

---

[107] Jordan to Langley, March 22, 1915, PRO, fo350/13/31.
[108] Jordan Annual Report to Foreign Office, 1919, PRO, fo405/229, 9.
[109] Waijiaobu to Minister Shi, May 12, 1915, in Zhongyang yanjiuyuan jindai shi yanjiusuo, ed., *Zhong Ri guanxi shiliao: ershiyi tiao jiaoshe*, I: 308.
[110] Waijiaobu letter to local governments, May 13, 1915, in ibid., I: 309.

concessions. In a move similar to its strategy for imposing the Twenty-one Demands, Japan enjoined China to the strictest secrecy. The Chinese, however, brought the issue to world attention.[111]

The Chinese government's use of public opinion and its disclosure of problems in foreign affairs constituted a point of departure in its approach to world affairs. The unprecedented publication of these cases "signified the determination" of China "to let the world hear also the Republic's side of the case, instead of waiting for truth eventually to proclaim its own tale."[112] Thanks to the new diplomacy, historians have recourse to a "white book" in English ("Official Documents Relating to the War") that covers the crucial year of 1917 and Chinese dealings with the powers and efforts to join the Great War.

A new world order as ideal and reality: the coming of the Great War

Despite China's determination to enter the new and West-dominated international system, its conceptions of the new world order and the West were not really clear and sometimes even contradictory. For many in the Chinese elite the new international system remained an abstract concept which was non-Chinese, and based on foreign norms of international law, the nation-state, and diplomacy. Ideally this world order promised an arena of justice in which every country would be welcome and entitled to equal treatment. While the Chinese had become brutally realistic about their traditional worldview, they fell into another trap by idealizing the Western system. This phenomenon might be termed diplomatic romanticism.[113] In China's case, the gap between a new world order in the ideal and in reality was large indeed. The Chinese had cherished the ideal of China's full membership in the new world order and were

---

[111] For detailed information on the incident, see Zhongguo di er lishi dangan guan, ed., "1916 nian Zhengjiatun Zhong Ri jundui shijiang jiaoshe wenjian xuan," *Minguo dang an* (Archives of Republican China) 2 (1992): 23–28. "Zhengjiatun jiaoshe qing xin," *Xin qingnian* 2, no. 2 (October 1916).

[112] Tyau Min-Chien, *China Awakened*, 268.

[113] As explained by Gurutz Bereciartu, romanticism "is not a movement resulting from rigorous doctrinal construction of a philosophical political nature; rather, it is a life concept, a world view, that seeks to influence each and every behavioral manifestation and expression of the human being. Romanticism is essentially intuition, sentiment, individual experience." See Gurutz J. Bereciartu, *Decline of the Nation-State*, translated by William A. Douglass (Reno: University of Nevada Press, 1994), 42. As Armstrong also reminds us, it is quite common in the world that "order in international affairs is as much a state of mind as a state of being" and "international order is not simply a condition that exists as a consequence of the effective working of various objective structures or institutions like the balance of power, diplomacy, or international law." Armstrong, *Revolution and World Order*, 6.

not quite ready to temper it. Sun Yat-sen's attitude serves as an example of this wishful thinking: He declared in 1912 that the only way to resolve the current Chinese diplomatic impasses was to welcome foreign capital and to completely transform the old conservative closed-door policy into an open-door policy. He argued that by doing this, the powers with designs on China would no longer be able to press their unreasonable demands.[114] On another occasion, Sun pointed out that an open-door policy could be used to safeguard sovereignty.[115] Not only Sun held this innocent view, of course. Many in the Chinese elite thought the same way. Such naiveté in the face of the Western countries' obsession with expanding their own unequal rights in Chinese territory largely explains why the story of China's quest to become an equal in the family of nations had many stormy twists and turns. Chinese romanticism about the West's abstract ideals prevented the elite from developing a clear and deep understanding of the West and the international system itself.

Furthermore, different people, or even the same people at different times, held varying understandings of the international system and the West. Few Chinese considered the possibility that the powers might not welcome China into their ranks, or might even obstruct its joining. They did not sufficiently attend to the fact that while the powers might be deadly enemies in Europe, they still cooperated to expand their interests in China – as for example, when in 1900 they sent combined military forces to suppress the anti-imperialism movement during the Boxer Rebellion. When members of the Chinese elite discussed their country's future, they did not always factor in the complexity of the international system and the nature of the West's dominance. And when reality did not live up to expectations, many suffered emotional devastation and protested their betrayal.

Their ambivalence about imperialism brings into sharper focus the paradox that Chinese elite members faced in their efforts to insert China into the new world order: on the one hand, China had to rid itself of both foreign and traditional homegrown imperialism to create for itself a new niche and a new identity; on the other, imperialism – defined in Social Darwinist terms – was also the main source and inspiration for Chinese nationalism, aimed at the ultimate goal of building national power. It was not just something to resist but also something to strive for. From the late nineteenth century, many Chinese had taken the doctrine of the survival

---

[114] "Sun Yat-sen's Speech on September 5, 1912," in Julie Lee Wei et al., eds., *Prescriptions for Saving China*, 90–92.

[115] "Sun's Speech on October 12, 1912 at a Reception Hosted by the Shanghai Newspaper Guild," in ibid., 106.

of the fittest to heart. Liang Qichao saw no difference between nationalism and imperialism, regarding the latter as resulting from "the overabundance of the energy of a nation. The energy spills over its boundaries." Liang was so confused about the difference between nationalism and imperialism that he coined a new phrase "nationalist-imperialism" (*minzu diguo zhuyi*) to indicate the deep interconnection between them.[116] Sun Yat-sen obviously agreed with Liang in this case, defining imperialism as the final stage in the development of nationalism.[117] This phenomenon of linking nationalism with imperialism necessarily turned Chinese attitudes toward Western imperialism ambivalent. Liang argued that the only way victims of imperialism like China could resist it was by following the law of Social Darwinism and mobilizing their populations, just as their enemies had.[118]

When Chinese elite talked about the international order as an abstract entity, they seemed to consider it fixed, although the international system was in fact never static. This was especially true at the turn of the twentieth century. Between 1895 and 1914, the international system experienced a tremendous change, with the "shifting balance of world forces."[119] The old system defined by a balance of power in Europe and Asia was collapsing. Interestingly enough, just as China was embracing nationalism in the late nineteenth and early twentieth centuries, most European states, including the United States and Japan, were doing the same. The two major factors in world politics were the impulse to nationalism and the spell of imperialism under the ideology of Social Darwinism.[120] With the rise of imperialism and rapid economic development resulting from the industrial revolution, Europe in the late nineteenth century found itself in an age of cross-border power struggles. Newcomers such as Germany, with its recently found economic and military strength, pushed at the existing international order by claiming their own *Lebensraum* and adopting *Weltpolitik*. Indeed, Germany was a leading player in the attempt to redefine the world order.[121]

---

[116] Li Huaxing and Wu Jiayi, eds., *Liang Qichao xuanji*, 189–93. Liang Qichao, *Xin Min Shuo*, 4.

[117] Cui Shuqing, *Sun Zhongshan yu gongcan zhuyi* (Hong Kong: Yazhou chubanshe, 1954), 77.

[118] About the introduction of Social Darwinism into China and its impact, see James Reeve Pusey, *China and Charles Darwin* (Cambridge, MA: Harvard University Press, 1983).

[119] I borrow the phrase from Charles L. Mowat, ed., *The New Cambridge Modern History: Vol. XII, the Shifting Balance of World Forces, 1898–1945* (Cambridge: Cambridge University Press, 1968).

[120] For a detailed analysis on this point, see David Kaiser, *Politics and War: European Conflict from Philip II to Hitler* (Cambridge, MA: Harvard University Press, 1990), 271–354.

[121] James Joll, *The Origins of the First World War* (London: Longman Group UK Limited, 1984), 34.

Meanwhile, two rival camps were beginning to take shape in Europe – the Allied powers and the Central powers. These rivals would soon orchestrate the demise of the existing world order because their struggles were no longer merely over European issues but over markets and territories that ranged across the globe.[122] But they went to war not only for economic, strategic, and political reasons, but for emotional reasons as well.[123] Two rising powers, the United States and Japan, also posed a challenge to the existing world order. Although not yet part of the great power system at the inception of World War I, the United States, with its economic clout, was transforming itself into a dominant player in the international system. As Paul Kennedy put it, by 1914, the economic power of the United States was probably *the single most decisive shift in the long-term global power balance*" (italics in the original). Even if World War I had not been fought, Kennedy argues, "four centuries of European predominance were swiftly coming to an end because of American economic muscle."[124] Japan, although still a marginal power geographically and industrially before 1914, would become a dominant player in East Asia while the old powers concentrated their attention elsewhere. Japan thus redesigned the political map of the international system in Asia. On the eve of the First World War, both Japan and the United States were poised to force a new international system based on their own interests and ideas when the opportunity presented itself.

By the early twentieth century, all these forces had come together to challenge the status quo. When an assassin's bullet in Sarajevo on June 28, 1914, set off the reaction that would become the First World War, these players were presented with the opportunity they had been waiting for to dismantle the existing international system. So were the Chinese.

---

[122] Paul Kennedy, *The Rise and Fall of the Great Powers* (London: Unwin Hyman Limited, 1988), 195.

[123] The best short survey on the origins of the war is provided in Joll, *The Origins of the First World War*; on the mood of 1914, the best book is by Robert Wohl, *The Generation of 1914* (Cambridge, MA: Harvard University Press, 1979).

[124] Paul Kennedy, "The First World War and the International Power System," *International Security* 9, no. 1 (1984): 23–24.

Part II

China attempts to join the war

It would be strange if the last power left out to mediate [the Great War] were to be China . . . The one people in the world who really believe in peace . . . What have we been fighting for? What are we fighting for? Do you know? Does anyone know?

H. G. Wells[1]

Although the Chinese elite showed some confusion about world affairs and the existing world order, the foreign policy public nonetheless responded quickly when the European war broke out in 1914. To date few historians have noted the presence of a foreign policy public in China at this point in time. This lack of knowledge has distorted historians' understanding of the real connection between China and the war. For many, China entered the war not of its own initiative but under pressure from the major powers. Few have recognized the great changes in China in this period or the strong desire of the Chinese to reclaim their country and join the international system through participation in the war effort. In fact, the push from within China to join the war was stronger than the pull from outside, but the internal pressures were so subtle, so diffuse, that the whole picture has been difficult to appreciate.

"Weiji" and China's initial response

The failure to recognize China's motivations to enter the war has prevented a clear understanding of what I would call the sense of *weiji* (crisis) experienced by the Chinese elite and government officials at the time. The term *weiji* combines two Chinese characters: danger (*wei*) and opportunity (*ji*). As Europe's generation of 1914, too young and innocent to suspect what bloody rites of passage awaited them, went gladly to war in August 1914, the new generation in China experienced a sense of *weiji* at the challenge of dealing with new developments in the international

---

[1] H. G. Wells, *Mr. Britling Sees It Through* (New York: The Macmillan Company, 1916), 201–02, 431.

system. Many Chinese recognized the dangerous likelihood of becoming involved in the war involuntarily, since the belligerents all controlled spheres of interest in Chinese territory. Moreover, with the collapse of the old international system, China could easily be bullied by Japan, and its development thwarted. As early as August 2, 1914, an editorial in *Shi Bao (Shanghai Times)* argued that if war broke out, other countries would focus on Europe and leave Japan a free hand in East Asia, and Japan would try then to control China. *Shi Bao* appealed to the European powers not to go to war.[2]

Yet despite the dangers China faced, some Chinese realized the European war also presented excellent opportunities. It could bring changes to the international system that would provide China a chance to join the larger world. China might even inject its own ideas into shaping the new world order. For contemporary Chinese like Liang Qichao and Liu Yan, the war offered more opportunity than danger. When the news of the European war reached China, Liu Yan, who later wrote a diplomatic history of Republican China and who in 1914 was an active member of the foreign policy public, immediately wrote several memoranda to the foreign ministry and the state council suggesting that China declare war on Germany and take back Qingdao. This, he thought, would forestall Japanese efforts to do the same. The other option he recommended was to regain Qingdao through negotiation.[3]

Liang, as a leader of the foreign policy public, also paid close attention to such issues. In 1910, he published an article entitled "Some Personal Comments on China's Foreign Policy Principles," in which he argued that even weak countries such as China could engage in active diplomacy. With the international system at breaking point owing to the intense antagonism between the major powers, it was a good time for China to advance its own national interests.[4] A keen observer of the war from the outset, Liang wrote several books and articles on the subject, including one entitled *On the History of European Battles*, which was published just three months after the war started. His purpose in writing these pieces was to help the Chinese understand foreign affairs. Greater interest in the war, Liang argued, "could help increase and strengthen Chinese self-awareness."[5] On November 6, 1914, Liang Qichao was invited by Beijing's YMCA to speak on intellectual change after the European war. According to *Shen Bao's* report, an audience of more than a thousand showed up for his lecture. Liang emphasized that the European

---

[2] *Shi Bao*, Editorial, August 2, 1914.
[3] Liu Yan, *Zhongguo waijiao shi* (Taipei: Sanmin shuju, 1962), 409.
[4] Liang Qichao, "Zhongguo waijiao fangzhen shiyi," *Yin bing shi he ji* (Beijing: Zhonghua shuju, 1989), III: 79–106.
[5] Liang Qichao, "Ouzhan Zhong ce," *Yin bing shi he ji*, IV: 12.

war was a war between nation-states. Since China was deeply influenced by world affairs, he urged the Chinese to learn to be citizens of a nation-state, and also citizens of the world. He expressed the hope that China would take advantage of the European war to change and reform its own society.[6]

In other occasions, Liang argued that the First World War presented the Chinese a once-in-a-thousand-years opportunity. They should use this opportunity to renew their country and get it on track to recover its national sovereignty. "We cannot justly condemn war as a sin pure and simple when it can be used as a purifying and caring agent. It is certain that every great war opens for the world a new era or a peaceful regime of hundreds or several scores of years. Seen from this point of view, it is quite probable that the seeds of great blessing have been sown during this year of disaster and misfortune."[7] For Liang, the key reason for China's joining the war was to enhance its status in the new international configuration – in this way, it would not only survive in the short term, but would have an easier time as it tried to enter the international community in the long term.[8] The problem was how best to take advantage of this opportunity. Liang argued that if China exploited the situation properly, it could finish the process of becoming a "completely qualified nation-state" and prepare for a quick rise in the world.[9]

Liang Qichao and Liu Yan were not alone in this view. Many writers for a very influential magazine, *Dong fang za zhi* (Eastern Miscellany), looked at the war in nearly the same way. Starting with its August 1914 issue, this magazine invited leading members of the foreign policy public to write columns on the war and its implications for China. In the lead article of the series, "The Start of a Great European War," one author argued that the conflict would have a direct impact on China: Once Britain joined the war, Japan would follow, and eventually China would become involved. He warned that China should be very careful not to let Japan gain control of the German sphere of interest in Shandong.[10] A September 1 lead article entitled "The Great War and China" argued that the war would serve as an extremely "strong excitant" to "Chinese patriotism and the national consciousness."[11] *Dong fang za zhi* continued to devote extensive space to war reports and commentary throughout the war period, with

---

[6] "Ouzhan hou sixiang bianqian zhi yanshuo," *Shen Bao*, November 11, 1914, 6.
[7] *Peking Gazette*, December 31, 1914.
[8] Liang Qichao, "Waijiao fangzhen zhi yan – can zhan pian," *Yin bing shi he ji*, IV: 4–13.
[9] Liang Qichao, "Ouzhan Zhong ce," *Yin bing shi he ji*, IV: 11–26; see also Ding Wenjiang, ed., *Liang Rengong xiansheng nianpu changbian chugao* (Life chronology of Mr. Liang Qichao) (Taipei: Shijie shuju, 1959), 439.
[10] Gao Lao, "Da zhanzheng kaici," *Dong fang za zhi*, 11, no. 2 (August, 1914).
[11] Cang Fu (Du Yaquan), "Da zhanzheng yu Zhongguo," *Dong fang za zhi* 11, no. 3 (September, 1914): 2–4.

a special focus on its effects on China. Other prominent journals also covered the war extensively. One article in *Da Zhong hua* (Great China), entitled "The European War and China," argued that the Chinese should pay close attention because the end of the war would definitely influence the balance of power in China among the great countries: after the war, the powers were likely to try to increase their hold in China to make up for losses elsewhere. Thus, China had to reform if it hoped to avoid the fate of Turkey and Egypt.[12] Another article, in *Jiayin zazhi* (The Tigers), entitled "The European War and Its Influence on China's Finance and Economy," suggested that China should use the war in Europe as an opportunity to reform its finance, increase commerce, and develop its industry.[13]

Using the war to enhance China's international status was especially appealing to the Chinese foreign policy public. Zhang Junmai (Carsun Chang, 1887–1969), who was Liang's close friend and a recently returned student from Germany, had observed the war effort first-hand and was especially interested in the idea that China might be able to secure the cancellation of the Boxer Indemnity, restoration of leased ports, and the like if it joined the Allied side and declared war on Germany. Zhang lived in Germany during the first two years of the Great War and while there, he followed military affairs so closely that his German landlady suspected him of being a Japanese spy and reported him. By 1915, from his close observation of military affairs in Europe, he had already reached the conclusion that Germany was going to be defeated. When he returned to China in 1916, he missed no opportunity to argue that China should declare war on Germany to recover its lost sovereignty. The Chinese had to contribute something (*li gong*) to the world to secure the cancellation of the powers' unequal treaties.[14] He wrote several articles advancing these arguments.[15] Other writers shared this kind of view. Liu Shuya wrote in *Xin Qingnian* that one lesson Chinese youth should learn from the European war was that might is right in the international system, and the country that fights for its rights will survive and be strong. He encouraged Chinese youth to fight for their future and to cancel their country's recent humiliations.[16]

---

[12] Ouyang Faxiao, "Ouzhan yu Zhongguo" (The European War and China), *Da Zhonghua* (Great China) (Shanghai) 2, no. 2 (1914): 4.

[13] Gao Bei, "Ouzhou zhanzheng yu woguo caizheng jingjishang suo shou yingxiang," *Jiayin* 1, no. 8 (August, 1915); see also Zhong Lang, "Ouzhan qijian nei chengji fazhan shiye wenti," *Da Zhonghua* 2, no. 12.

[14] See Zhang Junmai, *Zhong Xi Yin zhexue wenji*, ed. Chen Wenxi (Taipei: Xuesheng shuju, 1981), 1: 65–66, 165.

[15] Carsun Chang, "The Inside History of China's Declaration of War," *Millard's Review* 5, no. 12 (August, 1918): 464.

[16] Liu Shuya, "Ouzhou zhanzheng yu qingnian zhi jiaowu," *Xin qingnian* 2, no. 2 (1916).

Interestingly, Sun Yat-sen, who in 1917 strongly opposed China's entry into the war, was nonetheless enthusiastic when the Great War broke out. He saw the European war as a favorable opportunity for China from a different perspective: "Europe will not have time to bother about the East and the traitor [Yuan Shikai] will no longer benefit from foreign loans and military equipment," Sun wrote on September 1, 1914. "This is our chance to rise up and make our stand."[17]

China's interest in the First World War coincided with a new cultural moment that had started with Chen Duxiu's *New Youth*.[18] With this movement, Chinese intellectuals' mood of despair and discouragement gave way to a vigorous cultural renaissance that rapidly drew a whole generation into its orbit. The thrust of the new cultural movement was to compel China to thoroughly break with its past. About the search for a new national identity, said Chen in 1916, "the basic task is to import the foundation of Western society, that is, the new belief in equality and human rights. We must be thoroughly aware of the incompatibility between Confucianism and this new belief, the new society, and the new state."[19] Such ideas won many followers. Because of these powerful voices and pens, creating a national identity based on Western ideas became a serious goal for many members of the Chinese reading public in the era of the 1910s. Even Mao Zedong once characterized the intellectual climate of China during the First World War as a "search for truth from the West." He later recalled what he had in mind during the Great War period: "In order to save China, we had to reform; and to reform, we had to learn from foreign countries. At that time, among the foreign countries, only the Western capitalist countries were progressive ones."[20] Thus although a crisis of national identity was responsible for setting this search in motion, the First World War provided additional momentum for it. It is perhaps right to claim that this movement provided China with a social and cultural basis for participation in the war on the side of Allies. As Arif Dirlik notes, "Concern for China's destiny as a nation was an important element in many intellectuals' advocacy of a cultural revolution."[21] The evolution of a new Chinese mentality regarding world affairs provided an intellectual base for China's domestic renewal. One major reason why Chen Duxiu eventually supported China's

---

[17] Quote from Marie-Claire Bergère, *Sun Yat-Sen*, trans. Janet Lloyd (Stanford: Stanford University Press, 1988), 262.

[18] The magazine was founded in September 1915 and was renamed *Xin qingnian* in 1916.

[19] Lin Yu-sheng, *The Crisis of Chinese Consciousness: Radical Anti-Traditionalism in the May Fourth Era* (Madison: University of Wisconsin Press, 1979), 76.

[20] *Selected Works of Mao Zedong* (Beijing: Foreign Language Press, 1965), 1474–75.

[21] Arif Dirlik, "New Cultural Movement Revisited: Anarchism and the Idea of Social Revolution in New Culture Thinking," *Modern China* 11, no. 3 (July 1985): 290.

participation in the war was his belief that it would "shake off age-old lethargy" and set China on the road to "democracy and science."[22]

For all these reasons, when news of the European war reached it, the Chinese foreign policy public immediately took notice. Liang Qichao observed at the time that everyone, from high officials in Beijing to the rural gentry, discussed the war. Although their understanding was shallow, the strong interest of the Chinese in world affairs was considered progress.[23] The foreign policy public came to include groups such as the Oushi Yanjiuhui (Study group for European affairs), founded in Japan by Chinese elites exiled there. Once the Great War broke out, they gathered regularly to discuss its implications for China. Although this group was a political party focusing more on domestic politics than on foreign policy, its choice of name and its discussion of the war is another indication of increased public interest in foreign policy in general and the war in particular.[24]

Although many members of the foreign policy public realized the importance of the Great War to China and argued for action, few of them could provide a clear blueprint for how China should respond. This amorphous public not only lacked a consensus regarding China's war policy; more importantly, all the information and opinions in circulation introduced a degree of confusion into public discourse. For one thing, few could predict who would win the war, and not a few Chinese were deeply impressed with German military power and its victories. Liang Qichao and Chen Duxiu were among these. Chen Duxiu in his lead article for *Xin Qingnian*'s first issue of 1916 suggested that Germany might win the war in the new year.[25] Liang Qichao also first believed that Germany would win. In 1914 he noted that Germany had a better social structure and better soldiers, and, above all, that the whole country was united to carry out its war aims. Liang even claimed that if Germany lost, it would mean the known norms of evolution were not correct, since Germany was considered a model nation-state.[26] The Chinese military had been strongly influenced by the German military model, and many Chinese officers had confidence in the invincibility of German arms.[27] In one extreme case, Xu Shuzhen, a powerful general, secretly provided

---

[22] Chen Duxiu, "Our Policy toward Germany," *Xin qingnian* 3, no. 1.

[23] Liang Qichao, "Ouzhan Zhong ce," *Yin bing shi he ji*, IV: 12.

[24] For details on discussions of the study group for European affairs, see Li Xin and Li Zongyi, eds., *Zhonghua minguo shi, 1912–1916* (Beijing: Zhonghua shuju, 1987), II: 662–90.

[25] Duxiu Chen, "1916," *Xin qingnian* 1, no. 5 (1916).

[26] Liang Qichao, "Ouzhou zhanyi shilun," *Yin bing shi he ji*, VIII: 69–73.

[27] Morrison to Steed, Beijing, February 17, 1915, *The Correspondence of G. E. Morrison*, ed. Lo, Hui-min (Cambridge: Cambridge University Press, 1976), II: 375.

munitions to German forces in Qingdao when they faced Japanese attack in late 1914, to cultivate better Sino-German relations in the long term. Xu, although a confidant of the minister of army and later prime minister Duan Qirui (1865–1936) who would later play a major role in pushing China into the war, had not changed his views even in 1917 and argued against China's declaration of war on Germany (to be discussed in detail later). Some Chinese such as Zhang Shizhao took a middle position: Zhang predicted that no side would win a decisive victory, and this could be good for China because it would not upset the balance of power and China could avoid being swallowed up by either side.[28]

To be sure, some Chinese soon revised their pro-German stances. Liang Qichao was one of these: by early 1915 he realized that a prolongation of the war was not good for Germany, and he started to doubt that it could win. In late 1916, he openly advocated a Chinese declaration of war on Germany, arguing that China had several reasons for participating in European affairs and the war. If China wanted to design its future carefully and skillfully, it had to be in harmony with the main trend in world affairs. Liang argued that taking part in the European war represented a point of departure for China; it would demonstrate the seriousness of China's desire to take bold action and to move into the international community as a full member.[29]

As the foreign policy public debated the war and its implications for China, the government was trying to devise a strategy for dealing with war developments. Like the foreign policy public, the government was ambivalent about the war. It was eager to exploit the situation internationally yet apprehensive about the consequences of such action and its possible negative repercussions. But the government did not have the luxury of sitting idly by, and it quickly undertook a series of actions. First, the Foreign Ministry asked its diplomats abroad to pay close attention to local developments and report back every day to help the government monitor the conflict. According to Zhang Guogan, secretary-general to the State Council and a decision-making insider, Duan Qirui, minister of the army and later prime minister, read reports and materials on the war on a daily basis.[30] Second, on August 3, 1914, China's Foreign Ministry notified all belligerent powers that they should not engage in warfare in their spheres of interest in China or in Chinese territory. Third, the Chinese government deliberated about offering to mediate. This impulse came

---

[28] Zhang Shizhao, "Jiari Ouzhan zhi yijian" (February 10, 1917), in *Jiayin Zazhi cungao* (Taipei: Wenhai chubanshe, 1977), 46–48.

[29] Liang Qichao, "Waijiao fangzhen zhi yan – can zhan pian," *Yin bing shi he ji*, IV: 4–5.

[30] Xu Tian, "Dui De-Ou canzhan" (China's declaration of war on Germany and Austria), *Jindai shi ziliao* (Materials on modern history) 2 (1954), 53.

from Clause 1 of Article III in the 1907 Hague Convention, on the peaceful settlement of international disputes, which states that "Contracting powers, strangers to the dispute, should, on their own initiative, and as far as circumstances may allow, offer their good offices or mediation to the states at variance. Powers, strangers to the dispute, have the right to offer good offices or mediation, even during the course of hostilities. The exercise of this right can never be regarded by either of the parties at variance as an unfriendly act." Indeed, as a co-signatory of the convention, China had the right to offer mediation on its own initiative.

To have the right to mediate is one thing; whether that mediation will achieve anything is another. China, realizing its weakness and the fact that its voice might not carry much weight, contacted the American government about appealing to the contending powers.[31] On August 3, the Foreign Ministry asked the Chinese minister in Washington to see if the United States cared to take the initiative in appealing to the warring states to limit the war to Europe.[32] Coincidentally, the United States government was deliberating on the same issue. American ambassador to France Myron J. Herrick was the first to suggest to his government that a strong plea from the American president might delay and moderate the war situation in Europe.[33] On August 4 the American government, in the name of President Woodrow Wilson, sent a telegram to the belligerent powers officially offering his good offices to meditate the war.[34] The American government did try to act on China's behalf and in its own interest as well. On August 7, Secretary of State William Jennings Bryan authorized the American Legation in China to support China's proposal to neutralize all foreign settlements in China, not including leased areas.[35] However, China's expectations of the Americans were soon disappointed. The United States immediately backed down once Japan and Britain summarily rejected the appeal; John Jordan, British minister to China and doyen of the diplomatic corps in Beijing, reported later that the American effort to press for all concessions in China to be declared neutral ground did not commend itself to himself and several of his colleagues.[36]

---

[31] Guo Tingyi, ed., *Zhonghua minguo shi shi ri zhi* (Taipei: Zhongyang yanjiuyuan jindai shi suo, 1979), I: 151.

[32] Waijiaobu to Minister Xia, August 3, 1914, Taipei: Zhongyang yanjiuyuan jindai shi suo dang an guan, Ouzhan dan, 03–36/1–(1). Also see MacMurray to the secretary of state, August 3, 1914, Department of State, *Papers Relating to the Foreign Relations of the United States* [hereafter cited as *FRUS*], *1914, Supplement: The World War* (Washington, DC: Government Printing Office, 1928), 162.

[33] Herrick, "Telegram to the Secretary of State, Paris, July 28, 1914," *FRUS, 1914, Supplement: The World War*, 18–19.

[34] Ibid., 42.   [35] Ibid., 163.

[36] Sir John Jordan to Edward Grey, Beijing, August 28, 1914, confidential, in Kenneth Bourne and Donald Cameron Watt, eds., *British Documents on Foreign Affairs: Reports*

Japan had rejected China's suggestion to neutralize its territory as early as August 8 even though Japan itself was not counted a belligerent at that point.[37]

In accordance with its desire to prevent war from spreading to China, the Chinese government on August 6 declared its neutrality.[38] It repeatedly pressed Britain about Japan's intentions regarding the German-leased territory in the northeast. Britain assured China that it "need have no apprehension as to the results of any joint action which Great Britain and Japan might decide upon." China could rely "on Allied assurance" for getting Shandong back from Germany. In his long meeting with Wellington Koo on August 19, 1914, Jordan again promised that Qingdao would be returned to China without any conditions.[39]

The Chinese government also took the initiative to discuss with Germany the return of the territory it had leased. According to Yan Huiqing, Chinese minister to Germany, the Foreign Ministry had instructed him sometime in August to ascertain whether the German government would return the leased territory, to avoid possible bloodshed in the Far East. But Germany did not agree to take such action at the time.[40] On August 15 the Foreign Ministry itself contacted the German legation in Beijing to inquire whether Germany was willing to allow China to take back the Qingdao–Jinan railway. Since it realized the inevitability of war with Japan over Qingdao and felt that its main focus must remain Europe, the German government began to think returning Shandong to China might be a good idea, on the condition that China agree to pay for this early return. On August 16, German diplomat Baron Maltzan presented this proposal to the Chinese. Eventually the German deal was rejected by China for several reasons. First, buying back Qingdao was not a good idea even if China could have afforded it; second, China already had assurances from Britain regarding its eventual return; third, both Japan and Britain strongly objected to the scheme and pressured China

and Papers from the Foreign Office Confidential Print, Part II, series E, Asia, China, August 1914 – October 1918 (Bethesda, MD: University Publications of America, 1994), XXII: 1.

[37] See Ju ri gong shi Lu zongyu zhi waijiaobu dian, August 8, 1914, in Chen Daode, Zhang Minfu, and Rao Geping, eds., Zhonghua minguo waijiao shi zhi liao xianbian, 1911–1919 (Beijing: Beijing daxue chubanshe, 1988), I: 154.

[38] The original declaration can be found in Nanjing Zhongguo di er li shi dang an guan with the call number 1039–53.

[39] Jordan, 1919 Annual Report to the British Foreign Office, PRO, FO405/229, 9. See minutes of the meeting between Wellington Koo and Jordan on August 19, 1914, Zhongyang yanjiuyuan jindai shi yanjiusuo, ed., Zhong Ri guanxi shiliao:Ouzhan yu Shandong wenti (Zhongyang yanjiuyuan jindai shi yanjiusuof, 1974), I: 58–64.

[40] See Yan Huiqing, East-West Kaleidoscope: 1877–1944, an Autobiography (New York: St. John's University Press, 1974), 92–93.

not to accept the deal.[41] Jordan told the Chinese government flatly that the powers would not recognize it.[42]

In light of this situation, China decided to ask the United States to convince Japan and Britain that Germany should turn Qingdao over to the United States first, and the United States would immediately give it back to China. The United States categorically refused to get involved.[43] All China's efforts on this front proved unsuccessful. On August 23, Japan, citing its 1902 treaty with England, declared war on Germany and brought the war directly into China.[44] By November 7, 1914, Qingdao had fallen into Japanese hands.[45]

Until August of 1917, China was officially a neutral country. But its neutrality was only an expedient measure, or perhaps a strategy intermediate to making a better move; China was prepared to give up its neutrality the moment a new opportunity rose. Modern-minded Chinese officials were especially enthusiastic about the prospects of China's active involvement in the war. These officials, "with knowledge of foreign diplomacy," took an immediate interest and combined to exhort the conservatives to action.[46] Zhang Guogan was one of them. He suggested to Duan Qirui that the European war had such importance for China that it should take the initiative to declare war on Germany. This might not only prevent Japan from taking Qingdao in the short term, but would be a first step toward full participation in the future world order. Duan responded by saying he supported the idea of joining the war and was secretly preparing for this move.[47] Liang Shiyi, who had served in many powerful positions in government and was President Yuan's confidant,[48] also suggested that China join the war on the Allied side in 1914.[49] In one overnight

---

[41] Wu Dongzhi, ed., *Zhongguo waijiao shi*, 1911–1949 (Kaifeng: Henan renmin chubanshe, 1990), 38.

[42] Guo Tingyi, ed., *Zhonghua minguo shi shi ri zhi* (Taipei: Zhongyang yanjiuyuan jindai shisuo, Academica Sinica, 1979), I: 154–55.

[43] Ibid., 155–56.

[44] For a detailed analysis, see Tyau Min-Chien T. Z., *China's New Constitution and International Problems* (Shanghai: Commercial Press, 1918), 145.

[45] For details of the fall of Qingdao, see Edward P. Hoyt, *The Fall of Tsingtao* (London: Arthur Barker Limited, 1975); Charles B. Burdick, *The Japanese Siege of Tsingtau* (Hamden, CT: Shoe String Press, Inc., 1976).

[46] "China's Breach with Germany," *Manchester Guardian*, May 23, 1917.

[47] Xu Tian, "Dui De-Ou canzhan," 51.

[48] Liang Shiyi (1869–1933), besides being a confidant of President Yuan, held many important government posts such as director-general of the Railway Bureau, secretary-general to the president and prime minister. He was so powerful in Chinese politics that in private he was called "God of Wealth," "Co-President," and "the brains of China." For details on him, see Feng Gang et al., eds., *Minguo Liang Yansun xiansheng shiyi nianpu* (The Life Chronology of Mr. Liang Shiyi) (Taipei: Commercial Press, 1978), I: 197; *The Saturday Evening Post* (July 10, 1915), 5.

[49] Feng Gang, *Minguo Liang Yansun xiansheng shiyi nianpu*, I: 194–96.

discussion with Yuan Shikai sometime in August, Liang told Yuan that Germany was not strong enough to win the war in the long term, so China should seize the opportunity to declare war. By doing so, Liang reasoned, China could recover Qingdao, win a seat at the peace conference, and therefore the move served China's long-term interests. Liang was famous for his foresight and shrewdness; indeed, some close observers called him "the Machiavelli of China."[50] In his long political career, he probably never had a fixed view on any political issue. Yet on China's position during the war he never wavered, arguing that China should be on the side of the Allied Powers. In 1915 he argued again that "the Allied Powers will win absolutely. [That is why] we want to help them."[51] In one of his hand-written notes in November 1915, he insisted that the "time is right [for China to join the war now]. Otherwise, we won't get a second chance."[52]

The arguments of Zhang Guogan and Liang Shiyi must surely have influenced Yuan Shikai's attitude toward the war. In August 1914 Yuan informed John Jordan, the British minister, that China would offer 50,000 of its own troops to join the British military in taking back Qingdao, Chinese territory under German control since 1898. Certainly China was not powerful enough to attack the Germans by itself, and no doubt Japan was after this territory, so China needed the Allies' approval for this scheme. Unfortunately, Jordan rejected the idea outright, without even consulting his French or Russian colleagues. He indicated that Chinese cooperation was not needed. China's first offer to join the war was thus killed in embryo.[53]

---

[50] Michael Summerskill, *China on the Western Front: Britain's Chinese Worker Force in the First World War* (London: n.p., 1982), 30.

[51] Feng Gang, *Minguo Liang Yansun xiansheng shiyi nianpu*, I: 271–72.

[52] See ibid., 289; Su Wenzhuo, ed., *Liang Tan Yuying ju shi suo cang shu han tu zhao ying cun* (Hong Kong: 1986), 208.

[53] No official documents survive on this maneuver by Yuan. However, some secondary sources do exist. For example, both Morrison and Bertram Lenox Simpson mentioned it either in their personal letters or in official memoranda. Morrison mentions it several times in his personal letters; see Morrison to Mrs. Moberly Bell, May 8, 1916; Morrison to L. G. Fraser, Beijing, October 12, 1916, *The Correspondence of Morrison*, II: 515–16, 559. Simpson (1877–1930), pen-name Putnam Weale, was an Englishman who spent most of his life in China, first as an employee in the Chinese Customs Service; he then worked for the political section of the office of the president of China starting in 1916. His main responsibility there was to prepare reports for the Chinese president on foreign affairs. He also published widely on China. During the period from September 1916 to June of 1917, he had written at least thirty-eight reports on foreign affairs for Chinese government. Many of them were translated into Chinese by Wu Chaoshu and read by President Li Yuanhong. In his report to President Li Yuanhong on October 7, 1916 he cited Yuan's contact with Jordan. For the complete report, see Lai Xinxia, ed., *Beiyang junfa* (Shanghai: Shanghai renmin chubanshe, 1988), III: 131–36.

Jordan's blunt rejection caused the Chinese a humiliating loss of face, especially considering that the proposal came directly from President Yuan. On November 9, 1915, Yuan revealed his bitterness at Jordan's response to George E. Morrison when China made its second secret attempt to join the war.[54] Morrison, the former London *Times* correspondent in Beijing, then served as Yuan's political advisor. He called Jordan's response "a diplomatic blunder of the very worst kind."[55]

The failure of its first major attempt to enter the war on the Allied side and its declaration of neutrality meant that China must try harder to search for an effective war policy. Qingdao was attractive bait that would bring the war to China whether China liked it or not, and this dark prospect had to be dealt with somehow. The Chinese were especially apprehensive regarding Japan's intentions, since the Japanese, too, saw the European war as an opportunity and would doubtless take full advantage of it.[56] The Okuma Shigenobu cabinet declared that "Japan must take this chance of a millennium" to "establish its rights and interests in Asia."[57] When the First World War broke out, elder statesman Marquis Inoue Kaoru welcomed it as "a divine aid in the new Taisho era for the development of Japan's destiny." Another Japanese called it absolutely the most opportune moment to advance Japan's future standing in China.[58] As Baron Kato Takaaki, the Japanese foreign minister, explained to one American journalist in 1915,

Germany is an aggressive European Power that had secured a foothold on one corner of the province of Shan-tung. This is a great menace to Japan. Furthermore, Germany had forced Japan to return the peninsula of Liao-tung under the plausible pretense of friendly advice. Because of pressure brought to bear on us, Japan had to part with the legitimate fruits of war, bought with the blood of our fellow countrymen. Revenge is not justifiable, either in the case of an individual or a nation; but when, by coincidence, one can attend to this duty and at the same time pay an old debt, the opportunity certainly should be seized.[59]

---

[54] Morrison to Jordan, November 10, 1915, *The Correspondence of Morrison*, II: 469.

[55] Morrison to L. G. Fraser, Beijing, October 12, 1916, *The Correspondence of Morrison*, II: 559.

[56] J. Ingram Bryan, "The Shogun of Modern Japan," *New York Evening Post*, August 3, 1916. The whole article was reprinted in *The Peking Gazette*, October 12, 1916; for a detailed analysis of the Japanese government's policy on the war, see Tatsuji Takeuchi, *War and Diplomacy in the Japanese Empire* (New York: Russell & Russell, 1967), chapter 14.

[57] Ikuhiko Hata, "Continental Expansion, 1905–1941," in John W. Hall, ed., *The Cambridge History of Japan* (Cambridge: Cambridge University Press, 1988), VI: 279.

[58] Frederick R. Dickinson, *War and National Reinvention: Japan in the Great War, 1914–1919* (Cambridge, MA: The Harvard East Asia Center, 1999), 35–36.

[59] Samuel G. Blythe, "Banzai – and Then What?" *The Saturday Evening Post* 187, no. 47 (1915): 54.

It is clear that Japan was determined to take full advantage of the European war at China's expense and take revenge for the German role in forcing Japan to return the Liaodong Peninsula to China in 1895. The Chinese knew this and worked hard to prevent Japan from achieving its goal. The Qingdao episode also highlights two serious frustrations for the Chinese: on one hand, it wanted to join the war, but was not welcomed; on the other, it had a strong desire and compelling need to contain Japanese ambitions, but could not afford to irritate Japan. China and Japan were obviously on a collision course. When Japan used its alliance with England as an excuse to attack Germany in Shandong, the British minister Jordan wrote on September 4, 1914, to his superior and confidant in the Foreign Office, Sir Walter Langley, who had been a senior assistant undersecretary (1907–18), about a meeting with Liang Shiyi. Jordan reported that Liang asked Britain "to guarantee Japan's good faith in the matter of Jiaozhou and to save China from Japan."[60] In the meantime, China did everything it could to accommodate Japanese demands, such as allowing the Japanese to use the railroad in Shandong for military purposes. In a telegram to its minister to Japan, the Chinese Foreign Ministry bitterly recognized that China was forced to make concessions against its own will.[61] Japan repaid China by continually violating Chinese neutrality and committing atrocities in Shandong. Japanese soldiers robbed Chinese of their goods, raped local women, burned furniture from Chinese homes to warm their quarters and killed Chinese at random. Even Jordan, in a personal letter to his colleague Beilby Alston (1868–1929) on January 18, 1915, admitted that "we must always remember that the Chinese, especially those in Shantung [Shandong], have suffered a good deal by the present war and that our alliance inevitably exposes us to criticism by China."[62] The challenge of dealing with the Japanese threat and working out an effective war policy was soon brought to a crisis point when Japan issued its Twenty-one Demands. This finally compelled the Chinese to settle on a policy toward the war.

The Twenty-one Demands and their impact

On January 18, 1915, after it had already wrested control of Shandong from Germany, Japan, without any regard for diplomatic norms, directly presented Chinese president Yuan with the infamous Twenty-one

---

[60] Jordan to Langley, September 4, 1914, PRO, FO350/12, 81–82.
[61] Waijiaobu to Lu Zengru, Chinese Minister to Japan, August 30, 1914, in Wang Yunsheng, *Liushi nian lai Zhongguo yu Riben* (Beijing: Sanlian shudian, 1980), VI: 48.
[62] Jordan to Alston, January 18, 1915, PRO, FO350/13.

Demands through its minister to China, Mr. Hioki Eki.[63] The demands consisted of five sections with a total of twenty-one articles.[64] They were so severe that presidential advisor Morrison called them "worse than many presented by a victor to his vanquished enemy."[65] Obviously, the Japanese meant to reduce China to essentially a vassal state while the other powers were busy engaging in European battles.

Japan's demands presented the biggest challenge yet to China's survival and its desire to become a full-fledged nation-state. Jordan confided to Langley that it was "a pity for this unfortunate country, as it was just beginning to find its feet again under Yuan Shikai's guidance." Still, Jordan, like other Allied ministers to China, was no friend. As he frankly noted, China was "largely to blame for its own weakness, and might is right in these days. Therefore, weak states must pay the penalty of weakness or take the consequences."[66] Jordan obviously felt no real sympathy for the Chinese and was only concerned with British interests. Indeed, when the Japanese foreign minister Baron Kato voiced concern that Jordan might be pro-Chinese, Jordan professed to Langley that this "is a compliment I feel that I scarcely deserve."[67] What did concern Jordan was Japan's fishing in troubled waters. The Twenty-one Demands obviously had a seriously negative impact on British interests in China, yet Britain and other powers could not do much about it. As Jordan noted, the behavior of Japan "has proved particularly unpleasant for us in China and all we can do is to mark time."[68] On another occasion, Jordan even went further, complaining that Britain, because of its alliance with Japan, "may get ample compensation in other parts of the world, but I should be failing in my duty if I did not point out that the war and the Japanese intervention in it have hit us hard in China."[69] Britain had to swallow hard. "Only one thing would have saved us in China – a decided success in Europe," Jordan thus told his assistant Alston. "The Allied victory has been too late in coming and we must endeavour to make the best of a

---

[63] For a detailed study on Sino-Japanese negotiation regarding the Twenty-one Demands see Li Yushu, *Zhong ri er shi yi tiao jiao she* (Taipei: Zhongyang yanjiuyuan jindai shi yanjiusuo,1966); for the most recent work, see Zhitian Luo, "National Humiliation and National Assertion: The Chinese Response to the Twenty-one Demands," *Modern Asian Studies* 27, no. 2 (1993): 297–319.

[64] For the complete content of the Twenty-one Demands, see Chinese National Welfare Society in America, ed., *The Shantung Question: A Statement of China's Claim Together with Important Documents Submitted to the Peace Conference in Paris* (San Francisco: Press of Ramsey Oppenheim Co., 1919), 33–36.

[65] Cyril Pearl, *Morrison of Peking* (Sydney: Angus and Robertson, 1967), 307.

[66] Jordan to Langley, PRO, FO350/13.

[67] Jordan to Langley, October 2, 1914, PRO, FO350/12.

[68] Jordan to Langley, PRO, FO350/13.

[69] Jordan to Langley, March 5, 1915, PRO, FO350/13.

bad situation. It is a hard time for the British people everywhere, and we must face it like men."[70]

While Britain was marking time, France was making its own deal with Japan. The French minister in Beijing had approved all the Japanese demands apparently in the hope of successfully advancing the French government's appeal for Japanese military assistance in Europe. The United States was the only country in a position to do something about Asia, and some Chinese diplomats such as Koo were hoping that it might support China.[71] As early as January 22, 1915, Chinese government officials had leaked the general content of the Twenty-one Demands to Paul Reinsch, American minister to Beijing, although Japan had demanded that they be kept secret.[72] On February 19, the Chinese minister to the United States formally informed his host of the whole content of the demands.[73] But the United States chose to do very little. Its only important action was its so-called non-recognition policy.[74] On May 11, Secretary of State William Jennings Bryan instructed his minister in Beijing and ambassador in Tokyo to tell their host countries that "the government of the United States cannot recognize any agreement or understanding which has been entered into or which may be entered into between the Governments of China and Japan, impairing the treaty rights of the United States and its citizens in China."[75] This policy in fact originated with the counselor of the State Department, Robert Lansing, who even played with the idea of the United States making a deal with Japan at China's expense.[76] In fact, the US non-recognition position was only issued long after the Twenty-one Demands episode had been largely resolved.

During the Twenty-one Demands episode, the Chinese mood was somber and emotions ran high. A mixture of helplessness, anger, and also a new determination to renew China predominated. In his interview with Samuel G. Blythe on April 15, 1915, Yuan Shikai commented on Sino-Japanese negotiations over the Twenty-one Demands, "Whatever China can concede will be conceded, but she cannot help remaining firm

[70] Jordan to Alston, May 6, 1915, PRO, FO350/13.
[71] Gu Weijun (V. K. Wellington Koo), *Gu Weijun Huiyi lu* (Beijing: Zhonghua shuju, 1983), I: 123.
[72] Guo Tingyi, ed., *Zhonghua minguo shi shi ri zhi*, I: 173.   [73] Ibid., 177.
[74] For detailed analysis on the American response to the Twenty-one Demands, see Wang Gangling, *Ouzhan shiqi de Meiguo dui Hua zhengce* (Taipei: Xuesheng shuju, 1988), 35–65. For a recent study on US–Japanese relations during the First World War, see Noriko Kawamura, *Turbulence in the Pacific: Japanese–U.S. Relations During World War I* (Westport, CT: Praeger, 2000).
[75] Bryan to Reinsch, May 11, 1915, National Archive, College Park, MD, 10–15–6, M341, Roll 24.
[76] Lansing to Bryan, March 1, 1915, National Archive, College Park, MD, 10–19–2, T841, Roll 3.

on those articles which encroach on China's sovereignty or infringe upon the treaty rights of other Powers."[77] Yuan's government accepted all the demands but those of Section 5, which were the most damaging.[78]

The Chinese public reaction was rage at Japan's delivering so deadly a blow just as the country was in the process of transforming itself into a modern state.[79] A new and strong China was clearly contrary to Japanese interests, and the Chinese felt helpless because their country was so vulnerable and no other country would help. The bitterness expressed by Chen Youren (Eugene Chen) was shared by millions of Chinese: "The Japanese were not willing to give us the time necessary to adjust our old life to the new environment, which foreign intercourse and influence have set up in this region of Far Asia."[80]

Japan might have won the diplomacy battle, but it lost the war of public opinion. Widespread violent public response to the Twenty-one Demands proved to be a defining moment for the new Chinese foreign policy public. While Wellington Koo and his colleagues within the government executed a skillful secret maneuver to win foreign diplomatic support for China's battle against the Twenty-one Demands, Liang Qichao and others launched a brilliant public relations campaign on the domestic front. When news about Japan's demands came out, Liang wrote many powerful articles warning Japan not to treat China like Korea, which Japan had annexed in 1910, and appealed for public support. The campaigns of Liang and other members of the elite fanned public outrage at the Japanese demands to unprecedented levels. Merchants and students in Shanghai, Beijing, Tianjin, Hangzhou and many other cities immediately held rallies, wrote to magazines and newspapers, and sent the news in telegrams around the country. They demanded that the Yuan government reject the Japanese demands, and civic associations or societies soon emerged to orchestrate further civil protests.[81] On March 18, 1915,

---

[77] Samuel G. Blythe, "The Chinese Puzzle: A Talk on Policies and Conditions with the President of China," *The Saturday Evening Post* 187, no. 46 (1915): 4.

[78] In August 1916 Japan tried to use the so-called "Zhengjiatong Incident" to get what it wanted in group 5 of the Twenty-one Demands.

[79] Some officials such as Duan Qirui advocated fighting with Japan to resist the demands. However, after an evaluation of China's military strength, the option of war with Japan was not considered feasible. For the different attitudes within the government regarding the Twenty-one Demands, see Conty to Delcasse, June 2, 1915, Quai d'Orsay, NS, Chine, CLVII: 146.

[80] Eugene Chen, "The Menace of Japan," *The Peking Gazette*, October 12, 1916.

[81] The Chinese media's critical responses to the Twenty-one Demands were so strong that Morrison advised the Chinese government that it should take measures to cool them down in order not to further damage Sino-Japanese relations; see Morrison to Cai Tinggan, March 13, 1915, in *Minguo Dangan* (Archival materials of Republican China) (Nanjing, 1988), no. 3, 3.

about 40,000 people attended one anti-Twenty-one Demands rally in Shanghai.

Many societies and associations became involved in this effort: Shanghai's "Guomin dui Ri tongzhihui" (The Citizens' Group to Deal with Japan), "Waijiao houyuanhui" (The Association for Supporting [China's] Diplomacy), and "Jiuguo jijinghui" (The Radical Group for Saving the Nation); the "Aiguohui" (Patriots' Association) in Hangzhou; the "Jiuwantuan" (National Salvation Association) in Shandong; the "Funu jiuguotuan" (Women's Association for Saving the Nation) in Jiangxi; the "Zhonghua shangwu jiuwanhui" (Chinese National Merchants' Association for National Salvation) in Guangdong; and the "Guoshi yanjiuhui" (Association for Studying National Affairs) in Sichuan, among many others, gave active voice to the people's anger and dismay. Additionally, Japanese goods were widely boycotted. In Changsha, the capital of interior Hunan Province, all Chinese employees in Japanese shops resolved to quit their positions and work for the movement to boycott Japanese goods.[82] Some Chinese women even stopped wearing Japanese hairstyles, which had become fashionable in China after the Japanese victory over Russia in 1905. This was the first time in Chinese history that broad public opinion had weighed in so clearly on a foreign policy issue.[83] On May 9, 1915, the day that the Chinese government caved in to Japan's ultimatums, the Chinese National Education Association resolved that it should be memorialized as "a day of national shame." Beijing students resolved that the Japanese ultimatums be read on a daily basis to remind them of their national humiliation.[84] It was reported that people in Hankou were so stricken by the Twenty-one Demands and their government's capitulation to them that they proposed a day of no lights throughout the whole city on May 10. On that day, all of Hankou was pitch dark and dead silent after sunset.[85]

Japan's blatant bullying confirmed for many Chinese that this neighbor posed a major threat. "Japan is our country's strong enemy," wrote a young Mao Zedong in a letter to a friend on July 25, 1916. He predicted that China "could not survive without fighting within twenty years."[86] The broad-based response to the Twenty-one Demands in 1915 set the

[82] *Shi Bao*, April 26, 1915.
[83] See Tyau Min-Chien, *China Awakened* (New York: The Macmillan Company, 1922), 86.
[84] Li Xin and Li Zongyi, eds., *Zhonghua minguo shi*, II: 560, 566.
[85] Peter S. Jowe, "The Voice of an Oriental Nation," *Millard's Review* 5, no. 1 (Shanghai, June 1, 1918): 14.
[86] Mao to Xiao Zisheng, July 25, 1916, in Stuart R. Schram, ed., *Mao's Road to Power, Revolutionary Writings* (Armonk, NY: M. E. Sharp, 1992), I: 103.

stage for widespread public demonstrations that would be the hallmark of the May Fourth Movement of 1919.

The Twenty-one Demands fully exposed Japanese ambitions in China and helped the Chinese focus on the direction in which their country should head. If Japan provided China with a crisis of national identity by defeating it in 1895, the demands it presented in 1915 not only aroused Chinese national consciousness, but also helped the government identify its first specific goal in responding to the First World War: It had to attend the postwar peace conference.[87] Although China had earlier expressed its intention to join the war, it was only after the Twenty-one Demands that sufficient momentum had gathered for the government to act on its now almost irresistible desire to participate in the postwar peace conference. As Liang Qichao argued, Japan's demands had made obvious the necessity for China's attendance. He urged Chinese diplomats not to compromise, pointing out that China would be "one of the main issues" to be discussed at any peace conference held at the war's conclusion. Liang argued eloquently that Japan would have a strong voice there. Why, then, did Japan choose to present China with its demands now rather than at the postwar conference? The obvious answer must be that Japan knew it could be difficult to get what it wanted from the other powers. Therefore, China's diplomats must not surrender to Japan now. China must always keep the postwar conference in mind when responding to the Twenty-one Demands.[88] As soon as it had finally given in to Japan's ultimatums, the Chinese government decided to publish a tell-all document that explained how the Twenty-one Demands negotiations were conducted with hopes of abrogating them as soon as an opportunity presented itself.[89] Many Chinese assumed that the right moment would be the postwar peace conference.

The drive to attend the postwar peace conference

Liang Qichao's concerns were shared by many members of the foreign policy public and the Chinese government. Indeed, from early 1915, obtaining a seat at the conference became the firm goal of both the government and that public. Yet this idea had first emerged as early as the beginning of the war. Available documents indicate that the first suggestion of

[87] For an excellent article on this point, see Stephen G. Graft, "Angling for an Invitation to Paris: China's Entry into the First World War," *The International Historical Review* 16, no. 1 (1994).

[88] Liang Qichao, "Zai jinggao waijiao danju," in *Yin bing shi he ji*, IV: 108–09.

[89] For a complete declaration on the negotiations and China's attitude, see Waijiaobu guanyu Zhong Ri jiaoshe shi mu xuan yanshu, May 13, 1915, in Chen, Zhang, and Rao, eds., *Zhonghua Minguo waijiao shi ziliao xianbian (1911–1919)*, 206–14.

China attending the conference came from the French minister to China, Alexandre R. Conty. As early as August 17, 1914, a secretary from the Chinese Foreign Ministry visited Conty to discuss the implications of the European war regarding the future of Qingdao. Conty maintained that Japan would take Qingdao from Germany, and suggested that the only thing China could try was to attend the peace conference after the war. By sitting at the conference, China should be able to have its problems solved favorably.[90] In 1914 and early1915, even prior to the Twenty-one Demands episode, the idea of attending a peace conference appealed to many in the Chinese elite who argued that their country's destiny would surely be decided there. Various professional diplomats strongly advocated efforts to this end. As early as November 10, 1914, Wu Chaoshu (1886–1934), the son of Wu Tingfang and a high official in the Foreign Ministry himself, advised that China should avoid direct negotiations with Japan; it "would be to China's advantage if it were to wait for the end of the war and then bring the Shandong problem to the international peace conference."[91] The Chinese minister to the United States, Xia Xiefu, also advised in late 1914 that in order to turn the European war to China's benefit, the Chinese government should consider attending the postwar conference and start preparing for it.[92]

Perhaps the most detailed, if not the most convincing, argument was made by Xia Yiting, who was soon appointed counselor to the Foreign Ministry and later served as acting vice-foreign minister and acting foreign minister. In a long memorandum forwarded to the Foreign Ministry on January 15, 1915, Xia maintained that if China wanted fair treatment from the international system, especially to enhance its international prestige in the postwar world, its first priority must be to attend the postwar conference. He listed several possible ways China might win a seat. One involved cooperation with other neutral countries, especially the United States, in mediating the war. According to the third clause of the Second Hague Peace Treaty, a neutral country would automatically be invited to the postwar peace conference when it participated in mediation efforts. If this method did not work, China could try to force a wedge between the powers, as for example, when after the Napoleonic Wars, the French diplomat Charles Maurice de Talleyrand played on antagonisms among the victorious powers to get France into the Congress of Vienna. China could do the same by taking advantage of tensions between Japan and the

---

[90] A meeting report between secretary Liu Fucheng and Conty, August 17, 1914, Zhongyang yanjiuyuan jindai shi yanjiusuo, ed., *Zhong Ri guanxi shiliao: Ouzhan yu Shandong wenti*, I: 55.

[91] Memorandum from Wu Chaoshu, November 10. 1914, ibid., 436–37.

[92] Xia to Waijiaobu, December 25, 1914, ibid., II: 598–600.

other countries. Xia argued that timing was critical to the success of this strategy; China must wait for the moment when the powers needed it to check Japan at the peace conference. One thing it should do right away, according to Xia, was to select its best and brightest diplomats to prepare for this opportunity. A third option was to negotiate with Germany for entry into the conference. After all, Shandong was Chinese territory and China had the right to a voice if Germany agreed to sponsor its membership.

Xia pointed out that China had six possible issues to prepare for: (1) making China ready to deal with the charges from Germany that China had violated its neutrality; (2) annulling the Sino-German agreement regarding Qingdao because Germany had given it up to a third party without China's approval; (3) getting Qingdao back unconditionally; (4) taking control of the Shandong railways, which had been in German hands prior to the war; (5) collecting evidence of its losses and suffering in Shandong and elsewhere to support a demand for compensation and indemnities from the belligerents; and (6) dismantling all illegal railways and communication lines built by Japan.[93] To be sure, this kind of discussion was perhaps naive and lacking pragmatism given the urgency of the situation, but it indicates the beginning of serious consideration of the problems China faced diplomatically, should it be included in postwar deliberations.

Discussions of China's attendance at the peace conference were at this point limited to a small number of the elite and the policy making circle, and did not gain broad currency until the Twenty-one Demands had been presented. After that, the idea spread widely among both government officials and the non-official elite. Following its deliberation of all the proposals and inputs, the Foreign Ministry resolved in early 1915 to make a seat in the postwar conference a top-priority issue. On January 18, 1915, the same day Japan delivered the Twenty-one Demands, the Foreign Ministry sent a telegram to all Chinese ministers abroad explaining the push-to-attendance policy. The communication pointed out that the many crimes committed by Japan "could not be solved justly until our country attends the peace conference after the war." To prepare China's case, a high-level research group was convened on January 22, 1915, which included many influential officials from the Foreign Ministry[94] like Lu Zhengxiang,[95] Vice minister Cao Rulin, and Counselor Wellington Koo.[96] The Foreign Ministry also decided to send a special envoy to

[93] Xia Memorandum, ibid., 664–69.
[94] Waijiaobu to all China's legations, January 18, 1915, ibid., II: 678–79.
[95] Lu replaced Sun Baoji on January 27, 1915, as foreign minister.
[96] Minutes of the Lu Group meeting on January 22, 1915, found in Zhongguo di er li shi dang an guan beiyang wai jiao bu dang, 1039(2)–377.

visit Chinese diplomats abroad, coordinate their suggestions, and collect relevant documents. The special envoy's mission also included engaging in secret consultations with the world's distinguished international law experts.[97]

By 1915 Chinese intellectuals and other social elite members widely supported the official goal of attending the peace conference. *Jiayin Zazhi* published several articles by elite members of the foreign policy public that criticized Japanese "hooligan" behavior and argued that China's best chance was to wait until after the war, when the ultimate success of Japan's invasion would depend on the results of the European conflict.[98] This view was widespread in Chinese publications of that period.

Both the government and the Chinese foreign policy public were determined to link China's fate with the postwar world order and the international system; they would rely on the world community to regain what China had lost since the Opium War: its dignity, sovereignty, and prestige. The challenge was how to win a place at the table. Although Xia Yiting and others had proposed several strategies, none guaranteed China a seat. One stumbling block was presented by the Japanese foreign minister, Baron Kato, when he declared that China was not qualified to take part in the peace conference because it was not a belligerent power.[99] This made some Chinese think the most secure way to the conference was to join the war. Indeed, immediately after signing a series of treaties regarding the Twenty-one Demands, Lu Zhengxiang, the chief negotiator, told Yuan in May 1915 that only by joining the war could China hope to attend the postwar conference.[100] Even Cao Rulin, who would eventually be labeled a national traitor during the May Fourth Movement, suggested to Yuan in October 1915 that the best way to deal with Japan's ambition in China was to attend the war on the side of the Allied Powers. He argued that even if China could not send soldiers to Europe, it should still do everything it could to help the Allies so as to be rewarded after the war.[101] Cao was so serious about this idea that, in his capacity of vice minister for foreign affairs, he would ask the Chinese minister to

---

[97] Waijiaobu to all China's legations, January 18, 1915 / Waijiaobu to Minister Liu Shishun, January 21, 1915, *Zhong Ri guanxi shiliao: Ouzhan yu Shandong wenti*, II: 678–79 / 682–84, respectively.

[98] See Zhao Yun, "Ji Zhong ri jiao she" (News on Sino-Japanese Negotiations); Jiang Sheng, "Sanji Ouzhou zhanzheng" (Part III); and Duan Liu, "Zhanzheng yu caili," all in *Jiayin Zazhi*, July 1915.

[99] *The Peking Gazette*, November 28, 1914.

[100] See Lu Zongxiang, Wo suo jinshouqian ding ershiyi tiao, in Chen Zhiqi, ed., *Zhonghua minguo waijiao shiliao huibian* (Taipei: Bohaitan wenhua gongshi, 1996), I: 420; Luo Guang, *Lu Zhengxiang zhuan* (The biography of Lu Zhengxian) (Taipei: Shangwu yinshuguan, 1966), 105.

[101] Cao Rulin, *Yi sheng zhi huiyi* (Hong Kong: Chun Qiu chubanshe, 1996), 138.

Japan, Lu Zongyu, to inquire after Japan's possible response to Chinese participation in the war.[102]

It was this motivation to forge a link between China and the Allied side that made Wellington Koo, a young and brilliant diplomat, a strong candidate to be China's minister to the United States. In 1915 Koo was only twenty-seven years old, a returned student with a doctoral degree in international law from Columbia University. Since his rank was only that of a counselor in the Foreign Ministry, the Chinese government found a devious way to bolster his credentials by first appointing him minister to Mexico on July 11, 1915. Then it sent him out to Europe as a special presidential envoy to investigate and discuss the European war issue in London.[103] On October 25, 1915, Koo was finally appointed minister to the United States.[104]

China's desire to join the war gave rise to a number of policy issues. First, which side would China join? The German side? To be sure, since the outbreak of the war, especially after it lost Shandong to Japan, Germany's policies toward China had been relatively friendly compared with those of the Allied countries. The Chinese minister to Berlin, Yan Huiqing, once reported that the German attitude toward China was "extremely peaceful and friendly."[105] In his autobiography, he also wrote that in his tenure as minister to Germany during the war, the German government sometimes went out of its way "to meet our desires."[106] Certainly China may have felt less resentment toward Germany than toward Russia, France, or Britain. Further, China was more apprehensive about Japan than about any European nation. If the Chinese wanted a *casus belli*, they had a better case against Japan than against the Germans. But if they hoped to realize their dream of attending the postwar peace conference and thus gaining a solid footing in the international system, they had a far better chance of doing so by standing with the Allied side, since people like Liang Shiyi and Zhang Guogan were convinced that the Allied side would be victorious. If Germany won, it would simply retake Shandong, leaving China little chance to win back the province until the lease expired. Moreover, compared with Great Britain and some of the other powers, German interests in China were not significant. Therefore, Germany might not accord China much attention beyond the Shandong issue, and it might not be a key player in postwar East Asia whether it won the war or not. That being the case, Germany would not be much

---

[102] Guo Tingyi, ed., *Zhonghua minguo shi shi ri zhi*, I: 206.
[103] Koo, *Gu Weijun huiyi lu*, I: 141.
[104] Guo Tingyi, ed., *Zhonghua minguo shi shi ri zhi*, I: 202.
[105] Yan to Waijiaobu, September 5, 1914, Zhongyang yanjiuyuan jindai shi yanjiusuo, ed., *Zhong Ri guanxi shiliao: Ouzhan yu Shandong wenti*, I: 139.
[106] Yan Huiqing, *East–West Kaleidoscope*, 98.

use to China in either containing Japan or advancing its status in the international system.

Taking all these factors into consideration, the Chinese realized that siding with the Germans was unwise. Since whoever won the war would run the postwar conference, it was almost certainly in China's best interest to join the Allies. But here China faced a dilemma. Japan, which continued its effort to subsume China as its vassal state, was also a member of the Allied side. In addition, France, another Allied member, had strained relations with the Chinese. France was famous for having taught the code of diplomatic manners to the world; however, its minister to China, A. Conty, was notorious for his arrogance and hostility toward his hosts. Because of his frequently insulting attitude, Conty's relationship with Chinese officials, especially Wu Tingfang and his son Wu Chaoshu, both high officials in the Foreign Ministry, was often stormy. Conty was reputed to be the most expert of table-thumpers, whose classic method of clinching an argument at the Chinese Foreign Ministry was to beat an impressive rhythm. He sometimes sent official messages directly to the Chinese cabinet without first submitting them to the Foreign Ministry because of his hatred for its chief, Wu Tingfang.

Conty's hostility reflected his general contempt of the Chinese. One newspaper reported that even prior to Wu Tingfang's assumption of office as minister of Foreign Affairs, Conty's presence in the Foreign Ministry could always be detected by the resounding whacks issuing from the reception hall of the building.[107] Perhaps maintaining good relations with China had never been Conty's goal. As he once told William Rockhill, an American diplomat famous for his connection with the American Open Door policy, an axiom for a minister to China was that he ought never to be a *persona grata*![108] The French minister's anti-Chinese attitude was well known among his colleagues. Jordan, in his letter to Langley of February 29, 1916, wrote, "The French minister is decidedly difficult and is so detested by the Chinese that his opinion carries no weight. He takes a positive delight in being rude to the Chinese even when politeness could do no harm."[109] Conty's hostile attitude brought frequent protests from the Chinese government, which made him *persona non grata* and compelled his recall in the fall of 1917. When Conty was replaced in September 1917, it was observed that the Chinese government was "extremely happy."[110]

---

[107] *Peking Gazette*, April 6, 1917, Quai d'Orsay, NS, Chine, CCCLXXVII.
[108] Morrison to Alston, Beijing, April 11, 1917, *The Correspondence of Morrison*, II: 585–86.
[109] Jordan to Langley, February 29, 1916, PRO, FO350/15.
[110] De Martel to Quai d'Orsay, September 25, 1917, Quai d'Orsay, NS, Chine, DCXXIII, Protocole Corps Diplomatique Français, 1915–1917.

Conty, however, represented French official policy, not simply his own prejudices. The so-called Laoxikai Incident clearly indicates the general hostility and arrogance of the French toward China. This incident took place on October 20, 1916, when Conty was in Paris. On the orders of the French chargé d'affaires Damien de Martel (1878–1940), the French seized by force an area called Laoxikai in Tianjin. The point of this action was to extend the French concession, which had an original area of 250 acres. France had been eyeing the Laoxikai area for some time and in 1902 requested extension of its Tianjin concession by the inclusion of this locality, which would have tripled its size. The Chinese refused. With France's seizure of Laoxikai in 1916, the Chinese foreign policy public responded immediately by forming a Society for the Preservation of National Rights in Tianjin, in which both merchants and students were very active. At a general meeting held on October 23, the society decided to submit a petition urging the central government to break off commercial relations with France and prohibit further employment of Chinese workers in French enterprises, as well as the payment of wages in French currency. On November 2, a few days after a student demonstration, about 1,600 workers employed in French enterprises went on strike. A general boycott of French goods was also initiated in Tianjin. The boycott was actively supported by the Chinese chamber of commerce and other local groups which had been set up after the incident. They distributed funds and allocated coal and rice to the strikers. Messages of solidarity came from such far-flung places as Hankou, Chengdu, and Fujian.[111] A delegation of Tianjin businessmen visited the newly appointed foreign minister, Wu Tingfang, still in Shanghai, where he resided while in retirement (1912–16), and told him of the "true state of affairs." They pressed him for a plan of action. Another group of Tianjin businessmen called upon him in Beijing shortly after he had opened talks with the French to inquire about negotiations.[112] One upshot of this incident was its effect on the French recruitment of Chinese laborers for its home front (the recruitment issue will be examined in detail in the next chapter). At one point, it caused the supply of Chinese laborers to be cut off entirely.

Of course, Conty and France were not alone in their hostile policy toward China. As Jordan admitted, other ministers of the Allies were "all in the same boat" with Conty.[113] Policies toward China were anything but friendly. As Jordan confided to Langley, "I have, in fact, acted upon the plain assumption that China had to be subordinated and, if necessary,

[111] Jean Chesneaux, *The Chinese Labor Movement: 1919–1927*, translated from the French by H. M. Wright (Stanford: Stanford University Press, 1968), 132–33.
[112] *North China Daily News*, November 24, 1916; December 8, 1916.
[113] Jordan to Langley, February 29, 1916, PRO, FO350/15.

sacrificed to the main object of winning the war." He added, "In some respects things have gone rather further than I anticipated."[114] Some British officials who, according to Jordan, "clamour for treating China as part of British territory and forbidding all transactions with German commission agents, forget that China may have something to say. It will not help us much if China, owing to declining trade, is unable to maintain a stable administration or to meet her foreign obligations, and goes the way of Turkey." Because of this situation, Jordan called on all Allied countries, especially Britain, to "fight the enemy by all means by every weapon we can muster, but let us treat neutral countries, even China, fairly if we wish to avoid world-wide trouble. This is not a popular policy at present, but is nonetheless sound . . . China's amour propre has to be considered."[115] Despite this advice, Britain's attitude toward China did not change much. And Jordan himself was an effective representative of that policy. The Laoxikai Incident would have in fact been sorted out sooner had Britain not intervened. Britain was opposed to a French apology to China because of "the Allied humiliation involved." Furthermore, it worried that the agreement between France and China "formed a precedent for allowing the Chinese to restrict foreign trade and residence to areas of foreign concessions in treaty ports, the principle of which" Britain had contested for seventy-five years.[116] However, under insistent pressure of Chinese public opinion and the Chinese government's use of that opinion as a bargaining chip, France did eventually retreat from the Laoxikai area.

It is because of this background that Jordan was puzzled by China's desire to enter the war on the Allied side. He wrote to Alston in December 1915, "It is sometimes a wonder to me that the Chinese have not gone into the German camp altogether and that they still profess so much friendship for the Allies."[117] In his letter to Lord Bryce, Jordan also indicated that "the Chinese attitude towards the Allies has been more than friendly. They have given substantial assistance in ways I cannot mention and have contributed very large sums to the various war funds."[118]

Jordan's puzzlement can be solved only if we understand that China's pro-Allied policy was motivated by its great desire to use the war and the postwar peace conference as a vehicle for entering the international system rather than particularly friendly feelings for the Great Powers. It may seem strange that China should ally itself with a group of nations

[114] Jordan to Langley, April 16, 1916, PRO, FO350/15.
[115] Jordan to Langley, November 24, 1914, PRO, FO350/12.
[116] British Foreign Office Minutes on the incident, PRO, FO371/2914/10361.
[117] Jordan to Alston, December 21, 1915, PRO, FO350/13.
[118] Jordan to Lord Bryce, February 23, 1916, PRO, FO350/15.

to protect itself from the aggression of one of its members. "But such is the paradox of international politics," as noted in *Millard's Review of The Far East* in August 1917.[119] China had no real choice but to join the Allied side. But would the Allied Powers support China's move? Jordan had rejected China's first attempt in 1914; would the Allied Powers agree if China tried again? And what about Japan?

China again attempts to join the war

Just as the Qingdao issue compelled China to try to enter the war in 1914, and the Japanese Twenty-one Demands made China determined in 1915 to win a place at the postwar peace conference, the prospect of gaining membership in the international system was also an important motivation in ongoing Chinese efforts to actively participate in the war. As Jordan reported to the British Foreign Office, "China was willing to join with the Entente provided that Japan and the other Allies accepted her as a partner on a footing of at least nominal equality. This would have given her a measure of self-respect and a sense of security."[120] Yet how was China to effectively insert itself into the war? The Chinese government took several subtle diplomatic initiatives. These initiatives were conducted in secretive ways. For example, Liang Shiyi insisted to Jordan in 1915 that China's bid to enter the war not be exposed.[121] On another occasion, he had sent Jordan a message through the governor of Hong Kong urging that the governments of Great Britain, France, and Russia arrange for Japan to take the initiative in inviting China to join the Allies.[122] Both China and Allied Powers in Europe carefully disguised Chinese maneuvers, to allay and neutralize Japanese or German suspicion and sabotage. Yet, despite all the secrecy, we now have sufficient evidence to track these initiatives. One convincing but rarely cited piece of evidence is General Cai Tinggan's instructions to George E. Morrison, Yuan Shikai's foreign advisor. Cai, Yuan's secretary and confidant, played a role in foreign policymaking similar to that of Colonel Edward House for Woodrow Wilson, and often undertook important diplomatic activities for Yuan without the knowledge of the Foreign Ministry.[123] Cai wrote to Morrison on November 1, 1915 that "the President said this

---

[119] *Millard's Review* (August 4, 1917): 233.
[120] Jordan to Foreign Office, February 15, 1916, PRO, FO371/2647/30061.
[121] Jordan to Grey, November 6, 1915, PRO, FO371/2341/183325.
[122] Alston secret report to Balfour, March 1, 1917, PRO, FO371/2916/332.
[123] For Cai's role in foreign policymaking, see Tang Zaili, "Xinhai yi hou de Yuan Shikai," in Du Chunhe, Lin Binsheng, and Qiu Quanzheng, eds., *Beiang junfa shiliao xuanji* (Beijing: Zhongguo shehui kexue chubanshe, 1981), I: 85, 100.

morning he must have or find a good excuse or pretext for going in [the European war]. Find one for him and embody it in the memo, either signed or not as you please."[124] Morrison responded the same day. In his letter to Cai, Morrison cautioned that China should take every care not to give its declaration of war the appearance of being prompted by a desire to prevent Japanese aggression because "the Allies have for the time being ceded to Japan the foremost position in the Far East; their policy is apparently to be guided by Japan."[125] Morrison advised that China should simply renounce its neutrality, declare that it was on the side of right and justice, and offer its support to the Allies in the fight against the Germans. China could claim that it had itself experienced oppression, and so should stand before the world in support of the oppressed. China would do all it could to bring the war to a conclusion.[126]

On November 6, 1915, China advised the British that it was prepared to join the Allied cause if Britain, France, and Russia invited it to do so. China's decision to join the war in early November of 1915 is confirmed by a confidential report from Captain I. Newell, US military attaché in Beijing. In his "absolutely confidential" report of November 17 entitled "China proposes to join the Allies against Germany," he wrote that "[o]n or about November 10th several of the Chinese Ministers and influential advisors" held a conference and agreed China would declare war on Germany and thus force "herself in with the allies." According to the report, "When the above plan was submitted to the President of China, he returned it with the endorsement that it had his approval but that some good pretext for declaring war must be found." This report is highly reliable since the author obtained the information from one who was present at the conference with a promise to keep it "absolutely confidential."[127]

China took several bold yet subtle actions to help its bid. One was to provide the Allied countries with rifles. China knew that a shortage of weapons on the Allied side, especially in Russia, had placed the Allies in urgent need of help. In 1915 the British army's artillery shell shortages contributed to a political crisis at home and led to the fall of the liberal government. In early November the Chinese government suggested to the British that "with a view to placing on a wider and a more satisfactory footing the manufacture of arms and munitions of war in China

---

[124] Cai Tinggan to Morrison, *The Correspondence of Morrison*, II: 463.
[125] Morrison to Cai, November 1, 1915, *Correspondence of Morrison*, II: 464.
[126] Morrison memo, November 1, 1915, ibid., 464–67.
[127] I. Newell, absolutely confidential, "China Proposes to Join the Allies against Germany," November 17, 1915. National Archive (College Park): RG 165 Records of the War Department, General and special Staffs, entry 296 box 324.

for the supply of the Allied governments," the British and Russian governments "should address an official note to the Chinese government stating that they have been obliged, in order to meet the exigencies of the war in Europe, to remove military supplies from their possessions on the borders of China, and requesting the Chinese government, in the interests of peace and good order in China, to relax their neutrality provisions affecting the supplies of a military nature, so that public peace may be maintained in the regions on the frontier by the introduction of satisfactory measures." The Chinese further requested that the note from the two countries include language stating that "the two powers would assist China effectively in dealing with any unforeseen diplomatic difficulties which might ensue from the proposed action." The Chinese proposal was too attractive for the Allied countries not to consider. On November 18 ministers from Britain, France, and Russia discussed formally with China the case for its joining the war. But to accept China's bid would mean a giant step forward for China, leading eventually to its admission into the Allied club. The question remained whether Japan would support the move. To forestall Japanese disapproval, Britain and Russia made a presentation to the Japanese on November 22 to explain their case. The British Foreign Office asked the French government to also make a similar presentation. On the day he learned about China's intention, the Japanese minister to China immediately questioned the Chinese Foreign Ministry regarding China's move, but the Foreign Ministry declined to acknowledge that China intended to join the war. It was four days later that China finally admitted its intention to Japanese officials and asked for Japan's response.[128]

In its communication with Japan the British government hid certain important aspects of the munitions plan. On November 12 Grey told the Japanese ambassador in London that "in endeavouring to leave no stone unturned to assist her ally [Russia] in this respect, it has occurred to His Majesty's government that the Chinese government might be induced to spare some rifles, et cetera, from their reserves of military stores, and as a result of private communications with them it is hoped shortly to be able to purchase a small supply of these. His Majesty's government has realized, however, that instead of carrying on these negotiations privately, it would be more satisfactory in every way to place the transaction on a more formal footing."[129] Grey did not mention that China had already proposed to provide this material on its own initiative. So eager were the

[128] Guo Tingyi, ed., *Zhonghua minguo shi shi ri zhi*, I: 205.
[129] British Embassy to French foreign ministry, November 13, 1915, Quai d'Orsay, NS, Chine, CXXXII.

Chinese to assist the Allies that by late November, Liang Shiyi had worked out a detailed plan for China's providing arsenal support for Britain and Russia and sent several extremely confidential letters to the Russian and British legations to indicate Chinese willingness to cooperate.[130]

Early Chinese interest in joining the war had been noted by foreign diplomats in Beijing. Paul Reinsch, the American minister, reported in November 1915 that "in the utmost confidence I have been informed that Yuan and his three chief counselors are at present considering the possibility of checkmating the Japanese onset through a declaration of war against Germany. They believe that by this stroke they would force Japan either to act in good faith as an ally and to desist from interference in China or to declare herself openly as an enemy and side with Germany." But "the Chinese government will take the action only upon assurance from Great Britain, Russia, and France that Japan will not be allowed to use the alliance as a means to interfere in China."[131] The French chargé d'affaires in Beijing also acknowledged the arsenal and other war initiatives from China in his report to Quai d'Orsay.[132] Jordan indicated the same in a report to his government. He wrote that the Chinese had sent one shipment of rifles to the Allies after secret negotiation. "[F]rom these negotiations originated China's offer to enter the war. The president intimated to His Majesty's minister that it was impossible to continue secret help to the Allies, and that it would be much better for China to come out into the open, and to develop her arsenals with financial help from Great Britain and Russia in order to meet the military requirements of those countries." In the same report Jordan admitted that the whole diplomatic démarche which Britain sponsored started only at China's instigation.[133] The shipment of rifles involved considerable quantities. As Liang Shiyi confirmed to Conty in September 1917, about 30,000 rifles had been secretly transferred to the British through Hong Kong.[134]

Thus China signaled that it had adopted a new approach to international affairs by offering to help the Entente, and the Allied Powers

---

[130] See Quai d'Orsay, NS, Chine, CXXXII: 89–95.

[131] Reinsch to Secretary of State, November 9, 1915, National Archive, M341, Roll 25.

[132] De Martel to Briand, September 23, 1916, Quai d'Orsay, NS, Chine, CXXXIV: 137–39.

[133] Jordan annual report to FO, 1919, PRO, FO405/*Zhong Ri guanxi shiliao: Ouzhan yu Shandong wenti*, II: 678–79; 229/10.

[134] Conty's confidential note to Quai d'Orsay (November 12, 1917), Quai d'Orsay, NS, Chine, CXXXVII; *Sanshui Liang Yansun xiansheng nianpu* indicates that the shipment was ready in November 1915; the Chinese navy assigned two vessels to transport them to Hong Kong in January 1916. The shipment included 24,000 rifles and an undisclosed number of different types of cannons. For details, see Conty's confidential note to Quai d'Orsay, November 12, 1917, Quai d'Orsay, NS, Chine, CXXXVII; Feng Gang, *Sanshui Liang Yansun xiansheng nianpu*, I: 300–1.

were responding by engaging in negotiations with Japan. For the Allied countries, China's participation in the war would mean not only valuable material assistance but also that all Germans and German businesses would be forced to leave China. Thus Britain and its allies would be rid of a possibly strong commercial rival in this great market after the war. Concern about German intrigues in China was also a consideration for Britain. Edward Grey understood these to be the "substantial and moral advantages" of China's participation in the war.[135] Since Japan was key to the success of this scheme, Britain, France, and Russia discussed how to obtain its approval[136] and began to press the Japanese government for cooperation.[137] But Japan was unhappy with this development. It knew that China would use the opportunity to provide an arsenal and other services for the Allied side and thereby improve its international status. Japan was also alert to and feared "the moral awakening of 400 million Chinese that would result from China's participation in the war."[138]

For all their sincere attempts to persuade Japan, the Allies' efforts were in vain. On December 6, 1915, the Japanese foreign minister formally objected to the proposed policy on Chinese support in a memorandum to the Allied ambassadors. Although he used technical excuses such as diplomatic procedural problems, the real reason for the rejection, which Grey clearly understood, was that Japan was "alarmed by the idea of concessions which might be claimed by China as a reward for her assistance when peace has been declared." Grey let the Japanese know that Britain was "acutely disappointed" with their attitude.[139] But Japan did not blink. In another memorandum on February 25, 1916, Japan again told the Allied countries that it opposed the plan, but with a different rationale. China's direct participation in the actual warfare "cannot fail to create in the minds of the Chinese grave unrest and misgiving, and to give a chance to discontented and revolutionary elements already reported to be active in various parts of that country." The memorandum went on to state that the Japanese "cannot commit themselves to any action that is likely to bring China to a state of disorder and devastation." Japan also challenged the British argument that China's entry into the war could

---

[135] FO telegram to Regnault, Quai d'Orsay, NS, Chine, cxxxII/7.

[136] For details, see Quai d'Orsay, NS, Chine, cxxxII.

[137] Paul Cambon, telegram to Quai d'Orsay, November 15, 1915, Quai d'Orsay, NS, Chine, cxxxII.

[138] Eugene Chen, An Address delivered before the National Liberal Club, London, March 18, 1920, found in Zhongguo di er li shi dang an guan, beiyang wai jiao bu dang, 1039-2-400.

[139] British immediate and confidential memo to Quai d'Orsay, December 15, 1915, Quai d'Orsay, NS, Chine, cxxxII/171–73.

check German intrigues in Asia, claiming that reports of the so-called German intrigues were exaggerated.[140]

Britain retorted that "the main features of this German propaganda are so well known in the Far East that it is unnecessary to enlarge on them." Furthermore, Britain argued that Germans in China had been involved in fomenting rebellion in India, furnishing would-be rebels with arms and ammunition. Britain had evidence for this in intelligence obtained through the arrest of German agents.[141] Yet Japan was not persuaded. As Jordan wrote, "It did not suit Japan to allow China to join the Entente. That is all. Japan's interest is to see the European war prolonged as much as possible and to keep China in a state which will facilitate the attainment of her own objects."[142]

To make the situation worse, the Allied countries were alarmed in 1915 to see Japan responding to German advances when the Allied side was not doing well in the war. Japan's strategy was simple. By flirting with Germany, it could readily switch sides if the Allies lost. Japan could also use the German card to keep the Allies anxious. Either way, Japan gained. The Allied countries understood this all too well. The British War Office in a secret note pointed out that "in 1915, Japan was anxious as to whether she had not 'backed the wrong horse,' and for this reason she was opposed to any action which might force her to take further action against Germany."[143] In the meantime, Germany was pleased at the Japanese advances. In January 1915, Germany commissioned Admiral Paul von Hintze as the new minister to Beijing. Hintze, an influential German politician, had come to China seventeen years earlier as a lieutenant in the German navy and an aide-de-camp on Prince Henry of Prussia's famous cruise to East Asia. That mission had led to the selection of Qingdao as a German naval base in China and contributed to the emperor's schemes for a powerful German navy. That Germany chose to send Hintze to Beijing fully indicated the considerable importance it accorded to China. As soon as he was in Asia, Hintze generated strong diplomatic shockwaves by trying to pry Japan away from the Allied side and dissuading Japan from embarking on military operations in Europe in support of Britain and its allies.[144] Hintze informed the Japanese minister to China that Germany would let Japan keep not only Qingdao but also the Pacific Islands, and would be willing to give Japan a much freer hand in China than the Allies would. In due course, Japan "began to show unmistakable

---

[140] Quai d'Orsay, NS, Chine, CXXXIII/129.
[141] FO document, December 28, 1915, Quai d'Orsay, NS, Chine, CXXXIII/134–39.
[142] Jordan to Alston, February 1, 1916, PRO, FO350/15.
[143] War Office secret memorandum, March 7, 1917, PRO, WO106/36.
[144] Jordan to Grey, January 26, 1915, PRO, FO405/218.

signs of wavering in its allegiance to the Allied Powers" and "was dangling the bait of a separate peace in front of German eyes." The flirtation between Japan and Germany was a nightmare for the Allied side. The contacts between Japan and Germany, though they did not bear fruit, "had shown the Japanese government a means of putting pressure on its Allies."[145]

The Chinese failed to fully realize until it was too late that not only had China's hopes of joining the war been dashed in 1915, but its fundamental interests had been also compromised by Japanese actions. To avoid losing Japan at this critical juncture, the Allied Powers not only gave up on China's direct participation in the war, they let Japan dictate Allied policies in China. As early as December 10, 1915, Grey told Japan that it should not worry about any reward China might receive in return for its participation in the war, "as the grant of concessions of this sort was a matter to be decided by the Allies in concert with Japan."[146] On November 26, 1915, Grey further instructed Sir Coyningham Greene, the British ambassador to Tokyo, to deny that Britain had talked with China regarding its participation in the war, adding, "We have no intention of entering upon political negotiations with China except in consultation with Japan."[147] No wonder Jordan complained, "We all feel that we are so many puppets pulled by Japanese strings."[148]

By early 1916, Britain, France, and Russia had failed in their diplomatic intrigues regarding China's entry into the war, because the Allies deemed it unwise to offend Japan in exchange for China's participation. For them, Japanese assistance was more important, even though "It is quite horrible that active assistance may be offered in return for a free hand in China," as a high officer in the British Foreign Office commented.[149] But if the Allies had to concede something to Japan, "such a concession," the British Foreign Office told Jordan in its secret telegram, "can be found only in China."[150] Exchanges of opinion within the British Foreign Office indicate that Britain was prepared to let Japan take control of German concessions in China if Japan would provide the Allies with military,

[145] Frank W. Ikle, "Japanese–German Peace Negotiations during World War I," *American Historical Review* 71, no. 1 (October 1965): 62–76.
[146] British confidential memorandum to Quai d'Orsay, December 15, 1915, Quai d'Orsay, NS, Chine, CXXXII.
[147] Greene, Confidential report to Balfour, November 13, 1917, PRO, FO371/3176.
[148] Jordan was not a big supporter of China's joining the war effort; Morrison even called him the "chief opponent" of China's joining the Allies (Morrison to Fraser, October 12, 1916, *The Correspondence of Morrison*, II: 520). For Jordan's complaint, see Jordan to Alston, December 21, 1915, PRO, FO350/13.
[149] PRO, FO371/2646/223579.
[150] War Office secret memorandum, March 7, 1917, PRO, WO106/36.

especially naval, support.[151] Thus China's second push to join the war had failed, and more importantly, its treatment and fate at any future peace conference was also effectively sealed. Of course, Chinese officials did not yet realize the extent of the damage to their cause.

[151] See handwritten exchange between Edward Grey and other officials in the Foreign Office in the middle of February of 1916, PRO, fo371/2647/30061.

4   "Using laborers as soldiers" – China's alternative strategy

> Their emigration from the shores of Shandong will take its place certainly as one of the most important aspects of the Great European War.
>
> A British commander of Chinese laborers[1]

> What is worth remembering of this experience is the undoubted goodwill of the Chinese Government to take an active part in the conflict in which the very existence of France was at stake. This assistance was valuable. Thousands of Chinese workers in our factories allowed us to spare an equal amount of French workers for military service.
>
> Marius Moutet[2]

To establish a strong link with the Allied side and strengthen its case to eventually claim a part in the war, Chinese officials worked out a creative new strategy in 1915. The conventional view suggests that the "laborers as soldiers" program was an "elaborate recruiting scheme . . . launched by the Allies in 1916," in response to which "the weak Peking government proved unable to cure Allied exploitation of China's neutral resources in manpower."[3] This view, however, is mistaken. The labor plan was in fact launched in 1915 and it was the Chinese rather than the Allies who initiated it. The labor plan was to play a pivotal role in China's strategy to join the Allied cause and became a key mechanism for the Chinese entry to the international system.

The "laborers as soldiers" program

The idea of sending laborers to help the Allies was the brainchild of Liang Shiyi (1869–1933), who called it the *yigong daibing* (literally, laborers in the place of soldiers) strategy.[4] Liang and his associate Ye Gongchuo

---

[1] Lynn Pan, ed., *The Encyclopedia of the Chinese Overseas* (Singapore: Archipelago Press, 1998), 65.

[2] Marius Moutet was the French socialist politician. Quote from ibid.

[3] A. Philip Jones, *Britain's Search for Chinese Cooperation in the First World War* (London: Garland Publishing, Inc., 1986), 109.

[4] Feng Gang et al., eds., *Minguo Liang Yansun xiansheng shiyi nianpu* (Taipei: Commercial Press, 1978), I: 310.

worked out the detailed plan for using laborers as a crucial element in pursuing China's war policy.[5] The rationale behind the scheme in Liang's mind was this: The Chinese government wished to link China with the international system and the Allies; sending laborers demonstrated Chinese sincerity and an ability to help the Allies. Additionally, Germany could not charge China with violating its neutrality because these laborers would be hired through "private" companies.

The Chinese decision to send laborers to Europe was unprecedented. Both the Ming and the Qing dynasties had strongly discouraged Chinese people from going abroad and even persecuted those who had.[6] In 1712, when considerable numbers of Chinese were already residing abroad, an edict from the Qing court decreed, "Those who stay overseas permanently are liable to capital punishment and will be extradited from foreign countries by the provincial governors for prompt beheading." Emperor Qianglong called overseas Chinese "deserters of the Celestial Empire," who would therefore not receive protection from China when they encountered trouble in other countries.[7] This hostile practice remained official policy until 1893 when the Qing government finally abolished it.[8]

The anti-emigration policy was one manifestation of the Middle Kingdom syndrome and pointed to the isolationist mindset of Chinese society at that time. The decline of this sort of thinking in the late nineteenth century coincided with the new desire to join the Western world system. No longer was the West a land of demons, but an example for China to follow; going abroad had become a glorious privilege. As a result, the status of overseas Chinese was enhanced a great deal, and in 1912 Republican China passed a series of laws, including the Provisional Constitution and Organization Act of Congress, that legalized the representation of overseas Chinese in domestic politics.

In 1916, as Chinese laborers started to leave for France, the Ministry of Agriculture and Commerce and the Ministry of Foreign Affairs deliberated over a new law to protect those workers overseas.[9] The new law

---

[5] Ye Gongchuo held posts of chief of the Railway Bureau, manager of the Bank of Communications, and vice-minister of the Ministry of Communications during the period 1913–18.

[6] For a recent study on the Chinese overseas, see Wang Gunwu, *Chinese Overseas* (Cambridge, MA: Harvard University Press, 2000).

[7] Quote from Yen Ching-Hwang, *Coolies and Mandarins: China's Protection of Overseas Chinese During the Late Ch'ing Period, 1851–1911* (Singapore: Singapore University Press, 1985), 20–22.

[8] This policy was not compatible with several treaties the Qing court signed after the Opium War that allowed foreign countries to recruit Chinese to work abroad.

[9] See "Waijiaobu shou nong shangbu zhi, October 25, 1916," "Waijiaobu fa nong shangbu zhi, November 4, 1916," "Waijiobu shou nong shangbu zhi, November 17, 1916," in

was soon passed, and in 1917, with a huge number of Chinese laborers already in Europe, the State Council of the Beijing government set up a new office, the Bureau of Overseas Chinese Workers.[10] The government's 1915 laborers as soldiers program, therefore, should also be seen as further evidence of the new Chinese thinking and the transformation of Chinese society in general, as well as an expression of China's eagerness to join the war.

Liang Shiyi began discussing his labor idea with the Allied diplomats in mid-1915. According to the British military attaché in Beijing, Lieutenant Colonel David S. Robertson, Liang first put forward the idea to the British in early June. Liang's plan proposed that China supply Britain with 300,000 military laborers (along with 100,000 rifles), to serve under British officers wherever required. It is important to note here that Liang's original suggestion was the use of military laborers, not hired workers. If Britain had accepted this proposal, China would have been fighting on the Allied side in 1915. Unfortunately, no one in the British government except Robertson was interested. The British minister to China, John Jordan, termed the idea of using Chinese military help "hardly practicable."[11] The British War Office agreed with Jordan, claiming that "the proposal to utilize Chinese either as fighting troops or for labour purposes" was "considered not to be feasible, as any such step would involve China taking her place on the side of the Allies against the central powers, and this had for political reasons been considered an impossibility."[12] Britain rejected this idea immediately.

However, when similar but revised proposals ("laborers" without the adjective "military") were made by Liang to the French, they immediately drew positive attention. When the war started in Europe, Georges Clemenceau wrote in an article for the *Saturday Evening Post* that "France is once again nothing more or less than a great battlefield."[13] During wartime, the French had to mobilize nearly 7.2 million of its population for the war effort and almost 1.5 million French soldiers were killed (Britain suffered some 1 million dead and millions more wounded).[14]

Chen Sanjing, Lu Fangshang, and Yang Cuihua, eds., *Ouzhan Huagong shiliao* (Taipei: Zhongyang yanjiuyuan jindai shi yanjiusuo, 1997), 12–14, 16.

[10] For a detailed analysis of the Beijing government's overseas Chinese policy, see Jiang Shunxin, Du Yugeng, "Lun Beiyang zhengfu de Qiaowu zhengce," *Minguo dangan* 3 (1993): 68–72.

[11] Jordan to Grey, July 25, 1916, PRO, wo106/35.

[12] "Summary of Information Concerning the Recruiting of the Chinese Labour Corps," January 12, 1917, PRO, wo/106/33.

[13] Georges Clemenceau, "The Cause of France," *The Saturday Evening Post* 187, no. 17 (1914): 65.

[14] J. M. Winter, *The Great War and the British People* (London: MacMillan Publishers Ltd., 1986), 65–99.

The mobilization and casualties drastically exacerbated the labor short-age. Getting new human resources had become the key to winning or losing for France as it entered the summer of 1915, the second year of the war. Liang's proposal coincided with the French search for new human resources. To solve the manpower problem, France looked to China for help and responded quickly with the Truptil Mission to carry out Liang's plan.

The French mission

As early as March 17, 1915, the French Ministry of War had discussed the idea of using Chinese laborers to do roadwork for the military. But not everybody in the ministry supported this notion. For one, a senior general did not think it was a good idea. He argued that the use of Chinese in the French military zones presented a "serious disadvantage." "There is no room," in his opinion, "to authorize the cause,"[15] and the idea was dropped. Several months later, however, the War Ministry reconsidered the value of Chinese labor, given that the war had become prolonged and it was necessary to mobilize all possible resources to defend France.[16] By June, the same month Liang made his proposal, French military author-ities had decided to seek China's help. They formally asked the French minister in Beijing, Alexandre R. Conty, to investigate the possibility of recruiting Chinese laborers. Liang's proposal, therefore, came as a godsent opportunity for France.

After some discussion with Liang, Conty reported to his government on June 9, 1915 that the Chinese wanted to help, on one condition: Chinese laborers should only be hired "theoretically" by French private companies since China was still "officially" neutral. On November 4, 1915, Conty further told his government that a very high Chinese official (presum-ably Liang Shiyi) had confidentially told him that China could provide between 30,000 and 40,000 workers for France. On November 11, 1915, after some debate, the French War Ministry decided to go ahead with the recruitment plan. On December 1, it selected a retired lieutenant-colonel of the French army, Georges Truptil, to head a recruiting commission to China. Two weeks later, the Truptil Mission was on its way and arrived in Beijing on January 17, 1916.[17]

---

[15] Le Major Général à Monsieur le Ministre de la Guerre, Etat-Major de l'Armée, Service Historique de l'Armée de Terre, Château de Vincennes (hereafter cited as Vincennes), 7N398/Chine.

[16] Le Ministre de la Guerre à Monsieur le Général Commandant en Chef, Paris, October 27, 1915, Vincennes, 7N435/Main-d'Oeuvre Indigene.

[17] "French Foreign Ministry Report on Chinese Laborers," January 23, 1917, Quai d'Orsay, Ministre des Affaires Etrangères, 1918–1929, Chine, XLI.

To avoid German charges of China's violating its neutrality, the Chinese side set up a private organization, the Huimin Company, to handle the recruitment. The company was established in May 1916 by Liang Shiyi and the director of the Chinese Industrial Bank, Wang Keming. The Truptil Mission also pretended to be acting in a private capacity with Truptil himself taking the cover of an agricultural engineer. The French contracted Huimin to recruit laborers in China, and that contract was signed on May 14, 1916, after long negotiation. The Huimin recruiting area mainly consisted of the northern Chinese provinces. Truptil also signed a contract with another Chinese company set up to hire skilled workers in Shanghai, and by January 23, 1917, he had assembled 600 workers in this category.

Although Truptil pretended to be a businessman from a private French agricultural company and the French government promised that Chinese laborers were being recruited only for private purposes, the mission's military and official connections were obvious. From the mission's outset, administration of the Chinese laborers in France fell to the Direction des Troupes Coloniales, part of the French Ministry of War. This arrangement clearly violated the agreement between China and France. First of all, China was not a French colony; the Chinese government was doing France a great favor by offering workers. French minister to China Conty himself admitted that he was not comfortable and even felt shamed by the word "colonial."[18] Moreover, the French government recognized that the Chinese workers would be assisting with the French "national defense."[19] The Chinese government was fully aware of these issues but chose not to contest them.

As soon as Germany learned of the French recruitment scheme, it protested repeatedly to the Chinese government, charging violation of neutrality since one Chinese worker counted as equal to one soldier for the Allied side. The Chinese government responded mildly by saying the workers went to Europe in a private capacity and had been recruited by private companies.[20] Of course, in its secret communications with local government, the Chinese Foreign Ministry admitted that in reality the recruitment was being conducted by the government and it asked local

---

[18] Conty to Quai d'Orsay, March 1, 1916, Quai d'Orsay, Ministre des Affaires Etrangères, 1918–1929, Chine, XLI.

[19] France made similar statements several times. See, for example, Procès-Verbaux de la Conférence Interministérielle, Archive Nationale, Paris, 14F/11334.

[20] See "Waijiaobu shou de shi xing ce zhao hui," July 15, 1916; August 3, 1916, August 9, 1916, November 13, 1916, "Waijiaobu fu de shi zhao hui," August 9, 1916, "Waijiaobu fa de shi zhao hui," December 5, 1916, in Chen, Lu, and Yang, eds., Ouzhan Huagong shiliao, 8–11, 15, 17.

governors to understand and support this carefully designed policy (*wei chu qiu quan zhi ku xin*).[21]

The Truptil Mission was not the only entity engaged in recruiting Chinese laborers for France, however. Other organizations had also been set up to the same end. For example, on January 31, 1916, the French Ministry of Works agreed that the Société Franco-Chinoise d'Education, as its representative, would also begin to recruit Chinese laborers. In early 1917, with some connection to the recruitment plan of the Société, another recruiter, the so-called Louis Grillet Mission, arrived in China.[22] This mission also came under the French war machine's direct control, and was officially subordinate to the Truptil Mission. But in fact it acted quite independently, mainly focusing its recruiting efforts on the South, especially Yunnan and Sichuan provinces. When Truptil returned to France, Grillet took charge of both missions.[23] Although several French recruiting missions would be active in China over the course of the war, the Truptil Mission was the most effective and important among them.

The War Ministry's original plan was to recruit 40,000 Chinese workers, but by the time both sides entered final negotiations, French ambitions had expanded. The French decided they would recruit at least 50,000 Chinese workers instead and this was the figure recorded in the contract.[24] The laborers fell into two categories: the common laborers (*travailleurs*) and skilled workers (*spécialistes*) who could handle difficult jobs and received more compensation. The general contract was renewable for five years. However, because of disputes regarding issues such as compensation for Chinese laborers who died in France, the contract was later revised.[25]

In theory Chinese laborers under the French were legally equal to their French counterparts. They could celebrate both French and Chinese holidays with some benefits. For example, on Chinese holidays such as the Chinese New Year and National Day (October 10) they were provided with better food, and usually allowed to have those days off.[26] The French

---

[21] "Waijiaobu fa yan Jiang Yan hai Dong san sheng ge dujun sheng zhang mi han," January 30, 1917, in ibid., 20.

[22] "Le Ministre du Travail et de la Prévoyance Sociale à Monsieur le Ministre de la Guerre," October 14, 1916, Vincennes, 6N149/Fonds Clemenceau/Mission de Recrutement des Ouvriers Chinois.

[23] Note of Quai d'Orsay, Paris, January 17, 1917, Quai d'Orsay, Ministre des Affaires Etrangères, 1918–1929, Chine, XLI: 145.

[24] Naval attaché report, no. 2109, French Embassy, February 6, 1916, Archives de la Marine, Vincennes, SSEB119/Transport Personnel.

[25] "Note pour la Direction des Affaires Politiques et Commerciales," April 6, 1917, and Conty to Quai d'Orsay, March 31, 1917, Quai d'Orsay, NS, Chine, CXXXV.

[26] There are records of several orders given with regard to this treatment from the military authorities; see, for example, Vincennes, 17N156/Correspondance.

were serious and conscientious about understanding Chinese laborers' different tastes and customs, and the authorities prepared detailed general guidelines about how to accommodate Chinese culture and customs.[27] The French government even set up an inter-ministerial conference, which met frequently to coordinate foreign laborer issues.[28]

The first group of Chinese laborers arrived in France on August 24, 1916.[29] Prospects seemed bright with this boost to the French war effort, and the government congratulated itself on the idea that an additional 10,000 Chinese would become available to it each month. The French government calculated that by the end of 1917, there would be 100,000 Chinese laborers working for France. Officials had even decided how these laborers would be assigned. According to one document, the allotments were as follows: armament would receive 20,000 laborers, the Ministry of War 50,000, and transport 30,000.[30] Unfortunately, things did not work out so well. The French recruitment figure was actually much smaller because of complications, one being the lack of cooperation between the French Foreign Ministry (Quai d'Orsay) and the War Ministry, specifically between its Beijing legation and the Truptil Mission. The French minister A. R. Conty was not happy with a separate recruiting mission that operated beyond the jurisdiction of the legation. As early as December 3, 1915, two days after the Truptil Mission was selected, he charged that a recruitment mission under military jurisdiction would produce "a regrettable effect." Of course, this was only an excuse for Conty. He was not a man who really honored commitments with the Chinese. The bottom line was that he had already engaged in negotiations with Chinese officials regarding recruitment, and he felt that he should be in charge of the whole business. Conty was not fully cooperative with the Truptil Mission from the outset, and took every opportunity to complain.[31] Conty grumbled openly that the Truptil Mission did not handle contract disputes wisely and "from the beginning" the French War Ministry had made decisions that were completely contrary to the opinion of the French legation in Beijing. This being the case, Conty could only "strive to repair or relieve to the extent possible the consequences of the errors committed in complete ignorance

[27] See "Instruction Relative to Employment of Chinese Laborers," September 26, 1916, issued by Commander of Colonial Troops, Vincennes, 17N/156.
[28] For details on this, see "Procès-Verbaux de la Conférence Interministérielle," Archive Nationale, Paris, 14F/11334.
[29] "Procès-Verbaux de la Conférence Interministérielle," February 24, 1917, Archive Nationale, Paris, 14F/11334.
[30] Archive Nationale, Paris, 14F/11331/Chinois/Institution et Affaires Générales, 1917.
[31] Quai d'Orsay Report on Chinese Workers, January 23, 1917, Quai d'Orsay, Ministre des Affaires Etrangères, 1918–29, Chine, XLI.

of the Chinese environment in which the recruitment operations take place."[32]

Quarrels and the lack of close cooperation among the French of course hurt the recruitment business. Though in wartime the military had a louder voice and military control of recruitment continued, the Truptil Mission moved slowly and its work suffered from delays.[33] The lack of cooperation from Quai d'Orsay persisted even after the Truptil Mission ended. The French military authority made matters worse by terminating the recruitment of Chinese laborers in early 1918 without any advance consultation with the Chinese government. This unilateral and early termination violated the contract between China and France, and since the French legation in Beijing had guaranteed the contract in the name of the French government, Quai d'Orsay was left to clean up the mess.

At first, the French chargé d'affaires in Beijing, de Martel, sent several telegrams to Quai d'Orsay drawing its attention to the inappropriate action of the French military.[34] On February 9 and February 18, 1918, he warned of the cancellation's "inevitable consequences." He argued that since there remained a 15,000-man quota to meet, the unilateral termination of the contract by France legitimized the Huimin Company's demand for compensation of its loss. The French government had no justification for refusing to pay. De Martel also worried that the War Ministry's decision set a risky precedent, which might hurt France in the future. For example, French business could be hurt should China follow suit and cancel its contracts unilaterally. Furthermore, French prestige was at stake because the contract had the French government's guarantee. With these considerations in mind, de Martel suggested that France should pay an indemnity to the Huimin Company as soon as possible in accordance with the terms of the contract.[35]

Using arguments provided in de Martel's telegrams, Quai d'Orsay sent several memoranda to the War Ministry drawing its attention to the serious consequences of breaking the contract. The War Ministry, however, did not agree. Ministry officials responded that many of the Chinese demands for compensation were unjustified. However, it did recognize the legal problems its action gave rise to and agreed to settle with the Chinese in "a spirit of conciliation." Even with this admission, a

---

[32] Conty to Quai d'Orsay, February 12, 1917, Quai d'Orsay, Ministre des Affaires Etrangères, 1918–1929, Chine, XLI: 163.

[33] For disputes between Conty and Truptil, see Procès-Verbaux de la Conférence Interministérielle, March 3, 1917, Archive National, Paris, 14F/11334.

[34] For the opinion from the Huimin side on this, see Feng Gang, *Sanshui Liang Yansun xiansheng nianpu*, 448–53.

[35] Martel to Quai d'Orsay, February 9, 1918 and February 18, 1918, Quai d'Orsay, Ministre des Affaires Etrangères, 1918–1929, Chine, XLII.

close reading of the War Ministry's reply shows a lack of sincerity and an indifference to Chinese rights.[36] At one point, the ministry even argued that France could use the poor quality of Chinese laborers as grounds for refusing payment of the two million francs it owned to Huimin.[37]

Bickering between Quai d'Orsay and the War Ministry concerning compensation of the Huimin Company indicates how poorly coordinated France's China policy had become. There was no consensus on how to recognize China's contribution to the war or how to accommodate other Chinese ambitions. Then the Laoxikai Incident of October 1916, arising from the arrogance of the French legation in Tianjin, nearly destroyed the entire French recruiting effort in China.[38] After Laoxikai, public outrage made it impossible to recruit northern Chinese workers for a time, and the mission was forced to move south. However, public opinion in the South was not particularly friendly to recruitment either. In one telegram dated February 12, 1917, the governor of Guangdong Province suggested to the Chinese Foreign Ministry that since many people in his province opposed French recruitment, it should temporarily suspend activities in Guangdong. The Foreign Ministry agreed.[39]

The British mission

Britain refused to consider Liang's proposal until the second half of 1916. Even then, Jordan was suspicious of the Chinese plan. When he reported on this issue to the Foreign Office, he commented that the Chinese "new school of statesmen would not, in my opinion, view with favour the prospect of seeing their countrymen assisting European powers in a struggle on any terms which did not ensure them complete equality of standing and a voice in the subsequent settlement."[40] Jordan was right.

---

[36] War Ministry to Quai d'Orsay, July 15, 1918, Quai d'Orsay to War Ministry, July 28, 1918, Quai d'Orsay, Asie 1918–1929, Chine, XLII.

[37] For detailed differences between the two sides, please refer to Note pour le Cabinet Militaire/Affaire Truptil [without a date on it], and Secret Telegram from French Minister to China, Boppe, October 22, 1918; both documents are available in Vincennes, 6N149/Fonds Clemenceau/Mission de Recrutement des Ouvriers Chinois; for the best short summary of the differences, see Le rapport de M. Dubois in Vincennes, 6N111/Divers secrets/Fonds Clemenceau; for a detailed view of the French military side, please see Rapport Fait au Sous-Secrétaire d'Etat, Ministre de la Guerre, Analyse au Sujet de la Demande d'Indemnité du Syndicat Wey-min par suite de la Suspension du Recrutement de Main d'Oeuvre Chinoise, Vincennes, 6N111/Divers secrets/Fonds Clemenceau.

[38] For details of this incident, see chapter 1.

[39] "Guangdong shengzhang zhi wai jiao bu," February 12, 1917. Zhongguo di er li shi dang an guan beiyan wai jiao bu dang, 1039–1.

[40] Jordan to Grey, July 25, 1916, PRO, wo106/35.

If Britain was not prepared to accommodate China's position, it was not a good idea to accept Chinese assistance.

In early 1916 the British War Office had regarded the Chinese labor scheme with "the greatest apprehension." Of special concern was the opposition of organized labor at home. The War Office also felt uncomfortable about accepting help from the Chinese for the rescue of Western civilization, and therefore decided that until there was "a definite assurance that the trades unions, tribunals, etc., at home would agree to release a corresponding number of men for active service at the front, no steps should be taken to replace them by Chinese and black labour."[41] Obviously, domestic and racial considerations were major factors in the War Office's hesitation, but by the summer of 1916, everything had changed. The very existence of Britain was at stake and British arrogance had been replaced by desperation. The Battle of the Somme had inflicted enormous British casualties, and manpower on the home front was in such a state that it was impossible to spare anyone without hurting the war effort. In July alone, the first month of fighting at the Somme, 187,000 British soldiers were killed, wounded, or missing. By mid-August total casualties had reached 223,000 and the British were experiencing an acute manpower shortage. Clearly Britain needed outside help, even from a country like China. This dismal situation compelled the British authorities to reconsider their earlier position on the Chinese labor proposal.

David Lloyd George, in his capacity as head of the War Office, agreed in the summer of 1916 to the principle of employing Chinese labor for work "in France and in other theatres of war in order that the British labour now being employed in France etc may be released for work at home to mitigate the existing shortage of men in agriculture and industries."[42] On August 14, 1916, the British informed the French government that the British forces in France would soon also employ a considerable number of Chinese laborers.[43]

Beginning in August of 1916, Great Britain put its own recruitment plan into action. Like the French, the War Office selected a representative, Thomas J. Bourne (1864–1947), who had been engineer-in-chief for the Beijing–Hankou Railway, with twenty-eight years' experience in China, to head the recruiting mission.[44] He left London on October 9, 1916, and arrived in Beijing on October 28. Three days later, on October 31, he left

---

[41] Peter T. Scott, "Chinese in France in WW I," *War Monthly* 8, no. 76 (1980): 8–11.
[42] War Office Document, August 1916, PRO, wo32/11345.
[43] War Office Memorandum, August 14, 1916, PRO, wo32/11345.
[44] His official title was War Office Representative for the Purpose of Recruiting Labour in North China for the British Expeditionary Force in France.

with Robertson for Weihaiwei, a British sphere of interest that served as his recruitment base, and started to work immediately.

Weihaiwei was not the first place the War Office considered, but its choice was the result of consultation and compromise between the War Office and the Foreign Office. In mid-1916, when the British War Office decided to use Chinese laborers, it first proposed to enlist the Cantonese at Hong Kong. This proposal was submitted to Jordan, who was against the idea of recruiting workers in south China, based on the view that southerners were less suitable than northerners. The scheme of using Hong Kong as a base was eventually dropped and a follow-up proposal was put forward to recruit laborers at Weihaiwei.[45]

Each laborer was contracted to work for three years, but the army could terminate the contract after one year, giving six months' notice. Compared to the contract Chinese workers signed with the French, the British terms were not at all favorable. As one British governmental report boasted, of all the contracts made with the Chinese, this one "was, from our point of view, the most satisfactory. It gave us power to hold them for a long period of time with the option of getting rid of them in a moderately short time."[46]

At first the British mission was not effective, its recruitment complicated by factors different from those that plagued the French. In all it had recruited fewer than forty people for its first Chinese labor corps by late November 1916. Unlike France, Britain did not use Chinese contractors to do the recruiting; instead, its recruiting was carried out by agents of the British government. Without cooperation from the Chinese government, it was difficult for Britain to move ahead. Chinese cooperation, however, had conditions attached, as Jordan had pointed out earlier. The British chargé d'affaires in Beijing, F. Alston, described the situation in late 1916 to the British Foreign Office, "It seems quite clear that, if coolie recruitment is ever to materialize, some more active steps must be taken at once. We are quite ready to give the necessary assurances to the Chinese government that they will be protected against aggressive action by enemy powers for supposed breach of neutrality."[47]

The Chinese were quite ready to respond. In December 1916, with the British still having trouble jump-starting their recruitment scheme, the Chinese foreign minister told them that although the Chinese government could not openly assist their efforts it would help it any way it

[45] War Office Document, January 12, 1917, PRO, wo106/33.
[46] Michael Summerskill, *China on the Western Front: Britain's Chinese Worker Force in the First World War* (London: 1982), 94–95.
[47] Alston to Foreign Office, December 22, 1916, PRO, wo 32/11345.

could (*zi dang an zhong jin li, bu bian ming zhu ye*).[48] Supplying labor for the Allies was "very important" for Chinese international relations since it supported China's goal of winning a seat in the postwar peace conference and other benefits.[49] For this reason, the Chinese government provided the British with a list of demands in exchange for Chinese support in manpower.[50] In a telegram to the Chinese minister to London on January 25, 1917, the Foreign Ministry officially and openly linked its labor scheme with its larger plans. The dispatch asked Britain to agree to the following to obtain Chinese assistance in its recruiting effort:

1. Britain would allow China to delay payment of the Boxer Indemnity for fifty years with no increase in interest.
2. It would immediately allow China to raise taxes, an act of governance that had not been allowed by the Great Powers for some time.
3. Britain would help China secure a seat at the postwar peace conference.

Of these three goals, joining the peace conference was the most important, and the dispatch asked the Chinese minister to stress that point.[51] China also asked Great Britain to persuade the other powers to accommodate Chinese wishes. Although the Chinese government did not achieve any of the above goals with this dispatch, these points did provide the basis for later successes.

One problem the British recruitment mission shared with the French effort was too strong a military orientation. Jordan pointed this out clearly: "Unless the situation clears there is even a possibility of our recruiting being stopped . . . I feel bound however from my knowledge of the Chinese to express my opinion that the scheme as now being developed by the War Office appears to me to be assuming too military a character and I fear this may further militate against it. If the project is to succeed at all, every effort must be made to keep the military nature of the organization in the background out here."[52] As with the French mission, China eventually chose not to make a fuss over this issue. But even the French presented a problem for Britain's initial recruitment: the disastrous Laoxikai Incident made recruiting for *any* overseas service difficult. Alston reported that "the French incident at Tientsin [Tianjin] is primarily responsible for obstruction. It puts [a] stop to all recruiting for abroad in the province."[53]

[48] "Zong zhang hui wu Ying ai dai ban wen da," December 13, 1916, in Chen, Lu, and Yang, eds., *Ouzhan Huagong shiliao*, 456.
[49] "Shou guo wu yuan gong han," January 17, 1917, in ibid., 467.
[50] "Fan ju ying shi gong shi dian," January 25, 1917, "Shou ju yin shi gong shi dian," February 6, 1917, ibid., 469, 79.
[51] "Waijiaobu to Minister Shi Zhaoji," January 25, 1917, Taipei: Zhong yang yan jiu yuan jin dai shi yan jiu suo dang an guan, wai jiao bu dang, British Recruitment, E-1–4–2.
[52] Jordan, telegram to Foreign Office, November 12, 1916, PRO, wo32/11345.
[53] Alston to Foreign Office, December 3, 1916, PRO, wo32/11345.

Despite its many problems at the outset, the British recruitment effort soon took off. According to one report from the French military attaché in London, General de La Panouse, by late April 1917 the British had sent 35,000 Chinese laborers to France to work for the British military, a number which greatly surpassed those working for the French.[54] The French naval attaché in London reported on June 1, 1917, that he had information about the British even recruiting Tibetan workers to serve under the control of the British War Office.[55]

How can we explain the success of the British recruiting mission? Of course, one obvious factor was the gradual removal of earlier obstacles. But most important was the close cooperation that developed between the British Foreign Office and the War Office; the dialogue between the British legation in Beijing and the War Office representative was particularly productive.[56] First, the War Office kept Jordan closely informed about what was going on in its recruitment program. One of the War Office cables to Jordan stated that the provisional terms it communicated to Bourne were subject to Jordan's concurrence. It also told Jordan that Bourne was instructed to consult with him closely. It even explained to Jordan why the War Office had to assign someone else to be in charge of the mission. "[W]hile leaving the collection of the men in Shantung under legation control, it is necessary, however, for the War Office to have an agent at Wei-hai-wei itself who will be responsible for receiving, approving, enrolling, clothing etc., the coolies after they have been collected, but subject to any advice to the contrary from you, he will remain throughout at Wei-hai-wei and leave all operations outside that territory to be carried out under your direction." In the same telegram, the War Office expressed its desire to "set the [recruiting] machinery going as soon as possible" and asked Jordan to "take the preliminary steps forthwith."[57] Of course, widespread British interests in China and the enormous experience of the British minister Jordan also played some role in the success of the recruitment program.

The numbers issue

The question of how many Chinese laborers worked in France during the war remains unsolved, and can perhaps never be fully sorted out owing to

[54] La Panouse Report, April 27, 1917, Vincennes, 17N156; see also Procès-Verbaux de la Conférence Interministérielle, May 26, 1917, Archive Nationale, Paris, 14F/11334.

[55] Naval Attaché report, "Au Sujet des Cooliers Tibetains," no. 1589, June 1, 1917, Vincennes, marine, SSEB5/travailleurs coloniaux et étrangers/généralités.

[56] A. Philip Jones has mentioned the many problems that existed between the two sides; see his *Britain's Search for Chinese Cooperation in the First World War* (London: Garland Publishing, Inc., 1986), chapters 6 and 8.

[57] Foreign Office to Jordan, October 5, 1916, PRO, WO32/11346.

lack of data. There is a sizable discrepancy among the figures provided by different sources. The recently published *Dictionary of the First World War* indicates that Britain alone recruited 320,000 Chinese laborers during the war period.[58] If this figure seems high, the British scholar A. Philip Jones provides a much lower number: Jones puts the total number of Chinese laborers in France, Mesopotamia, and Russia at 150,000.[59] Chinese scholar Chen Sanjing indicates that the number recruited by the French and British together was about 200,000.[60] Gu Xingqing, who worked for the Chinese labor corps as an interpreter, indicates that 175,000 Chinese workers (including skilled workers) served under Britain and France.[61] Robert Lansing, secretary of state under American President Woodrow Wilson and a delegate to the Paris Peace Conference, stated at the Council of Ten that "China had furnished 200,000 men."[62] A telegram document dated June 1, 1918, found in the US National Archives' War Department files, indicates that Chinese laborers sent to the western front from China proper by the British government numbered 97,000; French government recruits numbered 40,000 laborers and 1,500 specialists.[63] One Chinese official document indicates that the total number of Chinese workers in France reached 150,000.[64]

Which figure is right and reflects reality? So far no scholar has tried to solve this issue, but since manpower was one of the most important factors in the war, it seems necessary for this study to establish at least roughly how many Chinese laborers worked in France during the war period. To settle on the total number of recruits for both Britain and France, we have to consider the recruitment records of each country. Let us begin with France.

The French recruitment record is quite messy. Even the Chinese government did not know exactly how many Chinese France had recruited. Li Jing, who was appointed by the Chinese government to take care of the French recruits in 1917, was himself puzzled by the number issue from the very beginning. His uncertainty is reflected in several reports he sent to the Foreign Ministry from France. For example, Li informed his boss

---

[58] Stephen Pope and Elizabeth-Anne Wheale, eds., *Dictionary of the First World War* (New York: St. Martin's Press, 1995).

[59] Jones, *Britain's Search for Chinese Cooperation in the First World War*, 108–09.

[60] Chen's figure is not fixed. In many places in his book, he cites the number as 200,000, but on one particular page, he mentions the number as being between 175,000 and 200,000; see Chen Sanjing, *Huagong yu Ouzhan* (Taipei: Zhong yang yan jiu yuan jin dai shi yan jiu suo, 1986), 34–35.

[61] Gu Xingqing, *Ou zhan gongzuo huiyilu* (Shanghai: Shangwu yinshuguan, 1937), 50.

[62] "Council of Ten," January 15, 1919, *FRUS*, The Paris Peace Conference (Washington, DC, 1919), III: 567.

[63] National Archives, College Park, RG165M1444 Roll 2, document nos. 2055–12.

[64] "Waijiaobu shou qiaogong shiwuju han," November 25, 1918, in Chen, Lu, and Yang, eds., *Ouzhan Huagong shiliao*, 413.

that by May of 1918, 53,109 Chinese workers recruited by the French had arrived in France.[65] In his next report, however, Li indicated that the total number stood at 36,925.[66] When confronted by his superiors about the discrepancy, Li Jing had to admit that the number of laborers had turned out to be nearly impossible to track given the way the men were recruited and managed.[67]

Archival materials may clarify the matter. A report prepared at the request of the French Ministre de la Marine on September 25, 1919, by the chef du Service des Travailleurs Coloniaux, which had charge of Chinese workers, not only clearly points out that 36,939 Chinese workers recruited by France had arrived, but also gives individual figures on an annual basis. It reports that in 1916, 5,979 Chinese had come to France; in the year 1917, the number was 18,117; and in 1918, 12,839; in 1919, four Chinese laborers arrived even though the recruiting plan had been terminated.[68] The French figure is almost identical to that given in a report by the Chinese government in April 1919. That record says the number of Chinese laborers recruited by the French government as of October 16, 1918 was 36,925.[69] The same Chinese report indicated the number was 36,965 as of October 19, 1918. However, it must be pointed out that the actual number recruited by France must have been greater because these reports did not count Chinese workers who died en route to France as a result of German submarine attacks and other causes. It is also questionable whether the figures include workers recruited by non-military agencies such as the Société Franco-Chinoise d'Education.

The best way to reckon the number of recruits deployed by the French is to look at a breakdown of recruitment by the different organizations. Let us consider the Huimin Company first. The French chargé d'affaires in Beijing, Damien de Martel, reported on February 18, 1918, that as of the date he submitted the report, the Huimin Company had provided 35,000 Chinese workers for France.[70] Another count that seems more reliable comes from the newly appointed French minister to China, Auguste Boppe (1862–1921), on October 22, 1918. In his report, the confirmed number of Chinese recruited by means of "embarqués or licenciés" by

[65] Li, The third report, ibid., 396.   [66] Li, The fourth report, ibid., 417.

[67] "Shou qiaogong shiwuju han, April 2, 1919," ibid., 441.

[68] Report from chef du Service des Travailleurs Coloniaux to Ministre de la Marine, September 25, 1919, Marine, SSEB7/Main d'oeuvre demandes statistiques.

[69] "Guowu yuan qiaogong shiwuju de wu ci diaocha zai fa hua gong qing xin shu," *Xin Zhongguo* (The New China) (Monthly) 1, no. 3 (July 1919): 261.

[70] Martel to Quai d'Orsay, February 18, 1918, Quai d'Orsay, Asie, 1918–1929, Chine, XLII.

the Huimin Company was 40,429.[71] Boppe's number does not actually conflict with the figure provided by Service des Travailleurs Coloniaux because the former possibly includes people who died on the way or disappeared for other reasons.[72] Given that the point of this report was to establish how much France should compensate the Huimin Company for the sudden termination of contract, the number here was presumably checked carefully by both sides. Therefore, we can reasonably conclude that this was the actual number recruited by the Huimin.

But how many Chinese laborers were recruited by non-Huimin agencies? According to preliminary Chinese official figures, the total non-Huimin recruitment added up to about 2,000–3,000 under the French.[73]

Given all the evidence cited above, I would argue that the Chinese workers recruited by France totaled somewhere between 43,000 and 44,000.

In the British case, according to one War Office document, from January 18, 1917 to March 2, 1918, Britain sent 94,458 Chinese workers to France.[74] Another War Office document indicated 95,000 Chinese workers operated under British military control.[75] On December 10, 1919, a member of the British Parliament, Aneurin Williams, asked Winston Churchill in Parliament about the number of Chinese workers who served Britain in France during the war. Churchill seemed to agree that the number was nearly 100,000.[76] On another occasion, when the British king paid a visit to British-run Chinese laborers' camps in France in early January 1918, it was reported that the camps contained 100,000 recruits and officers.[77] The Chinese government records show the figure recruited by the British government as 110,000.[78] From these various accounts, it appears that in the British case, the numbers are all reasonably close.[79]

---

[71] Boppe to Quai d'Orsay, Beijing, October 22, 1918, Vincennes, 5N216/Chine/January–December 1918.

[72] Chen Sanjing mentioned that 752 Chinese laborers died from German submarine attacks; see Chen, *Huagong yu Ou zhan* (Taipei: Zhong yang yan jiu yuan jing dai shi yan jiu suo, 1986), 72–73.

[73] Li Jing, "Second report," in Chen, Lu, and Yang, eds., *Ouzhan Huagong shiliao*, 382.

[74] "Report on Chinese Labour Corps," PRO, wo 32/11345.

[75] "War Office Report on Chinese Labor Corps," PRO, fo371/3682/125.

[76] PRO, fo371/3682/154.   [77] "Newspaper Clips," 1/18/1918, PRO, wo106/33.

[78] "Qiaogong shiwuju dafu zhanhou jingji diaochahui guanyu qiaogong diaocha shi xian (Bureau of Overseas Chinese Workers of the State Council's Reply Regarding Chinese Laborers to the Committee of the Post-war Economic Study)," *Xin Zhongguo* 1, no. 6 (October 1919): 237

[79] The number was so confusing that even the official publication *Statistics of the Military Efforts of the British Empire During the War*, published in 1922 by the British Government's War Office, was not sure about the real figure. It provided the number as 92,129 at its peak. For the details, see *Statistics of the Military Efforts of the British Empire During the Great War, 1914–1920* (London: H. M. Stationery Office, 1922), 160.

We can also check the British data against other sources. The French military attaché in London closely monitored and frequently reported on British-recruited foreign laborers, including the Chinese. In one report dated July 6, 1917, he stated that the British goal was to recruit 105,000 Chinese workers. The number 105,000 perhaps was a typing error for 150,000, since this figure appears consistently in his other reports. By the date the report was written, 44,000 men had already been recruited. In another report dated May 21, 1918, the attaché indicated that 94,458 Chinese workers of the projected 150,000 had been raised. But there are inconsistencies between the attaché's reports. For example, an April 8, 1918 report states that Britain had recruited 98,928 Chinese workers. By May, the number had somehow been reduced.[80] In his report of June 22, 1918, the number returned to 94,458.[81] Given the evidence from all sources, I conclude that the Chinese laborers working in France under British control numbered no more than 100,000, and the figure 94,458 well may be accurate. This number, however, does not represent all the men Britain recruited during the war, because Britain also sent Chinese workers to other places, such as Mesopotamia and Egypt, and the Chinese in Mesopotamia, according to the British official history of the war, numbered nearly 6,000.[82]

To conclude, the total number of the Chinese workers in France during the war was about 140,000, and one source from the Chinese government seems to support this estimate.[83]

It is worth pointing out here that when the United States entered the war, it considered recruiting Chinese workers as well. According to *The New York Times*, "It is believed that the combination of Chinese labor and American bosses will be most satisfactory for getting work expeditiously done."[84] However, transportation problems proved so severe that the plan was never carried out. Eventually the American Expeditionary Force arranged to borrow about ten thousand Chinese laborers from the French, employing them on the same terms.

---

[80] Secret Reports from General Panouse, Attaché Militaire to Ministre de la Guerre, Vincennes, 6N155/Dossiers 3.

[81] General Panouse, Military Attaché to London, "Secret Report to War Ministry," Vincennes, 6N155/1.

[82] Brig.-Gen. F. J. Moberly, *The Campaign in Mesopotamia: 1914–1918* (London: H. M. Stationery Office, 1923–27), IV: 329.

[83] "Qiaogong shiwuju dafu zhanhou jingji diaochahui guanyu qiaogong diaocha shi xian, *Xin zhongguo* 1, no. 6 (October 1919): 237. The difficulty of the numbers issue is also reflected in a recently published encyclopedia of the Chinese overseas. For example, in one place, it indicates the number is 150,000, in another 100,000, and finally gives the number as 140,000. See Pan, ed., *The Encyclopedia of the Chinese Overseas*, 64, 304, 11.

[84] *The New York Times*, July 21, 1917.

A comparison of the French and British recruitment missions

There are obvious similarities and differences when one compares the French and British recruitment of Chinese laborers. One aspect they shared was heavier recruiting in China's northern provinces, especially Shandong. Second, their main purposes were the same. For both countries, Chinese workers were to serve military needs and to help them win the war. With the French and British military authorities doing the recruiting, Chinese workers came primarily under military management, and were usually organized into military-type units commanded by officers. Even before they arrived in France, each Chinese laborer under the British was thumb-printed and assigned a number which was stamped on a brass identification card, or bracelet, in English and Chinese. These became the laborer's only identification – his name was of no importance. On their arrival in Europe, the Chinese were finger-printed several times again. One witness wrote, "when the coolies line up to be 'printed,' an impression of each digit is taken separately, then another impression of the whole five simultaneously, and the whole are taken in duplicate, making a total of twenty-four separate impressions for each coolie."[85]

The officer selected to command the Chinese labor corps for Britain was Lieutenant Colonel B. C. Fairfax. The Chinese, especially those working for the British, often worked in or close to the military zones. They marched to work each day, and their marching skills sometimes impressed those who saw them. According to one report, when the first group of Chinese laborers recruited by the British arrived in France in early April 1917, the French village near their camp "was agog with excitement, the whole po[p]ulation [sic] of about 200 old men and women and children turning out to welcome 'les chinoises.' The Chinese formed up outside the station and the order 'form fours' was given. Stepping out smartly in their new uniforms, their march from the station to the depot along the muddy French roads was really wonderful, and our N.C.O.s gasped with astonishment."[86] If they broke rules while in France, they could be court martialed,[87] and in fact, at least ten Chinese laborers under British control were executed under military law during the war.[88]

---

[85] Harry B. Wilmer, "Chinese Coolies in France," *North China Herald*, September 21, 1918.

[86] Ibid.

[87] "Le Ministre de Guerre Messieurs les Commandants de Groupements de Travailleurs Coloniaux," Paris, December 22, 1916, Vincennes, 16N/2450/6H/98/9.

[88] Summerskill, *China on the Western Front*, 82.

Even their mail service was under military control. The postal arrangements for the labor corps allowed each Chinese worker to write two letters per month. All these letters had to pass through the corps post office
at headquarters, where, after being censored, they were made up into
bags and dispatched to the British War Office recruiting agent in China.
Similarly, the British recruiting agent made up a bag at Weihaiwei and
forwarded it directly to the Chinese labor corps post office in France
whence the letters were distributed.

According to Li Jing's reports, most Chinese laborers employed by the
French worked away from the front for military industries under French
military control.[89] But after China officially joined the war in 1917, even
French authorities started to assign Chinese workers to military zones
more frequently and openly. However, there were some slight differences between the two countries on this issue. In the British case, almost
all Chinese laborers served at the front; some of the French-recruited
Chinese worked in civilian areas and for civilian companies, though these
companies worked for the French military authorities.

Given their broad similarity of purpose, a few differences between
French and British Chinese labor programs were notable. One big difference was in their method of recruitment. While France recruited mainly
through Chinese contractors, Britain did not. Second, Chinese workers under French control received better treatment than those under the
British. For example, France paid the Chinese higher wages, and French
rules governing the Chinese laborers were less strict. In general, Chinese
labor corps were worse off under British control, and the British authorities were not shy about admitting their tough attitude toward the Chinese;
they were even proud of it. One confidential report from the quartermas-
ter general of British troops in France and Flanders, R. Ford, recognized, "[P]erhaps the most striking discrepancy being the fact that whilst
a British Chinese coolie is not allowed to enter cafes or estaminets, the
French Chinese coolies are not subject to any such prohibition."[90] The
British military authority even complained that French people were too
friendly to the Chinese workers. The French "civilians, by their actions,
have rendered the enforcement of the British orders to the Chinese on
this subject most difficult," complained one official from British military headquarters in France.[91] The British boasted that Chinese laborers

---

[89] Li Jing, first report on the Chinese laborers under the French, December 4, 1917, the
second report, June 10, 1918; both in Chen, Lu, and Yang, eds., *Ouzhan Huagong shiliao*,
352–59, 79–92.

[90] "General R. Ford Report," September 18, 1919, PRO, FO371/3682/144.

[91] "Note from J. B. Wroughton, Headquarters of British Troops in France and Flanders,"
July 17, 1919, Vincennes, 7N1297/Chinois Evacuation.

under British control "are under the strictest discipline and are subject to far greater restrictions than are the coolies working under the French administration."[92]

Because of their harsh treatment by the British military, Chinese workers in British camps occasionally migrated to French camps without authorization. For example, one British document recorded that "[Chinese] Coolie 54857 lived in No. 9 French camp for about six weeks from March to May 1919; Coolie 68211, who was absent for over six months, had spent periods of weeks in several French camps. Two coolies from No. 149 British company, when arrested a short time ago, stated that they had been living in a French camp near Litte."[93]

To prevent the Chinese in different camps from having contact, the British authorities suggested that the French adopt the same strict management policy. "I would therefore most strongly urge that such steps as you may consider desirable and necessary may be taken to communicate these facts to the inhabitants and that special reference may be made to the extreme importance of their refraining at all times from association or communication with Chinese workers," wrote the British General Wroughton to his French counterpart in July 1919. At the same time, he tightened control over his Chinese camps. Wroughton justified the tough new regimen by claiming that "numerous cases of complaints as to the behaviour of Chinese workers employed by the British authorities in France have recently been brought to notice and it is evident that stricter supervision of these workers is called for."

New rules issued in the middle of 1919 for Chinese labor corps under Britain read as follows:

1. Passes should take the form of an entry on the back of the work ticket, dated, stamped and signed. The ganger who was in charge of the party should have a pass giving the regiment number of his party, which should be checked on return. Chinese labour corps are not allowed to leave their camps in the evenings.
2. Surprise roll calls should be frequently held, during which the camp should be searched for possible refugees.
3. Camp police should be held responsible for immediately reporting the arrival of any Chinese labourers visiting the camp.
4. More responsibility should be placed on gangers who are directly responsible for the presence and behaviour of all coolies under them, both at work and in camp. Any culpable delay in reporting the absence of any coolies should be severely dealt with.

[92] War Office Document, May 25, 1917, PRO, FO370/2906.
[93] From the British Troops Headquarters in France and Flanders, October 23, 1919, signed by Burrowes, Vincennes, 7N2289/Affaires Britanniques/Travailleurs Chinois.

5. Gangers and coolies should be forbidden to be in possession of civilian clothing [other than headgear] as such was frequently used for the purpose of disguise.
6. Gambling has become one of the chief causes of discipline problems. The proclamation forbidding this crime is being reissued from the Chinese labour corps headquarters and should be maintained prominently posted in each camp.[94]

The rules above treated Chinese workers, who left their homes to help the Allies, as if they were prisoners. Furthermore, the British authorities never considered these laborers the mental equals of the British. They maintained a firm policy forbidding Chinese to associate with either military or civilian Europeans. In their minds, Chinese men had never grown up and were not mature enough to be trusted or treated like adults; they were still essentially children. One proclamation by the head of Chinese labor in France, Colonel R. I. Furdon, addressed all Chinese workers under the British Armies in France with exactly this attitude. Furdon declared that because Chinese workers were "separated by distance from their mother-country, parents and kinsmen, [this led] him to look on them as children." The proclamation "clearly warned" Chinese laborers that "complaints as to quality and quantity of food, errors in pay and allotment, treatment by overseers, work, hours, etc., etc., will receive no consideration if accompanied by unlawful acts." What Britain wanted the Chinese to do was "respect and obey."[95]

Besides widespread British racism, cultural ignorance and misunderstandings on both sides also explain many management problems. The serious shortage of interpreters made the situation worse. How were the Chinese workers to communicate their complaints? The quality and quantity of Chinese-speaking officers were such that communication and disciplinary problems were inevitable. On numerous occasions labor companies had only two or three white officers, none of them speaking Chinese and without a reliable interpreter. Sometimes the commander had to rely on a phrase book prepared by an officer with common phrases in English and their equivalents in Chinese, with characters and phonetic pronunciation. The following incident provides a good example. A near riot broke out when one officer started the day's march by shouting "Let's go!" This command sounds in Chinese like "gou" or "dog," a serious insult to many Chinese, especially

---

[94] Headquarters of British Troops in France and Flanders, July 4, 1919, Vincennes, 7N2289/Affaires Britanniques/Travailleurs Chinois.

[95] "Proclamation by Furdon to All Chinese Labourers Under British Armies in France," June 16, 1919, Vincennes, 7N1297.

northerners.[96] When the workers assumed they were being basely insulted and refused to move, the British punished them for infraction of discipline. On October 10 of 1917, China's National Day, one Chinese labor company, forced to work, rioted and the company commander ordered an armed party to fire on the laborers, killing five Chinese and wounding fourteen. A court of inquiry determined that the "disturbance appeared to be due to a lack of appreciation on the part of the officer commanding . . . of the standard of discipline to be maintained among his officers and British NCOs as regards the treatment of the Chinese labourers." In December 1917 another Chinese labor company rioted at Fontinettes and the men were only subdued after four of them had been shot and a number wounded.[97]

Like these incidents, most "infractions" originated from a misunderstanding.[98] One confidential letter written on January 1, 1918 by Colonel C. D. Gray, who worked closely with Chinese laborers, says it all. It begins by complaining that things generally were not going well in the Chinese labor corps. Then it offers an insider's explanation, claiming that troubles in the British labor camps occurred not because of the workers but because of serious management problems. For example, companies were usually commanded by inexperienced and unsuitable officers appointed by the directorate without any consideration of qualifications. According to Colonel Gray,

It is in this way these companies are sent out under officers who know nothing whatever about the coolies; troubles arise, misunderstandings and grievances which these officers cannot settle and then drastic measures are taken whereby coolies are shot down, innocent and guilty alike, which leads to unrest and brings British prestige into danger among them. Practically every week these shooting affrays take place, and in almost every instance they are the outcome of the coolies' inability to make themselves understood by their superior officers.

The letter further reported that in some instances these group commanders seemed afraid of the Chinese and restricted them from any liberty outside their barbed-wire enclosure when not at work. On one occasion an officer was sent from General Headquarters to try a coolie by court martial and brought with him a supply of plates, because he had the idea that a Chinaman's way of taking the oath was by breaking a plate, after which he would speak the truth. Such ignorance of the Chinese and their language prevented officers from realizing what was going on among their men. In conclusion, Colonel Gray maintained that "from all

---

[96] Charles Hayford, *To the People: James Yen and Village China* (New York: Columbia University Press, 1990), 24.

[97] Scott, "Chinese in France in WW I," 8–11.   [98] Hayford, *To the People*, 24.

I have seen, the Chinese will work all right if guided properly. But these recurring shootings, beatings, and harsh sentences for field punishment by people who don't know how to deal with them are only heaping up trouble which will sooner or later assume a serious aspect."[99]

Racism was less pronounced in the French camps. But of course, incidents did occur, especially once the war was over. A police report from Le Havre, dated May 1917, noted that some local Frenchmen were not happy to see Chinese workers there and rioted against the Chinese. According to the report, the Frenchmen were disappointed with the high casualties sustained by France. "It is frequently said (in the munitions factories)," the report continued, "if this continues, there will not be any men left in France; so why are we fighting? So that Chinese, Arabs, or Spaniards can marry our wives and daughters and share out the France for which we'll all, sooner or later, get ourselves killed at the front."[100] From this anxiety sprang tensions between the Chinese and local people, but overall the French official attitude toward the Chinese was friendly. Jiang Tingfu (T. F. Tsiang), who later became a prominent Chinese educator and historian, observed the differences when he worked with the Chinese labor corps during the war: "From my observation the Chinese laborers with the French were more contented than those with the British. Besides discipline, the difference in the attitude of the officers toward the laborers was also an important factor. The French were much less race conscious, they were more democratic in their manners and took a more paternalistic interest in their laborers," while the British officers "stood on their dignity as officers, and perhaps as white men, most of the time."[101]

As mentioned earlier, instead of recruiting its own Chinese workers, the American expeditionary forces in France ended up borrowing nearly 10,000 Chinese laborers from the French. According to Li Jing, Chinese laborers were not happy to work for the Americans for the following reasons: (1) Chinese in the United States were treated badly, and Americans had the same attitude toward Chinese workers in France. (2) Some American soldiers were not educated and behaved with extreme arrogance toward Chinese laborers. (3) Americans were strong and hot-tempered. Whenever they were not satisfied, they became violent

---

[99] Confidential Letter from Colonel C. D. Gray, PRO, FO371/3178.

[100] John Horne, "Immigrant Workers in France During World War I," *French Historical Studies* 14, no. 1 (1985): 85.

[101] Jiang Tingfu (1895–1965), who received a Ph.D. in history from Columbia University, had served as professor of history at Nankai and Tsinghua Universities before becoming Ambassador to the Soviet Union and later to the United States. The quote is from his "Letter to the United States Bureau of Labor Statistics," October 16, 1922, quoted from Ta Chen, *Chinese Migration, with Special Reference to Labor Conditions* (Washington, DC: Department of Labor, 1923), 147.

and started to abuse the Chinese. According to the labor loan arrangement, Chinese workers borrowed from the French side should only be subject to French regulation, yet the Americans did not always comply and controlled the Chinese as they saw fit, sometimes punishing them unfairly.[102]

The Chinese government was not blind to the fate of its laborers in Europe, and in many cases it strongly protested against the Allies' mistreatment, demanding that the Allies respect Chinese workers' human rights and treat them the same as other people.[103] In 1917 the Chinese government appointed a special agent to be stationed at the Chinese Legation in France to look after the Chinese laborers. This official would negotiate with Allied authorities on issues regarding their welfare and fair treatment. Li Jing was responsible for men working under the French, while Pan Lianyu, assigned by the Chinese Legation in London, was assigned those under the British. It appears that Pan did not do very much; his reports, compared to Li Jing's, were nothing more than sketchy.[104]

Competition and conflict among the Allies

As Great Britain and France started recruiting Chinese laborers, competition and conflicts of interest arose between them. Because Britain could take advantage of its more widespread interests and breadth of experience in China, it usually had the upper hand over France. To make the situation worse for the French, British authorities were recruiting Chinese laborers to work on French soil, creating a rather uncomfortable situation for the government. To put a stop to the competition and foreign laborers working in France under another country's direction, the French authorities asked Britain to halt this practice in February of 1917, arguing that if British military camps in France needed help, they could use Chinese laborers already recruited by France.[105] Britain responded that it was a military problem and both countries' military authorities had already solved it. Britain then counter-proposed the creation of different recruitment zones to avoid competition.[106]

---

[102] Li, the third report, November 30, 1918, in Chen, Lu, and Yang, eds., *Ouzhan huagong shiliao*, 398.

[103] Boppe to Quai d'Orsay, Beijing, Nov. 24, 1919, Quai d'Orsay, Ministre des Affaires Etrangères, 1918–1929, Chine, XLII: 170.

[104] Pan's reports can be found in Chen, Lu, and Yang, eds., *Ouzhan Huagong shiliao*, 519–20, 34–37, 42–47, 57–59, 63–64.

[105] "Procès-Verbaux de la Conférence Interministérielle," February 10, 1917, Archive Nationale, Paris, 14F/11334.

[106] French Ambassador Paul Combon to Quai d'Orsay, October 9, 1917, Quai d'Orsay, NS, Chine, CXXXVII.

But France was still determined to change the recruiting situation. On February 21, 1917, the French government sent another memorandum to Britain proposing that the entire recruiting operation for both Britain and France be placed under the control of Colonel Truptil, who would hand over a certain portion of the Chinese workers to Britain. The British Foreign Office cynically noted in private: "Are we right in thinking that our recruiting scheme is now more successful than the French and that we are in a position to supply them with as many coolies as they can ship to France?"[107] In a handwritten comment on the French proposal, one official in the British Foreign Office angrily wrote, "It is very bad of the French to do this," and charged that they "want to nullify all our efforts."[108] In the end, the French proposal fell on deaf ears and the British stuck to their idea of separate zones.[109]

Once the French realized that Britain would not compromise and would continue to recruit its own laborers, France had to reconsider the British suggestion of separate recruitment zones. On September 7, 1917, France told Britain that the idea of separate recruitment zones was fine if Britain agreed that the French zone was in North China and the British moved to the South. This proposal was bound to fail, of course, since the British had given up the idea of recruiting southerners very early in their campaign. Britain also had an extensive and highly developed recruiting organization in the Shandong area and, according to the British authorities, its recruitment in the North had "met with such success that coolies are now being dispatched to France at the rate of ten thousand per month." The Chinese laborers "are well known to the French military authorities and are so highly valued by the Army Council that Her Majesty's Government would view with alarm any action which might prejudice the supply of recruits."[110] The negotiations went nowhere.

The finger pointing and competition continued between the two countries. The French even went to Qingdao, close to the British recruitment base, to woo Chinese laborers. This really angered the British, whose senior diplomat, Alston, declared, "All recruitment in China is for the same cause and it seems obvious that there should be no competition between Allies."[111] The British secretary of state for foreign affairs, Arthur Balfour, officially complained in his memorandum to the French

[107] Foreign Office to Alston, February 22, 1917, PRO, FO371/2905/28360.
[108] Internal Exchange Paper of Foreign Office, February 21, 1917, PRO, FO371/2905/28360.
[109] Foreign Office Document, May 25, 1917, PRO, FO371/2906/40.
[110] British Foreign Office to Quai d'Orsay, October 5, 1917, Quai d'Orsay, NS, Chine, CXXXVII.
[111] Alston to FO, October 5, 1917, PRO, FO371/2906/296–97.

government that the French should "recognize that all recruitment in China is directed to a common end." He warned the French that "any action which is calculated to retard or impair the united efforts of the Allies is much to be depreciated." He further claimed in the same document that the Chinese labor corps raised by the British for service with the British expeditionary force in France had "proved a great success." He asked the French government for "a free field in the zone which they have selected for their operations."[112] The quarrel continued into January 1918, when the British Foreign Office and the Army Council were considering whether it was still necessary to make further representations to the French government regarding the withdrawal of French recruiting agencies in Shandong.[113] The British Foreign Office was doubtful that further protest would lead to any resolution. Furthermore, since the war had reached its final moment, perhaps further protest was not justifiable.[114]

While French recruiting numbers remained low compared to Britain's, British competition in this area was not the only problem. Transportation proved another serious issue. Although the Allied countries tried to cooperate toward their common goal, from 1914 to the end of 1917 each country made its own arrangements for transport. By late 1917, France was running into serious difficulties transporting its recruits, and British assistance was not always forthcoming.[115] For example, in an agreement made between France and Great Britain on December 3, 1916, special provisions had to be inserted regarding a French request for assistance with transporting laborers from Asia.[116] To a great extent, the French recruiting program was held hostage to Britain's cooperation regarding transportation. The importance of transport is reflected in the fact that after the war, Britain used its preeminence in this area to influence American policy. "The two-million-man American expeditionary force in France," wrote David Kennedy, author of *Over Here*, "constituted a kind of hostage that could be marooned in Europe if the British should decide to deny the use of their transport vessels to the United States."[117] The transportation issue often led to clashes between the two countries despite the creation of the Allied Maritime Transport Council in late 1917. France's repeated request for more tonnage again

---

[112] Balfour to Combon, October 11, 1917, PRO, FO371/2906.
[113] War Office to Foreign Office, January 21 of 1918, PRO, FO371/3178/269.
[114] Foreign Office to Jordan, January 23, 1918, PRO, FO371/3178/271.
[115] For a detailed explanation of the Allied shipping issue, see J. A. Salter, *Allied Shipping Control: An Experiment in International Administration* (Oxford: Oxford University Press, 1921).
[116] See ibid., 138–39.
[117] David Kennedy, *Over Here* (New York: Oxford University Press, 1980), 333.

fell on deaf ears.[118] France even tried to enlist Japan's assistance to transport its Chinese workers; the Japanese government, however, was not interested. Germany's unrestrained submarine warfare, begun in 1917, further aggravated the French transportation problem. When the United States joined the war, the transport issue became increasingly delicate, since so much tonnage would be required to transport American soldiers. So, in the middle of January 1918, the French military authorities decided the recruitment mission should be ended completely because of the transportation shortfall,[119] and on February 10, 1918, the French government halted its recruiting program in China.[120]

It is only fair to point out that Britain also faced a transportation problem, but initially a less serious one. The shortfall of tonnage, however, eventually compelled Britain to stop its recruitment program as well.[121] A memorandum from Joseph Maclay, Britain's shipping controller, reveals the problem clearly. Dated January 17, 1918, it explains, "In view of the present tonnage situation, the question of stopping the entire import of coolies should be immediately considered. In addition to the great relief which would be afforded on the transatlantic run, where it was not at present possible to meet the American troops' requirements, there was the heavy transit across the American continent. Furthermore, it is estimated that 10,000 additional American troops might be brought per month if the coolie traffic was entirely stopped."[122] Great Britain terminated its recruitment mission in China on April 14, 1918, about two months after France had canceled its own.[123]

Laborers' contributions to the war effort and to broader Chinese interests

Yale historian Paul Kennedy argues that the main contribution of the United States to the First World War was not military. "American intervention in the war could not immediately affect the military balances." The vital contribution of the United States was on the economic front: it kept the Allied side fighting "without embarrassment of

---

[118] British Foreign Office to Quai d'Orsay, October 5, 1917, Quai d'Orsay, NS, Chine, vol. CXXXVIII.

[119] "Note Secrète sur la Question du Transport de Contingents Chinois," January 25, 1918, Vincennes, 16N3246.

[120] Quai d'Orsay to War Ministry, July 28, 1918, Quai d'Orsay, Asie, 1918–1929, XLII.

[121] Summerskill has given an excellent description of the British suspension of recruiting Chinese labor corps; see his *China on the Western Front*, 179–94.

[122] "Maclay to the War Cabinet," January 17, 1918, PRO, War Cabinet minute, CAB23/5/324.

[123] Foreign Office to Jordan, April 14, 1918, PRO, WO106/33.

bankruptcy."[124] I would argue that China's contribution to the war was its manpower: with 140,000 laborers in the field, China greatly strengthened the Allies' front and support industries.

The First World War was total war; it involved both the home front and the military. According to the (London) *Times*, "Modern war is modern industry, organized for a single definite purpose. Behind the army that fights the enemy with bomb, bullet, and shell and in some cases alongside of it" was "another army whose weapons are the pickaxes, crowbar, spade, and pulley."[125] The Chinese laborers helped keep the Allies fighting; they were young and strong. While in Europe, they worked at least ten hours per day, seven days a week, with few days off. To be chosen as a member of the Chinese labor corps, they had to pass strict medical examinations. Under the British regulations they had to be free of twenty-one health problems such as trachoma, tuberculosis, venereal diseases, and bad teeth. The French had similar requirements. Anyone suffering from any of these conditions was rejected. British secretary of war and prime minister during the war, Lloyd George, wrote in his *War Memoirs* that they "were immensely powerful fellows, and it was no uncommon spectacle to see one of the Chinese pick up a bulk of timber or a bundle of corrugated iron sheets weighing three or four hundred pounds, and walk off with it as calmly as if it weighed only as many stone!"[126]

Because of their work, they freed at least the same number of people on the Allies' side to undertake military combat. As one British newspaper commented,

The coming of the Chinese labour corps to France relieved our own men from an enormous amount of heavy and miscellaneous work behind the lines, and so helped to release a much larger proportion than otherwise would have been impossible for combatant duties. For not only did the Chinese fulfil multifarious tasks at the various bases, such as loading and unloading ships and trains, building railways, repairing roads, working in petrol factories and at various supply depots throughout the northern region, but they dug hundreds of miles of support trenches in the forward area, well within shell range.[127]

One can argue that the huge number of Chinese laborers was the equivalent of the same number of soldiers although they did not receive the same treatment or respect.

Chinese workers came to France to help the Allies' cause, and they won high marks for their performance. By the end of the war, and

[124] Paul Kennedy, "The First World War and the International Power System," *International Security* 9, no. 1 (Summer 1984), 24.
[125] [London] *Times*, December 26, 1917.
[126] David Lloyd George, *War Memoirs of David Lloyd George* (Boston: Little, Brown, and Company, 1937), II, 235.
[127] April 23, 1919, PRO, wo107/33.

for some considerable time thereafter, virtually all the cranes in Calais, Dieppe, Le Havre, and Rouen were operated by Chinese crane operators.[128] The French were quite pleased with the recruited Chinese laborers because they were "sober, strong, enduring, and peaceful."[129] General Ferdinand Foch (1851–1929) called Chinese laborers "first-class workers who could be made into excellent soldiers, capable of exemplary bearing under modern artillery fire."[130] The French officers in direct charge of Chinese laborers also made a positive assessment of their capabilities. Lieutenant-Colonel Gondre reported to his division commander that Chinese laborers were "docile, intelligent, and good workers."[131] Another officer reported that after finishing an inspection of labor camps he found the Chinese laborers very intelligent and much preferred.[132] Because of their good reputation, the French welcomed them with great enthusiasm. According to an article in the *Far Eastern Review*, a French crowd at Le Havre cheered when the Chinese arrived.[133]

Chinese workers in France under British control earned a good reputation as well. One report by H. R. Wakefield states that the Chinese laborer was "a splendid and versatile worker, inured to hardship and almost indifferent to the weather . . . [T]heir speed and endurance are phenomenal."[134]

There are many stories of bravery. One Chinese worker named Wang Yu-shan was awarded the meritorious service medal for his action. The official account of his story is as follows: Near Marcoing on June 6, 1919, Wang observed a fire near an ammunition dump situated close to a collecting station. On his own initiative he rushed to the scene with two buckets of water, which he threw on the fire. He then seized a burning British "P" bomb and hurled it to a safe distance. He continued to extinguish the flames that had spread to the surrounding grass in which rifle grenades and German shells were lying. By his initiative, resourcefulness, and disregard of personal safety this laborer averted what might have been a serious explosion.[135]

---

[128] Scott, "Chinese in France in WW I," 8–11.

[129] De Lapomarède to Commander-in-Chief of the French Army, Beijing, April, 1916, Vincennes, 16N2912/Chine.

[130] General Foch's Secret Report to Prime Minister, August 11, 1917, Vincennes, 16N2450/GQG/6498.

[131] Gondre Report, May 26, 1918, Vincennes, 18N107.

[132] General Taufflieb report, June 27, 1918, Vincennes, 18N207.

[133] "Story of the Chinese Labor Corps," *The Far Eastern Review* (Shanghai) 15, no. 4 (April, 1918): 126.

[134] Wakefield Report, PRO, WO106/33.

[135] "Chinese Labour Corps Bravery, a Very Gallant Act," *The North China Herald* 132 (1919).

Because of their adaptability and intelligence, Chinese laborers in general were more welcome than workers from other countries such as India and Egypt. The (London) *Times* wrote, "The Chinaman is more versatile and adaptable. They can handle stores and do other things for which a certain intelligence and initiative are required. He is a capable worker if his European superiors are careful to leave plenty of responsibility to his own headmen and overseers."[136] When one French maritime port needed workers, it chose to request Chinese workers after "examining several categories of foreign workers." The request report explained that Chinese workers dealt with the ocean climate better than those from Portugal and other countries. For the duration of the war, both the Ministry of Armament and the Ministry of War continued to press for Chinese workers because they believed the Chinese to be more effective laborers.[137] The official analysis of the work of Chinese labor corps concluded that "Chinese labour, properly handled, was undoubtedly most efficient."[138] In its official evaluation of all kinds of workers, the British War Office pointed out that "a great many of the Chinese workers were skilled or readily became so, and have been used freely in railway, ordnance, and tank workshops."[139]

Because Chinese labor corps usually worked in or near the battlefields, many died on European soil for the Allied cause. During the night of September 4/5, 1917, a number of German aircraft raided Dunkirk and bombs fell on a Chinese camp killing fifteen and wounding twenty-one others.[140] But they not only died in bombardments; some of the workers even had to fight Germans in close combat when emergencies arose. For example, during the German Offensive of 1918, companies of the Chinese labor corps caught in the German advance took up picks and shovels to fight the enemy, and many workers sacrificed their lives this way. One British newspaper reported, "A fair number of Chinese have been killed and wounded by enemy action since they went to France."[141] Even after the war, they continued to sustain casualties as they cleared the battlefields because such work involved locating mines and unexploded bombs. As late as October 1919, 50,000 Chinese laborers remained in British camps although they were being evacuated at the rate of 15,000 per month.[142]

---

[136] [London] *Times*, December 27, 1917.
[137] "Au Sujet de l'Emploi de la Main-d'Oeuvre Chinoise dans les Ports," Paris, July 18, 1917, Archive National, Paris, 14F/11331, XII/E/Sous-Secrétaire des Transports.
[138] Scott, "Chinese in France in WW I," 8–11.
[139] War Office Report, December 31, 1918, PRO, wo106/33.
[140] Scott, "Chinese in France in WW I," 8–11.
[141] Newspaper clippings, April 23, 1919, PRO, wo107/33.
[142] Vincennes, 7N1297/Chinois Evacuation.

We still do not know with certainty how many Chinese died in Europe during the war. The lowest estimate is two thousand. Gu Xinqing, who served as an interpreter for the Chinese labor camps, recorded this number of Chinese war dead in his memoir.[143] But according to another count, "between two and three thousand coolies were killed" near Calais alone.[144] According to an official Chinese government report of November 1, 1917, nearly 3,000 Chinese laborers died as a result of German submarine attacks on their way to Europe, though this number was perhaps exaggerated a bit.[145] The highest total death figure has been given at about 20,000.[146] A recent book published in China indicates that death casualties reached about 10,000.[147] These numbers bear close examination. They represent a death rate of roughly 7–14 percent. The higher percentage does not appear to be supported by existing evidence.

One way to calculate the casualty figure is to take a look at cemeteries in both France and Britain. In those near Folkestone and Plymouth in England lie nearly two thousand Chinese laborers who had died in the service of an alien society at war.[148] Their squat headstones in the cemeteries are inscribed in Chinese and English: "A Noble Duty, Bravely Done."[149] The French government buried deceased Chinese workers at various places among the French dead, according to local custom, and as provided in article 12 of the Huimin contract. A Chinese cemetery in the village named Noyelles near the mouth of the Somme is the final resting place of eight hundred Chinese workers who died from 1916 to 1920. Chinese cemeteries are located in other places as well. In Boulogne-Billancourt, not far from Paris, are about one thousand Chinese graves, and in the village of Les Baraques another 201. In other words, nearly two thousand Chinese laborers were buried in France alone. Therefore, the total number of Chinese deaths in Europe during the war was at least four thousand according to the cemetery evidence.

According to one British War Office report, the exact number of Chinese laborers under the British authority killed by German bombs in France was 147, and by enemy bombardment 20. This report claims

---

[143] Gu Xinqing, *Ou zhan gongzuo huiyilu*, 45. See also Wou Pen-chung, *Travailleurs Chinois et La Grande Guerre* (Paris: Editions A. Pedone, 1939), 13

[144] Judith Blick, "The Chinese Labor Corps in World War I," *Papers on China (from Harvard East Asia Regional Studies Seminar)* 9 (1955): 123.

[145] Feng Gang, *Sanshui Liang Yansun xiansheng nianpu*, I: 446.

[146] Li Huang, *Xue Dunshi huiyilu* (Taipei: Zhuanji wenxue chubanshe, 1973), 58.

[147] Yuan Li and Chen Dazhang, *Haiwai Huaren ji qi juzhu di gaikuan* (Beijing: Zhongguo Huaqiao chuban gongshi, 1991), 273.

[148] Lynn Pan, *Sons of the Yellow Emperor, the Story of the Overseas Chinese* (London: Secker & Warburg, 1990), 82.

[149] Scott, "Chinese in France in WW I," 8–11.

that given the strength of the Anglo-Chinese Labour Corps in France, the mortality from enemy action was "surprisingly light."[150] However, even if this number is correct, it cannot reflect the whole picture because it covers only a fraction of the losses documented elsewhere. In a British Parliament meeting of December 10, 1919, the number of Chinese workers under British authority who died from wounds and sickness was cited as two thousand.[151] This number is supported by the cemetery evidence. According to Ta Chen, a leading scholar of Chinese emigration, of the laborers in British employ around Isbergues and Noyon, sixty-five were killed in bombing raids between May and September 1918. Between August 4, 1918 and April 30, 1919, ninety-five suffered death from the same cause while working for the British army around Dunkirk and Calais. Ta Chen further points out that nearly three thousand Chinese laborers killed by German bombardment while working in the vicinity of Calais were buried in a special cemetery, side by side with the British dead, by order of the British government.[152] Chen's figures come very close to the four thousand assessed from the cemetery evidence.

How many Chinese lost their lives at sea en route to France? One source suggests that at least 752 Chinese laborers died from German submarine attacks.[153] One Chinese official document indicates that the Chinese laborers killed by German submarines numbered 713.[154] Although these sources do not agree perfectly, we may still safely conclude that at least 700 lost their lives before they reached France. Therefore, the sources suggest that approximately five thousand Chinese workers died either on their way to Europe or in service in France.

It is worth pointing out that these five thousand deaths are still not the whole picture. Thousands of Chinese sailors worked for Britain, and according to the Chinese minister to Britain, 448 of them died in action.[155] The Chinese general consul to London reported to the Foreign Ministry in December 1918 that a total of 863 Chinese seamen serving on British ships had died in the war.[156]

---

[150] Emigration Agency, October 9, 1919, PRO, FO371/3682/125.
[151] British Parliamentary Meeting Minute, December 10, 1919, PRO, FO371/3682/154.
[152] Chen Ta, *Chinese Migrations, with Special Reference to Labor Conditions, 1919–1927* (Washington DC: Government Printing Office, 1923), 152.
[153] Chen Sanjing, *Huagong yu Ouzhan*, 72.
[154] See "Waijiaobu fa guo wu yuan han, January 8, 1919," in Chen, Lu, and Yang, eds., *Ouzhan Huagong shiliao*, 38.
[155] Waijiaobu, "Shou ju ying Gongshi dian," December 7, 1918, Zhongguo di er li shi dang an guan, beiyang wai jiao bu dang, 03–36/4–(5).
[156] Zhongguo di er li shi dang an guan, 1050–12.

But Chinese sacrifices were not meaningfully recognized after the war. According to the British Parliamentary Record, though Chinese workers had "borne greater risks than other coloured labourers," they were the last to receive even a few minor war medals.[157] At the Paris Peace Conference, British secretary for foreign affairs Balfour claimed that China's contribution during the war had involved neither "the expenditure of a single shilling nor the loss of a single life," completely discounting the sacrifice made by Chinese laborers.[158] One report issued at the war's end even suggested that China actually harmed the Allies because its laborers had brought the deadly "Spanish flu" that swept through Europe and the world in 1918.[159] Instead of appreciation, the Allied countries tried to quickly rid themselves of the Chinese workers, claiming that the Chinese disturbed "local stability." From time to time, both the French and Belgian governments had expressed the view that the Chinese should be removed from their countries immediately once the war had ended. The British government began the repatriation of Chinese laborers in the fall of 1919 and completed it on April 6, 1920. The French repatriation program ended in March 1922.[160] At the end of the war, about three thousand Chinese laborers remained and eventually settled in France, including 1,850 qualified men who signed new contracts to work in the metallurgical industries. Other workers found employment in the mechanical or aeronautical sectors. Many of those who remained married French women. Two of them lived long enough to receive the French Legion of Honor in 1989.[161]

Because of the sacrifices, contributions, and lack of recognition given these laborers the Chinese scholar Chen Sanjing has characterized their being sent to Europe as "a great tragedy,"[162] However, if we look at the

---

[157] British Parliamentary Meeting Minute, December 10, 1919, PRO, FO371/3682/154.

[158] Balfour to Curzon, May 8 1919, Woodward, *Documents on British Foreign Policy, 1919–1939*, Series I, VI: 565–66.

[159] Ellen Newbold la Motte, *Peking Dust* (New York: The Century Co., 1919), 240. So far there is no scientific evidence to suggest that the Chinese brought the virus to Europe. As a matter of fact, although from 20 million to 100 million died from the 1918 flu, to the present day nobody really knows for sure how it started and where it came from. For details, see Gina Kolata, *Flu: the Story of the Great Influenza, Pandemic of 1918 and the Search for the Virus that Caused it* (New York: Farrar, Straus and Giroux, 1999), and Alfred W. Crosby, Jr., *Epidemic and Peace, 1918* (Westport, CT: Greenwood Press, 1976 [this book was later published by Cambridge University Press in 1989 under a different name]). For a later study on the subject, see Mark J. Gibbs, "Recombination in the Hemagglutinin Gene of 1918 'Spanish Flu,'" *Science* 293, no. 5536 (2001), and John Pickrell, "The 1918 Pandemic: Killer Flu with a Human-Pig Pedigree?" *Science* 292, no. 5519 (2001).

[160] Ta Chen, *Chinese Migrations*, 156.

[161] Pan, *Sons of the Yellow Emperor, the Story of the Overseas Chinese*, 82. Pan, ed., *The Encyclopedia of the Chinese Overseas*, 311.

[162] Chen Sanjing, *Huagong yu Ouzhan*, preface, 1.

labor scheme as an important part of China's war plan, its results were still significant. Working, if not fighting, side by side with the Allies, China determinedly signaled its desire and ability to play a role in world affairs, and this signal was recognized, if reluctantly, by the rest of the world. *The Far Eastern Review* in 1918 predicted that Chinese laborers' emigration from the shores of Shandong

will take its place in history certainly as one of the most picturesque and interesting, possibly as one of the most important aspects of the great European War. For never before this war has the East provided the West with manpower on anything approaching the same elaborate scale. It has hurled itself against the West many times, compelled the West to unite more than once and, of course, colored European life and thought in a variety of ways, but it has never before, practically the whole of it simultaneously, taken sides in a huge European conflict.[163]

It was also the first time such a large number of ordinary Chinese had personal contact with the West. Without a doubt, this experience provided an opportunity for them to observe and experience life in another civilization and to reflect on their Chinese way of life and society. When they returned home, they brought with them new ideas, new thoughts, and the inspiration to change. These laborers who came to the rescue of the Allies were more than hired workers, therefore; they were the first wave of new Chinese participation in world affairs and the vanguard of China's new national identity.

The link between sending Chinese laborers abroad and the formation of national identity must be understood in terms of the Chinese social elite's involvement in the plan. Many Chinese elite members had been active advocates of and a moving force behind the migration scheme. They believed it presented an unusual opportunity for poor Chinese to acquire new knowledge and broaden their horizons. They also hoped that when these laborers returned home they would play an important part in China's renewal. Li Shizeng, Cai Yuanpei, Yan Yangchu (James Yen), and Wang Jingwei, among others, were representative of this elite. For them, the success of reforming Chinese society would be bolstered by these returned laborers. They advised the government to put in place a standard policy for dealing with the foreign recruitment of Chinese laborers and emphasized the importance of their education on foreign soil. In a joint letter to government officials, these men argued that the success of the labor recruitment program had deep implications for China and its relations within the international system.[164] They soon found ways to put their ideas into action.

---

[163] *The Far Eastern Review*, 15, no. 4: 126–27.
[164] "Waijiaobu shou nei zheng bu zhi, November 11, 1916," in Chen, Lu, and Yang, eds., *Ouzhan huagong shiliao.* 14.

In June 1915 in Paris they organized the Qinggong Jianxuehui (Society for Frugal Study by Means of Labor) that was to cooperate in the French recruitment effort. The society would promote "diligence and perseverance in work, and frugality (in order to save money) for study, thereby advancing the laborers' knowledge." Li Shizeng claimed that Chinese workers in France would not only contribute to the transmission of industrial skills on their return to China, but would also help in the reform of society and the elimination of undesirable social customs by having been exposed to European civilization.[165] The next year they became directly involved in the recruitment plan by organizing the Société Franco-Chinoise d'Education in March 1916, also in Paris.[166] The aim of the association was to "develop relations between China and France and, especially, with the aid of French scientific and spiritual education, to plan for the development of China's moral, intellectual, and economic well being."[167] As noted earlier, this organization accepted the French government's invitation to go to China to recruit laborers on its behalf.

To better understand the role of the Chinese laborers in advancing China's larger national goals, it might help to look at the origins of the idea of sending Chinese laborers abroad, from the perspective of the elite. Li Shizeng for one had been adamant about the idea since the turn of the twentieth century. Li was an influential intellectual, entrepreneur, and politician, who had himself studied in France and translated many French books into Chinese. An advocate of reform, he was interested in bringing the Chinese into personal contact with the West and thus encouraged them to study and work abroad. As early as 1902, when he went to France for the first time, he and Wu Zhihui had discussed the possibility of sending ordinary Chinese to Europe.[168] For him, the key to reforming China was education and learning from Western countries. Sending Chinese students to the West as laborers would be a perfect means of gaining that experience. Wu Zhihui described Li's strategy this way: the main point of sending thousands of Chinese to France was the expectation that if a huge number of Chinese workers did go and subsequently return, they would make an enormous impact on Chinese society.[169] On this understanding, Li Shizeng, Wu Zhihui, Wang Jingwei, and Cai Yuanpei organized the Society for Frugal Study in France (Liu-Fa Jianxuehui) in

---

[165] Paul Bailey, "The Chinese Work-Study Movement in France," *The China Quarterly* 115 (1988): 448.

[166] The Société was officially founded in June 1916.

[167] Bailey, "The Chinese Work-Study Movement in France," 449.

[168] Yang Kailing, ed., *Minguo Li Shizeng xianshen nianpu* (Taipei: Taiwan Shangwu Yinshuguan, 1980), 15.

[169] Quote from Chen Sanjing, *Huagong yu ouzhan*, 13.

1912. The main purpose of this organization was to encourage young Chinese to go to France to study and work. Working was the means and learning was the end. The major purpose of the society was to expand educational opportunities, to introduce the Chinese to world civilization and advanced learning, and to develop the Chinese national economy.[170] Under its sponsorship, 120 young Chinese went to France during the period 1912–13.[171] Although the Society was dissolved very soon under political pressure from Yuan Shikai, leaders of the group such as Li, Cai, Wang, and Wu Yuzhang never gave up on their vision. In 1914, they founded a new work-study program. Cai Yuanpei, its Chinese president, explained that the Society's functions included educating Chinese workers in France, promoting Sino-French friendship, and especially learning from French scientific and intellectual achievements to "help China develop her morality, knowledge, and economy."[172] Li, Cai, and others not only advocated the idea of working abroad and actively helped Chinese laborers in France, they also used their influence and prestige to push the Chinese government to better organize and systematize the migration program.[173] Cai himself carefully prepared lecture notes and taught Chinese workers in France. For Cai, the first minister of education for the Republic of China, if China meant to advance its position in the world it was imperative to understand Western civilization. "China has an opportunity to absorb European civilization. The Chinese in Europe are the first learners," he wrote.[174] Li Shizeng had founded *The Chinese Labor Journal* (*Huagong Zazhi*) in Paris in 1917 to provide vital information for Chinese laborers. In January 1919 Li Shizeng and Wu Zhihui founded the Society for Study and Work in France (Liu-Fa Qinggong Jiangxuehui) which helped many future Chinese leaders go abroad.[175] Zhou Enlai, Deng Xiaoping, among many others, went to Europe thanks to this social elite and its programs.

Besides the above-mentioned organizations under Cai and Li, the Chinese Youth Association in Shanghai also assisted Chinese workers in France. It provided them with Chinese books, magazines, and tools

---

[170] Beijing Liu-Fa Jiangxuehui, "Beijing Liu-Fa Jiangxuehui jiangzhang," *Xin qingnian* 3, no. 2 (1917), Yang Kailing, ed., *Minguo Li Shizeng xiansheng nianpu*, 32.

[171] Yang Kailing, ed., *Minguo Li Shizeng xiansheng nianpu*, 28–29.

[172] Gao Pingshu, ed., *Cai Yuanpei quanji* (Beijing: Zhonghua shuju, 1984), III: 219.

[173] See Li's "Yimin yijianshu" (Proposal for allowing emigration), in Li Shizeng, *Li Shizeng xiansheng wenji* (Taipei: Zhongguo Guomindang zhongyang weiyuan hui, 1980), I: 220–25.

[174] Gao Pingshu, ed., *Cai Yuanpei quanji*, III: 219.

[175] For an excellent collection of original thoughts on this, see Liu-Ou Zazhi she and Chen Sanjing, eds., *Liu-Ou jiaoyu yundong* (Taipei: Zhongyang yanjiuyuan jindai shi yanjiusuo, 1996).

from China, keeping them well informed about affairs at home. Furthermore, both the French and British governments realized the importance of Chinese laborers for Europe in the future and provided a few education programs as well. As early as the summer of 1917, the British legation in China reminded the British government of the potential implications of the laborers' presence. In one of its memoranda, the legation officials wrote, "The time has come to consider the very important political effect which the sojourn of some hundred thousand Chinese in France will have." The memorandum further argued that these Chinese laborers would play an important role in China when they returned home, and therefore it was "most important" for the British government to provide educational programs to make the laborers "preachers and exponents of British fairness and efficiency."[176] Although neither government did enough, at least they both understood the issue and made some effort.

Perhaps the most successful organization in transforming these young, strong, and innocent Chinese laborers was the Young Men's Christian Association, which sent about 150 people (40 British and 109 American and Chinese Christian workers connected with missionary societies and the YMCA in China) to France to help Chinese workers during the war.[177] Activities which the YMCA organized included entertainment, education, writing letters, and religious meetings; it also provided courses on national conscience, civil rights, and modern government. A major motivation of the YMCA was to help shape China's new sense of place in world affairs.[178] A comment on the YMCA's program for the Chinese labor corps in France says it all:

[I]f our programme is comprehensive and statesman-like enough, they will return to their own country to become disseminators of a better understanding between the West and the East among their relatives and friends. Whereas, if we do not undertake this service for them it is almost certain that as a result of their coming to Europe misunderstanding between the East and the West will be increased.[179]

---

[176] Jordan to Balfour, August 14, 1917, PRO, wo106/33.

[177] Their ignorance in the beginning was reflected in a presumably heated discussion among the laborers about why the United States entered the war. Some argued that the United States entered the war because the Crown Prince of America had become engaged to a Princess of France, and thus it was bound to support the cause of its newly acquired ally; see Captain Harry L. Gilchriese, "Managing 200,000 Coolies in France," *Current History* (December 1919), published by the New York Times Company, 324; I. H. Si told the same story in his article "With the Chinese Laborers: Somewhere in France," *The Chinese Students' Monthly* 13, no. 8 (June 1918): 452. See also "What the Chinese Learned in the War," *The Literary Digest* 62, no. 11 (1919).

[178] For a detailed study on the YMCA and Chinese workers in Europe, see Chen Sanjing, "Jidu qingnianhui yu ou zhan Huagong," *Zhongyang yanjiuyuan jindai shi yanjiusuo ji kan* 1, no. 17 (1988).

[179] The statement was dated around April 1918, PRO, FO/371/3179.

Another important aspect of the YMCA's program was to give the future Chinese elite who worked through the YMCA experience with the Chinese workers. Shi Yixuan (I. H. Si), a Ph.D. student at Harvard, was the first Chinese student to come to France to work with the laborers in October 1917. Many others such as Yan Yangchu and Jiang Tingfu soon joined him. They came to Europe because these Western-educated Chinese had fallen under the spell of Woodrow Wilson's call for a new world order and the promise of a better world system from which China could benefit. They wanted to use their knowledge, energy, and experience to help bring about the early inception of this new world order. Yan, a new graduate of Yale University, came to France in the summer of 1918. He read, translated, and summarized foreign newspapers for the workers, and taught them in popular literacy classes. He even edited a paper for all Chinese in France, *The Chinese Laborers' Weekly* (*Huagong Zhoubao*, founded on January 15, 1919), with a paid circulation of 15,000. Through his work with the Chinese labor corps in France, Yan found the solution for China's problems and identity crisis; more importantly, he found his career for life: mass education. He realized that only through education from the village level, and reform from the bottom up, would China have a chance of renewing itself and qualifying as an equal member of the world community.[180]

In short, the people involved in helping the Chinese labor corps tried to help these poor Chinese better understand their experience in Europe and urged them to play a role in building a new China when they returned home. They had high expectations for these workers, who themselves were eager to live up to them. It was an eye-opening experience for all Chinese who came to Europe at this critical moment. One Chinese interpreter wrote in 1919 that in France they "gained an insight into the social conditions of the West, and their ideas have undergone a great change since they came to Europe . . . It is certain that every one of these labourers will desire to see strong reforms made on his return to China."[181] By coming to the West, some of them even discovered a new God and embraced their new religion with enthusiasm. According to the *Missionary Review of the World* (New York), about thirteen Chinese workers converted to Christianity and declared their purpose was to devote their lives to Christian service on their return to their native land.[182] On another

---

[180] The best book on this subject is by Charles Wishart Hayford: *To the People: James Yen and Village China* (New York: Columbia University Press, 1990).

[181] C. F. Summers, "The Chinese Labour Corps; What They Learned in France," *The North-China Herald* 132 (1919).

[182] "What the Chinese Learned in the War," *The Literary Digest* 62, no. 11 (September 13, 1919): 33–34.

occasion, the Religious Tract Society sent Christian books to Chinese labor corps in France. One of the books was entitled "The Church's Welcome to Chinese Workmen at the Front," and consists of a few introductory words of cheer, a selection of scriptural passages and a number of short prayers. According to a reader's letter, one Chinese worker happened to be Christian and was so pleased with the booklet that he sent a donation of twenty francs, two thirds of a month's pay, to the society.[183]

More importantly, Chinese workers learned and developed a new perspective about themselves and about their country, and even about the world. China as a nation had been an abstraction but now it became directly relevant to them. These laborers became notably patriotic when they were overseas. When Li Jing reported to them that a damaging flood had struck North China and asked them to help, many workers immediately donated their hard-earned francs. Within less than two months, 10,138 francs were collected. One worker alone donated 200 francs.[184] The total donation for this relief program had reached 14,906 francs in November 1918.[185]

If national identity emerges when one country compares itself to others, then these Chinese saw with their own eyes what a Western country looked like, and how people in other countries worked and lived. They obviously shared their fellow countrymen's sense of crisis and wanted to do their part. According to one witness, when President Wilson, on his way to Paris to attend the peace conference, arrived in Le Havre, Chinese laborers nearby sent a delegation to welcome him. One laborer donated his entire savings from two years in France to the Chinese delegation for the peace conference and asked them to use the money for anything which would benefit China most. This laborer was not the exception. In each issue of *The Chinese Laborers' Weekly*, one can find records of donations to Chinese national causes such as the National Salvation Fund and the Patriot Fund. Upon hearing that Japan might compel China to recognize its control of German interests in Shandong, the laborers sent a petition to Lu Zhengxiang urging him not to accept. A pistol was even included with the petition, which threatened that "if [Lu] agrees to Japan's demands, [he] should commit suicide with this pistol. Otherwise we will kill him." On another occasion, when the British army in Belgium organized an international sporting event to celebrate the end of the war, Chinese laborers sent 6,000 of their members to attend. When

---

[183] John Darroch, "The China Labourer's Reading," *The North China Herald*, August 3, 1918.
[184] Li Jing's fourth notice to Chinese workers in France, December, 1917, Li Jing's second report, in Chen, Lu, and Yang, eds., *Ouzhan Huagong shiliao*, 288, 391.
[185] Li, "The fourth report," ibid., 418.

they entered the field to find no Chinese flag among all other countries' flags, they felt China's national dignity had been affronted and immediately left the event in protest.[186]

When the Chinese laborers returned home after the war, they were indeed new persons with new ideas, and a new worldview; their horizons had been broadened enormously. As a consequence, they wanted to do their share in shaping the new world order and improving China's status in it. One laborer, Fu Shengsan, explained the changes well in an article entitled "Chinese Laborers in France and Their Contribution to the Motherland" (*Huagong zai Fa yu zhouguo de sunyi*) that appeared in *The Chinese Laborers' Weekly*. He wrote that Chinese laborers had not really understood the relationship between an individual and a nation, or between a family and a nation before they came to Europe. When they witnessed the Europeans fighting for their country in the Great War, their own nationalism and patriotism were aroused as well. The same article also declared that the laborers were determined to educate their fellow Chinese with the new knowledge they had acquired in Europe. Fu even wrote that the laborers' experience in Europe helped them realize that Westerners were not superior to the Chinese and made them confident that China might become as strong as the West.[187]

The workers' new nationalism and patriotism found further expression when they returned to China after the war, with some of them coming back from France via the Pacific. They actually refused to leave ship when their vessels called at Japanese ports, claiming that Japan "had behaved unfairly to China; being Chinese, they could not land and enjoy themselves." As a contemporary Chinese commentator, M. T. Z. Tyau, wrote, when they returned they brought a new spirit with them. "The returned laborers no doubt find splendid soil for the sowing of their transplanted seeds." These men were a strong force for changing China. In the early 1920s, Chinese workers frequently held strikes and the charge was made that the "returned laborer from the scene of recent conflict in Europe may be said to be the stormy petrel of the Chinese labor world." And in some official quarters, the returned laborer was even dreaded as a potential Bolshevik.[188] Chow Tse-tsung, in his authoritative study of the May Fourth Movement, points out that the experiences of these workers helped shape the organization and activities of labor unions in Shanghai during the May Fourth period. They were "instrumental in driving the

---

[186] Gu Xinqing, *Ouzhan gongzuo huiyilu*, 50–51.

[187] Fu Shengsan, "Huagong zai Fa yu Zhongguo de shenyi," *The Chinese Laborers' Weekly* 7 (March 12, 1919).

[188] See Tyau Min Chien, *China Awakened* (New York: The Macmillan Company, 1922), 240.

May Fourth Movement to extremes in both socialism and nationalism early in the twenties."[189] For Chow, the underpinnings of the new labor movement were "more of nationalism than Bolshevism."[190]

In conclusion, although a recent book continues to suggest that Chinese laborers in Europe "did not fulfill the expected foreign policy objectives during the First World War,"[191] I argue they not only provided a valuable contribution to the Allied side but, more importantly, served Chinese national interests well indeed, playing a critical role in China's early efforts to take its rightful place on the world stage.

[189] See Chow Tse-Tsung, *The May Fourth Movement: Intellectual Revolution in Modern China* (Cambridge, MA: Harvard University Press, 1960), 40.

[190] S. K. Sheldon Tso, *The Labor Movement in China* (Shanghai, 1928), 20.

[191] Marilyn A. Levine, *The Found Generation: Chinese Communists in Europe During the Twenties* (Seattle: University of Washington Press, 1993), 71.

5 China's formal entry into the war

War is not only a political act, but a real political instrument, a continuation of political transactions, an accomplishment of them by different means. That which remains peculiar to war relates only to the peculiar nature of its means.

Karl von Clausewitz[1]

Like Moses of old, she [China] is now stretching forth her arms; but who are they who uphold those arms?

Ellen N. LaMotte[2]

Commenting on the significance of China's entry into the war, French prime minister Aristide Briand expressed his view that Chinese participation had "at least two indisputable advantages of far-reaching consequences for all the Allies." First of all, it destroyed the power of German trade in Chinese markets and provided "first quality and unlimited" manpower. More importantly, it "would not be insignificant that the most ancient civilization in the world should take sides" with the Allies.[3]

Among the many countries that participated in the war, China was perhaps the most unusual. No neutral country had linked its fate with the war so closely, had such high expectations, and yet had been so humbled by the experience. China's declaration of war on Germany and Austria-Hungary in August 1917 might not be considered significant in world affairs, but it was an extremely important event for China. The war declaration in 1917 was the culmination of two decades of transformation in China, which included the emergence of an active and vigorous foreign policy public that supported the formulation of a new Chinese diplomacy. The outbreak of the war abroad coincided with and accelerated

---

[1] Quote from Lawence Stone, *The Causes of the English Revolution 1529–1642* (New York: Harper Torchbook, 1972), 5.

[2] La Motte made this statement regarding China's protest note to Germany on February 9, 1917 and its note to Paul Reinsch about China's German policy. See Ellen Newbold La Motte, *Peking Dust* (New York: The Century Co., 1919), 143.

[3] Marianne Bastid-Bruguière, "France and the 1915–1916 National Protection Movement," Paper presented to the Taipei Symposium, November 19–23, 1994.

155

these domestic developments, leading to various strategies for maneuvering China out of its old crippling relationships and into a new role within the world community.

The United States serves as a catalyst

After the developments in China's domestic political culture, perhaps the most important aspect of its new diplomacy was the decision to use the United States as a stepping-stone for its entry into the international system. A key feature of the Qing government's foreign policy had been "playing the powers off against each other," but Republican China made a clear break from that stance with its new strategy of alliance with the United States. Playing the powers one against the other was not real diplomacy, but a practice born of the traditional worldview that had encouraged China's isolation; it was a passive stratagem that allowed other countries to take the initiative even when Chinese interests were at stake. The new strategy was based on rational choice, focusing on active Chinese participation in world affairs. The United States enjoyed a better image in China than the other Great Powers, and many Chinese believed it supported China's territorial and political integrity.[4] In their opinion, the United States had no territorial ambitions in China and had been the first country to return some of the Boxer Indemnity. It was also the first major power to recognize the Republic of China. These gestures had enhanced America's formal image and led to the belief that the United States might be helpful.[5] This is exactly the point of one Chinese Foreign Ministry document entitled "Some Ideas on [China's] Foreign Policy Principles." This document was composed sometime around 1912, and it argued that if the recently established Republic of China was to find an ally in foreign affairs, the United States, which had "showed a favorable policy toward China," was the best candidate. The same document pointed out that this alliance would be in both countries' national interest.[6] The pro-American leanings of the Republican government were held by most Chinese officials when the First World War broke out. The Chinese elite considered the United States best suited to providing China with an opportunity to enter the war; indeed, many regarded the United

---

[4] Zhongyang yanjiuyuan jindai shi yanjiusuo, ed., *Zhong Ri guanxi shiliao: Ouzhan yu Shandong wenti*, II: 653.

[5] Brazil and Peru recognized the Republic of China in April 1913; the United States did so on May 2, 1913. Other countries did not recognize China until October 1913.

[6] The original date for this document was mistakenly put at 1921. Given its context, it was more likely written in 1912. See Zhongguo di er lishi danganguan, ed., *Zhonghua minguo shi zhi liao huibian: Di san ji, waijiao* (Collections of archival materials of Republican China: III, foreign relations) (Nanjing: Jiangsu guji chubanshe, 1991), 20–25.

States as China's "best friend."[7] Echoing this sentiment, Wellington Koo told his government that "the United States has been speaking out for China from a sense of justice and has treated China as a best friend."[8] Wang Zhengting, who later was appointed a member of the Chinese delegation at the Paris Peace Conference, wrote, "Besides political assistance, America is also in an excellent position to aid China financially, of which she stands so much in need."[9] Liang Qichao suggested to the Duan government that "the United States, after all, is the most reliable . . . for China." Liang hoped "that the United States would help China as it had earlier. [Therefore, reliance on America] should be considered a fundamental part in our plan of nation building."[10] In 1916 a young man by the name of Mao Zedong also fancied the idea of a Sino-American alliance against Japan. In a letter to a close friend, Mao wrote that "the two republics East and West will draw close in friendship and cheerfully act as reciprocal economic and trade partners." He called this alliance "the great endeavor of a thousand years."[11]

The popularity of an alliance with the United States was clearly reflected in China's new diplomacy with respect to foreign affairs in general, and the First World War in particular. China's initial response to the war indicated this expectation, when, on August 5, 1914, Yuan Shikai privately asked the United States to increase its military presence in China. The next day China invited the United States to call for belligerents not to expand the war into East Asia.[12] On August 19 the Chinese government came out with a new scheme. It naively hoped that, with help from the United States and England, Germany would agree to transfer its interest in Shandong to the United States. The United States would then return it to China. On September 10, the Chinese again requested the United States' assistance, asking that its navy help repel the Japanese invasion. But these proposals, with only one exception, fell on deaf ears in the

---

[7] For example, the Chinese Minister to the United States, Xia Xiefu, suggested that of all countries only the United States could be China's friend. At the postwar peace conference, China could benefit from American friendship; see Xia to Waijiaobu, March 22, 1915, in Zhongyang yanjiuyuan jindai shi yanjiusuo, ed., *Zhong Ri guanxi shiliao: Ouzhan yu Shandong wenti*, II: 788–89.

[8] Ibid., 175; see also Koo, *hui yi lu*, I: 152.

[9] Wang Zhengting, "How America Can Help China," *Millard's Review* (July 28, 1917): 207.

[10] Li Huaxing and Wu Jiayi, eds., *Liang Qichao xuanji* (Shanghai: Shanghai renmin chubanshe, 1984), 713. Ding Wenjiang, ed., *Liang Rengong xiansheng nianpu changbian chugao*, II: 512.

[11] Mao, Letter to Xiao Zhishen, July 25, 1916, in Stuart R. Schram, ed., *Mao's Road to Power: Revolutionary Writings, 1912–1949* (Armonk, NY: M. E. Sharpe, 1992), I: 104.

[12] Minutes of meeting between Wellington Koo and the American Legation in Beijing, August 6, 1914, Zhongyang yanjiuyuan jindai shi yanjiusuo, ed., *Zhong ri guanxi shiliao: Ouzhan yu Shandong wenti*, I: 9–11.

United States. Only the proposal for excluding East Asia from the war, a proposal which China itself withdrew in the face of serious obstruction by Japan, attracted the United States' interest.[13]

The United States may not have responded as hoped to these diplomatic efforts, but the Chinese desire to take part in international affairs kept the government trying to cultivate a close relationship with it. China was perhaps the first neutral country to respond to American president Woodrow Wilson's peace proposal in December 1916; the Chinese government immediately expressed its willingness to join the international effort to eradicate wars of aggression "to assure the respect of the principle of the equality of nations, whatever their power may be, and to relieve them of the peril of wrong and violence." In his note to Reinsch, the Chinese foreign minister declared that "China cannot but show satisfaction with the views of the Government and people of the United States of America" and would act "in conformity with not only her interest but also with her profound sentiments."[14]

China's new diplomacy was further reflected in the prompt Chinese response to another American-initiated diplomatic action. For the first three years of the European war, most Americans refused to believe that their country had any stake in the war, and the United States pursued a policy of so-called complete neutrality, in which Wilson asked his fellow Americans to be "impartial in thought as well as in action."[15] But in early 1917 this policy changed.[16] On February 3 the United States, responding to unlimited German submarine warfare, broke off relations with Germany and invited all neutral countries to join together.[17] When Reinsch forwarded this invitation to the Chinese government, the Chinese jumped at the opportunity, expressing to the United States its firm intent to join the action. For China, this invitation was a godsent opportunity to revitalize its campaign to enter the war, and more importantly, to put its new diplomacy into full motion.

After receiving the US invitation, the Chinese government organized four special meetings to discuss its response for three days. In the meantime, the Chinese Parliament also held secret sessions to discuss the war.

---

[13] For China's initial response, see Huang Jiamu, "Zhongguo dui Ouzhan de chubu fanying," *Zhongyang yanjiuyuan jindai shi yanjiusuo jikan* 1 (1969).

[14] Reinsch to Lansing, January 9, 1917, US Department of State, ed., *FRUS, 1917, Supplement 1; the World War*, 400–01.

[15] Reinsch to Waijiaobu, Beijing, February 4, 1917; Waijiaobu, ed., *Official Documents Relating to the War, for the Year of 1917* (hereafter cited as *ODRW*), printed by Peking Leader Press (Beijing), 1918, 5. See also Papers of Woodrow Wilson, xxx, 393–94.

[16] For a good analysis of US policy, see Ernest May, *World War and American Isolation, 1914–1917* (Cambridge, MA: Harvard University Press, 1966).

[17] Reinsch to Waijiaobu, Beijing, February 4, 1917, *ODRW*, 5.

To develop a better war policy, the Parliament organized many study groups, as did the Duan Qirui cabinet. Among them, the State Council established a Committee of Foreign Policy (Waijiao weiyuanhui), which consisted of both government officials and the social elite, and worked exclusively on China's war policy. Other groups included the Group for Supporting Diplomacy (Waijiao houyuanhui), the Discussion Group for Foreign Policy Issues (Waijiao shangquehui), the Association for International Affairs (Guoji xuehui), and the Group for Backing Up Foreign Policy (Waijiao houdunhui).

Even before receiving the US invitation, the Chinese government had been interested in following the United States' lead with respect to the war; Chinese foreign minister Wu Tingfang declared in a cabinet meeting that took place before America severed its relations with Germany, "The United States has protested to Germany. Therefore, China should follow suit. If the United States breaks off relations with Germany, China shall do the same. If the United States declares war on Germany, China shall declare war as well . . . In short, China shall do the same as the United States does."[18] On February 7, the Chinese government announced, "Since Germany has violated international law and hurt our national interest, China, for the sake of its status in the world, should not remain silent. China will take this opportunity to enter a new era of diplomacy, become an equal member of the international community, and through a firm policy [on Germany], win favorable treatment from the Allies."[19] The Chinese therefore told Reinsch that they had decided to protest Germany's submarine policy and indicated that diplomatic relations would be severed unless Germany abandoned unlimited submarine warfare. Beilby Francis Alston, a senior diplomat in the British Legation in Beijing, reported on February 7 in his "very confidential, urgent" telegram to Arthur James Balfour that an absolute majority in the Duan cabinet was in favor of China's severing relations with Germany, but no decision had been made "owing to unknown attitude of British and Japanese Legations. Public opinion is also said to be 80 per cent in favour" of severing relations with Germany.[20]

Despite the fact that China very much wanted to follow the United States, it insisted that it would not sever relations with Germany until the US had given it certain assurances. Accordingly, when Reinsch

---

[18] Zhang Guogan, *Zhang Guogan wenji* (Beijing: Beijing Yanshan chubanshe, 2000), 205.
[19] Yi ming, "Zhong De jie jiao shimu ji lihai" (The story of China's breaking off relations with Germany, March 18, 1917), in Zhang Bofeng et al., *Beiyang junfa, 1912–1928* (Wuhan: Wuhan chubanshe, 1990), III: 58; Ping Yi, "Dui De jie jiao zhi jingguo" (On China's breaking off relations with Germany), in *Dongfang zazhi* 14, no. 4.
[20] Alston to Balfour, February 7, 1917, very confidential, PRO, FO405/222/20.

approached the Chinese government, the Chinese asked Reinsch three questions: (1) Could assurances be given that Chinese arsenals and military forces would not come under foreign control? (2) Could assurances be given that China would be admitted to full membership in the peace conference? and (3) How would the powers now entering the war relate to the London agreement not to make a separate peace?[21] The fundamental concern of the Chinese was whether they could join the postwar peace conference.[22] Eventually Reinsch provided these and other assurances, telling China that if it participated in the American action, "China would improve its standing among the nations, she would have to be consulted during the course of the controversy and at the conclusion of the war; she would, in all this, be most closely associated with [the United States]."[23] In his official note to Chinese Foreign Ministry, he promised to help China further with the following message:

I have recommended to my government that, in the event of the Chinese government's associating itself with the President's suggestion, the Government of the United States should take measures to put at its disposal funds immediately required for the purposes you have indicated, and should take steps with a view to such a funding of the Boxer indemnity as would for the time being make available for the [purposes] of the Chinese government at least the major portions [of] the current indemnity installments.[24]

Unfortunately for both China and Reinsch, the American government did not share Reinsch's enthusiasm, and his assurances did not receive Washington's official sanction.[25] He was even reprimanded by Robert Lansing of the State Department in a sharply worded cable which

---

[21] Reinsch to Lansing, February 5, 1917, *FRUS, 1917, Supp. 1*, 401–02.

[22] Ibid., 404–07.

[23] Paul Samuel Reinsch, *An American Diplomat in China* (Garden City, NY: Doubleday Page & Company, 1922), 252.

[24] *FRUS, 1917, Supp. 1*, 403–04; also see Reinsch, *An American Diplomat in China*, 242–44.

[25] The question is why Reinsch acted as he did. To understand his motives, it may be helpful to take a look at his background. Born of German parents, he studied and taught in Germany for several years before becoming a leading political scientist at the University of Wisconsin (Madison). He married a German woman, and his mother-in-law, who stayed in Beijing with Reinsch, was still a German citizen. He was therefore understandably considered by the Allied representatives in China to be "pro-German" (Conty to Quai d'Orsay, September 13, 1917, NS, Chine, CCVII). He was not President Woodrow Wilson's or Secretary of State William Jennings Bryan's top, or even second, choice for the post of American Minister to China. At the beginning, Reinsch's name did not emerge as a candidate for this post. (For details on this point, see Bryan to Wilson, June 2, 1913, the Manuscript Division, Library of Congress: William Jennings Bryan Papers: Correspondence with Wilson, 1913–1915, 66.) Reinsch, a political scientist by training and for several years deeply interested in East Asian affairs, understood China's mood and aspirations. China finally found in him an active "Open-Door diplomat," an effective go-between for its new foreign policy initiatives. For the point on "China's devoted friend," see Burton F. Beers, *Vain Endeavor: Robert Lansing's Attempts to End the*

demanded that Reinsch use the utmost caution "lest China through our advice should become involved in difficulties from which we shall be unable to extricate it."[26]

Reinsch's enthusiasm nonetheless served as an excellent catalyst for pushing China's war policy, and the Chinese took advantage of it to take a first step toward eventually joining the war. Reinsch might have been naive to claim that it was he who single-handedly wooed China to break off relations with Germany, but his unauthorized promises did engage official Chinese interest and encouraged the Chinese to act quickly.[27]

Historian Noel Pugach is perhaps right when he writes, "It is more likely that Reinsch served as a useful catalyst for those Chinese who had been thinking of involving China in the war in order to gain specific benefits for their country."[28] On February 9, China quickly delivered its strongly worded official protest to Germany.[29]

On the same day, the Chinese Foreign Ministry sent a note to Reinsch expressing the Chinese government's concurrence with the principles set forth by the US government and declaring China's intention to associate itself firmly with the United States.[30]

The American connection to the Chinese protest against Germany and to China's war policy as a whole can be more fully appreciated by examining an important but secret Chinese document made available to scholars only recently – a State Council telegram to military governors dated February 9, 1917. This communication reveals that China's protest cited only "open" reasons, but that the real reasons, which were "not appropriate to reveal," were more important in the thinking of the Chinese government. First, the postwar peace conference was bound to affect East Asia, and if China did not do something with respect to the

---

American–Japanese Rivalry (Durham, NC: Duke University Press, 1962), 93–101; for a study of Reinsch as an open-door diplomat, see Noel H. Pugach, *Paul Reinsch: Open Door Diplomat in Action* (Millwood, NY: KTO Press, 1979) and Reinsch, *An American Diplomat in China.*

[26] *FRUS, 1917, Supp. 1,* 408–11.

[27] Samuel G. Blythe, the editor of the *Saturday Evening Post,* went even further by claiming certain foreigners including Reinsch had played a crucial role in pushing China's war policy. He wrote that for the first time "in five thousand years," although China was reluctant, afraid, to take part in world affairs, it was up to "half a dozen Americans, headed by Paul S. Reinsch . . . and assisted by two Australians [George Morrison and W. H. Donald, who was editor of the *Far Eastern Review*] of exceptional force and ability" to ask China "to formulate a definite foreign policy" and "to get into step with the march of the universe." Blythe considered himself one of these important Americans who "drove China relentlessly over the line of self-sufficiency and into world affairs." See Samuel G. Blythe, "The First Time in Five Thousand Years," *Saturday Evening Post* 189, no. 44 (1917): 28–34.

[28] Pugach, *Open Door Diplomat in Action,* 228.

[29] Wu Tingfang to Hintze, Feb. 9, 1917, *ODRW,* 5–6.   [30] Ibid., *ODRW,* 6–7.

war, it would not "have an opportunity to participate in the conference, and therefore China [would] face the prospect of having no voice at the conference." If China followed the American war policy, "China [would] attend the conference with the United States and henceforth any attempt to damage China's interest by any other countries at the conference can be contained." Second, the United States, as a leader of the neutral countries, had broken off relations with Germany, and most neutral countries would follow suit. The American minister to China had repeatedly invited China to do the same. "If China rejects America's invitation, its position will become an isolated one" in the postwar world (*you zhong li bian gu li*), and "its future diplomacy will be more difficult to manage." But if China "befriends the United States, its international status will be improved a great deal." Third, "China's diplomacy has lacked direction in the past and [China] has no Allies." If China was determined to follow a war policy similar to that of the United States, "the latter will provide a base for all China's diplomatic initiatives in the future." One week later, in another secret telegram to the same group, the State Council made its point much clearer, stressing that China's war policy was made not because it was hostile toward Germany or because it followed other countries blindly; the bottom line, the telegram read, "is to avoid an isolated position" in the international arena.[31]

The most eloquent and authoritative argument made for the Chinese alliance with the United States came from the Chinese minister to Washington, Wellington Koo. On April 9, 1917, Koo, in one of his long telegrams to Prime Minister Duan Qirui, strongly emphasized the importance of the American connection in China's new diplomacy.[32] He argued that a Chinese declaration of war on Germany would be a natural development of its foreign policy after the protest, but actively joining the war on the side of the United States or the Allies was fundamentally different (*qianli zhi bie*). He argued that there were four dangers to the Chinese national interest if it joined the Allies. First, because China had promised to proceed hand in hand with the United States, if it now turned to the Allied side, it would look insincere, and so would lose the trust of the United States. Second, Japan had taken advantage of the European war to expand its influence in China. If China joined the same side as Japan, this would provide an opportunity for Japan to tighten its control there further in the name of the Allied cause. Third, the Allied countries such as

---

[31] "Guowuyuan zhi gesheng dujun deng midian" (Secret State Council telegrams to provincial military governors), February 9, 16, 1917, in *Mingguo dangan* 1 (1991): 5–6.

[32] Koo, in his memoir, emphasized the importance of this report. Unfortunately he could not cite it in his memoir because he did not have a copy. This report did not become available to scholars until 1979.

Britain and France needed China's help in the form of human and material resources, and they would try to win that support by every means at their disposal, including pressure. If China compromised owing to their pressure, its sovereignty would be threatened; if not, it would be charged as a less reliable member of the Allied side. Fourth, the Allied countries, especially Britain and France, had allowed Japan a free hand in East Asia and consulted Japan first about any issues regarding China. If China did join the Allied camp, Japan would have the chance to further manipulate China's relations with the major powers and make China a complete Japanese dependant. In contrast to these four dangers, Koo claimed that China would enjoy four advantages if it joined the war on the US side as a member of associating powers in the Allied camp. The first advantage would be freedom of action in helping the Allies. The second advantage would be support from the United States in the form of promised economic aid. Compared to the Allies' many demands upon China, the United States had made none. Third, the United States might help stem Japanese incursions, whereas Britain and France were not willing or able to do that. Fourth, the United States would become a dominant world power after the war and could have a great impact on China's future international status. On the strength of these arguments, Koo suggested to Duan that if China decided to join the war, it should follow the United States rather than the Allies.[33] Koo's arguments are important because they not only took into account China's dilemma about entering the war but, more importantly, recognized the vital role of the United States in China's war policy. Koo's position was supported by Vice-president Feng Guozhang.[34]

Unfortunately, Koo's policy suggestion was never followed. Washington's reluctance to support China's entry into the war and a sudden change in Japanese policy regarding China's war participation attempt explain, to a certain extent, why China eventually went over to the Allied side. Yet the idea of Chinese alliance with the United States clearly indicated that China genuinely wished to enter the war and took the American invitation and Reinsch's assurances seriously. The Chinese government seemed to believe that by associating itself with the United States, it could certainly achieve the goals that prompted it to enter the war in the first place.

[33] Koo, telegram to Duan, April 9, 1917, in *Jindai shi ziliao* 38 (1979): 184–86.
[34] "Feng Guozhang guanyu bu jiari xieyaoguo, yu Mei yizhi xingdong zhi Zhu Qinglang diangao" (Feng's draft telegram to Zhu regarding the issue of not joining the Allies rather than following the US, April 30, 1917), in Zhongguo lishi di er dangan guan, ed., *Zhonghua minguo shi dangan ziliao huibian: Di san ji, zhengzhi* (Collections of archival materials on the history of Republican China: III, politics[2]) (Nanjing: Jiang su gu ji chu ban she, 1991), 1190.

China's war aims

After its initial protest note to Germany, China moved in a firm direction. On March 14, 1917, the government officially severed diplomatic relations with Germany "in the cause of international law and in the interests of the protection of the lives and property of our people" and "by the desire to further the cause of world peace."[35] China might have entered the war immediately had the Duan government handled domestic politics more skillfully; but only after several months of the political chaos triggered by the clumsy communication of the war policy did China finally declare war on Germany and Austria-Hungary on August 14 (the domestic implications of Duan's war policy will be discussed in detail in Chapter 6). Interestingly, the declaration coincided with the eighteenth anniversary of the eight major countries' military forces including Germany's entering Beijing during the Boxer Rebellion. The coincidence is especially striking because Germany had played a leading role in that expedition. In the declaration of war, China's president informed Germany and the world that

What we have desired is peace; what we have respected is international law; what we have to protect are the lives and property of our own people . . . I cannot bear to think that through us the dignity of international law should be impaired, or our position in the family of nations should be undermined or the restoration of the peace and happiness of the world should be retarded. Let the people of this entire nation do their utmost in this hour of trial and hardship to safeguard and develop the national existence of the Republic of China, so that we may establish ourselves amidst the family of nations and share with all mankind the prosperity and blessings drawn from our common association.[36]

One cannot discount these high-sounding pronouncements as mere lip service. Given China's long suffering under imperialism, we can easily understand why it was eager to pursue a policy that would put it on the same footing as other countries. China was sincere in its desire for a new world order and in its intention to work with the United States to make that a reality. By pursuing its desire to win a seat at the peace conference China also created an opportunity to help build the new world order based on the equality of nations and justice over might.

A close reading of the Chinese notices of protest and declaration of war exposes several important characteristics of China's new diplomacy. For instance, China based all its arguments on international law. Given its

---

[35] "Da Zongtong bugao" (Presidential Proclamation), March 14, 1917, in Zhongguo di er li shi dang an guan, beiyang wai jiao bu dang, "Ouzhan wenjian an zhi san," 03–36/6–(1); see also Alston to Waijiaobu, August 14, 1917, *ODRW*, 17: 19.

[36] "Presidential Proclamation, August 14, 1917," *ODRW*, 12: 13–15.

weak status, its desire to enter and transform the international community, and, above all, its grand plan to use the war as an opportunity to join a fair international system, recourse to public opinion and international law gave China its best chance at achieving its goals.[37]

A new world order based on international law would serve China's interests. Wellington Koo explained this link on November 2, 1918, at the dedication of the Altar of Liberty in New York. Koo told his audience that China had joined the war because it was vitally interested in the world struggle. From 1897 on, Germany had acted aggressively in Shandong Province. The atrocities of 1900 were still remembered as examples of the brutal character of German militarism. But it was not a desire for vengeance that moved China to declare war. China saw clearly from Germany's crimes in Belgium and on the high seas what would befall the rest of the world if the Teutons should emerge victorious in the conflict.[38] Liang Qichao, a major player in formulating China's war policy, elaborated this point very well. He argued that "the peace of the Far East was broken by the occupation of Kiaochow by Germany. This event marked the first step of the German disregard for international law. In the interests of humanity and for the sake of what China has passed through, she should rise and punish such a country that dared to disregard international law."[39] A Chinese expert on international law, Dr. M. T. Z. Tyau, also held out hope for world justice when he wrote that "the injustices, the inequalities, the inconsistencies of the past, must be abolished, and rational bases of mutual intercourse substituted." To help achieve this end, China had to enter the war.[40] Even some of the foreign media, to some extent, appreciated the war aims of China's new diplomacy. For instance, in the *Manchester Guardian* in late spring of 1917, an article argued that China's purpose in entering the war "through many channels" was to ensure its international position and to bring "China more intimately into touch with the family of nations than in any other phase of modern history."[41]

Clearly China entered the war to enhance its international status and break the spell of diplomatic isolation on the basis of international law. Unlike its declaration of war on the major powers in 1900, the

---

[37] Huang Fu, *Ouzhan zhi jiaoxun yu zhongguo zhi weilai* (Lessons of the European war and China's Future) (Shanghai: Zhonghua shuju chubanshe, 1918), 102.

[38] "China's Part in the European War," *Current History*, a monthly magazine published by *The New York Times*, May, 1919, 357.

[39] W. Reginald Wheeler, *China and the World War* (New York: The Macmillan Company, 1919), 80–81.

[40] Tyau Min-chien, *Legal Obligations Arising out of Treaty Relations between China and Other States* (Shanghai: Commercial Press, 1917), 217.

[41] "China's Breach with Germany," *Manchester Guardian*, May 23, 1917.

declaration of war on Germany and the Austro-Hungarian Empire in 1917 was a rational and well-considered policy. If the Qing's declaration of war on the major powers during the Boxer Rebellion conjured up xenophobia, irrationality, and barbarism, then China's war policy during the First World War was progressive and internationalist-minded, and reflected the careful consideration of its national interest and destiny, argued from the point of view of international law.[42] Chen Youren wrote in *The Peking Gazette* that "the [war] decision arrived at is in every sense a victory of the younger intellectual forces over the older mandarinate, whose traditions of laissez faire and spineless diplomacy have hitherto cost China so much."[43] Even Chen Duxiu and Li Dazhao, both esteemed scholars and subsequent founders of the Chinese Communist Party, supported China's participation in the war. Li said that China's protest to Germany symbolized "the first ray of morning sunshine in the decades of China's [sad] diplomatic history." He encouraged the government to take quick action to join the war and called on all Chinese to support the war policy with "iron and blood."[44] By its declaration of war, China had finally become a member of the Allied side.

While China's attitude toward world powers was usually conciliatory, its protest and declaration of war were both dignified in tone and firm in attitude. These proclamations told the world that China would no longer be merely silent in the international arena, easily pushed around by others; it was now pursuing a new diplomacy and working to become an independent member of the family of nations. One contemporary American China watcher, Gardner L. Harding, wrote in 1917 that the Chinese note to Germany on February 9 "not only took the first step toward breaking off relations with Germany," but "for the first time in her modern history, [China] assumed in a diplomatic note a position of active interest and presumptive interference in the affairs of European nations."[45]

Germany was fully aware of these changes in China, complaining on March 10 in its official response to the note of protest that "the Imperial Government is greatly surprised at the threat used by the Government of the Republic of China . . . Many other countries have also protested,

---

[42] For studies on the Boxer Rebellion, see Joseph W. Esherick, *The Origins of the Boxer Uprising* (Berkeley: University of California Press, 1987) and Paul A. Cohen, *History in Three Keys: The Boxers as Event, Experience, and Myth* (New York: Columbia University Press, 1997).

[43] Wheeler, *China and the World War*, 71–72.

[44] Li Dazhao, *Li Dazhao wenji* (Collected writings of Li Dazhao) (Beijing: Renmin chubanshe, 1984), I: 284, 296, 330–31.

[45] Gardner L. Harding, "China and the World War," *Current History*, July 1917, 100.

but China, which has been in friendly relations with Germany, is the only state which added a threat to its protest." Interestingly enough, given the firm tone and uncompromising message of the Chinese note, the German response was mild and conciliatory. Although the response indicated that it was "difficult for Germany to abandon her blockade policy," it did promise to "comply with the wishes of the Government of the Republic of China by opening negotiations to arrive at a plan for the protection of Chinese life and property."[46] German mildness in light of the strongly worded protest indicated a sea change in its response to China; contrast this to Germany's response in 1900 in the period of the Boxer Rebellion: The German Kaiser Wilhelm, in a speech at Bremerhaven on the occasion of the departure of the first contingent of German troops for China, declared he would order the German army to punish the Chinese so severely that none of them would dare to look at a German directly again, and this would open the way for German *Kultur* in China once and for all.[47] Now, less than twenty years later, China was declaring war on Germany. As Tyau wrote,

By accepting Germany's challenge to ride roughshod over all considerations of law and humanity, China is vindicating its prestige in the council of nations. She is no longer the negligible quantity that men used to know before the fateful days of August 1914, and as to her future one can only now hazard a guess. It is scarcely two decades since her actual dismemberment was regarded as inevitable; today, to quote further from Reuter's message, China has only by her adhesion to the great principles of international law, and from the very first, been on an equal footing with the nations fighting for civilization.

Tyau further wrote that "thanks principally to Germany," China "has been drawn into the limelight of *Weltpolitik*." Although the major powers did not treat China fairly, Tyau asserted, "We remain confident that at the postbellum peace conference full justice will be done to her rightful claims" and looked forward to "the day of China's complete rehabilita-tion."[48]

Although the Chinese war policy clearly indicated a desire to follow the United States in trying to build a new world order, this was only a means to an end. As one Chinese newspaper declared in an editorial on the eve of the Chinese government protest to Germany under the headline "Now or Never,"

[46] Hintze to Waijiaobu, March 10, 1917, *ODRW*, 7–8.
[47] For Wilhelm II's speech, see John S. Kelly, *A Forgotten Conference: the Negotiations at Peking, 1900–1901* (Geneva: Libraire E. Droz, 1963), 52.
[48] Tyau Min-Chien T. Z., *China's New Constitution and International Problems* (Shanghai: Commercial Press, 1918), 188, 195, 221.

This is the time for action. We must range ourselves on the side of justice, of humanity and of international law. We must also win a place for ourselves, friends, in the council of nations by prompt and decisive action. Now, Germany's submarine policy and the United States' resolute stand against lawlessness and wholesale atrocity have given us the opportunity. In the present state of the world, it is impossible for any nation to stand alone. We must have allies, if not so sanctified in treaties, yet in a mutual bond of sympathy. This is the best opportunity for us to win friends among the powers. Possibly we will have only a little say in the peace conference, but since we have been willing to help [the Allied countries], our appeal will not be unheeded when we should be in difficulties . . . Cultivate friendship when our friends are in need, and not when they are above wants. Now or never must we show the world that this is a nation which is not always on the sick list, but living, pulsating and with a fighting spirit.[49]

To serve its own ends, China did not simply follow the United States, but sometimes pursued a different option. Unlike the United States, China declared war on both Germany and Austria-Hungary almost simultaneously.[50] Liang Qichao explained the difference this way: "America can afford to ignore Austria because there is no Austrian concession or Austrian consular jurisdiction in America," but Austria had certain unequal rights in China, and China could not ignore it.

By entering the war, China was finally able to recover some degree of sovereignty, one of its major war aims. As Liang Qichao, a key player in China's 1917 entry into the war, explained,

It is impossible for China to take the necessary steps to safeguard itself against Germans residing in China unless the old treaties are canceled. For unless war is declared it is impossible for China to cancel the consular jurisdiction of the Germans in China . . . It will be advantageous to China if the old treaties be canceled by a declaration of war and new treaties be negotiated after the conclusion of peace . . . This is not reluctantly yielding to the request of the Entente Allies. It is the course we must take in our present situation.[51]

After breaking off relations with Germany and Austria, the Chinese navy confiscated German vessels in Chinese ports and its police immediately took over German and Austrian concessions. One American newspaper, commenting on the occasion of China's taking over German and Austrian settlements, wrote, "This is a memorable day for China. For the first time since Western powers established extraterritoriality within her borders, China has ordered two European nations to give up that privilege."[52] With its declaration of war, China went a step further

---

[49] Wheeler, *China and the World War*, 71–72.
[50] The United States did not officially declare war on Austria-Hungary until December 7, 1917.
[51] Liang Qichao, *Yin bing shi wen ji* (Beijing: Zhong hua shuju, 1989), xxxv: 3–7.
[52] *The Evening Post* (New York), October 3, 1917.

toward recovering national sovereignty and national dignity by pronouncing that

All treaties, agreements, and conventions, heretofore concluded between China and Germany and between China and Austria-Hungary, as well as such parts of the international protocols and international agreements as concern only the relations between China and Germany and between China and Austria-Hungary are, in conformity with the Law of Nations and international practice, hereby abrogated.

China also immediately declared that Germans in China would be judged by Chinese courts if they committed crimes, rather than by their own consuls. "For the duration of the war all civil and criminal cases in which enemy subjects are concerned shall be tried by the Chinese Courts of Justice."[53]

China had drawn up several laws or regulations to monitor Germans and Austrians residing in China; their residences and mail were to be inspected and their travels had to be reported to local Chinese officials. "All laws, rules and regulations enacted by China may also be enforced" in the newly recovered concessions.[54]

Not surprisingly, the Chinese attempt to recover national sovereignty did not go entirely smoothly. One of the major obstacles was the Dutch minister to China Beelaerts van Blokland, who was asked to take care of German interests in China after March 14, when China broke off relations with Germany. He tried hard to keep German interests there intact, given the old treaty system.[55] But in most cases Chinese officials firmly withstood his protests and although the recovery of sovereignty in the German concessions was not complete, China's first successful effort to rid itself of unequal treaties is nevertheless too significant to ignore.

China had hoped that its declaration of war would be a catalyst for the eventual complete recovery of sovereignty. The war enabled China to recover German and Austrian concessions; and it was hoped that it would also provide an opportunity to negotiate the cancellation or revision of unequal treaties with the Allied Powers and the United States. Many Chinese in both official and unofficial circles entertained the hope that by throwing its weight against Germany, China might eventually bring the Allied Powers to reconsider the terms of the most oppressive treaties,

---

[53] "Shengli de renxing shishuo song zhan xin zhang cheng," Zhongguo di er li shi dang an guan, beiyang wai jiao bu dang, 03–36/6-(1).

[54] See *ODRW*, documents nos. 122–26, 132: 112–20, 126–27.

[55] "Beelaerts van Blokland to Waijiaobu, April 11, 1917," *ODRW*, 134; "Beelaerts van Blokland to Waijiaobu, August 18, 1917," *ODRW*, 167–68.

particularly the Boxer Protocol of 1901.[56] As Wu Tingfang said, "We have heard the public pronouncements of the statesmen of the powers, that after the war, justice and equality will rule among the nations. We believe in them, and have great hopes of them. We expect that in carrying them out in practice in China, one of the first things that will be done will be a reasonable and equitable revision of our treaties."[57] China proceeded to ask the major powers to "favour the independent development of China, and in no way to seek in China, either singly or jointly, advantages of the nature of territorial or preferential rights, whether local or general." China further insisted that the powers accord to China their full assistance, to "help it obtain the enjoyment of the advantages resulting from the equality of powers in their international relations."[58]

After receiving news of its war declaration, all the Allied countries and the United States gave China an "assurance of their solidarity, of their friendship, and of their support" and vowed that they "will do all" to help China "have the benefit in her international relations of the situation and the regard due to a great country."[59] The Allied countries even agreed to ensure that China would receive equal status after the war. The French minister at Beijing had been authorized by his Allied colleagues to sign an official exchange with China on the following grounds: First, the Allies assured that China would be guaranteed against claims by the central powers on account of its participation in the war and especially guaranteed against measures taken in regard to enemy subjects and property. Second, the Allies promised in general terms that at the peace conference, the interests of China would be taken into consideration on a footing equal to those of the other Allies.[60]

Besides its desire for equal status, China also had several other important aims in mind when it decided to declare war. As we noted earlier, obtaining a seat at any postwar peace conference had been China's obvious motive for joining the war, and after it had joined the war, this aim became a concrete objective. This can be seen in, among other sources, one Chinese Foreign Ministry draft of an undated internal document, entitled "War Aims," which was prepared around 1917. This document

---

[56] According to the Boxer Protocol, no Chinese soldiers could be stationed within twenty *li* of Tianjin, while foreign troops could stay along the Beijing–Tianjin railroad and around the Legation Quarter in Beijing.

[57] Wu's preface for Tyau's *Legal Obligations Arising Out of Treaty Relations Between China and Other States* (Shanghai: Commercial Press, 1917), viii.

[58] Reinsch, *An American Diplomat in China*, 287–88.

[59] Allied and American Ministers to Waijiaobu, August 14, 1917, Zhongguo di er li shi dang an guan, beiyang wai jiao bu dang, 03–36/15-(1); see also Presidential Proclamation, August 14, 1917, *ODRW*, 14.

[60] Lord Bertie, telegram to FO, February 9, 1918, PRO, FO371/3173/257.

points out that since Japan had violated China's neutrality by sending troops to attack Qingdao and assuming possession of all the rights formerly possessed by Germany in Shandong Province, it had become necessary for China to move in this direction: "In no other way than by entry into the war on its own account did the Chinese Government consider that it would be certain of a seat at the conference."[61] By associating itself with the Allied Powers against Germany, China expected to be accorded an independent voice when the disposal of German rights in Shandong came up for consideration. It seemed to Chinese officials that the United States and the Allied Powers confirmed this reasoning. When in late January of 1918 China promised to deport the enemy subjects, Britain indicated that it was "of the opinion that the Allied governments should give an assurance in general terms that China's interest will be considered equally with those of all her Allies at the peace conference."[62] Given such assurances, many Chinese believed that their goal of attending the postwar conference and receiving reasonably fair treatment was within reach.

Economic gains were also an important part of China's war aims. John Jordan observed that "as the declaration of war against Germany and Austria has profound influence upon China's political status, so has it great effects upon her financial conditions."[63] The economic gains China hoped for included loans and an increase in tax income, as well as cancellation of the Boxer Indemnity. As Lu Zhengxiang clearly informed the Allied ministers,

The Chinese Government could not undertake the responsibility of taking any further steps in the direction of war without having the assurances of the powers that they would allow China certain financial benefits, particularly the postponement of the Boxer indemnity installments during the remainder of the war, and an increase of the customs duties to which China is entitled by treaty.[64]

China was further promised that if it followed the United States or joined the Allied side, it would receive outright financial support. With the breakdown of its control over domestic revenue, especially after the death of Yuan Shikai, the Beijing government was eager to secure foreign loans. Entry into the war seemed the best way for China to avoid taking potentially compromising loans from Japan, since by joining the war effort it could attract loans from elsewhere. Chinese officials were led to believe the government would receive financial support from the Allies. Reinsch

---

[61] Chinese Second Archive, 1039-2-399.
[62] FO Telegram to Greene, February 2, 1918, PRO, FO371/3173/212.
[63] Jordan to Balfour, February 27, 1918, PRO, FO371/3188/100049.
[64] *FRUS, 1917, Supp. 1*, 441–42.

observed this very clearly in his memoir. He wrote that after the declaration of war on Germany, "The time has come for China to put money in her purse. She was sure she could do it, and sure that the United States, her great, rich sponsor and friend, would help her . . . commensurate with her needs of development for war."[65]

China had good reason to believe such support was forthcoming. Besides the earlier promises from Reinsch, China also received assurances from Robert Lansing, the US secretary of state, who plainly told the Chinese minister in Washington that "if China should be among those engaged in war with our enemies, she might have some reason to expect such financial assistance."[66] In the meantime, in early February of 1917, the British government also notified China that "Britain in consultation with the other Allied Powers interested in China" would "no doubt favourably" consider China's request to postpone the Boxer Indemnity and to secure other financial assistance "should China take any steps hostile to German interests."[67] In its telegram to Alston on April 27, 1917, the British Foreign Office instructed, "You should take an early opportunity of letting [the] Chinese government know that, in the event of their acting as suggested and unconditionally ranging themselves on the side of [the] Allies, His Majesty's government has every intention of subsequently meeting China's reasonable requests in a generous spirit and that she may count on their assistance in endeavouring to persuade the other powers to do likewise."[68]

With all these assurances, China officially presented its concrete requests to the Allied Powers in March 1917:

1. Postponement of the Boxer Indemnity for ten years without accumulation of interest;
2. Recognition by the Allied Powers of China's right to immediately increase the customs tariff to an effective 5 percent and gradually modify its tax; an immediate surtax of 50 percent should be levied on import duties, preliminary to raising the tariff to an eventual 12.5 percent;
3. Permission for the Chinese army to be stationed in Tianjin and Legation areas at least temporarily.[69]

---

[65] Reinsch, *An American Diplomat in China*, 296.
[66] Lansing to Reinsch, April 23, 1917, *FRUS, 1917, Supp. 1*, 431–32.
[67] FO to Alston, February 23, 1917, PRO, wo106/35.
[68] Kenneth Bourne and Ann Trotter, eds., *British Documents on Foreign Affairs: Reports and Papers from the Foreign Office Confidential Print: Part II, From the First to the Second World War, Series E, Asia, 1914–1939*, XXII (Bethesda, MD: University Publications of America, 1994), 279.
[69] Ibid., 266–67.

China's demands for the postponement of the Boxer Indemnity and the revision of tariffs were both a just and a smart move. These two issues had haunted China for many years, presenting major obstacles to independence and equality in the international arena. Both issues had been at the top of its diplomatic agenda for some time. The Chinese had tried hard to convince the Great Powers to revise the tariff in 1915, but this attempt went nowhere because of the powers' lack of interest. After its entry into the war, China immediately resumed this effort, trying to raise the current 5 percent customs duties on imported goods to 7.5 percent, and then to 12.5 percent after abolition of the *likin* or transit dues system.

As for the Boxer Indemnity, for which the Great Powers had exaggerated their claims to an exorbitant and shameful level, Liang Qichao, China's financial minister in 1917, held that if payment could be delayed, the country's finances would benefit greatly.[70] The indemnity represented a tremendous burden for the Chinese people and was a serious insult to national dignity and sovereignty. The Chinese had repeatedly demanded prior to the war that the indemnity be at least postponed. In 1912, China had made serious and sincere efforts to negotiate with the Great Powers about this issue. As they had on the issue of tariff revision, the Great Powers simply turned a deaf ear. But by 1917, the government felt it was time to push for change once again. The Chinese social elite felt that if the Allied countries were really fighting, as they claimed, for humanity and for a fair world, the Boxer Indemnity was an injustice they should relieve. The Allies had the moral, if not diplomatic, obligation to redeem China by showing it positive consideration. As one Englishman put it to Balfour, "Would it not be a just, as well as a graceful act, for us to take the lead in passing the sponge over this old and rather discreditable sore?"[71]

Although not all of its requests bore fruit and the powers would not accommodate all China's desires, its war policy nonetheless led to some immediate economic gains. All claims for repayment of debt and the Boxer Indemnity by Germany and Austria were *ipso facto* canceled or suspended.[72] Upon declaration of war, the Chinese government immediately liquidated the Deutsch-Asiatische Bank, which had been organized in 1889 and had since served as the German government's financial

[70] Ding Wenjiang, ed., *Liang Rengong xiansheng nianpu changbian chugao* (Taipei: Shijie shuju, 1959), 531.

[71] George Lynch to Arthur Balfour, March 17 1917, PRO, FO371/2907.

[72] "[Mi] yu chuoxuan zhanhou ge yuan bu qu ying banshi yi qing danbing fujian" (Secret: Things should be taken care of by ministries and their branches in case China declares war) in *Dui de ao xuan zhang wen juan*, Zhong guo di er li shi dang an guan, beiyang wai jioa bu dang, 1049(2)–58.

agent in China, with its main office at Shanghai and branches at Tianjin, Beijing, Hankou, Guangzhou, Qingdao, and Jinan. Given China's terrible financial situation at the time, even this meant a substantial gain.

Except for these concrete gains, however, the promised financial assistance from the United States and other countries was a long time coming, and negotiations with the Allied Powers for postponement of the indemnity and tariff revision did not go as well as the Chinese had hoped.

Betrayals on many fronts

It was one thing for China to have high expectations about benefits from its war involvement, but whether those expectations would be met was something else. The powers, of course, were not happy to see China asserting itself, even though they wanted Chinese help. Moves to reassert Chinese sovereignty and national dignity in relation to Germany and Austria-Hungary were both welcomed and feared by the Allied side. After all, such actions undermined the treaty system on which the powers had long based their unequal rights relationship with China.

Worried that the new Chinese confidence in its right to assert sovereignty might affect their interests, the Allies devised the idea of "internationalizing" the German and Austrian concessions. The French first proposed this strategy in March 1917. It included two provisions: (1) that disposal of enemy persons and property from the international settlement at Shanghai should be handled by the Allied consuls, meaning that the Chinese government would not be able to interfere; (2) that German concessions at Tianjin and Hankou should become international settlements based on the Shanghai model.[73] But the Allied side had trouble justifying this move. They realized that "[t]he internationalisation of the German and Austrian concessions which would mean the ejection of the Chinese and a serious loss of face for China would further militate against the object in view. China is being invited by the Allied Powers to take part in the war, and it is unreasonable and unfair that the latter should at the same time pursue local aims of their own at her expense, and doubly so, when the effect has all the appearance of maintaining her in tutelage and emphasizing her inferiority."[74]

The powers' internationalization scheme did not hold China back, and the government eventually went ahead to recover the German and Austrian concessions in 1917. But with the Allied Powers' foot-dragging,

---

[73] Bourne et al., *British Documents on Foreign Affairs: Reports and Papers from the Foreign Office Confidential Print, Series E, Asia 1914–1939*, XXII, 266.
[74] FO to Greene, April 5, 1917, PRO, wo106/35.

China did run into obstacles pursuing its other war aims. Although the Allied countries readily made promises, most of them unfortunately proved empty. For instance, the Allied side promised the Chinese government that "once they have severed diplomatic relations with the Germans . . . the Allied governments will be ready to discuss in a friendly spirit all the demands they have made." Yet the negotiations were not carried out "in a friendly spirit" at all.[75] The Allied side told China that they assented in principle to Chinese demands for the postponement of the Boxer Indemnity and tariff issues, but the detailed terms had to be worked out later. As early as February 16, 1917, the powers had reached a consensus on the French initiative that China should first declare war if it wanted to put itself on firm ground for negotiating its demands.[76] Russia, owing to its preponderant share of Boxer indemnities, only agreed to defer one-third, thus bringing the annual payment down to about 13,000,000 Mexican silver dollars. The Italian government, for domestic and administrative reasons, did not want to postpone getting its share of the Boxer Indemnity either. The Japanese suggested that the Allied countries reply to the Chinese demands with the following promises:

1. Postponement of the Boxer Indemnity only up to the end of the war;
2. Consent in principle to modify the customs tariff to an effective 5 percent;
3. Consent, as regards the protocol of 1901, to Chinese troops having access for the duration of the war to areas within 20 Chinese *li* of Tianjin, as necessary for surveillance of the Germans.

The Japanese government further indicated to the Allies that numbers 1 and 2 would only take effect on the day China formally declared war on Germany.[77] But when China actually joined the war in August the Allied Powers did not want to meet Chinese demands. The French for instance would favorably consider a Chinese government loan, an increase of the Chinese customs tariff, and temporary suspension of part of the Boxer protocol that would enable the Chinese to expel the Germans: that is, permission for Chinese troops to pass through the foreign concessions. But France thought it necessary to postpone decision on China's request about the Boxer Indemnity until it was satisfied with China's detailed proposal of actions against Germany.[78]

In general, there was enormous disagreement among the Allied countries about how to accommodate China's aims. The gap was so large

[75] Balfour to Quai d'Orsay, February 27, 1917, Quai d'Orsay, NS, Chine, CXXXV: 130–34.
[76] Conty, telegram, Beijing, February 16, 1917, Quai d'Orsay, NS, Chine, CXXXV.
[77] Foreign Office Memo to France, March 20, 1917, Quai d'Orsay, NS, Chine, CXXXV: 227–29.
[78] Quai d'Orsay Telegram, February 18, 1917, Quai d'Orsay, NS, Chine, CXXXV.

that the British Foreign Office complained, "If China's entry into the war is really the object of the Allied Powers, it is quite evident that the attitude adopted by many of their representatives at Peking is calculated to defeat their object."[79] The proposed postponement of indemnity payments proved especially difficult. Britain admitted that China's entry into the war "would justify the total remission of indemnity payments, though they [the Allies] recognise that such a step required lengthy consideration both by themselves and the other powers. But certainly, pending a general decision as to this, the only course with any chance of success is to postpone indemnity payments unconditionally for such a period as would make it worthwhile for China to join in the war."[80]

One major obstacle was Japan, which had its own plans. In September 1918, Japanese officials told the Chinese that Japan might remit its share of the Boxer Indemnity. Of the 80 million dollars still owed to Japan, according to this plan, about 30 million was to be spent on education and the remaining 50 million on the development, under Japanese auspices, of China's resources in cotton, iron, and wool. A Japanese advisor was to be appointed to supervise the resolution of the issues brought up by China at the peace conference. Furthermore, China could not borrow money from any other country to pay the loans contracted from Japan, nor could it cancel the loan agreements. The conditions attached were what China had been trying hardest to avoid. Not only would these conditions preclude China's getting back Shandong at the postwar conference, but also they made a joke of Chinese war aims and undermined the very basis of its new diplomacy. The conditions Japan set out were so extreme that even its legation in Beijing tried to soft-pedal them. But given devious Japanese behavior in the past, especially the episode of the Twenty-one Demands, the other powers grew suspicious. Chinese public opinion immediately denounced the Japanese proposal. As Jordan commented, "In view of the past history of Japanese negotiations with China, the public generally refuses to entirely disbelieve them and they have aroused considerable attention in the presses."[81] The Chinese suspected that Japan intended to "induce China, by the proposal to return their share of the Boxer Indemnity, not to present her case at the international peace conference in a way detrimental to Japanese national interests."[82] The Chinese government firmly refused to accept the Japanese conditions and let the issue die. This refusal, according to Jordan, "showed clearly the attitude taken up in this

[79] FO to Greene, April 5, 1917, PRO, wo106/35.
[80] FO to Greene, April 5, 1917, PRO, wo106/35.
[81] Jordan to Balfour, October 30, 1918, PRO, fo371/3175/167–75.
[82] See Hollington Tong, "Japan's Conditions for Remitting Her Share of Boxer Indemnity," *Millard's Review* 6, no. 8 (October 26, 1918): 303–06.

matter by the more intelligent classes of young China."[83] This episode is another example of how public opinion had an impact on China's foreign policy-making.

Besides taking different positions on the Boxer Indemnity, the Allied countries had serious conflicts over China's request for a revision of the tariff. Once again, Japan and Russia did not want to give China an easy way out. Russia wanted to retain the system of duties for goods transported by land, and the Japanese claimed that the tariff changes were "the last concession" they were prepared to make.[84] Japan insisted that the duties should be decided according to the quality of goods and proposed only a 30 percent surtax on import duties, which seemed too low even to the British government.[85] Jordan complained,

The Japanese are the great sinners in the matter of the tariff. It is hard to characterize their attitude in moderate language and it seems simply to amount to a denial of bare justice. It is no wonder, therefore, that the Chinese desire some assurance about the tariff as a condition precedent to the deportation of enemy subjects.[86]

In consequence, the negotiations on tariff revision did not bear real fruit until the 1920s when the Allied Powers and also the United States only agreed in principle to revise the customs tariff on the basis of an effective 5 percent and set up a commission on tariff revision, composed of delegates from all the powers concerned, for discussion of the matter.[87]

As noted earlier, one of China's direct motives for seeking a seat at the postwar peace conference was to take back Shandong, which Japan had seized from German hands. Unfortunately, it is here that China suffered the biggest blow to its war aims. Although the Allied Powers had promised to allow it to attend the postwar conference, as noted earlier, the Allies' secret deals with Japan made that almost impossible. China's dream of a seat as a full partner at the postwar conference had been betrayed by the Allied side from the very beginning.

In early 1916, Edward Grey, then British foreign secretary, had already promised Japan that in the event of a discussion of German rights and concessions in China at the peace conference, Britain would stand by the Japanese.[88] This deal was finalized in early 1917. On February 14, 1917, Britain officially told Japan that it

---

[83] Jordan to Balfour, October 30, 1918, PRO, FO371/3175/167–75.
[84] Jordan to Balfour, April 9,1918, PRO, FO371/3174/28360.
[85] FO to Greene, April 5, 1917, PRO, WO106/35.
[86] Jordan to Langley, February 17, 1918, PRO, FO350/16/59.
[87] Jordan to Balfour, February 27, 1918, PRO, FO371/3188/100049.
[88] Grey dispatch to Tokyo, February 4, 1916, PRO, WO106/34.

accedes with pleasure to the request of the Japanese government for an assurance that they will support Japan's claims in regard to the disposal of Germany's right in Shantung and possessions in islands north of the Equator on the occasion of a peace conference, it being understood that the Japanese Government will . . . treat in the same spirit Great Britain's claims to the German islands south of the Equator.[89]

Besides the deal with Britain, Japan also made arrangements with France and Russia. When the United States sent its famous invitation note to China to join the war effort, the French foreign minister Briand argued that the Allied Powers "should not allow the opportunity to escape" (*ne doivent pas laisser échapper l'occasion qui se présente*). Still remembering how they had fallen short in 1914 and 1915 of having China participate in the war because of Japanese opposition, the French, eager to see China in the war, concluded a secret deal with Japan, as had Britain; Russia made a similar deal as well. In their secret agreements with Japan, all included the clause promising, in case of China's admission to the post-war peace conference, that Japan would be supported by France, Russia, and Britain "on the questions of Shandong and the Pacific Islands."[90] In consequence, Jordan reported that Japan by February of 1917 had "induced those powers, at a time when their fate hung in the balance, to recognize the position she had thus acquired and the reversion in her favour of German rights in Shantung."[91] In his comment on Japan's activity in China during that period, Jordan told Langley that "with all our worldwide preoccupations at present . . . we cannot afford to antagonize the Japanese, and without antagonizing her, we cannot get the principles for which we are fighting in Europe extended to the Far East."[92]

Since Japan had gained everything it wanted from China, it was not hurt by allowing China to pursue its war policy, especially since the United States had invited China to do so. In this way, Japan calculated it might regain the diplomatic ground it had lost for standing in the way of China's new diplomacy and earlier war effort. Furthermore, by supporting China's entry into war, Japan might kill two birds with one stone since it could use the Duan cabinet's war policy to destabilize Chinese domestic politics and accordingly create more room and opportunity for Japanese intervention. This, in addition to the assurances it had obtained from the Allies, suggests why Japan's policy toward Chinese participation

---

[89] Memorandum to the Japanese Ambassador, February 14, 1917, PRO, FO371/2950.
[90] About the French attitude toward American China policy, see Quai d'Orsay, NS, Chine, CXXXVII: 122–24; see also Jordan to Langley, April 16, 1916, PRO, FO350/15.
[91] Jordan Annual Report to Foreign Office, 1919, PRO, FO405/229/9.
[92] Jordan to Langley, August 28, 1918, PRO, FO350/16.

in the Allied cause took a 180-degree turn in February of 1917. Five
hours prior to its protest to Germany on February 9, China had asked
for Japan's view. To the surprise of Chinese officials, the Japanese had
not only supported China's protest, but even suggested that China go
further by breaking diplomatic relations with Germany once and for
all.[93]

The tragedy for China was that although it was finally welcomed by
the Allied countries into the war effort, it had already lost the major
objective of its war policy: recovery of its territory and sovereign rights in
Shandong. The Chinese innocently believed a declaration of war would
bring justice and international prestige, and the assurances of Allied countries gave the Chinese government and people a false expectation of fair
treatment. Even some officials in the Allied countries realized the moral
dilemma presented by their China policy. For example, in view of the
commitment to Japan's postwar claims, John D. Gregory, Assistant Head
of the Far Eastern Department in the British Foreign Office, felt that "we
must . . . decide whether we are morally justified in giving [the Chinese]
any sort of encouragement . . . in regard to possible advantages to be
derived from throwing in their lot with us."[94] But moral arguments did
not carry any weight.

The Allied Powers, however, were not alone in betraying China; the
United States, which had recently joined the war as an associated power
and on whom China depended as a supporter of its new diplomacy, also
perpetrated a number of betrayals. Although the US had professed its
special friendship many times over many years, it failed time and again
to give credible assistance to the Chinese government. Looking at Sino-
American relations during the war, one can argue that America's self-
proclaimed friendship with China was merely a bubble that vanished
when China turned to it for help. At the war's inception, Secretary of
State William Jennings Bryan wrote to President Woodrow Wilson, "We
shall avoid anything that can possibly bring us into collision with the
belligerent powers."[95] This, of course, included assisting China. Robert
Lansing, Bryan's successor in 1915, was even more frank.[96] He told
Reinsch, "It would be Quixotic to the extreme to allow the question of

---

[93] Zhang Zhengxiang to Waijiaobu, February 9, 1917, Wang Yunsheng, *Liushi nian lai
Zhongguo yu Riben* (China and Japan over the last sixty years) (Beijing: Sanlian shudian,
1980), VII: 79.

[94] Minutes by J. D. Gregory, February 16, 1917, PRO, FO371/2910.

[95] Bryan to Wilson, August 29, 1914, Library of Congress, Bryan Papers, General Correspondence, 30.

[96] For a study on Lansing and Japan and China, see Burton F. Beers, *Vain Endeavor: Robert
Lansing's Attempts to End the American–Japanese Rivalry* (Durham, NC: Duke University
Press, 1962).

China's territorial integrity to entangle the United States in international difficulties."[97] Lansing's admission was not an aberration, but an extension of long-standing American policy. Almost one century earlier, John Quincy Adams had declared,

Wherever the standard of freedom and independence has been or shall be unfurled, there will her heart, her benedictions, and her prayers be. But she goes not abroad in search for monsters to destroy. She is the well-wisher to the freedom and independence of all. She is the champion and vindicator only of her own.[98]

The promised American financial aid for China never was implemented; in fact, the United States did not provide one cent for China after it finally joined the war. As Reinsch wrote in his memorandum to Wilson, "The United States, though assisting all other Allies financially, could not contribute one dollar toward maintaining the financial independence of China as undivided attention was needed to the requirements of the west front."[99] Reinsch further commented that China's gaining financial support from the United States "was undreamt of" by the US, and it received no assistance whatsoever.[100] What China got from the US was the Lansing–Ishii agreement, which the United States signed with Japan in early November 1917. In that agreement, the United States government recognized that Japan had special interests in China.[101]

The State Department even kept its minister in Beijing in the dark about the contents of the agreement. When Reinsch was told by his Japanese counterpart, he angrily sent a telegram to Lansing on November 4, 1917 to complain.[102] Moreover, China had not been consulted or informed by the United States despite the fact that its national interests were keenly affected. When confronted by Wellington Koo, the Chinese minister to Washington, Lansing justified his silence with a bizarre excuse. He told Koo, "In order to avoid any question of China giving assent to the understanding reached in the notes, I had abstained mentioning the negotiations to him [Koo] during their progress or advising his government in any way of the subjects being discussed." His silence "had been deliberate and because I wished to keep China from an embarrassing situation." Regarding the phrases "special interests," Mr. Lansing was evasive, telling Koo that the phrase "was merely stating an axiom and nothing more."

---

[97] Lansing to Reinsch, *FRUS, 1914, Supp. 1*, 189–90.

[98] John Q. Adams: "Fourth of July Oration," 1821, *Niles' Weekly Register*, July 21, 1821, quoted from Ernest R. May, ed., *American Foreign Policy* (New York, 1963), 64–67.

[99] Reinsch, *An American Diplomat in China*, 337.

[100] Ibid., 296.   [101] Department of State, ed., *FRUS*, II: 432–51.

[102] State Department, Washington DC: National Archive, 10-15-6 M341, Roll 25, 793.94/589.

Koo retorted that "if it was an axiom, why was it stated?"[103] Lansing himself knew perfectly well that this phrase was what Japan wanted most and Japan took full advantage of it. Lansing was haunted by its repercussions for quite some time.[104] To many in the Chinese social elite and their government, China had been sacrificed to American self-interest.[105] Naturally, the Lansing–Ishii agreement was a huge blow to China's new diplomatic efforts, and it is amazing that Chinese determination was not shaken. After learning of the existence of this agreement, the Chinese government declared that "[t]he principle adopted by the Chinese government towards the friendly nations has always been one of justice and equality" and "the Chinese government will not allow herself to be bound by any agreement entered into by other nations."[106] This response was still quite in tune with China's ongoing diplomatic efforts to counter further injustice.

How can we explain the Lansing–Ishii agreement? The United States, like the Allied countries, seemed to have made a deal with Japan at the expense of China to solve problems in US–Japan relations. Like the Allied countries, the United States wanted Japan to stay in the war, especially after Russia had withdrawn. One reason for the Lansing–Ishii agreement was the United States' assumption that Japanese cooperation in the war was vital. As Lansing wrote happily, "Complete and satisfactory understandings upon the matter of naval cooperation in the Pacific for the purpose of attaining the common object against Germany and her Allies have been reached between the representative of the Imperial Japanese Navy, who is attached to the Special Mission of Japan, and the representative of the United States Navy."[107] For the United States, consideration of China's sovereignty and territorial integrity was of only secondary importance to securing Japanese cooperation.

---

[103] Robert Lansing, *War Memoirs of Robert Lansing* (Indianapolis and New York: The Bobbs–Merrill company, 1935), 303–04.

[104] Ibid., 302.

[105] This agreement contained a secret protocol, however, declaring that the two nations would "not take advantage of the present conditions to seek special rights or privileges in China which would abridge the rights of the subjects or citizens of other friendly states." For the content of the protocol, see Department of State, *FRUS, the Lansing papers, 1914–1920*, 450–51. According to Akira Iriye, this secret protocol "was more in accordance with Wilsonian principles. To have had to keep it a secret was ironical and unfortunate, for not being aware of its existence," Iriye comments, "the Chinese would protest vehemently against the Lansing–Ishii agreement." See Iriye, *The Cambridge History of American Foreign Relations*, vol. III: *The Globalizing of America, 1913–1945* (New York: Cambridge University Press, 1993), 48.

[106] "Declaration of the Chinese Government Concerning the Notes Exchanged Between the Governments of the United States and Japan During November 2, 1917," November 12, 1917, Washington DC: National Archive, State Department, 10–15–6 M341, Roll 25, 793.94/603.

[107] Reinsch, *An American Diplomat in China*, 309.

The terms of the Lansing–Ishii agreement are confusing. The State Department realized this and authorized Reinsch to deliver an explanatory note to the effect that the Japanese interests referred to "were of an economic, not a political nature."[108] But as Reinsch points out in his memoir, the agreement easily gave the impression that it "might include also certain political influence or preference" for Japan. Its signing was "unfortunate" and unnecessary.[109] Moreover, Japan might explain the terms as it wished. Commenting on the American explanation that Lansing–Ishii agreement merely gave Japan special interests in China with respect to commercial and industrial relations, British Foreign officials laughed in private, pointing out that "it looks as if the US government were naive enough to believe so. Obviously, Japan had a different definition of this special interest."[110] The British ambassador to Japan, Sir Coyningham Greene, also commented in his confidential report to Balfour, "Indeed, it almost looks as if the US government, after setting out with a disposition to confine Japan's special interest to those portions of China to which her possessions are contiguous, had thought better of this intention at the last moment and had decided to admit them in the whole of China, but with the addition of a somewhat lame qualifying rider, which does not amount to much more than 'saving face' in drafting the agreement." Greene concluded that the agreement had become more a source of embarrassment than of agreement to the contracting parties. The whole declaration turns upon the interpretation of its phraseology, and this was likely to open the door for argument, not to say controversy. In fact, the agreement raised more questions than it decided. According to Greene, when one high Japanese official was asked what would happen if neither party could agree in an argument as to the interpretation of any "special interest," the Japanese (Viscount Motono) laconically replied "ce sera le plus fort qui aura le dessus" which may be loosely rendered as "it will be the top dog that gets the bone."[111]

Conflicting Allied goals create deadlock

Although the Allied Powers did their best to hobble China's efforts to achieve its war aims, they were very focused on pursuing their own aims in China. Significant differences among the Allied countries' goals in China, and between those of the United States and the Allies, meant

---

[108] Reinsch to Lansing, November 4, 1917, Washington DC: National Archive, State Department, 10–15–6 M341, Roll 25, 793.94/587.

[109] Reinsch, *An American Diplomat in China*, 310–13; see also Washington DC: National Archive, State Department, 10–15–6 M341, Roll 25, 793.94/586–1/2.

[110] PRO, FO371/3176/410.   [111] PRO, FO371/3176/412-14.

that, in many cases, their goals simply were not compatible. Lansing made this point clear when he informed Reinsch, "While desirous of cooperating in a general way with the governments at war with Germany, it is not always possible for us to support their policies entirely since our situation as belligerents is not identical with theirs."[112] One good example was the reversal of American support for China's joining the war in late spring 1917. The United States had become unhappy with Japan's sudden change of heart on China's entry into the war and the fact that Chinese society was being torn by internal fighting over the issue of its war participation. On June 4, 1917, the United States sent a diplomatic note advising China that its declaration of war was only of secondary importance to its domestic stability. This note outraged the Allied countries, especially Japan, and clearly indicated a cooling of American support for China's entry into the war.[113]

The lack of a coherent policy in the Allied camp presented problems for China's war effort. The inability of the Allies and the American governments to agree among themselves regarding Chinese participation was, to a great extent, responsible for the final meagerness of China's contribution. This lack of cooperative spirit and of respect for China was especially evident in the case of Japan. The Japanese endeavored to keep China alienated and suspicious of the Western powers so as to isolate it. Having first prevented China's entering the war, Japan then discredited the Chinese by preventing their being of any real use or service to the Allies. Japan also engaged in wholesale misrepresentation of Allied war aims.

As had been the case with the labor recruitment programs, it was not only the Allied governments who varied in their China policy; different agencies within the same government sometimes pursued incompatible agendas. This situation made it difficult for one member of the Allied camp to determine what it really wanted to achieve with its China policy. A case in point is Britain. The Foreign Office and the War Office held different views regarding China's participation in the war; this created uncertainty among British policy makers and largely explains why the British did not take a decision on the issue until April of 1917. The War Office was especially suspicious of Japan's sudden change of heart.[114] In a top-secret memorandum, War Office officials argued that Britain should not support China's entry into the war because it would give the Japanese an opportunity to extend their control in China. The memo

[112] *FRUS, 1917, Supp. 2*, I: 689–90.
[113] See State Department, 10-15-6 M341, Roll 25, 793.94/589, in National Archive, College Park, Lansing to Reinsch, June 4, 1917, *FRUS, 1917*, 48.
[114] War Office, March 8, 1917 PRO, wo106/36.

criticized the Foreign Office for having "gone rather light-heartedly to work with China in the last few weeks, but it is not too late to draw back and tell China what the American Ambassador [*sic*] told her, that she should remain content with the severance of diplomatic relations with Germany and not be carried away with enthusiasm which will result in her becoming an active ally of the Entente." In the margin of the same memo, one official from the general staff further commented, "As far as I am aware, the Foreign Office has consulted neither the General Staff nor the War Cabinet before taking steps to get China to declare war on Germany." He suggested that the Foreign Office "be asked to support the American Minister in advising the Chinese government that their action should go no further than the rupture of diplomatic relations."[115]

The War Office's memorandum obviously challenged the China policy established by the Foreign Office, which had declared earlier that the British government had "considered the advantages and disadvantages under present circumstances, of China eventually coming into the war, have decided that the former outweigh the latter, and that it would be impossible to reverse their policy of 1915, even were there any reason for so doing."[116] After reading the War Office memo, members of the Foreign Office tried to set the record straight by replying that "proposals amounting to conditions for China's entry into the war began to emanate from Peking, and the Japanese and French governments began to press their consideration on us. On February 17 it was clear that we had to make up our minds whether or not we were prepared to welcome China's intervention." As for the Japanese motive, which the War Office memorandum emphasized, the Foreign Office realized that "it appears very desirable to review the situation in the light of the delay that has occurred and of the considerations brought forward by the War Office."[117] Given this challenge, the Foreign Office understandably hesitated to go further and welcome the Chinese declaration of war. The Foreign Office conceded that "It is not therefore clear why we are trying to make China become a belligerent. Would it not be much better to let Germany declare war in any case on China? There might be less trouble in China in consequence."[118]

For a moment, the Foreign Office seriously considered reversing its existing policy. On March 12, 1917, the Foreign Office Secretary Balfour telegraphed Alston in Beijing, to ask his evaluation regarding the question whether "it would be desirable to reverse the policy which this country has favoured since the early days of the war. It may perhaps be still possible

---

[115] March 7, 1917, PRO, wo106/36.
[116] Balfour to Alston, February 20, 1917, PRO, fo405/222.
[117] FO memo, March 9, 1917, PRO, wo106/36.
[118] FO memo, March 14, 1917, PRO, wo106/36.

to do so, but I am very unwilling to take this course without good reason. And I should be glad to have your appreciation of the whole situation."[119] Alston immediately responded by saying that "matters are progressing as satisfactorily as can be expected and that at no time have I seen any reason to sound a note of alarm with regard to the Allied policy." Alston concluded that "reversal of our policy at present stage would however in any event be as disastrous as it seems to me unnecessary."[120]

Despite the firm answer from its diplomat in China, the Foreign Office did not make up its mind until April of 1917 when both the Foreign Office and the War Office found they shared the same strong desire to get rid of Germans in China. On the strength of this common ground, both agencies finally agreed that Britain should go ahead and welcome China's entry into the war. This background also points to why Britain eventually refused to support China's military expedition to Europe.

If the major consideration behind Britain's support for China's participation in the war was to get the Germans out of China, the most important goal of French support was gaining Chinese military assistance. France had been particularly keen to get China into the war. General Ferdinand Foch, the French field marshal and commander in chief of Allied forces during the war, was a major advocate for bringing a Chinese military force to Europe.[121] Even before China had declared war on Germany, he had argued, in a letter to the French prime minister,

The entry of China into the struggle will allow this recruitment [of laborers] to come to an end and to be replaced by the dispatch to France of Chinese military units which would be used at the Front. It seems, in effect, that China must be asked to establish for us pioneer battalions of 1,200 to 1,500 men each. The battalions would be manned by Chinese, taken into the regular army, and helped only by some French staff officers, non-commissioned officers, and interpreters. Some Chinese senior officers would be needed for general supervision of the battalions. Given the population of China, the number of battalions which can be raised is theoretically limitless, even by recruiting in the north. It seems that we could ask the Chinese government to send us henceforth seventy to eighty battalions of 1,200 to 1,500 men each. These battalions would be used at first on work in the support zone, then used, progressively, in the firing zone on road and rail works and above all on fortifications . . . Perhaps it would be possible to attach one or two battalions to each of our army corps, perhaps, later, to attach one to each infantry division . . . Furthermore, this great military step would free for us a certain number of territorial battalions. It seems to me that this idea is particularly interesting, and that it should be implemented and pursued.[122]

[119] FO to Alston, March 12, 1917, PRO, wo106/36.
[120] Alston to FO, March 13, 1917, PRO, wo106/36.
[121] Ferdinand Foch (1851–1929), French marshal and commander in chief of Allied forces during the First World War.
[122] General Foch's secret report to the prime minister, August 11, 1917, Vincennes, 16N2450, GQG, 6498.

Foch's enthusiasm for Chinese military forces, to some extent, grew out of his high opinion of the Chinese laborers who had already been active in France since 1916. At the request of French military authority, and especially owing to Foch's urging, the Foreign Ministry at Quai d'Orsay had, on August 29, 1917, presented to China the general idea of using a Chinese contingent.[123]

The Chinese government, as a matter of fact, was willing and even eager to send troops to Europe. As we have seen, China placed enormous stock in participating in the war. Its high expectations for the postwar world order, its hopes for membership at the postwar peace conference, and its strong desire and motivation to prove itself a responsible member and player in the world arena all caused China to take joining the war seriously. As early as April, before China's official entry into the war, Prime Minister Duan had told Reinsch that "China was ready to do her part in the war, that she could furnish a force of 100,000 or 200,000 men, or a million or even more, if only the armament could be provided."[124] Later Reinsch further confirmed that Duan "was quite willing to send a big army to Europe."[125] In his telegram to Robert Lansing of October 2, 1917, Reinsch reported that Duan "personally and through his Vice Minister of War, Hsu [Xu Shuzheng], has had long conversations with me on the question of sending troops to Europe. He considers it inopportune to announce an extensive program because of probable diplomatic opposition, but he is willing to begin immediately preparations for sending to Europe from 10 to 50 divisions, 12,000 men each."[126] For China to participate militarily in the war was, as Koo confided to his government, "a brilliant move" (*miao zhuo*). It only stood to gain, especially with respect to enhancing its international position.[127] On September 1, 1917, Prime Minister Duan Qirui clearly told Conty that China wanted to cooperate effectively with the Allied side militarily. China was willing to send hundreds of thousands of soldiers to France if other Allied countries, especially Japan, did not oppose this and if the United States would provide some financial support. Quai d'Orsay immediately consulted Japan, the United States, Britain, Italy, and Russia for their opinion. These countries expressed agreement with the principle of Chinese military cooperation.[128] On September 14, the Chinese cabinet officially

[123] Quai d'Orsay, NS, CXXXVII: 19–20; Vincennes, 7N389/Chine/1917–1918.
[124] *FRUS, 1917, Supp. 1*, 447.   [125] Reinsch, *An American Diplomat in China*, 299.
[126] *FRUS, 1917, Supp. 2*, I: 691–92.
[127] Koo to Waijiaobu, Extremely Secret, September 11, 1917, Zhongguo di er li shi dang an guan, beiyang wai jiao bu dang, 03-36/18-(1).
[128] Conty to Quai d'Orsay, September 3, 1917, Quai d'Orsay, NS, Chine, CXXXVII: 19–20; Vincennes, 7N389/Chine/1917–1918, "Fa Ma dai ban hui wu zong zhang wen da" (Questions and Answers between the French and Chinese foreign minister), September 13, 1917, Zhongguo di er li shi dang an guan, beiyang wai jiao bu dang, 03–36/18–(1).

declared that it was in favor of sending troops to France. In a secret telegram to its minister in Paris, the Waijiaobu indicated that if the detailed negotiations went well, China could send about twenty or even thirty thousand Chinese soldiers to France within six months. China even said that it could send more if France so desired.[129] In early September 1917, in addition to the offer of sending soldiers to Europe, China proposed to offer two cruisers and three destroyers for patrolling eastern waters.[130]

Thus, from the outset, it was clear that the Chinese were willing to dispatch troops. The major obstacle was that none of the Allied Powers but France were ready to accept a Chinese military expedition to Europe. Only one man on the British side was interested, the military attaché of the British legation in Beijing, D. S. Robertson (1874–1919). When he pushed the idea of using Chinese labor he also supported involving the Chinese army. In his letter dated May 17, 1917, he wrote, "I am firmly persuaded that we could do a lot with the Chinese rank and file. They are excellent material, as can be seen by a visit to one of the coolies' battalions." He also had in mind not only the military value of the Chinese, but also the possible extension of British influence in China by including Chinese troops in the fighting. He argued that by Britain's supporting China's military presence in Europe, "we are being given a unique chance now to extend our influence in China after the war, and if we don't take it now we shall pay the penalty later."[131] However, the consensus within the British government was that bringing in Chinese troops would be counterproductive from the perspective of their military value, the British relationship with Japan, transportation logistics, and more importantly, the fact that use of Chinese troops "would presumably be most prejudicial to our prestige" since it would indicate Western weakness and could undermine the British position in its colonies.[132] When the French suggested using Chinese troops, the British privately ridiculed them for "becoming too fertile of ideas."[133] They argued that having Chinese soldiers in Europe was "wasting Allied tonnage for which they will receive no military return whatever" because, according to the British, even the best Chinese troops would not "stand shell fire on the western front for five minutes."[134] The British officials concluded, "It is impossible to imagine a greater waste

---

[129] Attaché Militaire à Ministre de Guerre, September 15, 1917, Quai d'Orsay, NS, Chine, CXXXVII: 51–52; "Fa ju Fa Hua gongshi dian, September 15, 1917" (Telegram to Chinese minister in France), "Zong zhang huiwu Fa Ma dai ban wen da, Sept. 21, 1917" (French Interviews with Chinese foreign minister), Zhongguo Li Shi di er dang an guan, beiyang wai jiao bu dang, 03–36/18–(1).
[130] PRO, FO371/2913/173091.
[131] Robertson to WO, May 17, 1917, PRO, WO106/35.
[132] PRO, FO371/2913/173327.   [133] PRO, FO371/2913/175633.
[134] PRO, FO371/2913/198562.

of time, trouble, equipment, money and tonnage" than using Chinese troops in Europe.[135]

Britain never revealed this internal consensus to the French; it simply put the ball back in their court. On November 13, the British War Office told France that it raised no objection to the French scheme, subject to the following reservations:

1. The Chinese force should be raised as far as possible from existing Chinese military formations.
2. The draftees should be organized in such a way that the British legation at Beijing was satisfied that recruiting Chinese labor for the British armies would not be adversely affected.
3. Transportation of the force should be arranged in such a way that the British naval authorities were satisfied that the program already arranged for the transportation of coolies to England for work in France would not be interfered with.[136]

These conditions were framed in such a way that would make it extremely difficult for China and France to carry out their plans. But once again, it was the Japanese who presented the biggest obstacle. Initially, the Japanese foreign minister told France that Japan "had no objection to this operation."[137] But Japan soon changed its tune. On October 13, 1917, the French ambassador to Tokyo reported, "I am afraid that Japan will not welcome it and it would be opportune if our demand was at least supported by England."[138] Since Japan itself had not sent soldiers to fight for the Allied cause on European battlefields, it follows that it would not want China to have the honor of doing so.

However, with even this lukewarm response from its Allies, China and France were determined to pursue the idea of using Chinese military forces in Europe. General Foch pushed especially hard. On September 29, 1917, in close cooperation with China, especially its military attaché in Paris, the French War Ministry worked out a detailed plan for engaging Chinese troops in France. It was entitled "Note on the Subject of Military Aid to be provided to France by China." The note began by claiming that "the principle of Chinese military aid for France was acknowledged by the French and Chinese governments." The tone of the note was optimistic, although it admitted a possible transportation challenge, and the main focus was how many Chinese soldiers France needed. The note suggested that once transportation was worked out, France might request forty pioneer battalions (40,000 soldiers). The note also suggested that China send a mission to France to make the scheme run smoothly. It

---

[135] PRO, FO371/2913/205881.   [136] Quai d'Orsay, NS, Chine, CXXXVII.
[137] Ibid., 54.   [138] Ibid., 104.

even discussed such concrete issues as where Chinese soldiers should be drafted and how many officers and interpreters should be in each battalion.[139]

After the plan was completed, negotiations on technical issues were immediately undertaken. China again made it clear to France that it could easily provide at least forty pioneer battalions and accepted the French suggestion to establish an advance military mission. In late 1917, China did send a mission to France with General Tang Zaili at its head.[140] In early November, the Chinese vice minister of war informed Prime Minister Duan Qirui that 40,000 soldiers were ready to go. They could be on their way to France immediately if the promised financial support from the United States was forthcoming.[141] The French military attaché confirmed their readiness. In a report to his superior in Paris, he wrote that as far as the Chinese government was concerned, not only had the project of the military expedition been agreed to, but also it was very near realization, for it only depended on American financing to facilitate it.[142]

Even though the powers would not object outright to the expedition plan, the success of the project still depended on adequate transportation and financial support. France and China tried hard to gain both, but they were not successful. The Chinese engaged in intense negotiations with the United States about the possibility of a loan. In the beginning, Prime Minister Duan hoped to secure 200,000,000 Mexican dollars from the United States to cover the expense of armaments and transportation for half a million troops. The United States promised to give this proposal "careful consideration."[143] China soon reduced its request to 25 million dollars, initially sending only 40,000 soldiers.[144] By late December 1917, Lansing told Reinsch that "The President, and State, War and Treasury Departments all favor financial assistance to China for the military expedition. The matter awaits approval of the Allied council."[145]

But hopes for financial support for the program were destined for disappointment. The United States position seemed to keep changing, and China never received any financial support for its operation to Europe.[146] The search for transportation also failed. France negotiated with Britain and Japan on this issue, arguing that an effective Chinese military operation would give the Allies real advantages. From the political perspective,

---

[139] Ibid., 62–63.   [140] Vincennes, 4N63/cooperation/Chinois.
[141] De Martel, confidential telegram to Quai d'Orsay, November 9, 1917, Quai d'Orsay, NS, Chine, CXXXVII.
[142] PRO, WO106/35 French Liaison Office.   [143] *FRUS, 1917, Supp. 2*, 692.
[144] Martel, telegram, Beijing, October 12, 1917, Quai d'Orsay, NS, Chine, CXXXVII: 100.
[145] *FRUS, 1917, Supp. 2.*
[146] Chen Sanjing, "Zhongguo pai bing canjia Ouzhan zhi jiaoshe," in *Zhonghua minguo lishi yu wenhua taolunji* (Taipei, 1984), 111.

it would associate the Chinese government more closely with the action against Germany. From the military perspective, it would obtain educated and well-trained soldiers that the crisis of strength did not permit the Allies to ignore. "Besides, these men are particularly apt at excavation work and at mine work that is now required in the preparation of every attack – their output would incontestably be much superior to that of workers who are not militarily trained."[147]

By the late 1917, there seemed little chance of Britain and Japan assisting with transportation, and France realized that it had to rely on itself if it wanted the project to work. Arranging the transport through its own resources was beyond its capability, and yet France persisted because the failure of this project not only meant that France would not receive Chinese military support; more importantly, French prestige was also at stake. As its military attaché in China argued, total abandonment of the scheme would bring the French representatives' efforts to nought and would be a severe blow to French military influence in China.[148]

As for the Chinese, the failure was a great loss of face, especially for Prime Minister Duan who was fully involved in the project. It was also an obvious blow to China's new diplomacy because the military expedition had become a central part of China's war policy. Because so much was at stake, neither side gave up easily.

With strong lobbying from both governments, especially from General Foch, the plan appeared to have been resuscitated in January of 1918. Foch happily informed the French military attaché in China that, "the question of sending Chinese engineer battalions to France has not been abandoned. On the contrary, the principle has been acknowledged by the Superior War Council and the United States. Realization depends on the means of transport, which are currently under consideration. I will keep you informed of the results of this study."[149] In another letter to the same attaché in January, Foch expressed further optimism: he wrote that the transportation of the Chinese contingents could begin in early April and would be carried out gradually.[150] In the middle of February of 1918, the French also notified General Tang Zaili that in a meeting of January 21, 1918, France had won a favorable consideration on the Chinese military forces in France. "The inter-Allied staff headquarters in Versailles put forward the opinion that the Chinese cooperation was useful and that financial aid from the United States was desirable." Moreover, "according to a recent communication with our embassy in Washington,

[147] Quai d'Orsay, NS, Chine, CXXXVII: 127–28.   [148] PRO, wo/106/35.
[149] Vincennes, 16N3012/Chine–Japon.
[150] Foch to French military attaché in Beijing, January 1918, Secret, French Liaison Office, War Office, PRO, wo/106/35.

the British government made it known to the federal government that it is willing to favor this transport" and the United States also indicated that its financial support seemed in order. Japan had expressed no further objections. All this prompted France to happily declare to Tang, "In these conditions, one can presume that the first echelon of 10,000 men will be able to embark from China as soon as next April."[151]

But the French optimism proved premature. The major powers gave lip service to the project without taking any concrete action. Neither funding nor transportation materialized. In desperation, France at one point even toyed with the idea of financing the Chinese contingent itself. The French military attaché pressed on March 7, 1918, for the provision of the credits necessary to enable the Chinese government to organize the first Chinese contingent for France as soon as possible: A sum of 1,500,000 dollars was required for the first contingent of 10,000 men. Unfortunately, this effort, too, was in vain. Given the many disappointments it had experienced in this project, the Chinese government finally lost patience. On March 22, 1918, the Duan Qirui government asked the French for a definite reply within ten days as to whether a Chinese military expedition was still feasible.[152]

On April 4, 1918, the French military authority admitted to Quai d'Orsay that "the executive committee of importation has decided it is impossible to set aside the tonnage asked for to transport the Chinese contingent to France; the program which had been drawn up for Chinese cooperation on the western front is not realizable, and in consequence the offer of the Chinese government has had to be refused." De Martel, the senior French diplomat in China, suggested to Quai d'Orsay that if a Chinese expeditionary force could not be sent to the French front, one or two model Chinese battalions should be transported. De Martel stated that this measure would enable Duan to "save face" and would also reduce the possible loss of French prestige in China because of its failure to manage Chinese troop dispatch. His advice was rejected.[153] On April 6, Quai d'Orsay instructed its minister in Beijing to tell the Chinese that "in the present circumstances, it is impossible to find the loan necessary for these transports. Thus, we must, to our great regret, give up on seeing courageous Chinese troops take their place next to ours on the French front."[154] The French Ministry of the Army also asked its military attaché in Beijing to inform Prime Minister Duan that the French government "regretfully finds itself obliged to give up on Chinese cooperation

---

[151] Vincennes, 7N398/Chine/1917–1918.   [152] PRO, wo/106/35.
[153] Quai d'Orsay, 1918–1929, Chine, XL: 80.
[154] Quai d'Orsay, 1918–1929, Chine, XL: 75.

because of the impossibility of allocating the necessary tonnage to the transport of Chinese contingents."[155] Accordingly, the French government bluntly admitted to the Chinese that "it is in the common interest to leave the Chinese government free to dispose of its troops as it may seem fit and to forego the prospect of Chinese military co-operation in France."[156]

The saga of a proposed Chinese military expedition thus ended in quiet disappointment.[157] Obviously, China had made a sincere effort to make it succeed. The Chinese government's genuine intention to help the Allied cause was also reflected in its leasing of almost all confiscated German vessels for Allied use even though its own merchants could have used them to enhance Chinese trading capabilities.[158] Sir Charles Addis, British director of the Hong Kong and Shanghai Banking Corporation, summarized China's contribution this way:

It was a memorable day in the history of the war when China deliberately took her place by the side of the Allies in this great world conflict of right against might. The material assistance which China was able to render was not inconsiderable. The work done by the Chinese labour corps in France did much to facilitate the advance of our troops, and in our mercantile marine Chinese subjects gave up their lives in order that our men might be supplied with food and with the equipment of war.[159]

China's attitude toward the repatriation of Germans further indicated its intent to accommodate the Allies. Although all the Allied countries except for France had only a lukewarm interest in China's military participation, they all shared a common interest in sweeping German interests out of China and repatriating the Germans. In this way, German competition in China would be eliminated and the business that Germans had built up would fall into Allied hands. Bertrand Russell observed that what the Allies wished was "to confiscate German property in China, to expel

---

[155] Quai d'Orsay, 1918–1929, Chine, XL: 79.
[156] PRO, WO 106/35/French Liaison Office; Quai d'Orsay, 1918–1929, Chine, XL: 69–71; Quai d'Orsay, 1918–1929, Chine, XL: 87.
[157] China did send troops to Siberia in 1918.
[158] Waijiobu, "Shou Xie Tianxi Chen" (Report from Xie Tianxi), October 3, 1917; "Shou Shanghai Zongshanghui dian" (Telegram from Shanghai Commercial Association), October 17, 1917, "Shou Shanghai Zongshanghui dian (Telegram from Shanghai Commercial Association), August 16, August 31, 1917, Zhongguo di er li shi dang an guan, beiyang wai jiao bu dang, 03–36/30–(6), 03–36/30–2. China detained three German warships in the South China sea (one was destroyed by Germany) and captured nine commercial vessels. It rented all nine of them to the Allies.
[159] The League of Nations and China: Extracts from Speechs Delivered by Viscount Bryce, Wang Zhengting, and Others, at Caxton Hall, Westminster, May 15, 1919 (a booklet published in London, 1919), 14.

Germans living in China, and to prevent, as far as possible, the revival of German trade in China after the war."[160]

After China officially broke off relations with Germany, the Allied countries collectively presented China with their own definition of a complete and effective rupture; it was drawn up by the French minister on March 31, 1917, and received the general approval of Allied diplomats in China. The document described the actions China should take:

1. Declare war;
2. Abrogate Chinese–German and Chinese–Austrian treaties regarding customs tariffs and Boxer indemnities;
3. Intern or expel enemy subjects;
4. Liquidate in agreement with the Allies German and Austrian concessions;
5. Sequester German firms;
6. Requisition enemy ships, to be either sold or leased to the Allies;
7. Settle outstanding claims presented by the respective Allied legations.[161]

From this definition, one can easily see that the top Allied priority was to get rid of the Germans. The British foreign secretary Balfour made this point very clear by further stipulating how the French requirements should be carried out: All Germans in China should be expelled or interned; the German concessions at Hankou and Tianjin should be liquidated; and all German properties of whatever kind in China should be sequestered.[162] In its further instruction to its diplomats abroad, the British Foreign Office indicated that the United Kingdom

attach[ed] increasing importance to the development of measures threatening Germany's economic recovery after the war as a means of hastening the conclusion of a satisfactory peace . . . it is essential that Allied firms and subjects abroad should take the fullest advantage of war conditions and the effect . . . to destroy or capture the trade of their German competitors and to prevent accumulation of supplies for post-war shipment to Germany.

The Foreign Office further expressed its confidence in the expectation of "full cooperation" from other countries, including the United States, on this issue. "In countries which are at war with Germany or which have severed relations with her, it is highly desirable to create movement in favour of effective liquidation of enemy undertakings as a definite

---

[160] Bertrand Russell, *The Problem of China* (New York: Century Co., 1922), 148. See also British Foreign Office to Jordan, Secret, February 11, 1916, PRO, FO371/2647.
[161] Alston to Balfour, April 1, 1917, PRO, FO405/222/45–46.
[162] Foreign Office Memo to France, March 20, 1917, Quai d'Orsay, NS, Chine, CXXXV: 227–29.

contribution to the Allied cause."[163] As Minister Jordan stated, "The one outstanding question which dwarfs all others is the deportation of enemy subjects."[164]

China's general policy was to cooperate with the Allies and try to repatriate as many enemy subjects as possible, and their effort depended on the Allies furnishing transport for repatriation. But cooperation did not necessarily mean that China let itself be pushed. From the beginning China insisted that internment or expulsion would only be adopted if the necessity for such measures was proven. The Chinese government would be prepared to consider the removal of specified enemy subjects who were certified by the Allied ministers to be undesirable. China claimed that its regulations were based on the same rules enforced in the United States of America and Japan. Unless Japan and the United States changed their deportation policies regarding the Germans, it would be unfair to press China to do more.[165] As a matter of fact, the Chinese were right to believe that the Allies' measures were discriminatory. As Jordan reported, the Chinese "see enemy subjects comfortably settled across the water in Japan" and ask why "the Allies did not press Japan to adopt similar measures of repatriation."[166] But the Allied countries only pushed China, charging that the latter's deportation policy was "unsatisfactory with regard to the questions of interning enemy subjects and disposing of their property." Balfour supported the French initiative to press the Chinese government "to deport all enemy subjects with a view to their internment in Australia."[167] On October 30, 1917, representatives of the seven Allied Powers presented to China twelve complaints, most of them relating to Germans in China. The Chinese government was reminded that "instead of devoting its energies single-heartedly to performing in the fullest manner its duties toward its associates," it had "engaged its force almost entirely in internal affairs in an attempt, by military means, to solve the internal difficulties." This note was a frank warning that China's official inaction during the war would be to its disadvantage at the peace conference.[168]

However, slow progress in deporting enemy subjects from China was not only caused by the Chinese. China worked hard at the task, as Jordan admitted: "the Chinese have committed themselves to the task and are

---

[163] FO Circular to its Ministers or Ambassadors, November 15, 1917, PRO, FO371/3177/475–476.

[164] Jordan to Macleay, January 15, 1918, PRO, FO350/16/54.

[165] Boppe to Quai d'Orsay, November 26, 1917, Quai d'Orsay, NS, Chine, CXXXVII.

[166] Jordan to FO, February 4, 1919, PRO, WO106/34.

[167] Bourne and Trotter, eds., *British Documents on Foreign Affairs: Reports and Papers from the Foreign Office Confidential Print, Series E, Asia*, XXII, 299–300.

[168] *The Eastern Miscellany* 15, no. 12: 207.

quite willing to carry it out, but not until the Allies make good the promises they gave when China entered the war. These related chiefly to the suspension of the indemnity and the revision of the tariff. In neither case have the Allies as a body kept faith with China."[169] Despite the fact that China received only "a very meagre and doubtful concession and the tariff revision has so far produced nothing except months of fruitless discussion," as Jordan further pointed out, the Chinese had "not sought to evade their obligations to take restrictive measures against enemy subjects. It is true that they favoured general internment and only agreed to deportation to Australia when they were convinced by us that they had themselves no effective means of enforcing internment. It is no fault of theirs that deportation has fallen through and in now reverting to internment we cannot expect them to guarantee it as an effective remedy." Jordan therefore concluded, "the Chinese government in spite of internal weakness has so far loyally carried out their obligations in the matter of preparation for deportation but added difficulties which have been imposed on them by provision of inadequate, and as they consider unsuitable, transport have produced an unfortunate impression."[170] Jordan reminded his government, "The Chinese have behaved very well in the matter and I hope in times to come it will always be remembered to their credit that at a moment when our fortunes were at their lowest ebb they took a step which not only committed them very deeply to the Allied cause, but exposed them to considerable risk in the future."

Jordan was right. The Allies should have blamed themselves rather than the Chinese for the series of deportation problems they encountered. The Allied countries themselves had great difficulty figuring out a firm and effective deportation policy. As Jordan complained, it was extremely difficult to "get the Allied representatives to adopt a common point of view." He was highly critical of the French attitude on this issue, pointing out that the French chargé d'affaires, de Martel, "has a remarkable gift for blundering."[171] Owing to lack of cooperation among the Allied countries, the deportation plan kept changing. For some time, they were interested in transporting Germans to Australia. China was cooperative and its minister for foreign affairs formally communicated to Jordan on January 31, 1918 that the Chinese government had decided to deport all enemy subjects to Australia as suggested by the Allies. In this note, China indicated that preparations would be commenced forthwith and "it is essential for [the] success of [the] scheme that shipping arrangements should now be

[169] Jordan to Langley, February 17, 1918, PRO, FO350/16/59.
[170] Jordan to FO, June 2, 1918, PRO, WO106/34.
[171] Jordan to Langley, April 15, 1918, PRO, FO350/16.

definitely settled."[172] But as the Chinese moved ahead to implement the plan, the Allied side abandoned the whole scheme because of problems which it should have foreseen. The first of these problems was deficiency of tonnage. As the British Foreign Office later admitted, "it was not foreseen, when the plan was first agreed to, that all the available tonnage in the Pacific would be required for transporting Czecho-Slovaks on their way to France." The second reason for the breakdown of the plan was a threat by the Germans: The German government let its enemies know that if German civilians were interned in Australia, Germany would make reprisals. This threat gave the Allied countries serious second thoughts. After all, the entire civil population of Belgium, as well as the population in the occupied parts of France, was under German domination.[173] The British government realized that "if the Chinese government were to proceed to repatriate all or any part of this German community against their wish they would at once resort to the same tactics as in the case of deportation and threaten violent reprisals against Belgians and civilians of other Allied nationalities in their power."[174]

The German threat was so serious that even the Vatican and the King of Spain appealed to the Allies not to carry out the proposed deportation plan on grounds of humanity, to avoid the suffering which retaliatory measures threatened by the German government would inflict on innocent persons.[175]

Under these circumstances, by June of 1918, the Allies had to give up the Australia scheme, intending to negotiate with Germany regarding an exchange of prisoners.[176] Jordan was very angry at the efforts wasted pursuing such an irresponsible Allied policy:

---

[172] Jordan to FO, January 31, 1918, PRO, FO371/3173/205; see also British Embassy to French Government, Paris, February 3, 1918, Quai d'Orsay, Asie 1918–1929, Chine, XXXVIII: 41–42.

[173] FO to Jordan, July 2, 1918, PRO, wo106/34; the German Government, through the Swiss, told the British government that if the Allies carried out the deportation plan [to Australia], Germany would "in the event of the measure being put into execution, hold not only the Chinese Government but also the British government responsible for all injuries which may thereby be caused to the lives, health and property of the Germans concerned" and "the German government will be compelled to resort to the severest retaliatory measures without any consideration whatever." Berlin, March 11, 1918, Quai d'Orsay, Asie 1918–1929, Chine, XXXVIII: 136–37.

[174] British embassy to the French government, Paris, June 29, 1918, Quai d'Orsay, Asie 1918–1929, Chine, XXXVIII: 211.

[175] British embassy to the French government, May 30, 1918, Quai d'Orsay, Asie 1918–1929, Chine, XXXVIII: 150–51; for the appeal from the Spanish king, see Spanish ambassador to Pichon, May 17, 1918, Quai d'Orsay, Asie 1918–1929, Chine, XXXVIII: 164; for Vatican appeal, see Vatican note to the French government, May 24, 1918, Quai d'Orsay, Asie 1918–1929, Chine, XXXVIII: 178.

[176] Britain to France, May 30, 1918, Quai d'Orsay, Asie 1918–1929, Chine, XXXVIII: 152.

Deportation is still hung up through lack of tonnage and the Chinese are naturally sick of the whole question. We have been spinning ropes of sand for the last three or four months and expect them to be made use of as a convenience. There is a limit to this sort of thing and it has nearly been reached in the present case. I know very well that every ton of shipping is probably far better employed in carrying American soldiers to France than in taking German women and children from China to Australia, but we ought to have foreseen this long ago and not to have yielded to the outcry for deportation unless we were prepared to carry it through.[177]

Even so, the Allied countries were soon pressing China to undertake another deportation scheme. According to British Secretary for Foreign Affairs Balfour, "The best course would be for the Allied ministers at Peking to consider whether . . . to insist on the Chinese government taking steps to intern the enemy civilians under a vigorous and effective system of supervision and control, and to suggest the most practical means of effecting such an internment."[178] Under Balfour's instruction, Jordan came up with an idea: interning Germans on a Chinese island called Liugongdao. But this plan failed for the same reason the first had, from fear of German retaliation. Jordan complained to Langley, "To me personally it was a bitter disappointment as I had practically carried on all the negotiations and had never anticipated the possibility of our yielding to German threats of reprisals. The Chinese have behaved very well and did not 'rub it in' as they might well have done."[179] In another personal letter, Jordan complained that "we cannot, in homely language, eat our cake and have it too." He specially blamed Japan's lack of cooperation on this issue and characterized the Japanese attitude as "criminal folly," which had "a huckstering spirit unworthy of a great nation."[180]

When the war ended, Britain and France were still pursuing the idea of deporting Germans from China. On December 14, 1918, the British Foreign Office told Jordan that he "should strongly urge the Chinese government to agree to repatriation of all enemy residents before peace is concluded."[181] Britain was "prepared to go even further . . . The expulsion should be enforced against enemy residents generally and not only against those whom the Chinese government may consider undesirable."[182] Therefore, by the beginning of 1919, the deportation scheme

---

[177] Jordan to Langley, May 7, 1918, PRO, FO350/16.
[178] British embassy to the French government, Paris, June 29, 1918, Quai d'Orsay, Asie 1918–1929, Chine, XXXVIII: 211.
[179] Jordan to Langley, August 14, 1918, PRO, FO350/16
[180] Jordan to Langley, August 2, 1918, PRO, FO350/16.
[181] FO to Jordan, December 14, 1918, PRO, FO371/3175.
[182] British Memo to French, December 20, 1918, Quai d'Orsay, 1918–1929, Chine, XXXIX: 55.

was resumed. This time it met with some success. Again, the Chinese government fully cooperated, agreeing in January to repatriate all enemy subjects from China.[183] The sequestration of enemy property was ordered to take effect from February 1, and repatriation of enemy aliens from March 1. The total number of Germans and Austrians in China when war was declared was not over 3,000, many of whom were interned only after a long delay.[184] In late February of 1919, 600 German women and children had been repatriated.[185] According to one newspaper report, in mid-March, nearly 1,000 German men, 400 women and 406 German children had been deported to Europe.[186]

In late June 1919, after its heartbreaking experience at the Paris Peace Conference, China notified the Allies that their scheme for further deportation of enemy subjects must be abandoned for the following reason: Repatriation measures hitherto adopted had only been acceptable to China because of its belief that the Allies would assist it in obtaining favorable consideration at the peace conference. Since China had been deeply disappointed in this expectation, the Chinese government did not want to resume the deportation.[187] The Allied deportation scheme ended on this bitter note.

China's involvement in the First World War is thus a story of frustrations. When China tried to contribute militarily, the lukewarm or confused British and American responses and Japan's lack of cooperation effectively stymied the Chinese efforts. But although China failed to send troops to Europe, it did manage to participate militarily in Siberia. In a report submitted to Reinsch on January 10, 1918, Major Walter S. Drysdale wrote, "Two thousand Russian soldiers were disarmed by Chinese troops on December 26, 1917, and escorted to the Siberian border." Afterward, many more Russian troops were disarmed and sent to their homes in Siberia by the Chinese. According to Drysdale, "All Russian soldiers disarmed and removed showed Bolshevik sympathies, [they] were considered a menace to good order and proper government in Harbin and in the zone of the Chinese Eastern Railway, and could not be depended on to protect the Allied interests in

---

[183] FO to Quai d'Orsay Memo, January 20, 1919, Quai d'Orsay, 1918–1929, Chine, xxxix: 86; Boppe to Quai d'Orsay, Beijing, January 24, 1919, Quai d'Orsay, 1918–1929, Chine, xxxix: 87–88.

[184] *New York Times*, February 26, 1919.

[185] Deutsche Gesandtschaft zum Auswärtigen Amt, Gesandtschaft file, March 5, 1919, Bundesarchiv, Koblenz, R85/vorl.4004, nr.183.E China.

[186] *The North China Daily News*, March 15, 1919; see also Chinese Minister in Paris to Quai d'Orsay, March 27, 1919, Quai d'Orsay, 1918–1929, Chine, xxxix: 154.

[187] See FO to Jordan, July 2, 1919; Jordan to FO, February 28, 1919; Jordan to FO, June 17, 1919, PRO, wo106/34.

Manchuria."[188] Moreover, some Chinese did join the war in France in a private capacity and volunteered to fight in Europe. One man from Shanghai named Zhu Yongzhang joined the French military where he served as a pilot when the war broke out. The French military authorities later awarded him a medal for his courageous action.[189] Yet, at the Paris Peace Conference both Japan and Great Britain charged that China had chosen not to contribute to the Allied cause during the war. In this they not only ignored the sacrifices made by Chinese laborers at the front, but also chose to forget their roles in the failure of the Chinese military expedition. Even more ironically, although the declared war between China and Germany did not bring the two sides to a direct military confrontation, the war policy ignited an undeclared civil war among Chinese warlords at home.

[188] Report of Major Walter S. Drysdale, on the military situation in north Manchuria, National Archive, College Park, war department files, document no. 2055-1RG 165, M14444, roll 2.

[189] "Ouzhou fei ji zheng zhong zhi zhong guo qing nian" (Chinese youth in European air war), *Xin qingnian* (New Youth) 2, no. 3 (1916).

Yuan Shikai: President of China, 1912–16. Yuan tried secretly to bring China into the Great War in 1914 and 1915.

Duan Qirui: Prime Minister of China during the First World War. Duan Qirui was the driving force behind China's war policy.

Liang Shiyi: an influential politician in early Republican China. He argued for China's entry into the war when the war had just started in Europe. The "Laborers as Soldiers" plan was his brainchild.

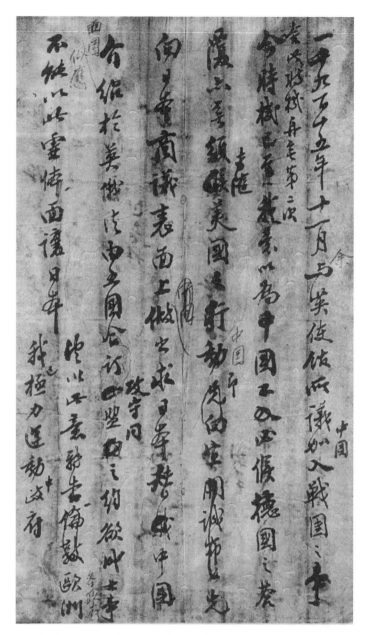

Handwritten note of Liang Shiyi: In this note, Liang indicated that he discussed with the British legation about China's entry into the war in 1915 and pushed for China's immediate action.

Liang Qichao: he was an influential leader of China's foreign policy public and played a crucial role in China's war policy in 1917. He went to Paris to push for China's case at the postwar peace conference.

Liang Qichao's handwritten letter to Duan Qirui on December 22, 1917 regarding Duan's plan to send Chinese military forces to Europe during the Great War.

Wellington Koo: Chinese diplomat. As a member of the Chinese delegation to the Paris Peace Conference, Koo was most instrumental and influential in bringing China's voice to world attention.

Part III

The Great War in Chinese domestic politics and foreign relations

6   The war within

What man is to blame for all this? The War Lord with his overweening
ambitions.

Charles Edward Russell[1]

Perhaps no single foreign policy initiative had a stronger impact on
China's domestic politics and society than its policy on the First World
War. Instead of enjoying the fruits of its first major independent diplomatic program China tasted bitter social disorder, political chaos, and
national disintegration. Disputes over the war participation policy exacerbated factionalism, encouraged warlordism, and led to civil war. In the
wake of China's war entry policy in 1917, China was a stage set for a
tragic drama. A series of bizarre episodes – the dissolution of parliament,
the restoration of the Qing emperor, repeated turnovers in government,
the dismissal and return of Prime Minister Duan Qirui, and the resignation of President Li Yuanhong – all took place in the wake of China's
announced plan to participate in the First World War. The situation was
described by contemporary Chinese this way: the country experienced a
"declaration of war abroad without fighting, and a fight at home without
a declaration of war."[2]

How can we make sense of all this? Given its domestic repercussions,
was China's war policy a bad one? Or can we argue that the policy itself
was sound, but the politicians bungled it? Can we go even farther and
conclude that Chinese society as a whole was at a "lower level of political
culture," to employ S. E. Finer's phrase, and was not mature enough to
deal successfully with political crises? Internal politics and foreign policy
were closely intertwined in China as we have seen, so just how did developments in one arena set off reactions in the other? A close analysis of

---

[1] Arthur Waldron, "The Warlord: Twentieth-Century Chinese Understandings of Violence, Militarism, and Imperialism," *The American Historical Review* 96, no. 4 (1991):
1076.
[2] Li Jiannun, *The Political History of China*, trans. and ed. by Ssu-yu Teng and Jeremy Ingalls
(Princeton: Princeton University Press, 1956), 373; see also Tao Juyin, *Dujun tuan zhuan*
(Biographies of corps of military governors) (Taipei: Wenhai chubanshe, 1971), 138.

the debate in China about its entry into the Great War will shed light on these questions and their impact on modern Chinese history.

The great debate of 1917

After China had protested to Germany regarding its submarine policy in February of 1917, direct Chinese participation in the war seemed imminent. The formal declaration of war, however, would not come until the middle of August, six full months later. Prime Minister Duan had not expected that publication of his protest note would set off a tremendous debate among interest groups and concerned citizens over the war policy. This debate not only upset what had been anticipated to be a smooth entry into the war, but more importantly, Chinese society itself. As President Li Yuanhong observed, "upon the diplomatic rupture suddenly taking place political crises have followed each another."[3]

Policy debates, especially regarding major issues, can be a natural and healthy process. But in early twentieth-century China, the new society and political structure were not yet established enough to withstand controversy over such a crucial policy as entry into war, and the political debate turned dangerous and destabilizing. In the past, this level of policy-making had been carried out by top leaders without consultation. Even when debates did take place, the emperor had had the final say. But in the era of the First World War, and especially after the death of Yuan Shikai, no Chinese leader enjoyed such paramount power; moreover, a broader Chinese public had become interested and active in politics. Yet, to judge by the political crises that grew out of the war issue, that public was not quite ready for this role. The new republican political structure, still fragile and unstable, could be shaken by any political crisis that might threaten it. If the politicians were unable to operate effectively within this new multidimensional political culture, and could not make compromises or wield the skills needed to steer China through uncharted waters, disasters could hardly be avoided.

New civic interest groups, ubiquitous across China, played a critical role in this war policy debate. The Chinese United Association of Industry and Commerce, for example, did not favor China's participation in the war owing to concerns that it would disrupt Chinese society and hurt business. Other business groups such as the General Chamber of Commerce of Shanghai, the Cantonese Guild, the Zhejiang Students' Society at Shanghai, the Ningbo Society, the Shaoxin Society, the

---

[3] Li Yuanhong, "Declaration by the President of his Policy," *The Peking Gazette*, June 1, 1917.

Foreign Goods Dealers' Guild, the Chinese Dealers' Association, the Society to Study Industries and Commerce, and the Society to Support Chinese Merchants all shared this concern. In early March of 1917, these groups wired a joint message "to the President, the Vice-President, the Cabinet, the Parliament, the Military Governors and the Civil Governors, the Provincial Assemblies and Chambers of Commerce of all provinces":

The existence or downfall of the state depends greatly on the people's responsibility. In the present state of this country the government could clearly see that if China once joins either one of the belligerents it will cause harm to China but no benefit, whichever belligerents might win. Therefore it is much better to remain strictly neutral at all times so as to maintain national rights and humanity.[4]

Although it is difficult to assess with any precision the impact of such interest groups on foreign policymaking, their eagerness to participate in the debate and engage in lobbying is unmistakable. The effectiveness of their efforts depended on circumstances and timing. Of the many different interests that opposed the war policy, the opposition can be generally divided into four main groups, with considerable overlap between them. The first I call the *Status Quo Group*, a set of interests that included industrial and commercial organizations, such as those mentioned above. This group argued that might exercised a louder voice than justice in the world and the protest of a weak country like China would have no impact except to embarrass that country since the protest would carry no weight. China was in no position to maintain or fight for international law, and it made no sense to antagonize either side and risk causing needless harm to itself once the war was ended. Furthermore, the German submarine policy did little damage to China, so since no crucial Chinese interests were involved in the European War, why should China bother?[5]

A written inquiry from twenty-three members of the House of Representatives asking Duan's government to account for its war policy echoed this view. It argued that the government by protesting to Germany was engaged in an unwise war policy, that China's protest was not justified since Germany did not harm Chinese interests during the current war, and that the protest did not make sense because China lacked the strength

---

[4] *The China Press*, March 8, 1917. For the originals, see "Shanghai Zongshanghui deng tong dian" (Telegrams from Shanghai General Association of Merchants and others), March 4, 1917, in *Minguo dangan* (Archival materials of Republican China), 1991, I: 7.

[5] A good example of this argument was expressed in "Tang Baoe deng dui De kangyi zhi wenshu" (Inquiry regarding China's protest to Germany from Tang Baoe and others), March 8, 1917, in Zhongguo lishi di er dangan guan, ed., *Zhonghua minguo shi dangan ziliao huibian: Di san ji, zhengzhi* (Collections of archival materials on the history of Republican China: vol. III, politics[2]) (Nanjing: Jiangsu guji chubanshe, 1991), 1152–60.

to back it up. Therefore, China's termination of diplomatic relations with Germany could yield no concrete or even potential gains for China.[6]

The second opposition group can be called the *Germany Factor Group*. For members of this group, Germany was the national model China should follow if it wanted to renew itself and grow strong and rich. Moreover, Germany had some chance of winning the war, and even if it lost eventually, it would still have power enough to punish China. More importantly, China's survival depended on the great powers balancing their interests in Asia. If China joined the war against Germany, it could actually help destroy that balance of power. Kang Youwei, Liang Qichao's former teacher, was the major figure in this group. Contrary to his famous student's position, Kang was strongly against China's entering the war and was notoriously pro-Germany. In early 1917 Kang Youwei sent several telegrams to Li Yuanhong and Duan Qirui to express his opposition to China's entry into the war. He argued that it was stupid and irresponsible to declare war on Germany since Germany could exact revenge on China. Kang Youwei's reasoning for his position was very clear if not altogether convincing. He declared, "If we ourselves cannot improve our internal administration to become a strong country, it is absurd to expect our admission to the ranks of the first-class powers simply by being allowed to have a seat at the peace conference and by taking sides with the Entente!" Kang was greatly concerned that China's severing of its diplomatic relations with Germany and contemplation of entry into the war might "cause grave peril."

Although Kang professed that he was not in a position to predict who would win the war, he did hazard the following observations:

Should Germany be victorious, the whole of Europe, not to mention a weak country like China, would be in great danger of extinction. Should it be defeated, Germany still can – after the conclusion of peace – send a fleet to fight against us. As the powers will be afraid of a second world war, who will come to our aid? Have we not seen an example in Korea? *There is no such thing as an army of righteousness which will come to the assistance of weak nations.* I cannot bear to think of hearing the angry voice of German guns along our coasts!

Like the Status Quo Group, Kang insisted that China was too poor and weak to fight Germany, and therefore it should focus on domestic development and avoid German retaliation after the war. He concluded that "we have nothing to do with the European war" and asserted that China should give up "its idea of a so-called opportunity of one thousand years and joining the ranks of first-rank nations with one jump" by

---

[6] "Tang Baoe deng dui De kangyi zhi wenshu," February 25, 1917, in Zhongguo di er li shi dang an guan, beiyang wai jiao bu dang, 1011(2)/39.

participating in the war.[7] It has to be pointed out that Kang's position on the war issue might not have been based on his objective consideration of Chinese national interest. It was fundamentally influenced by his obsession with the imperial restoration and his close connection with German agents in 1917. Kang's German link will be discussed further below.

Congressman Ma Junwu and others based their opposition on the same grounds. They argued that severing relations with Germany might have serious consequences for China.[8] Some of them even charged that Liang Qichao, the major force behind the war participation campaign, had committed the crime of "national subjugation" for having sponsored this policy.[9] Important people such as Li Jingxi, prime minister for a short time, and Feng Guozhang, who was vice-president then, had strong reservations about the Duan government's war policy as well. Li Jingxi, in a confidential letter to Duan, complained that China had issued its protest note to Germany too hastily, and he expressed doubts about the wisdom of this move.[10] Feng was especially worried about the consequences of a German victory.[11] Even Xu Shuzheng, Duan's closest associate and confidant, belonged to this group and opposed the war policy. According to Cao Rulin, an influential politician in early Republican China, Xu's reason for opposing it was that he did not think Germany would lose, and so China should not declare war before the outcome of the conflict was clearer.[12] Hoping to cultivate good relations with Germany in the long term, Xu had secretly provided German troops in Qingdao with a trainload of munitions to help them fight the Japanese in the summer of 1914.[13]

To be sure, not everyone was as consistent as Xu in his attitude toward Germany. Some Chinese initially belonged to the Germany Factor Group

---

[7] Tang Zhijun, ed., *Kang Youwei zhenglunji* (Kang Youwei's writings on politics) (Beijing: Zhonghua shuju, 1981), II: 976–78, 982–89.

[8] "Ma Junwu deng zhi gesheng dujun deng dian" (Ma Junwu and others' telegram to military governors, February 28, 1917), in Ding Wenjiang, ed., *Liang Rengong xiansheng nianpu changbian chugao* (Taipei: Shijie shuju, 1959), 511.

[9] "Wu Zhuan yu Ren xiong shu" (Wu Zhuan to Liang Qichao, March 27, 1917), ibid., 513–14.

[10] "Li Jingxi wei dui De guangxi zhi Duan Qirui han" (Li Jingxi to Duan Qirui, February 20, 1917), in Zhongguo lishi di er danganguan, ed., *Zhonghua minguo shi dangan ziliao huibian: Di san ji, zhengzhi* (Collections of Archival Materials on the History of Republican China: vol. III: Politics[2]), 1149–51.

[11] "Feng Guozhang guanyu geguo weiyi jue wofang tiaojian xuan zhan yi shengzhong zhi Shi Jingyun deng diangao" (Feng Guozhang, telegram to Shi Jingyun and others, March 16, 1917), in ibid., 1165–66.

[12] Cao Rulin, *Yi Sheng zhi huiyi* (The memoirs of Cao Rulin) (Hong Kong: Chun Qiu chubanshe, 1966), 160.

[13] Xu Daoling, ed., *Xu Shuzheng xiansheng wenji nianpu hekan* (Collections of Xu Shuzheng's writings and chronology) (Taipei: Shangwu yinshuguan, 1962), 159.

but later switched their position. Chen Duxiu was one of those; he was pro-German when the war first started. In 1915, as Germany was emerging victorious in the battlefields, Chen expressed hope that this newly developed country "could provide leadership to the colonial peoples of the world." But Chen soon lost faith and became a strong advocate of participation against the Germans.[14] In a series of articles published in *Xin qingnian* (New Youth), Chen argued that the war declaration was not simply a diplomatic issue, but a life-or-death matter for China. He argued that the advantages of China's entry into the war far surpassed its negative impact. For Chen, China's declaration of war would indicate that it supported justice over might. To rebut the Status Quo argument, Chen maintained that the existing situation was hostile to the Chinese national interest, and it was better to destroy it rather than to keep it intact.[15]

The third opposition group can be called the *Japan Factor Group*. According to its position, Japan was China's most dangerous enemy, always waiting for the least opportunity to seize control of more Chinese assets. Chinese participation in the war might provide an excuse for Japan to inflict further damage through its loans and other means. In any case, joining the war on the same side could only serve Japanese interests, so China should stay out of the war altogether.

The positions of these opposition groups are easily understandable. The position of the fourth group, which I called the *Political Opposition Group*, by contrast, is both complicated and crucial to our understanding the impact of the war on Chinese society. This group opposed China's participation in the war not because it disagreed with the war policy *per se* but mainly because that policy was a policy of the Duan government. Sun Yat-sen, the leader of the Guomindang (GMD) and an opponent of Duan, was perhaps the most important figure in this group. In a letter to Duan, he claimed that weak countries should not follow the great powers and join the war because the eventual losers would always be those weak countries.[16] In a booklet entitled *The Question of China's Survival*, published in 1917, Sun vigorously challenged both the wisdom of China's declaring war and, more importantly, the motives of the Duan government for wanting to do so. Sun argued that for the sake of China's survival it should maintain strict neutrality. To declare war on

---

[14] Lee Feigon, *Chen Duxiu: Founder of the Chinese Communist Party* (Princeton: Princeton University Press, 1983), 108–09.

[15] Chen Duxiu, "Dui De waijiao" (Foreign policy with Germany), in *Xin qingnian* 3, no. 1; for Chen's detailed arguments, see also his articles "Russian geming yu wo guomin zhi jiaowu" (The Russian revolution and our citizens' awakening), *Xin qingnian* 3, no. 2, and "Shiju zagang" (Random thoughts on current affairs), in *Xin qingnian* 3, no. 4.

[16] Sun Yat-sen, *Sun Zhongshan quanji* (The complete writings of Sun Yat-sen) (Beijing: Zhonghua shuju, 1985), IV: 29–30.

Germany was "utterly absurd" because it was the Allied countries rather than Germany that had inflicted the most damage on China. Therefore, Sun argued, if China were to enter the war, it should declare war on Russia, Britain, and France, not Germany. He argued for neutrality because China's entering the war would only lead to its destruction. He also expressed fears that entry into the war would cause domestic trouble that would allow Japan to take further advantage. Since the new diplomacy on which Duan's war policy was based focused on an alliance with the United States, Sun tried to discredit it by arguing that the United States was not reliable, even though Sun himself had been instrumental in this diplomacy.[17]

In addition to raising opposition to Duan's policy, Sun tried to dissuade foreign countries from supporting China's participation in the war. Sun sent a telegram in early March to British prime minister Lloyd George to appeal to him not to allow China to join the war.[18] On June 8, he sent a telegram to American president Woodrow Wilson arguing for American intervention in Chinese politics:

A band of traitors, under the pretext of declaring war for the benefit of China's interests, but whose real purpose is the restoration of the monarchy, are endeavoring to enlist the sympathies and support of the Entente allies and to obtain from them loans, nominally by joining them as faithful allies, but actually for attaining their own selfish ends . . . Although the militarists have the upper hand, we are able to vanquish them forever and preserve our republic provided your excellency will only now make known the real situation to those friendly powers and exert your influence to gain their cooperation in preventing China from being dragged into the European war.[19]

On June 9, when he heard the American advice to China, which will be discussed in detail later in this chapter, Sun expressed to Wilson the "deepest gratitude for your excellency's foresight and timely warning."[20]

Given all the arguments *for* Chinese participation that arose from a view of national interest, Sun's position appealed to few of the foreign powers or the Chinese themselves. In a telegram to the British Foreign Office, Alston plainly advised his government that Sun's arguments in his appeal to Lloyd George were "inaccurate and [that] the whole message is obviously enemy inspired. I suggest no notice be taken of it."[21] Alston might be wrong in suggesting that Sun was motivated by the "enemy,"

---

[17] Sun Yat-sen, *Zhongguo cunwang wenti* (The question of China's survival) (Shanghai, 1928), 7, 10, 113–14, 122, 110.
[18] Sun Yat-sen, *Sun Zhongshan quanji*, IV: 19–20.
[19] Sun to Wilson, June 8, 1917, in Arthur Link, ed., *The Papers of Woodrow Wilson* (Princeton: Princeton University Press, 1966–1994), XXXII: 466.
[20] Ibid., 468.   [21] PRO, wo106/35.

but Sun and his followers were clearly driven by narrow partisan politics in their opposition to Duan's war policy. Sun Yat-sen was more interested in establishing a power base for his own party's rise than pursuing what was clearly in the national interest by inserting China into the world war. In other words, he was not primarily motivated by opposition to China's entering the war. His main concern was that if Duan's war policy succeeded, his government would be greatly strengthened. According to a memoir by Zhong Boyi, a member of the Guomindang, the GMD had paid special attention to the outbreak of war in Europe from the very beginning. As mentioned earlier, Huang Xin and other leading GMD members, including Li Gengyuan, Zhang Shizhao, Li Lijun, Gengyi, Zhang Xiaozhun, Ouyan Zhengsheng, Chen Qiang, and Chen Zhikai, had organized a Society for the Study of European Affairs as early as the summer of 1914. When the European war moved to the crucial year of 1917, most members of the GMD supported China's declaring war on Germany. Wang Jinwei, one of Sun Yat-sen's close followers and a leading member of the GMD, was one of the strong supporters of war participation. Zhong Boyi claimed that even Sun did not actually oppose China's declaration of war before he realized it might strengthen Duan's government.[22] Zhong's view is supported by the GMD's declaration, published in July 1917:

While a few prominent members of the Mintang [GMD] have believed that a departure from neutrality might increase the internal difficulties of China, it is undoubted that a majority of Mintang members favor Chinese intervention in the war. And we are in a position to state that even those of our party who have been opposed to war would at once acquiesce in a war-decision made by a government whose loyalty to republican principles and whose opposition to militarism were not in doubt. Instead of saying that the political creed of Mintang logically and inevitably commits the party as a whole to support a policy which ranges China with the liberal powers at war with the Germanic states, we hold that if China is to survive as a modern state, she must grow strong.[23]

From this, we can see clearly that Sun and his followers opposed China's participation in the war only after they considered the issue from a purely political angle. This view is further confirmed by the fact that after Sun and other opposition figures declared independence from the Beijing Government and founded their own government in the South, they also declared war on Germany.

[22] Guo Tingyi and Shen Yunlong, *Zhong Boyi xiangsheng fangwen jilu* (Record of interviews with Zhong Boyi by Guo Tingyi and Sheng Yunlong) (Taipei: Zhong yang yan jiu yuan jing dai shi yan jiu suo, 1992), 47, 58.
[23] *Millard's Review* (July 21, 1917): 173.

If Duan's war policy was naive, as argued above, the opposition groups operated under their own brand of naiveté. They contended that if China did nothing, the great powers would leave it alone. This wishful thinking simply had not been supported by recent history. A good case in point is Japan's pressing the Twenty-one Demands in 1915 when China was still officially neutral. The argument that China was not strong enough to sustain international law also contradicts historical fact. China had been isolated and passive for so long in the late Qing, its strength and prestige had deteriorated day by day. But now opposition groups argued, ironically, that China would be better off sticking its head back in the sand and ignoring world events.[24]

My classification of these opposition groups is largely for purposes of discussion: in reality, they were not clearly differentiated and in many cases overlapped. Moreover, the members of these groups did not always stick to one position. They occasionally changed their minds and switched camps from opposition to conditional or unconditional support. After China officially severed its relations with Germany, Feng Guozhang, earlier cautious about the prospect of China's participation in the war, called on his fellow Chinese to support the central government's diplomacy.[25] Like Feng, Zhang Shizhao, another key member of elite society, had a change of heart about severing diplomatic relations with Germany. In February 1917, Zhang cited China's weakness as the main reason for his opposition to China's protest against Germany and argued that preserving the main countries' balance of powers in China was key to China's continuing existence. But by mid-March, he had become a strong supporter of Duan's war policy, claiming that he was "changing his mind for the sake of the nation's future." He even used his legal expertise to argue that Duan's war policy was right.[26]

Despite the existence of opposition groups, the majority of Chinese social elite members supported the idea of participation in the war,

[24] For an excellent analysis on opposition and why China should join the war, see Liu Yan, "Zhongguo jiaru xue yueguo shang que" (Questions regarding China's joining the Allied countries), Zhong guo di er li shi dang an guan, beiyan wai jiao bu dang, 16/101.

[25] "Feng Guozhang li Zhong De jiejiao shimu ji qi lihai yijiang shugao" (Draft memorandum from Feng Guozhang regarding China's breaking off diplomatic relations with Germany and its impact), March 18, 1917, Zhongguo lishi di er danganguan, ed., *Zhonghua minguo shi dangan zhi liao huibian: Di san ji, zhengzhi* (Collections of archival materials on the History of Republican China: III, Politics[2]), 1168–88.

[26] For Zhang's opposition to severance, see his articles, "Jia ru Ouzhan wenti zhi yijian" (Some thoughts on China's entry into the European war), "Lin ya le ma zhi waijiao" (Dangerous foreign policy), in *Jia yin rikan* (Jia Yin Daily), February 11, 15, 16, 1917. For his ideas supporting joining the war, see his articles such as "Yuefa shang xuan zhan tongyi zhi jieshi" (A constitutional explanation of the war declaration), "Yu zhi waijiao zhengce guan" (My views on foreign policy), "Waijiao wenti" (Foreign policy issues), in *Jia yin rikan*, March 10 and April 4, 1917.

arguing that no country could maintain neutrality while trying to enhance its international status. As one contemporary pointed out, "Every politically important element in China's limited but energetic sphere of public life was in favor of breaking off with Germany." As to declaring war, "Scattered elements opposed it, such as a group of radicals led by the famous ex-president Sun Yat-sen, but the southern parties as a whole approved and backed it."[27] Jiang Tingfu, who observed the controversy closely, insisted that when Chinese military and civilian factions were debating war policy in 1917, "Most of them argued that [China] should join the Allied side. Few insisted on neutrality. None suggested joining the German side."[28] The fact that a majority supported China's rupture with Germany and even its participation in the war explains why, on March 11, the parliament supported Duan Qirui's policy, voting 158 to 37 in the Senate and 331 to 87 in the House. This gave the Duan government an immediate mandate to break off relations with Germany.[29]

But the consensus on the war policy was soon to be dashed, and a personal clash between Prime Minister Duan and President Li Yuanhong would deal it the first blow.

Breakdown of the war policy consensus

To analyze this breakdown, we must start with the key figure Duan Qirui. Duan had studied military subjects in Germany from spring 1889 to winter 1890, an experience that helped him gain first-hand knowledge of Western society and civilization and made him realize quite clearly the depth of China's backwardness. According to his biographer, this experience was a turning point in his life. "His mental horizon had been greatly broadened, his worldview became more and more modern and

---

[27] "Zhong De jiejiao shimu ji qi lihai" (no author, presumably written by a high official within the government), March 18, 1917, in Zhang Bofeng et al., *Beiyang junfa, 1912–1928* (Wuhan: Wuhan chubanshe, 1990), III: 61; "Feng Guozhang li Zhong De jiejiao shimu ji qi lihai yijian shugao" (Draft Memorandum from Feng Guozhang regarding China's breaking off diplomatic relations with Germany and its impact) (March 18, 1917), in Zhongguo lishi di er danganguan, ed., *Zhonghua minguo shi dangan ziliao huibian: Di san ji, zhengzhi* (Collections of archival materials on the history of Republican China: III, politics[2]): 1172.

[28] Jiang Tingfu, *Jiang Tingfu huiyilu* (The memoirs of Jiang Tingfu) (Taipei: Zhuangji wenxue chubanshe, 1979), 65.

[29] "Zhong De jiejiao shimu ji qi lihai" (The inside story of China's breaking off its diplomatic relations with Germany and its implications), March 18, 1917, in Zhang Bofeng et al., *Beiyang junfa, 1912–1928*, III: 61; "Feng Guozhang li Zhong De jiejiao shimu ji qi lihai yijian shugao" (Draft memorandum from Feng Guozhang regarding China's breaking off diplomatic relations with Germany and its impact), March 18, 1917, Zhongguo lishi di er danganguan, ed., *Zhonghua minguo shi dangan ziliao huibian: Di San Ji: zhengzhi*, 1172.

liberal. He was determined to help his motherland stand on her own feet." After his German stint, Duan became interested in the relationship between China and the world, and frequently discussed world affairs and ways of helping China join the international system.[30]

It was not only his modern-mindedness and Western training that set him apart from conservative politicians; his personal character also placed him head and shoulders above the others. Unlike many Chinese politicians and warlords of his time, Duan was an honest man not interested in making money or pursuing personal pleasure. He refused gifts and lived simply. Because of his nationalist attitude, the great powers did not have a high opinion of him. Jordan, commenting on Duan's return to power in 1916, declared that he "is hardly a man fit to guide his country through a crisis like the present one. The Japanese minister who had not previously known him was not favourably impressed with his appearance, and came to the conclusion that he was waiting upon events rather than seeking to control them." But Jordan acknowledged that the "Chinese generally consider him an honest and well-meaning man."[31] Reinsch felt more positive about Duan, commenting in his memoir that Duan "is no politician and is bored by political theory . . . His personality, however, with its simplicity and pensiveness, and his real wisdom when he lets his own nature guide him, make him one of the attractive figures of China."[32] Reinsch's observations allow us to go beyond the conventional view that Duan's clash with Li was motivated by his seeking Japanese support while his opponent Li Yuanhong would prefer backing by the Americans in Duan's and Li's separate pursuit of a viable Chinese war policy.

Duan was foremost a man of principle. If some proposed course of action ran contrary to his personal principles, he would not do it, no matter what the cost. His opposition to Yuan's monarchical ambitions is a good case in point. Duan protested Yuan's scheme to make himself emperor by resigning his government post in August 1915, supposedly because of illness. He also advocated resistance to the Twenty-one Demands and argued for fighting the Japanese. Both actions were courageous because these positions could have put him in great personal and political danger. If he thought something was good for the country, such as China's entry into the European war, he would use every means at his disposal to make it happen. Liang Qichao's comment on Duan is typical:

---

[30] Fei Jingzhong, *Duan Qirui* (The biography of Duan Qirui) (Shanghai: Shijie shuju, 1921), 5.

[31] Jordan Confidential Report to Grey, May 9, 1916, PRO, FO371/2645/511.

[32] Paul Samuel Reinsch, *An American Diplomat in China* (Garden City, NY: Doubleday Page & Company, 1922), 243.

"He does have shortcomings. But he pursues bold policies and takes risks in the country's interest, regardless of personal concerns. Perhaps nobody in China can do the same." Liang even claimed that there was no hope for China if the Chinese failed to support Duan.[33]

Duan was convinced from the start that China could use the European war as a vehicle for renewal, and he harbored a secret wish that China had entered the war at its outbreak. Two points are worth mentioning here: First, Liang Qichao might have been the force behind China's drive to participate in the war in 1917, but it was Duan who actually carried out the policy.[34] Second, a point often missed by historians, is Duan's attitude toward his associate Xu Shuzheng in this matter. Xu was Duan's confidant, and Duan relied heavily upon him in many things. Yet Duan did not listen to Xu with respect to China's war policy, for Xu strongly opposed the declaration of war on Germany.[35] In early 1917 Xu wrote seven long letters to Duan expressing his opposition, but after reading two of them, Duan did not bother to open the rest.[36] This rarely noted fact is important not only because it shows that Duan's policy was consistent and did not suddenly take shape in 1917, but also because it challenges the conventional view that Duan did not have his own policy and simply agreed to whatever his confidants, especially Xu Shuzheng, asked him to do.

In early 1917, with the American invitation for joint action and pushed by Liang Qichao, Duan believed the time for quick action had arrived. But from the very start the prime minister found himself clashing with President Li Yuanhong over how to handle the war. When the Duan cabinet decided to break off relations with Germany, it also intended to ascertain Japan's response to China's war aims. This made sense to Duan since China had failed twice before in its efforts to join the war because of Japanese opposition. When Duan and all his cabinet members visited Li Yuanhong in early March, asking for his signature on a telegram to the Japanese government, Li suggested that these were important issues and advised them to take parliament's opinion into account. President Li thought it improper to inform a foreign country of such vital decisions before parliament had given its approval. Since such a proposal meant a definite step toward China's declaration of war, Li insisted on the prior

[33] Ding Wenjiang, ed., *Liang Rengong xiansheng nianpu changbian chugao*, 527.
[34] To use Conty's words, "The idea of China's entry into the Allied camp had been supported at the beginning by Liang Qichao . . . Marshall Duan did his best to put it into execution." See Quai d'Orsay, NS, Chine, LXIV: 120.
[35] Xu Daoling, ed., *Xu Shuzheng xiansheng wenji nianpu hekan* (Xu Shuzheng's Writings and Chronology), 120.
[36] Xu Tian, "Dui De-Ou canzhan." See also Tao Juyin, *Dujun tuan zhuan* (Biographies of the corps of military Governors), 51.

approval of parliament, which alone had the power to declare war. Duan resigned immediately to protest Li's lack of cooperation and mistrust of his cabinet's judgment.[37]

Why did Duan choose to resign rather than negotiate with Li? Duan's personality and his relationship with Li may help explain his decision. Duan had never greatly respected President Li and considered his refusal to sign a personal insult. Moreover, at this juncture there was still enormous confusion regarding the new republican political structure. In Duan's mind, presidential functions were mainly ceremonial and symbolic, and the president had no call to intervene in the cabinet decisions. But Li Yuanhong thought and acted differently. A cautious man, Li insisted that the war question was so important that it should be considered carefully. As president, he believed he should insist on handling the war policy legalistically by carefully briefing parliament and getting the latter's approval. Li was also appalled by the political nature of the debate over the war. He once commented to reporters that "today's fellow Chinese have a tendency to look at the issue [of China's joining the war] as an issue of different parties and party relations. This is not good." Li declared, "If China wants to join, it should do so for the national interest," and he warned that "we Chinese should never enter into the war in a spirit of risk-taking opportunism."[38] Duan, however, did not worry about legal issues, so long as he could achieve his goal. Because of his personal confidence, he believed that if something should be done, he would pursue it despite any risks.

Although Conty characterized Li Yuanhong as a man of "weakness, fickleness, and faintheartedness" (*faiblesse, inconsistence et pusillanimité*), this was not always the case.[39] Like Duan, Li opposed Yuan's planned restoration of the monarchy, resisting it after his usual passive style. Li might have had his own ambitions and principles but, unlike Duan, he knew his weaknesses and when to compromise. Indeed, his capacity to compromise allowed this first political obstacle to a Chinese war policy to be hurdled. Two days after Duan resigned, through the mediation of Vice-president Feng Guozhang, Li acceded to the condition set by Duan about his return as prime minister: that Li not interfere in diplomatic affairs and the cabinet's foreign policy. Duan returned immediately to Beijing to resume his duties. On March 10 and 11, the parliament approved the breaking of relations with Germany by a large margin. Everything seemed to be working in Duan's favor and moving along smoothly. But another problem soon arose.

---

[37] *Minguo Ribao*, March 8, 1917.   [38] *Zhonghua Xinbao*, March 3, 1917.
[39] Conty to Ribot, July 24, 1917, Quai d'Orsay, NS, Chine, LXIV: 84.

To ensure that his war policy would encounter no further resistance, Duan began soliciting support from the military governors in April. He assumed that if he could win their support, he could use it to pressure his opponents, especially those in the parliament, as well as the president. To this end, Duan called a conference, which convened officially on April 25, with more than twenty military governors or their representatives attending. Duan himself chaired the opening session. Once Duan assured them that war participation was in both their own and the national interest, the *dujun* or provincial military governors became advocates of Duan's war policy and did what they could to support it. But during their sojourn in Beijing, they also began to intervene in national politics by attending a cabinet meeting, and even in foreign affairs by collectively visiting ministers from the Allied countries.[40] Given the intimidating power of the *dujun*, the controversy regarding Duan's advocacy of participation in the war against Germany stirred strong chain reactions within Chinese political circles in general and within the Beiyang military clique in particular which soon shook the whole fragile political system. Problems around Duan's effort to secure regional support for participation in the war soon sparked intrigues within the parliament, conflicts between the president's secretariat and the cabinet, and a dispute over the constitution.

Having gained the support of the *dujun*, Duan's cabinet felt confident enough to decide to declare war on May 1. Under pressure from Duan and the military governors, President Li agreed to pass Duan's war declaration on to the parliament for consideration. On May 8, the House of Representatives started to debate the issue. Given the prior support of both houses, parliament should have easily passed this bill. According to Tao Juying, a scholar of politics in early Republican China, a majority of members of parliament supported Duan's declaration of war.[41] Indeed, as Wang Zhengting, vice-president of the Senate and a leading member of the GMD, wrote in July 1917, "The severance of diplomatic relations with Germany was approved by both houses with a large majority. An equally large majority would have voted for war against Germany had there been no interference from the military governors."[42] Li Jiannong, another leading scholar of the political history of early Republican China, has also suggested that "if the Peiyang military clique had not used harsh methods, the bill [for participating in the war] would have passed

---

[40] *Dujun* literally means "supervisor of military affairs," a post that was first used in 1916. For details, see Arthur Waldron, "The Warlord: Twentieth-Century Chinese Understandings of Violence, Militarism, and Imperialism," *American Historical Review* 96, no. 4 (October 1991).
[41] Tao Juyin, *Dujun tuan zhuan*, 61.   [42] *Millard's Review*, July 14, 1917: 150.

without trouble." Li wrote that in the parliament "all parties (except the 1916 Club, a leftist wing) intended to pass the bill."[43]

But Duan and his cronies had badly miscalculated the situation by trying to get the bill passed this way. The *dujun*, taking matters into their own hands, chose to use threats to assure its passage. On May 10, as the House of Representatives was holding a committee meeting on the issue, a mob of several thousand people calling themselves "Citizens' Petition Corps," the "Petition Corps of Military, Political, and Commercial Circles," and other such names, gathered in front of the House. Secretly under the direction of the *dujun*, their goal was to "persuade" representatives to pass the war declaration immediately. They distributed circulars to members containing veiled and not-so-veiled threats such as "we are ready to sacrifice our person" and "we will deal with you eventually." A delegation of six persons declaring themselves to be citizens' representatives even approached the speaker of the House and demanded that the war declaration should be passed that day; otherwise, they would burn down parliament and murder the members. Three thousand members of various "petition corps" surrounded the building and refused to disperse until the bill was passed. Ten or more congressmen were beaten and harassed.

Was Duan involved in this fiasco? Although his enemies of the time attacked him for direct involvement, some evidence suggests that the incident was organized without Duan's knowledge. According to one source, Duan's close assistant General Fu Liangzuo orchestrated the whole episode without Duan's authorization.[44] Regardless of whether Duan was directly involved in the planning, he could not avoid direct and full responsibility. After all, his assistants and associates had acted on his behalf, and he was the one who had encouraged military intervention in civil politics in the first place.

The Congressmen were so angry at Duan and the *dujun* that they decided to delay voting on the war question and demanded that Duan explain the spectacle of mobs surrounding the parliament building. The GMD members of parliament refused to attend further sessions until they were guaranteed protection against mob violence and intimidation. But Duan continued to play a dangerous game, allowing the military

---

[43] Li, *Political History of China*, 365–66.

[44] Zeng Yujuan, "Li Duan maodun yi fuyuan chongtu" (Clashes between Li Yuanhong and Duan Qirui and the conflicts between the Presidential office and the Cabinet," in Du Chunhe, Lin Binsheng, and Qiu Quanzheng, eds., *Beiyang junfa shiliao xuanji* (Selected materials on the Beiyang warlords) (Beijing: Zhongguo shehui kexue chubanshe, 1981). See also Ji Yu, *Duan Qirui zhuan* (Hefei: Anhui renmin chubanshe, 1992), 272–73.

governors to become increasingly involved in central policy and even foreign affairs. In mid-May, the *dujun* made further threats at a reception they themselves gave for the members of the parliament.[45]

These repeated threats outraged the members of parliament. On May 19, the House of Representatives passed a resolution to the effect that the war bill would be passed only if Duan's government were reorganized. This action actually meant a no-confidence vote for Duan and in effect called for his dismissal. It soon became clear that the gridlock between parliament and Duan Qirui would not easily be resolved. As Tao Juying indicates, after Duan's so-called "public groups fiasco" and his continuing use of the military governors, the parliament decided it had to deal with his cabinet before passing the war act.[46]

This was an enormous blow to Duan. The war act was stalled and his government was itself in grave danger. Duan's cabinet members resigned in protest over the embarrassing "public groups" fiasco, leaving the Duan government a "one-man cabinet" consisting only of the prime minister. Standing alone with only the *dujun* to back him, Duan was faced with a terrible situation.

In response, Duan chose to further threaten to dissolve Parliament to secure his political survival and his war policy. More than ten military governors or their representatives voiced support for this move, and because the cabinet lacked the power to dissolve Parliament, the *dujun* openly pressured President Li to do so.[47] This immediately brought Li back onto a collision course with Duan. Li, unmoved by the *dujun*'s pressure, claimed that the president had no constitutional power to dissolve Parliament. On the evening of May 21, with no prospect of any progress with Li, all the *dujun* left Beijing for their own power bases. On May 23, President Li took the bold action of dismissing Duan and appointing Wu Tingfang to act temporarily in his stead in order to break the gridlock. But Duan refused to accept the dismissal and called Li's action illegal and lacking the endorsement of the prime minister, namely himself. Duan declared he would take no responsibility for any consequences that might arise.[48] This was tantamount to calling on the military governors to stage a rebellion, and accordingly, eight of the military governors declared independence from Li's central government in late May.

[45] "A Coup d'Etat in the Making," *Peking Gazette*, May 17, 1917.
[46] Tao Juyin, *Dujun tuanzhuan*, 61.
[47] "Beifang ge sheng dujun cheng qing Li Yuanhong jie Shangguohui wen" (Memorandum from the Northern provinces' military governors asking Li Yuanhong to dissolve the Parliament), in *Dong Fang Zazhi* 14, no. 7.
[48] *Zhonghua Xinbao*, May 24, 1917.

Thus a new and even more serious crisis emerged, putting Li Yuanhong in the hot seat. The country faced danger of division and disintegration. Li found, ironically, that the only source of help was a warlord – Zhang Xun (1854–1923), who had not declared independence and had in fact volunteered his services. Zhang, the very conservative military governor of Anhui, was known as the "pigtail general" because his army still wore the queue as a gesture of loyalty to the Qing. On June 1, Li officially asked Zhang to mediate. Li's reliance on Zhang turned out to be a terrible mistake, like Duan's earlier soliciting of help from the *dujun* collectively. In Zhang, Li found no savior but rather a destroyer of the republic. On June 7, Zhang turned around to demand that the president dissolve Parliament immediately even before he and his army reached Beijing, otherwise he would not take on the responsibility of mediation. Li, now on the back of a tiger, reluctantly agreed. After much confusion and haranguing, the president did dissolve Parliament on June 13, 1917.[49] But this move did not satisfy Zhang because his real goal from the moment he had accepted the role of mediator was the restoration of the Manchu emperor. On July 1, by Zhang Xun's arrangement, the Qing court reassembled to declare a restoration. That day became the third of the fifth month in the ninth year of Xuantong.

With the Qing restoration, Li had not only failed to solve the problem of the *dujun* rebellion, he had unwittingly helped to bury the republic. He resigned immediately in great shame and embarrassment. The restoration, however, provided an excellent opportunity for Duan to return to power as a defender of the republic. But Duan again missed his opportunity. He, the GMD, and the southern provinces had become entangled in a serious dispute over the constitution and this led to a further breakdown in the consensus on the war.

To explain how the constitution got tangled in the war debate we have to realize that Republican China, although trying hard to project itself as a respectable member of the world community, had not yet established itself at home as a full-fledged constitutional nation. In fact, it did not even have a real constitution. As *Millard's Review of the Far East* (published in Shanghai) correctly observed, "A difficulty is that, in China, there is no recognized constitution; a temporary instrument exists, but its legality and application are matters of dispute."[50] At issue was the 1912

---

[49] For details, see "Dui De shijian yu junshi huiyi" (Sino-German affairs and the military conference), "Xuan zhan an yu zhengchao" (The war declaration case and the political current), "Dujun cong bing yu fubi" (The use of the military by military governors and the imperial restoration), in *Xin qingnian* 3, no. 3 (May 1917), 3, no. 4 (June 1917), 3, no. 6 (August 1917).

[50] *Millard's Review*, June 9, 1917.

("old") provisional constitution, which Yuan replaced with his own 1914 ("new") constitution. Sun and his followers and the southern provinces had strongly opposed Yuan's move and argued for restoration of the old constitution, a symbol of republicanism. After Yuan's death, the South insisted that the old constitution be restored. In the summer of 1916, after a serious clash with the South regarding this issue, Duan had agreed to restore the old constitution and Parliament too, which had been dissolved by Yuan in 1913. But the same issue haunted both sides again one year later after Duan's return to power in July 1917. Once Li had dissolved Parliament in June at the demand of Zhang Xun, Duan and his opponents again argued about whether the old Parliament was to be restored. Since Duan had clashed with Parliament in May over the war policy and *dujun* interference, he was not in favor of restoration. Instead, he pushed to bring in a completely new parliament. Sun and his followers, along with some of the southern provincial governments, immediately protested. On August 25, 1917, congressmen who supported the restoration of the old constitution convened in Guangdong and decided to set up a military government in the South under the banner of "protecting the constitution." On September 1, Sun was elected head of that government. China was once again divided, north and south.

We can see that although Duan finally did manage to bring China into the First World War on August 14, 1917, the country suffered domestically having weathered political crises brought on in the course of sorting out the institutional basis of the war policy. President Li had gone, Parliament had been dissolved, and the nation was divided. The goal of the war declaration had subsequently changed. Before the political crisis, Duan's main motive for joining the war was advancing China's national interest, but in the process of bringing the young republic into the First World War, another more pressing project had emerged. Now the reunification of China appeared at the top of Duan's agenda. To become a unifier of the nation, Duan would use the issue of participation in the world war to strengthen his own legitimacy and power.

What are we to make of this series of one crisis after another and the breakdown of the republic itself in the wake of the war policy debate? The dissolution of the government obviously started with the dispute between Duan and Li. Although they had many institutional and personal reasons to clash, including the power struggle between the president's office and the council of state, they chose the issue of declaring war on Germany to be "the main one."[51] Yet in fact there was little difference

---

[51] Zeng Yujuan, "Li Duan maodun yi fuyuan chongtu" (Clashes between Li Yuanhong and Duan Qirui and the conflicts between the Presidential Office and the Cabinet, in Du Chunhe, ed., *Beiyang junfa shiliao xuanji*, I: 263.

in their attitudes toward China's proper position on the European war. Both Duan and Li wanted to put China on the right track and help it to join the international community, thereby enhancing its status. Contrary to the conventional view, Li did not oppose China's participation in the war. According to Zhang Guogan, Li Yuanhong once confided to him that "he in fact supported the idea in his heart."[52] One might argue that Li and Duan's war dispute was not really *about* the war – both sides in fact wanted to benefit from the war policy and used the war issue to undermine the other. According to one source, Zeng Yujuan, Duan's secretary and confidant, on learning that Li's group was for declaring war in early 1917, quickly reported the news to Duan's circle and suggested that "we should push our war policy quickly. The presidential office might get ahead of us with the same policy. If this happens, the other side will get the credit and we will end up with the short end of the stick." Li's people actually had the same thought. They argued, "If it is Duan who declares war on Germany, then Duan gets the kudos. So let us get rid of him first. When Duan is gone, if we let his successor carry out the same war policy, then the glory and credit belong to us."[53]

The Duan and Li camps both saw the opportunity to participate in the war as an avenue to personal victory. Neither wanted the other to have glory. Ding Fuyan (1888–1930), who served as secretary-general in the presidential office from August 1916 to February 1917, expressed this partisanship with particular clarity, openly declaring that his opposition to a declaration of war was completely based on political considerations.[54] "To be honest, I am for China's participation in the war. But since it is Duan's policy, I will oppose it to the end."[55] Duan's side took an equally hostile position. One key member of Duan's faction maintained that "as long as Li is not cooperative, he is a big obstacle to Duan's war policy. And so we first have to get rid of him. Then all things will go smoothly."[56] Duan's bringing in the military governors and Li's dismissal of Duan were both aimed at achieving the other's downfall.

But power clashes cannot entirely explain the breakdown. One reason for Li's refusal to cooperate with Duan's war policy, according to his

---

[52] Zhang told the same story in at least two different places; see Xu Tian (Zhang Guogan), "Dui De-Ou canzhan" (China's declaration of war on Germany and Austria), 61–63; Zhang Guogan, "Zhonghua minguo neige pian" (Chapter on the cabinet of republican China), in Du Chunhe, ed., *Beiyang junfa shiliao xuanji*, I: 206.

[53] Zhang Guogan, *Zhang Guogan wenji* (Beijing: Beijing Yanshan chubanshe, 2000); see also Xu Tian, "Dui De-Ou canzhan," 69.

[54] Ding was an active member of President Li's faction. As a returned student from Japan and editor-in-chief of *The Asia Daily*, he was very liberal and active in politics. He had served as a senator and secretary-general of the presidential office.

[55] Tao Juyin, *Dujun tuan zhuan*, 62.   [56] Xu Tian, "Dui De-Ou canzhan," 69.

inner circle, was that he did not want it to be carried out by Duan's cabinet, which he feared was too influenced at that moment by Japan. Zhang Guogan later commented that it was a pity that the real intentions underlying Li's opposition to joining the war were not understood.[57] Furthermore, although Duan and his followers tried to pursue a foreign policy aimed at China's renewal, they failed to understand the new China, with its spirit of nationalism and a broadened and more complex political base. Duan had joined a bold, new forward-looking foreign policy public with an apparent contempt for power sharing and popular support. This was key in Duan's failure: his refusal to compromise crippled his initiatives, just as Woodrow Wilson's refusal to compromise with his congressional opponents cost him his own country's membership in his cherished organization, the League of Nations. Duan's personal failures led to the forfeiture of a sound policy. Duan sacrificed his wish to make China united, strong, and equal in the family of nations. Like the "best and brightest" American leaders of the 1960s – to use David Halberstam's famous phrase – who led the United States into the disastrous Vietnam War, the "can-do" arrogance of Duan and his followers pushed China to the brink of national disintegration.[58] Like Richard Nixon, Duan had an obsession with suppressing opposition, and this led him to overreach and overreact. Duan and his cronies destroyed, discouraged, and disrupted all legal dissent. By so doing, they brought discredit on themselves and their war policy as well.

The rise of warlordism feeds political disintegration

The invitation of the military governors to Beijing in April 1917 over the declaration of war on Germany signaled the start of local warlords' intervention in central politics and the rise of warlordism across China. If Duan had given birth to the warlordism monster, Yuan Shikai had been its midwife. He had played a twofold role: First, as father of Chinese military modernization, he had organized the Beiyang army, instituting a structure in which personal loyalty rather than the defense of the national interest was the key adhesive. It can be argued that although the Beiyang army was founded on the idea of state-building and dealing with outside threats, it behaved more like a private army than a national one.[59] Its patronage-based structure explains why this force fell apart so quickly after the

[57] Ibid., 61–63.
[58] David Halberstam, *The Best and the Brightest* (New York: Random House, 20th anniversary edition, 1992).
[59] For an inside and contemporary analysis of the Beiyang army, see Wu Qiu, "Beiyang zhi qi yuan ji qi bengkui" (The origins of the Beiyang and its collapse), in Lai Xinxia, ed., *Beiyang junfa* (Documents on the Beiyang warlords) (Shanghai: Shanghai renmin chubanshe, 1988), I: 961–1036.

death of Yuan. Second, Yuan's scheme in 1915 to make himself emperor provided a major impetus to the rise of modern Chinese warlordism. To understand the link between this scheme and warlordism, we must address the question of why Yuan wanted to become emperor in the first place.

Most scholars have pointed to Yuan's selfish ambition. Without denying the role of that ambition, I would like to draw attention to other factors as well. One was Yuan's great interest in making China strong and united. Jerome Chen noted this in his biography of Yuan, which was generally very critical. According to Chen, Yuan "wanted a strong China. Strength came from unity; unity from obedience to him."[60] For Yuan, a polity such as republicanism or monarchy was only a means toward the ends of national wealth and power. Yuan's conviction that a strong center was required for modernization, strengthening the nation, and maintaining order was shared by other political leaders, including Sun Yat-sen, who believed that too much democracy would impede the "rapid, peaceful and orderly" mobilization of resources.[61] Liang Qichao, a leading reformer, even advised Yuan to "be the servant in appearance but the master in reality."[62] To achieve national strength, Yuan would not hesitate to establish a different polity if he thought republicanism could not work. This perspective sheds light on his behavior during the Twenty-one Demands period. When the Twenty-one Demands were put forward, Yuan was so outraged that he immediately ordered all activities regarding the imperial restoration to be stopped. According to his confidential secretary Xia Shoutian, who worked closely on that scheme, Yuan stormed, "If I am going to be emperor, I will not be one under Japanese control!" Xia claimed that this thinking was not known by outsiders. Only after the Twenty-one Demands negotiations had ended was the monarchical scheme revived.[63] After the humiliation of the Twenty-one Demands, Yuan believed even more that a strong central government under a strong leader was the only formula to keep China out of similar trouble in the future. Wellington Koo, who had worked closely with Yuan before being appointed minister to the United States, explained to the American Academy of Political and Social Sciences in January of 1916 that the decision in favor of a monarchy reflected the need for a "government able to hold the country together, develop its wealth and

---

[60] For details on this point, see Jerome Chen, *Yuan Shih-Kai* (Stanford: Stanford University Press, 1972), 164, 201, 210.

[61] Edward Friedman, *Backwards toward Revolution: The Chinese Revolutionary Party* (Berkeley: University of California Press, 1974), 169, 78.

[62] Ding Wenjiang, ed., *Liang Rengong xiansheng nianpu changbian chugao*, 579–620.

[63] Xia himself told this story to Zhang Guogan. See Zhang Guogan, "Jindai shi pian duan de jilu" (Random memory of certain portion of modern history), in *Jindai shi ziliao* (Materials of Modern History) (Beijing: Zhonghua shuju, 1978), 152.

strength, and help realize the intensely patriotic aspirations of its people."[64] As Li Jiannong noted, one of the major justifications for restoration of the monarchy was that "republicanism does not suit the national
condition . . . Unless there is a great change of policy, it is impossible to
save the nation."[65] Even John Jordan noted this rationale. He wrote to
Langley, "One driving motive behind the Chinese is that they will be in a
better position to withstand Japanese aggression under a monarchy than
under a Republican form of government."[66] Jordan, who was not happy
with Yuan's restoration scheme, still wrote highly of him after his death,
calling him "a great man and a true patriot."[67]

If Yuan's scheme grew out of the Chinese desire for renewal, ironically his fall was caused by those same forces. Among those who opposed
Yuan's restoration scheme, considerations of China's international status were paramount.[68] The main reason Liang Qichao opposed Yuan's
scheme was his conviction that a sudden change of polity would neg-
atively impact China's quest to join the world community. He argued
that the monarchy scheme would derail China's efforts to attend the crucial postwar peace conference and so provide further opportunities for
Japan to thwart Chinese interests.[69] Liang attacked what he called Yuan's
seven major mistakes, the first being his lack of a modern concept of the
nation-state.[70] To Liang and General Cai E, the first general to take military action against Yuan, the anti-monarchical war had to be waged for
nothing less than the human dignity of four hundred million Chinese.[71]

Liang attached such importance to the implications of Yuan's scheme
that he risked his life to write an extremely powerful article entitled "How
Strange Is This So-called National Polity Problem!" (*Yi zai suowei guoti
wenti*), in which he roundly denounced Yuan. Liang told his daughter,
"Unless heaven takes away my pen, I will write and denounce Yuan and
his cronies."[72] Liang not only used his pen, he also joined the military

---

[64] *Peking Daily News*, March 14, 1916.   [65] Li, *The Political History of China*, 309.

[66] Jordan to Langley, October 20, 1915, PRO, wo350/13/101–103.

[67] For Jordan's general appraisal of Yuan, see Jordan to Langley, June 13, October 6, 1916, PRO, Jordan papers, FO350/15.

[68] Liang Qichao provided a good example. Liang's public appeal was key to the success of the anti-Yuan movement. His enormous influence on public opinion made him entirely irreplaceable. According to one newspaper, "the adhesion of Liang Chichao to the repub-lican cause and his open defiance of Peking [Yuan] are equivalent in value to at least another army corps to the republicans." *The South China Morning Post*, April 20, 1916.

[69] Liang Qichao, "Yi zai suowei guoti wenti zhe" (How strange is this so-called polity issue), in Liang Qichao, *Dun biji*, 156; see also *Yin bing shi he ji: zhuanji*, 33

[70] Liang Qichao, *Yin bing shi he ji: wenji*, 34.

[71] Liang Qichao, *Yin bing shi he ji: wenji*, 39, 89.

[72] Zhang Pinxing, ed., *Liang Qichao jiashu* (Family Letters of Liang Qichao) (Beijing: Zhongguo wenlian chubanshe, 2000).

action by traveling south to work with Cai E, who was taking the lead in fighting Yuan. The trip south was extremely dangerous and difficult. "I will go although I risk my life because the whole nation's fate and destiny might depend on this trip," Liang wrote to his daughter.[73]

One direct result of the open military opposition to Yuan was that China was divided with two governments, one in the North and one in the South. Guangdong formally declared its independence from Yuan on April 6, 1916. On May 1, Guangdong and Guangxi established a military government, which was soon expanded with the inclusion of the Yunnan and Guizhou provinces under a new cabinet, the Military Council, formally established on May 8 at Zhao Qing, Guangdong, under the name National Protection Army. The southern government insisted that Yuan resign even after he gave up his scheme and yielded his authority. Even Yuan's death on June 6 did not resolve the split; rather, it made the situation worse because Yuan had been the only figure with sufficient prestige and status to hold the warlords together.

Yuan's death deprived the Beiyang faction of a leader and "caused internal dissension" among China's regional warlords.[74] This may be his single most powerful legacy. Yuan's exit from the national stage opened an era in which military leaders in every province acted without restraint to pursue provincial or personal goals, blighting the country with incessant warfare, rapacious exploitation, and banditry. As Ernest P. Young has noted, it was in the wake of the Yuan government's collapse in 1916 that "military men, without significantly sharing power with civilian politicians, were asserting their predominance and independence in the provinces."[75]

Local military rulers grouped and regrouped into competing factions, intercepted taxes earmarked for the central government, interfered in civilian government, and subjugated China's political and social life. Jerome Chen maintains that "the existence and influence of these warlords reduced China to the status of a pariah nation."[76] Warlords big or small like Zhang Zuolin, who controlled Manchuria, and Tang Jiyao, who controlled Yunnan, came to assert their control over the entire country. The central government, under the presidency of Li Yuanhong, who was not a Beiyang military man, rapidly lost its grip.

This was the situation Duan faced when he returned to power in the summer of 1917. Determined to unite China, he found his worst problem was the rebelling South under the leadership of Sun Yat-sen and

[73] Ibid.   [74] Li, *The Political History of China*, 345.
[75] Ernest Young, *The Presidency of Yuan Shih-k'ai*, 242.
[76] Li Jiannun has further pointed out, "The practice of the occupation of provinces by generals, set up during the war, resulted in the building of many military bases for smaller lords." See Li, *The Political History of China*, 345; Ch'en, *Yuan Shih-kai*, 215.

warlords Lu Rongting of Guangxi and Tang Jiyao of Yunnan. Almost simultaneously with China's declaration of war on Germany, Duan initiated military campaigns to suppress the rebellions of the South and reunite China. Fighting first broke out in September in Hunan province, between Duan's army and the southern forces. Hunan had declared its independence from Duan's government, and the government in Guangdong decided to provide military support for Hunan's resistance. The fighting in Hunan soon became a wide-ranging civil war between North and South.

But Duan was not to succeed in this endeavor. His military unification policy clashed with the peaceful unification plan of Feng Guozhang, also a military man who had succeeded Li as president. Without the cooperation and support from Feng, Duan suffered a disastrous defeat in Hunan, and on November 15 he resigned. Yet his resignation did not keep him from power; Duan still controlled decision-making through influence and his followers. Thus the civil war was still on. On December 18, Duan was appointed supervisor of the (European) War Participation Bureau, a powerful position that gave him complete control of all military and foreign affairs. Under his leadership, the civil war continued even after the First World War had ended in November 1918. Moreover, serious disputes between the Hebei and Anhui factions would cause warlords on both sides to launch a large-scale war in 1920, even though their leaders were supposed to belong to the same Beiyang system.

How to reconcile Duan's seemingly conflicting domestic and foreign policies? To an extent, they were strategically compatible. Duan wanted to use entry into the war as an opportunity to increase his military forces which would then be available for domestic use. He also saw in the European war an opportunity to secure loans which could be used for China's reunification. Since financial support from the United States was not forthcoming, Duan had allied himself with Japan after the outbreak of the civil war. From August 1917 to January 1918, Duan received a huge number of loans from Japan, the largest of which was the so-called Nishihara loan. According to Li Jiannong, Liang Qichao, in his capacity as Minister of Finance, was directly involved in the loan negotiations. Although a large amount of the Nishihara loan was expended on the training of an army for participation in the European war, a considerable part was poured into the domestic battle.[77]

For Duan, uniting China under an effective central government was a crucial step toward a proper Chinese entrance onto the world stage. That he assumed charge of the War Participation Bureau indicated his intention to carry forward his own war participation policy.[78] In terms of domestic affairs, the Duan government felt compelled to use authoritarian and military methods to overcome individualism and political conflict. As Duan told Reinsch on August 22, 1917, "We must first of all establish the authority of the central government . . . This can be done only through the defeat of the opposition. My purpose is to make the military organization in China national and unified, so that the peace of the country shall not at all times be upset by local military commanders."[79] In his later years Duan realized what a disaster having the military intervene in civil politics had been. He expressed "great regret for his role in it."[80] In his handwritten will, perhaps speaking from his own mistakes, he wrote that China would still enjoy a great future if its leaders followed his "eight Nos." His first "no" was that politicians should not try to "solve political disputes [by military means] to force through their own ideas."[81]

Duan's policy must also be understood in light of the times. Both Yuan and Duan were men of their era, a time of transition lacking a clear, well-defined political structure and values, and a well-charted direction. Their policies, and especially their resorting to military intervention in civilian politics, are understandable in this light. The warlordism problem had perhaps more to do with the times than with individuals. After all, it can be traced back to the imperialism of the late nineteenth century. In fact, Beiyang-style warlordism, which clearly defined the era of 1916 to 1928, first emerged during the Western incursion following the Opium War, when Zeng Guofan's Xiang army and Li Hongzhang's Anhui army were formed in the 1860s to respond to an internal threat caused by rebellions like those of the Taiping, the Nian, and the Muslims. The Beiyang army, however, grew in response to external threats and the drive for national survival. After the first Sino-Japanese War of 1895, the then governor of Hebei, Yuan Shikai, decided to build a modern Chinese army. In this sense, the Sino-Japanese War, which prompted the Chinese move toward military modernization, was directly responsible for the establishment of the Beiyang army.

Warlordism was also in tune with China's changing attitude toward military affairs after the late nineteenth century. Prior to that time,

---

[78] The French, who saw Duan's new post as a clear sign that he was serious about sending forces to Europe, asked its Foreign Ministry to attempt to try and hasten the American loan to China. See Martel to Stephen Pichon, January 2, 1918, "Le Président du Conseil et Ministre de la Guerre au Ministre des Affaires etrangères," Quai d'Orsay, 1918–1929, Chine, XL: 3; and XL: 5–6.

[79] Reinsch, An American Diplomat in China, 293.

[80] Rong Mengyuan and Zhang Bofeng, eds., Jindai bi hai (Materials of modern times) (Chengdu: Sichuan renmin chubanshe, 1985), II: 191.

[81] Ibid., IV: 697.

legitimate state-sponsored violence was associated with preserving the social order, and was described in terms of "pacification" rather than victory. Its targets were mainly internal rebels. The word "military" (*wu*) in Chinese derives from the graphic "he who acts to stop the clashing of spears." But, as Henrietta Harrison points out in a recent article, Chinese society underwent a great change in response to the foreign threat and, particularly after the Sino-Japanese War, militarization became "the root of China's self-strengthening." The desire for a new China and in particular the wish for a strong China helped to make the pursuit of military power a national priority. This in brief is the social background of the rise of warlordism. In the late nineteenth century, when militarism and militarist values began to be promoted in the new schools, military violence, once seen as peripheral in a world which considered violence primarily a means of preserving order, "now . . . became central to ideas of society and was sanctioned both by public opinion and the state."[82] Cai E argued in 1902 that militarist education had a positive connection to China's developing national identity, since "to train a good soldier is actually to train a good citizen."[83] The Shangxi warlord Yan Xishan (1883–1960), who was trained at the Japanese Imperial Military Academy, spoke for many Chinese when he declared in 1915 that "China can save herself only by embracing militarism."[84]

Not only the military men supported militarism; leading civilians held the same attitude. In Liu Shuya's article "Junguo zhuyi" (State militarism) published in *Xin qingnian*, he lauded the military state as the true solution to China's problems. He argued, "There is no other way to protect our national territory and people . . . today's world is a world of militarism."[85] Although Liu tried hard to differentiate militarism from warlordism, the emphasis on fighting was there. Chen Duxiu also argued that the relation of warfare to a society was similar to the relation of exercise to a human body: warfare played an important role in maintaining a society's vitality and vigor.[86] Liang Qichao published an article encouraging the Chinese to become more appreciative of martial spirit as well.[87]

---

[82] Henrietta Harrison, "Martyrs and Militarism in Early Republican China," *Twentieth-Century China* 23, no. 2 (April 1998): 43–46.

[83] Hans Van de Ven, "The Military in the Republic," in Frederic Wakeman, Jr., and Richard Louis Edmonds, eds., *Reappraising Republican China* (Oxford: Oxford University Press, 2000), 103.

[84] Donald G. Gillin, *Warlord Yen Hsi-shan in Shansi Province, 1911–1949* (Princeton: Princeton University Press, 1967), 11.

[85] Liu Shuya, "Junguo zhuyi," *Xin qingnian (New Youth)* 2, no. 3 (1916).

[86] Chen Duxiu, "Dui De waijiao," *Xin qingnian* 3, no. 1 (1917).

[87] Liang Qichao, "Shang wu lun"(On appreciating martial qualities), *Ying bing shi cong shu* 1 (1916).

The emergence of militarism in China was deeply connected to the rise of nationalism in the late nineteenth century. Militarism had wide appeal in China; it had made Japan and Germany strong, so it might help China to achieve the same. The nationalism of the late nineteenth and early twentieth centuries directly linked martial values to national survival and played a critical role in improving the status of the military. "In the context of this broader nationalist-inspired reassessment of the military," Edward McCord reminds us, "it would not be unexpected for China's military men to have developed a nationalist justification for their political interventions." These changing political circumstances would "in fact drive China's military towards political action."[88]

These circumstances introduced a new element into Chinese politics: a pro-military ideology and the legitimacy of generals in political society. Nationalism was a major force in Chinese society in the period under discussion, and for reasons outlined above this turned out to be favorable to Chinese career soldiers. Nationalism, according to S. E. Finer, "provides the military with a civic religion and an overriding set of values." It encourages military men to regard themselves as "the ultimate repositories and custodians of the nation's values." Finer further explains that highly significant consequences flow from this point. "First, where nationalism has gripped the masses, the armed forces tend to become the visible symbol and the pledge of nationhood and independence and to attract an esteem for that reason. Secondly, nationalism provides the military with an ideology and possibly even a programme."[89] In the Chinese case, the nation's desire to become rich and powerful could be used by both politicians and military men to justify intervening in politics when chaos threatened. In addition to motives of regional, factional, and individual self-interest, warlords considered the duty of the army to be saving the nation. This was especially true when external troubles were closely linked to internal ones. McCord examines the same phenomenon from a different perspective. He argues that "the underlying cause of warlordism in China was a crisis of political authority grounded in a lack of consensus in the early Republic over the organization of political power. Republican politics was militarized when different political forces turned to the military to resolve seemingly irreconcilable political conflicts."[90] McCord points out that "[w]arlordism did not originate simply in the rejection of

---

[88] Edward A. McCord, "Warlords against Warlordism: The Politics of Anti-Militarism in Early Twentieth-Century China," *Modern Asian Studies* 30, no. 4 (1996): 797–99.

[89] S. E. Finer, *The Man on Horseback: The Role of the Military in Politics* (London: Penguin Books, 1976), 189–91.

[90] Edward A. McCord, *The Power of the Gun: The Emergence of Modern Chinese Warlordism* (Berkeley: University of California Press, 1993).

legitimate political authority by military commanders, but rather in the difficulty of defining which authority was legitimate." He further argues, "The militarization of politics that resulted from the crisis of early Republican political authority created the environment essential to the rise of warlordism."[91]

Whether from Finer's perspective or from McCord's, we can conclude that the Chinese situation was ripe for military intervention in politics, and the generals used such slogans as "protect the nation" and "protect the constitution" as their rallying cry. Finer observes that unlike a dynastic state in which military loyalty to the state and to a ruler were synonymous, the nation-state "no longer necessarily" operated in such a way. "There," he explains, "it must first be demonstrated to the military that the government they serve is the reason why they should not regard an alternative government, and even themselves, as more representative and more worthy of the nation than the government in office; and since their transcendent duty is loyalty to the nation this may entail a duty to be disloyal to the government." Under this logic, the military could become, as Finer calls it, "the insurrectionary army," working for the liberation of national territory or for the replacement of the social order with its own ideology. Finer makes it clear that a new state with passionate nationalism on the one hand and the need for strong central government on the other was "a sure invitation to military intervention."[92]

Finer's arguments highlight a central controversy in Chinese political history: Warlords such as Wu Peifu (1887–1939) and Feng Yuxiang (1882–1948) considered themselves custodians of the national interest and did not hesitate to use force to pursue that interest. And we have seen that a civilian government like Duan's frequently resorted to the army in the name of national interest. These men held power "in the name of national aspirations for modernization, even though modernization is a means for establishing a national identity and national sovereignty." In the process of directing social change, they had "a political choice as to the relative balance of coercion versus persuasion that will be used in the effort to modernize."[93] It seems unexceptional, from the perspective of the mandate of heaven, that Chinese politicians and warlords desired more power and convinced themselves that it was not a selfish ambition, but one identical to the welfare of the country. Both Yuan and Duan were believers in this sort of mandate; for them unifying the country was the government's most urgent task. Even Sun Yat-sen had relied on warlords

[91] Ibid., 310.
[92] Finer, *The Man on Horseback: The Role of the Military in Politics*, 189–191.
[93] Morris Janowita, *The Military in the Political Development of Nations: an Comparative Analysis* (Chicago: University of Chicago Press, 1964), vii.

to set up a separate government in southern China in 1917 using the same logic. Only when he had been ousted by these same warlords did Sun lament, "The most serious pitfall our country faces is the struggle for power among the warlords who, in the North as well as in the South, show the same characteristics as badgers in a lair."[94]

Not every warlord acted completely from personal ambitions. Some were quite patriotic. Feng Yuxiang is a case in point. Feng had witnessed Japanese atrocities as a teenager during the Sino-Japanese War, and promised himself that "if he some day became a soldier he would fight the Japanese to the death."[95] To instill an anti-imperialist attitude in his men, Feng held a meeting every May 7 to commemorate Japan's imposing the Twenty-one Demands and his soldiers and officers all wore belts which bore the inscription "In Memory of the National Humiliation of May 7."[96] Furthermore, the *dujun* were not necessarily narrow-minded about foreign affairs; many of them had given considerable thought to China's war policy and had been carefully briefed by the Foreign Ministry and central government officials at every step. This can be clearly seen in the telegram exchanges between the central government and military governors in the provinces.[97] Some warlords maintained their own information sources about foreign affairs, hiring experts to do research and follow the development of the war in Europe. Feng Guozhang, the military governor of Jiangsu, is a good example of this. Although he held the post of vice-president in the central government, he remained in Nanjing and followed the war closely by having people collect information for him. Jiang Shili was one of Feng's people in Japan who sent several secret reports to Feng on the development of the war and advising him on a possible policy for China.[98] Even the ultra-conservative military governor Zhang Xun felt the need to pay attention to the war and asked his confidants and advisors for reports on its progress from time to time. On February 10, 1917, one of these confidants advised him to oppose

---

[94] Sun Yat-sen, *Sun Zhongshan quanji* (Complete writings of Sun Yat-sen) (Beijing: Zhonghua shuju, 1985), IV: 471–72.

[95] Feng Dali, *Wo de fuqin Feng Yuxiang* (My Father Feng Yuxiang) (Chengdu: Sichuan renmin chubanshe, 1985), 15.

[96] James E. Sheridan, *Chinese Warlord: the Career of Feng Yu-hsiang* (Stanford: Stanford University Press, 1966), 88, 23.

[97] For example, most telegrams regarding the war question which have been released recently are ones between the state council and military governors. See Liangning sheng danganguan lishibu (Department of History), "You guan Zhong De dunjiao de Yizhou zhi liao (Several Documents Relating to Sino-German Relations)," *Minguo dangan* 1 (1991): 5–13; also see Ji Di, "Feng Guozhang wanglai han dian" (Telegrams and letters from and for Feng Guozhang), *Jindai shi ziliao* (Materials of modern history) 40 (1979): 63–124.

[98] For details, see Jiang's four secret reports to Feng, in *Jindai shi ziliao* (1962), II: 1–10.

China's joining the war, arguing that the existing neutrality posed the best option for China. In fact, almost all of the secret letters or reports he received argued against China's declaration of war on Germany. Surely this advice lay behind Zhang's trenchant opposition to the war policy.[99]

Above all, the rise of warlordism was closely linked to the Chinese political structure and culture. Huge problems in the political system, especially the endless disputes about constitutional issues, pushed Chinese politics in a military direction because the only option a politician had for enacting policies was to solicit military help. Yuan Shikai had always relied on military forces to enforce his political will and this left his opponents no choice but to do likewise, as the anti-monarchical war showed. Under Li Yuanhong, the civil service became fragmented and docile when faced with military pressure. This compelled Li to turn to a warlord in mid-1917 in hopes of resolving his seemingly irreconcilable conflicts with Duan. Parliament was influential but its importance was secondary since it could be dissolved at any time, legally or illegally. There was no institutional framework for settling political disputes, and with no stable constitutional or legal framework, the Chinese military easily became politicized and politics militarized. As Edward A. McCord notes, "Warlordism thus describes not only a political condition but a political process."[100]

Because of Republican China's unstable political structure, the military was the only effective political force in China during the era of the First World War.[101] With one political crisis following another in the wake of the war declaration controversy, the military had an ongoing opportunity to intervene in politics. Moreover, as mentioned previously, the Chinese warlords seemed in many instances to have both the means and the moral appeal to intervene in national politics in this period. Furthermore, if military "professionalism" is the key factor keeping generals out of politics, as Samuel Huntington proposes, I will argue that such professionalism was not evident in the Chinese armies of the early Republic.[102]

---

[99] Shi Hua, "Zhang Xun Cang Zha" (Letters Collected by Zhang Xun)," *Jindai shi ziliao* (Materials of modern history) 35 (1965): 19–20, 22–23, 24–26; 28–38, 41–43, 50–51.

[100] Edward A. McCord, "Civil War and Warlordism," in *War and Society* 10, no. 2 (October 1992): 26, 51; see also his *The Power of the Gun: The Emergence of Modern Chinese Warlordism*, 11.

[101] According to Finer, there is a clear distinction between military interventions resulting from political vacuums and those responding to political crises. For the military to intervene in politics it must have "both occasion and disposition." The Chinese military did not face the two "political weaknesses" of civilian politics delineated in Finer's analysis: "the technical inadequacy of the armed force" and "the moral inadequacy of military intervention." Finer, *The Man on Horseback*, 3, 75–80, 20, 12–19.

[102] Samuel Huntington, *The Soldier and the State* (Cambridge, MA: Harvard University Press, 1957); see especially 80–97.

Perhaps the most important reason for China's domestic disintegration was what Finer has called the "lower level of political culture." That Chinese society tolerated military intervention in civil politics and the intimidation of opponents clearly shows that its political culture had not yet stabilized into a system of enduring institutions. Although elections were carried out and strong men such as Duan were expected to resign if something went terribly wrong, regardless of their military backers, military strength was the dominant power in this period. Huntington, in his classic *Political Order in Changing Societies*, has made an excellent point about the political connection to military intervention: "The most important causes of military intervention in politics," he argues, "are not military, but political and reflect not the social and organizational characteristics of the military establishment, but the political and institutional structure of the society." He further emphasizes that military interventions in politics "lie not in the nature of the group but in the structure of society." In the absence of effective political institutions "capable of mediating, refining, and moderating group action . . . social forces confront each other nakedly; no political institutions, no corps of professional political leaders are recognized or accepted as the legitimate intermediary to moderate group conflict. Equally important, no agreement exists among the groups as to the legitimate and authoritative methods for resolving conflicts." Huntington argues that military intervention in politics is a coherent part of the politicization of social forces in developing countries or, in his terminology, a "praetorian society." While in an institutional society the participation of new groups in the political system reduces tensions, in a praetorian society such as China it intensifies them.[103]

The Great Powers and Chinese politics

If warlordism contributed to China's domestic problems, the great powers must claim their share of responsibility as well. As Hans J. Van de Ven notes, China's fiscal crisis was central to the rise of warlordism. The fiscal crisis meant that the central state remained unable to construct a modern national army.[104] This crisis initially arose from the heavy burden imposed by the powers through many claimed indemnities and damaging loans.

Although many powers intervened in China's domestic affairs during the First World War period, Japan was the one that fished most in these

---

[103] Samuel Huntington, *Political Order in Changing Societies* (New Haven: Yale University Press, 1968), 192–98.

[104] Hans J. Van De Ven, "Public Finance and the Rise of Warlordism," *Modern Asian Studies* 30, no. 4 (1996). For a detailed study on Chinese militarism, see his recent book, *War and Nationalism in China: 1925–1945* (London: RoutledgeCurzon, 2003).

troubled waters. This was especially true during the war, when the other major powers were focused on European battles and did not want China to descend into chaos. Japan, however, loved to see China in trouble and was deeply involved in creating chaos at every opportunity. Obviously a weak and divided China served Japan's interest handsomely. Japan's behavior toward Yuan's scheme to restore the monarchy is a good example. From the very beginning, when China was undergoing transformation and beginning to pursue an entry into the world community, Japan tried hard to destroy its unity. This explains why Japan let Yuan think at the outset that it did not oppose his monarchical ambitions, and then, as soon as the scheme was in full motion, encouraged and supported his opponents. According to Liang Qichao's letter to his daughter, Japan made every effort to help Liang join Cai E's campaign against Yuan. As Liang put it, "The Japanese facilitated my trip and provided me with much assistance."[105]

Even after the failure of Yuan's scheme and his death, Japan continued to work toward China's domestic instability apparently with the object of bringing about a definite split between North and South. For instance, Japan supplied Cen Chunxuan, a warlord in the South, with 10,000 rifles and 200,000 dollars for his attempt to make Yunnan Province independent from Beijing.[106] No wonder Jordan reported confidentially that the Japanese "are masters of the situation in the Far East and are in a position to cause or avert trouble in China. They consider, and probably have good grounds for considering, that this [monarchy] movement will meet with opposition in south China."[107]

Japan obviously benefited from the turmoil diplomatically and economically. A weaker and more chaotic China would need more loans from the outside to function. For example, to re-unite China and to build a strong central government, Duan had to fight the regional warlords; but to do so, he needed money to finance campaigns and raise larger forces. From 1916 to 1918, nine provinces in China experienced large or small campaigns, and the size of military forces overall increased dramatically. In 1914 the Chinese national army had 457,000 soldiers. By 1918, the number had nearly doubled to 850,000. In 1919 it had further increased to 1,380,000. Accordingly, the military budget had to grow. The Beijing government's military budget in 1916 was 153 million yuan; in 1918 it

---

[105] Liang Qichao to Liang Sishun, March 12, 1916, in Zhang, ed., *Liang Qichao jiashu* (The family letters of Liang Qichao), 234.

[106] Jordan to Grey, June 28, 1916, FO371/2646/303; see also Jindai shi ziliao, 50: 171; Rong Mengyuan and Zhang Bofeng, eds., *Jindai bi hai* (Materials of Modern Times) (Chengdu: Sichuan renmin chubanshe, 1985), I: 109.

[107] Jordan to Langley, October 20, 1915, PRO, WO350/13/101.

was 203 million. Military expenses posed such a heavy burden that they took more than half of government revenue.[108]

The Duan government, determined to continue fighting the South, could only look to Japan for the loans it so desperately needed. By so doing, it fell victim to Japan's intent to destabilize and control, and sacrificed the national interests and considerable resources in the process. Lu Zongyu, who was branded a national traitor during the May Fourth Movement, himself acknowledged that some of the loans made under the Duan regime were guaranteed against the forests and mines in Helongjiang and Jilin provinces, and thus were contracted under "selling the nation" conditions.[109] Through these loans, Duan managed to compromise his long-term goal of joining the European war even as he endeavored to secure the means to achieve it.

By providing loans to China, the Japanese were able to compel the Duan government to make further concessions. This strategy was marvelously employed by Japan when in early 1918 it extracted the Sino-Japanese Military Agreement for Common Defense from Beijing. In late 1917 when the Bolsheviks swept to power in Russia, the existing order in Asia was changed dramatically. First, the Russo-Japanese alliance collapsed, and the Russian Revolution presented a new opportunity for Japan to extend its interest into Siberia. Japan could leverage this into gaining further control in Manchuria. While Japan was busy preparing its military expedition into Russia, it was also pressuring China to sign a treaty giving Japan full control of Manchuria and the Chinese army, using the excuse of dealing with German soldiers in Russia and preventing the spread of revolutionary currents from Russia to East Asia.

In early February 1918 when Japan first pressed this issue, China made it clear that if the so-called German threat came at its Russian border, China would itself manage the situation. Regarding affairs occurring outside Chinese territory it was admitted that "China may deal jointly with Japan."[110] But Japan pushed hard.[111] On March 2, the Chinese Foreign Ministry agreed in principle that China would negotiate with Japan regarding the joint defense if the latter was really sincere in its promise that

---

[108] The military budget in 1919 took 80 per cent of the country's financial income. For details, see Huang Zheng, Chen Changhe, and Ma Lie, *Duan Qirui yu wan xi junfa* (Zhengzhou shi: Henan renmin chubanshe: Henan sheng xinhua shudian faxing, 1990), 163–64.

[109] Lu Zengyu, *Wushi zishu* (Memoir of the fifty-year-old man) (n.d., n.p.), 18–19.

[110] Waijiaobu to Zhang Zongxiang, February 22, 1918, no. 3, in Chinese Ministry of Foreign Affairs, ed., *Diplomatic Documents: Sino-Japanese Agreements for Common Defense* (Beijing: The Waichiopu Press, 1921) (quoted hereafter as *Waijiao wendu*).

[111] For details, see Zhang Zongxiang to Waijiaobu, no. 4, February 23, 1918, *Waijiao wendu*. Zhang Zongxiang to Waijiaobu, no. 5, February 23, 1918, *Waijiao wendu*.

afterwards the Japanese troops within Chinese territory would be entirely withdrawn.[112] As it did with the Twenty-one Demands, Japan asked China to keep the discussions and alleged agreements strictly secret. Viscount Motono told Zhang Zongxiang, Chinese minister to Japan, that "before the joint defense agreement is made known, we shouldn't disclose anything in words to the Allied countries, but should wait until such a time when the two countries can jointly confer with them."[113] In mid-May, the Terauchi Masatake government and Beijing concluded and signed the joint defense agreements; the army section was signed on May 16, the naval section three days later. Its provisions enabled Japanese troops to move freely throughout most of China.[114] To continue receiving its financial support, the Duan government even agreed that Japan could keep its interests in Shandong in a secret agreement signed on September 24, 1918.

These secret arrangements were important for two reasons. First, they sowed the seeds of China's failure at the Paris Peace Conference regarding the Shandong issue. Second, the joint defense agreement aroused strong opposition among China's foreign policy public, especially college students, with nationwide demonstrations coming as a forerunner of the May Fourth Movement. Indeed, when the news regarding the secret treaty with Japan leaked out, the Chinese people immediately protested. Thirty-seven groups in Shanghai alone sent a telegram on April 23 to the Duan government, declaring their opposition to the alleged treaty. Many influential social groups including the United Association of National Commerce and provincial education commissions openly expressed their dissent. Many societies sent delegates to Beijing to petition the government directly not to sign the treaty. They all pointed out that such agreements would only damage China's national interest and claims to sovereignty. Some protesters felt this was worse than the Twenty-one Demands. Among the protesters, students were the most active and vocal. Chinese students in Japan demonstrated, refused to go to class, and many returned to China. Beijing students organized demonstrations in front of the presidential office, demanding rejection of the treaty. Students in other places such as Tianjin and Shanghai also took similar actions. To make their opposition more effective and influential, the students set up their own organizations such as "Students' Society for National Salvation," which published its own magazines *Citizens* and *National*

---

[112] Waijiaobu and the Cabinet to Zhang Zongxiang, no. 7, March 2, 1918, *Waijiao wendu*. See also Waijiaobu to Zhang, no. 8, March 2, 1918, *Waijiao wendu*.

[113] Zhang to Waijiaobu, no. 9, March 6, 1918, *Waijiao wendu*.

[114] The agreement did not last long. On January 27, 1921, Japan was compelled to cancel the agreement under strong pressure from the Chinese anti-imperialist movement.

Salvation Daily.[115] The zeal and strength of the students' response to this agreement showed that the May Fourth Movement did not come out of the blue.

Japan, of course, was not the only country to meddle in China's internal politics. The United States also played a role in Yuan's monarchical scheme. As British minister Jordan wrote, the "American government has a measure of responsibility as it was one of their eminent citizens who came to China for the express purpose apparently of starting this movement."[116] He went on to observe with some irony: "Strangely enough, one of the American advisers has been called in to champion the change from republic to monarchy."[117] The American whom Jordan referred to was Frank Johnson Goodnow (1859–1939), first president of the American Political Science Association, founded in 1904. Goodnow was at the time referred to as "the father of American administration" for his emphasis on the administrative aspect of government.[118]

This eminent scholar was keenly interested in adapting constitutional provisions to social and cultural realities. Goodnow believed in Yuan, seeing him as "honestly desirous of saving his country" and bought Yuan's idea that China could be saved only by a "practically autocratic government."[119] Having served as Yuan's constitutional advisor (appointed in 1913) provided Goodnow with an opportunity to put his theory into practice. In the summer of 1915, at Yuan's request, he prepared a memorandum on the relative merits of republicanism and monarchism for

---

[115] *Minguo Ribao*, May 7, May 23, May 24, 25, 27, June 1, 1918; Zhang Bofeng et al., *Beiyang junfa, 1912–1928*, III: 975–92.

[116] Jordan to Langley, October 20, 1915, PRO, wo350/13/101–103.

[117] Jordan to Langley, August 19, 1915, PRO, wo350/13/85.

[118] Goodnow completed his undergraduate work at Amherst College in 1879 and also received the Ll.B. degree from Columbia University in 1882. Following this, he studied at the Ecole Libre des Sciences Politiques, Paris, and at the University of Berlin, where he specialized in administrative law. Goodnow started to teach at Columbia University in 1883, was the Eaton Professor of Public Law and Municipal Science at Columbia University, and served as the president of Johns Hopkins University from 1914 until his retirement in 1929. Historian Charles Beard called him "the first scholar in the United States to recognize the immense importance of administration in modern society and to sketch the outlines of the field." "With study, Mr. Goodnow combined practice. His services on President Taft's Efficiency and Economy Commission revealed Mr. Goodnow as a scholar interested in the application of his science and as a leader in the rationalization movement, associated with institutes for administrative research." His major books include *Comparative Administrative Law* (1893), *Politics and Administration* (1900), *Principles of the Administrative Law of the United States* (1905), *Social Reform and the Constitution* (1911). Charles G. Haines and Marshall E. Dimock, *Essays on the Law and Practice of Governmental Administration: a Volume in Honor of Frank Johnson Goodnow* (Baltimore: The Johns Hopkins Press, 1935), vi–vii.

[119] Goodnow to Nicholas Murry Butler, February 26, 1914, quote from Noel Pugach, "Embarrassed Monarchist: Frank J. Goodnow and Constitutional Development in China, 1913–1915," *Pacific Historical Review* 42, no. 4 (November 1973): 507.

China. Goodnow declared that it was "not susceptible of doubt," that a monarchy "is better suited than a republic to China" because republicanism did not suit the present conditions there owing to the country's history, traditions, and social and economic circumstances.[120]

Although Goodnow's argument does not hold water from a historical perspective, Yuan could not have found a better man. Having the backing of such a distinguished scholar from an influential republic justified Yuan's move and greatly enhanced the respectability of his scheme. Yuan underscored the "scientific" basis of his plan by pointing to Goodnow, and bought a whole page in the *Manchester Guardian* to publicize Goodnow's ideas. In the meantime, he arranged for the Chinese version to be printed and circulated widely in China.[121] It is said that Yuan's presidential office provided every one of its visitors with Goodnow's article.[122]

Liang Qichao suggested that Yuan's monarchical campaign started with Goodnow's supposed support of the imperial system, or at least that seemed to be the case "on the surface."[123] Within less than a week, the main organ to carry out Yuan's scheme, the Peace Planning Society, had been organized. Yang Du, a central figure in this society, wrote a long essay entitled "National Salvation by a Constitutional Monarchy" in April of 1915.[124] There he strongly argued that a republican government would be inefficient for China. If China wanted to be rich and powerful, it had to change its polity, and only a constitutional monarchy could save it. That article did not, however, attract wide attention. But when Goodnow's article came out, Yang realized the time to be ripe for carrying out the imperial plan. In its manifesto, the Peace Planning Society built its case mainly on Goodnow's ideas, claiming that the "leading political science scholar of the leading republic," Goodnow, was of the same opinion that a monarchy was a better form of government than republicanism. The society sent copies of Goodnow's article to each provincial official and asked them to send delegates to Beijing to discuss monarchical issues.[125] Goodnow tried to distance himself from the Peace Planning Society and refused to allow further use of his name in support of the latter's political views. No matter what his original motivation for writing the

---

[120] "Dr. Goodnow's Memorandum to the President," US Department of State, ed., *FRUS, 1915*, 53–58.

[121] Li Xisuo and Yuan Qing, *Liang Qichao zhuan* (Beijing: Renmin chubanshe, 1993), 340–41; the full text of his memorandum was published in the *Peking Daily News* on August 20, 1915.

[122] Bai Jiao, *Yuan Shikai yu Zhonghua minguo*, 246.

[123] Liang Qichao, "Yi zai suowei guoti wenti zhe," in *Dun bi ji*, 138.

[124] For the complete essay, see Yang Du, *Yang Du ji* (Writings of Yang Du), 566–84.

[125] Xie Benshu, *Yuan Shikai yu Beiyang junfa* (Yuan Shikai and the Beiyang Warlords) (Shanghai: Shanghai renmin chubanshe, 1984), 70.

memorandum, Goodnow's name and its prestige had been used to great advantage by Yuan's plotters and the Peace Planning Society.[126]

Goodnow's role in Yuan's scheme was crucial and irreplaceable. Certainly, other foreigners had voiced the same or similar ideas, but no one had received the same degree of attention or was as influential. If his ideas and actions did not necessarily represent official American policy, at least Goodnow represented various elite American groups' interests in China. He had been nominated for his position as Yuan's advisor by the Carnegie Foundation, at the recommendation of a Harvard president emeritus. From the perspective of international history, as long as such a position made an impact, it did not really matter whether it was an individual initiative or official policy. Goodnow's case shows how non-governmental organizations, and even individuals, can affect the history and direction of a country's development. His case also indicates the strong impact of ideas on policy-making, since Goodnow drew on his expertise to push his point. This case clearly supports the view that the First World War period was for the Chinese public an age of innocence, since a single foreigner's idea widely publicized could so fundamentally affect China's polity and its development. The fact that Yuan and his cronies fully embraced Goodnow's view not only reflects Chinese naiveté, but also the fragility of the evolving Chinese political culture.

The United States government also came to be directly involved in China's domestic affairs. In early June 1917 the American government proposed to France, Britain, and Japan that they make identical representations to the Chinese government "expressing regret for the factional discord that has arisen." The representation should make it clear to China that "the maintenance by China of one centrally united and responsible government is of first importance both to China itself and to the world," that "the entrance of China into the war against Germany is of quite secondary importance as compared with unity and peace of China," and that the Allied countries "hope that wise counsels will prevail and that harmony be restored which is so essential to China's welfare."[127] The Allied countries gave the American proposal a cold reception. For instance, the French protested, "It seems indeed excessive and useless to say that we consider China's entrance into the war against Germany as entirely of secondary importance."[128]

---

[126] "A Statement by Dr. Goodnow," *The Peking Gazette*, August 18, 1917, in *FRUS, 1917*, 59–60.

[127] American Ambassador to French Foreign Minister, June 6, 1917, Quai d'Orsay, NS, Chine, CXXXVI: 54–55.

[128] French Foreign Minister, telegram to French Ambassadors in Washington, London, Tokyo, Rome, and Minister in Peking on June 8, 1917, Quai d'Orsay, NS, Chine, CXXXVI: 65.

If the French suggestion was an indirect refusal of the American proposal, Britain and Japan more openly opposed it.[129] Robert Cecil told the American ambassador in London that he considered China's entry into the war "of very great importance," that "China's entry would deal a hard blow to Germany in trade relations after the war," and that he regarded "German fear of complete commercial isolation as one of the strongest kinds of pressure to bring peace." On June 14, the British Foreign Office officially responded to the American proposal by saying that the British government would "abstain from the step proposed" by the United States.[130] Japan simply let the United States know that it would not support the proposal.[131]

Even without the support of other powers, the United States went ahead single-mindedly. Secretary of State Robert Lansing asked Reinsch to let his host know that the American government considered Chinese entry into the war with Germany of secondary importance. Moreover, "the principal necessity for China," Lansing maintained, "is to resume and continue her political entity and to proceed along the road of national development on which she has made such marked progress." Lansing especially directed Reinsch to communicate this message to the Chinese "leaders of the military party opposing the President."[132]

Why did the United States choose this moment to send this note to China and suggest that other powers do the same? According to the State Department's official explanation, the major reason was that the United States wanted "China to stay [a] republic" and was "anxious not to see the monarchy restored."[133]

Lansing soon realized that the American note counseling internal peace in China did not have any positive result. The *Washington Post* even termed it a "blunder," and there is some truth to this characterization. First of all, American good wishes did nothing to stop the chaos in China. Second, the statement soured America's relations with the Allied countries, especially Japan. The Japanese government let the United States government know through official channels that it was not at all pleased with the step taken by the American government. It promptly questioned the right of the

[129] See Conty telegram, June 11, 1917, NS, Chine, CXXXVI: 74–76; French Foreign Minister to French ambassadors in London, Rome, Peking, and Tokyo, telegram, June 14, 1917, NS, Chine, CXXXVI: 82ab; French Government to American ambassador in Paris, expédié, June 14, 1917, Quai d'Orsay, NS, Chine, CXXXVI: 84–85; Rome, June 15, 1917, French ambassador to Rome, Barrère to French Government, June 15, 1917, Quai d'Orsay, NS, Chine, CXXXVI: 86; French ambassador to USA, Jussurand to Ribot, June 19, 1917, Quai d'Orsay, NS, Chine, CXXXVI: 93.

[130] Page to Lansing, June 5, 1917, *FRUS, 1917*, 50, FO to Page, June 14, 1917, *FRUS, 1917*, 75.

[131] The Japanese ambassador to Lansing, June 15, 1917, *FRUS, 1917*, 72.

[132] See Lansing to Reinsch, June 4, 1917, in *FRUS, 1917*, 49.

[133] *The Washington Post*, June 9, 1917.

United States to interfere in Chinese affairs and reminded the United States that the Japanese commanded the paramount position in East Asia. Japan also complained that the United States had sent its note to China without consultation in advance with Japan and other Allied nations. Given all these problems, The *Washington Post* commented that "the affair has left a very pronounced ripple on diplomatic waters." According to the same article, "Washington officials regarded the whole episode as a disturbing one, when it became apparent that the incident persists in surviving the State Department explanation that the whole thing is a misunderstanding brought about through the publication in Japan of a 'bogus note' before the correct text was received there." Yet, there was no "misunderstanding" that containing the increasing Japanese influence in China had actually been the impetus behind the American note. Given the wider global situation – Germany was out of the picture because of the war; Great Britain, as an ally, was forced to steer a cautious course; Russia was in revolution, and France absorbed in the defense of its own dominion – the United States was extremely concerned that should chaos prevail in China, "Japan might well attempt to justify her assumption of the prerogative of a special protector."[134] It was imperative that the US do something to stabilize the situation between Japan and China. Although the United States had good reason to think this way, its note achieved nothing concrete.

Some Chinese elite members welcomed the American note and asked for American intervention. Foreign Minister Wu Tingfang appealed to the United States, through Reinsch, for support: "In view of the present dangerous situation and the attitude of the rebellious Tuchuns [*dujun*], I earnestly request that President Wilson, as the defender of the cause of democracy and constitutionalism all the world over, be moved to make a public statement on the subject of the American attitude toward China and earnestly supporting President Li Yuan-hung [Li Yuanhong]."[135] After Parliament was dissolved in early June, Wu Jingliang, the Speaker of the House of Representatives, and Wang Zhengting, the Vice-president of the Senate, also sent a joint telegram to the American Congress: It read, "As a nation determined to be governed as a democracy, we appeal to the American people and their congress for support."[136]

As with Yuan's use of Goodnow, and Duan's and Li's turn to the military, Wu's request for foreign intervention indicates the naiveté and inexperience of Chinese politicians at the time.

---

[134] *The Washington Post*, June 17, 1917.
[135] Reinsch to Lansing, June 5, 1917, *FRUS, 1917*, 50.
[136] *China Press*, July 27, 1917. For the Chinese parliament, see Guan Meirong, *Wu Jingliang yu minchu Guohui* (Wu Jingliang and the Parliament in Early Republican China) (Taipei: Guoshi guan, 1995).

Germany was also deeply implicated in Chinese politics. Even as China was debating the war participation issue in the spring of 1917, Paul von Hintze, the German minister to China, realizing that China would soon join the war against his country, hired a lobbyist by the name of Yong Jianqiu, a rich and well-connected merchant who had close ties to both Chinese high officials and the Germans. Yong, with a four-million-yuan fee provided by Hintze, was to lobby Duan Qirui for at least a six-month delay of the Chinese declaration of war on Germany. Yong did manage to see Duan, but Duan immediately rejected Hintze's plea.[137] Evidence also suggests that Germany provided direct support for Zhang Xun's scheme to restore the Qing court. The French insisted, "There is much evidence to show that Zhang Xun worked hand in glove with the official representatives of Germany."[138] This charge is in fact confirmed by other sources. According to Zhang Zongxiang, Germany provided Zhang Xun with a large supply of weapons and money in 1917. Moreover, Germany let the restorationists know that it would recognize a restored Qing that was neutral in the European war.[139] The strongest evidence of German intervention in Chinese politics comes from the Germans themselves. In his report dated December 20, 1917, to Paul Hintze, Mr. Kuipping, German consul-general to Shanghai, who had secretly remained in China after it broke off its relations with Germany, wrote in detail about how his government tried to intervene in Chinese domestic politics to influence China's German policy. Kuipping, under instructions from Hintze, established a direct and close relationship with Sun Yat-sen through an intermediary, Mr. Schirmer, a former interpreter. Germany provided about two million dollars between March and August 1917 to Sun for his efforts to sabotage and possibly overthrow the Beijing government. Cao Yabo, a friend and partisan of Sun's, acted as intermediary between Sun and the German consulate general in Shanghai. To please Germany, Sun even volunteered to go to Japan to lobby pro-German sentiment. Mr. Kuipping politely asked him not to do so. Later when Sun set up a separate government in

---

[137] Yong Dingcheng, "Jun huo maiban Yong Jianqiu de yisheng" (Life of Arms and Munitions Merchant Yong Jianqiu), in *Wenshi ziliao xuanji* (Selected materials on literature and history) (Beijing: Wenshi ziliao chubanshe, 1981), 84. This was confirmed by Hintze's reports to the German Foreign Ministry; see Politisches Archiv des Auswärtigen Amts, Bonn, Hintze report, July 3, 1917, R18024 China No. 9, A24099. Please also see Li Guoqi, "De guo dang an zhong you guan zhong guo can jia de yi ci shi jie da zhan de ji xiang ji zai," in Li Guoqi, *min guo shi lun ji* (Taipei: Nan tian shu ju, 1990), 311–25.

[138] Quai d'Orsay, NS, Chine, LXIV: 131.

[139] Zhang Zongxiang, "Dongjing zhi san nian" (My three years in Tokyo), *Jindai shi ziliao* 38 (1979): 27; Zheng Xiaoxu, "Zheng Xiaoxu bingding riji" (Diary of Zheng Xiaoxu)," *Jindai shi ziliao* 35. See also Rong Mengyuan and Zhang Bofeng, eds., *Jindai bi hai*, IV: 198.

Guangzhou, he invited his German friends to join him there. Kuipping reported that he and Schirmer "did not consider it wise to accept the invitation." The same report also mentioned that a German agent had maintained close contact with Kang Youwei. Mr. Kuipping reported that an "excellent relationship" had been established between the two. Kuipping also revealed that through a secret messenger he maintained contact with Zhang Xun, and Zhang had assured him of "his friendship toward the Germans," promising that Kuipping and Schirmer "could remain in the country for as long as [they] wished."[140]

According to Li Dazhao, a professor at Beijing University and later a co-founder of the Chinese Communist Party, all Chinese "lived under the phenomenon of contradiction" during the First World War.[141] Li's observation is well founded. On the personal level, contradictions can be found across the board. Yuan Shikai, once considered China's best hope for stability and prosperity, brought shame and disaster on himself and China by trying to become emperor. Sun Yat-sen was thought to be a symbol of Chinese nationalism and national consciousness. Yet it was this same man who later tried to do everything and anything to get back into power. Sun Yat-sen's willingness to "follow any available trail, even of the most risky nature, and his acceptance of any and every condition set by his partners in return for possible aid, even if those conditions directly restricted the sovereignty and independence of the Chinese republic," make his legacy a mixed one.[142] As previous pages demonstrate, the actions and thinking of Duan Qirui, Li Yuanhong, and many others are full of contradictions. As China considered entering the First World War, its political groups competed bitterly for supremacy and each pursued its own interests. Duan Qirui's policies were not so much partial as stubbornly pursued at any cost, and it was – perhaps most tragically – his way of dealing with opposition rather than the policies themselves that explains why he eventually ended up as a defeated politician.

---

[140] Kuipping to Hintze, December 20, 1917, Potsdam Archives, Bestand: Deutsche Botschaft China, R9208, Document reference R17981.
[141] Li Dazhao, "Xin de! Jiu de!" (Something new! Something old!) *Xin qingnian* 4, no. 5.
[142] Marie-Claire Bergère, *Sun Yat-Sen*, 196.

The 1919 Paris Peace Conference and
      China's search for a new world order

"Great year! You will be the *regenerating year*, and you will be known by
that name. History will extol your great deeds."

Louis-Sébastien Mercier[1]

And so it comes about that we begin to conceptualize matters of identity
at the very time in history when they become a problem.

Erik H. Erikson[2]

False dawn: Wilsonianism in China

Given all the misfortunes and mishaps China experienced in connection
with its attempts at engagement in the First World War, it is perhaps
surprising that the Chinese people were excited and genuinely jubilant
when the fighting ended with the Allies' victory. Nonetheless, when the
news reached China, the government in Beijing immediately declared a
three-day national holiday to commence upon the armistice. Many people
gathered before the Presidential Palace in Beijing on November 17 to celebrate the victory; they cried out with one voice, "Long live justice, long live
national independence!" Meanwhile, the government resolved to immediately dismantle and relocate the Von Ketteler Memorial in Beijing –
a symbol of national humiliation for many Chinese – to a central park
and rename it Monument of the Right Over Might.[3]

When the war ended, many Chinese asked themselves such questions
as "Who will be China's champion . . . at the peace conference? What are

[1] Louis-Sébastien Mercier (a literary anatomist of eighteenth-century Paris), *Farewell to
the Year 1789*, quote from Roger Chartier, *The Cultural Origins of the French Revolution*
(Durham, NC: Duke University Press, 1991), xix.
[2] Erik Erikson, *Childhood and Society* (New York: Norton, 1963), 282.
[3] Von Ketteler was a German minister to China killed during the Boxer Uprising. As
punishment for his murder, the Chinese government was compelled to erect a three-arch
stone pailou (gateway) bearing inscriptions of official apology in Chinese, German, and
Latin in the center of the capital across the entire width of the main street. This was done
in the summer of 1901 and the gateway became a landmark, an everyday reminder of
Chinese humiliation and helplessness in the face of the powers.

the remedies for the wrongs from which China has suffered for the last two decades? Is China prepared for this [postwar peace] conference, which will offer an opportunity for the redressing of her grievances?" Veteran journalist Hollington Tong reported, "Thinking Chinese are looking to President Wilson for his leadership." For these Chinese, according to Tong, "Wilson is the best qualified statesman to assume the role of champion of human rights generally and of the rights of China in particular."[4] Although not every Chinese believed in Wilson, feelings ran high at the dramatic conclusion of the war. Chinese students in Beijing went to the American Legation where they chanted "Long Live President Wilson!" Some of them had memorized and could easily recite his speech on the Fourteen Points. The Chinese translation of his Fourteen Points speech was an immediate bestseller and a collection of Wilson's war speeches, translated by Jiang Menglin, was popular as well. It was not only young Chinese students who were deeply attracted to Wilsonianism. The established social elite believed in him enormously. General Huang Fu, a revolutionary general who played an important role in the Xinhai (1911) Revolution, visited the United States during the First World War and initially considered the war a hegemonic struggle between Germany and Great Britain, had a high opinion of Wilson and his Fourteen Points. He argued that America's impartiality and insistence on justice should make any country admire and agree with it. Without American participation, the Allied countries would not have achieved their victory, Huang concluded in his popular book on China and the First World War, published in the last days of 1918.[5]

For many Chinese, therefore, Wilson had become China's best hope. He was the world leader of "spiritual democracy."[6] Even Li Dazhao, a co-founder of the Chinese Communist Party, wrote that Wilson was "famous for his deep love of world peace," and that he had "single-handedly shouldered the future" of a fair world.[7] Chen Duxiu was so convinced of Wilson's sincerity that he called Wilson "the number one good man in the world."[8] For Chen, the end of the First World War was a turning point in human history. From now on, "might is no longer reliable, justice and reason can no longer be denied," wrote Chen.[9] Cai

---

[4] Hollington Tong, "What Can President Wilson Do for China," *Millard's Review* 6, no. 11 (November 16, 1918): 431–34.

[5] Huang Fu, *Ouzhan zhi jiaoxun yu Zhongguo zhi weilai*, 99–100.

[6] Fu Sinian, Luo Jialun, eds., *Xin Chao* (New Tide) 1, no. 5 (1919).

[7] Li Dazhao, "Wei Erxun yu pinghe" (Wilson and peace), in Li Dazhao, *Li Dazhao wenji* (Writings of Li Dazhao) (Beijing: Renmin chubanshe, 1984), I: 285.

[8] Chen Duxiu, *Duxiu wencun* (Surviving writings of Chen Duxiu) (Hefei: Anhui renmin chubanshe, 1987), 388.

[9] Chen Duxiu, "Fa kan ci" (Preface for a new magazine), *Meizhou pinglun* (Weekly Review) 1, no. 1 (1918).

Yuanpei, the president of Peking University, declared that the Allies' victory signaled the end of an age of "darkness" and the coming of an age of openness in the world.[10] Liang Qichao also lauded the Allied victory as representing "progress of the new age," because the war had been fought for "the purpose of securing permanent peace for the world."[11] Jiang Tingfu attested that during World War I, he had "believed in every word which President Wilson uttered."[12]

Thus, trusting Wilson and consumed by the prospects of a League of Nations and a new world order, the Chinese had extremely high hopes for the coming peace conference, especially when the news came that Wilson himself would go to Paris.[13] One Chinese spoke volumes when he wrote a letter to the editors of the *New York Times*:

The world is tired of wars, and China is tired of humiliations. The spirit of the glorious victory of the war indicates the birth of a universal feeling that imperialism of any description must be totally condemned and cast away as a dead theory of the bygone generation. The goal of the peace conference now assembled in Paris, exemplified by President Wilson's lofty ideals and enlightened principles, promises . . . to usher in an upright new regime of nationalism and internationalism, based on right and justice. With this spirit and toward this goal China has ample justification to claim a readjustment that would give her an honorable place among the family of nations. Such a readjustment China claims not only in her own interests, to which she is legally and morally entitled, but also in the interests of world peace.[14]

Such high expectations for Wilson and the postwar peace conference brought many of China's best and brightest to Paris either as official members of the delegation or as semi-private or private citizens who would push for China's goals at the conference during the first six months of 1919. The Chinese delegation to the historical gathering had over sixty members. Lu Zhengxiang, Wang Zhengting, Wellington Koo, Shi Zhaoji, and Wei Chenzhou were the plenipotentiaries of the delegation. Except

[10] Tang Zhengchan, *Cai Yuanpei zhuan* (The biography of Cai Yuanpei) (Shanghai: Shanghai renmin chubanshe, 1985), 159.

[11] *Dongfang Zazhi* 16, no. 2 (February 1919).

[12] Min-Chien T. Z. Tyau, *China Awakened* (New York: The Macmillan Company, 1922), 268.

[13] Not only many Chinese had high expectations of Wilson; the Europeans did as well. According to the *New York Times*, "Mr. Wilson sets foot on the soil of France amid such a tumult of acclaim as, perhaps, no other statesman, no other ruler, has been privileged to receive. The enthusiasm of the French people is that of every other people of the Allies, that of all the nationalities soon to be erected into nations . . . We all look forward with confidence or with hope!" See *The New York Times*, December 13, 1918. Another American newspaper reported that when Wilson arrived in Brest, the town was bedecked with banners proclaiming "Vive Wilson! Hail the champion of the rights of man!" See *The New York Tribune*, December 14, 1918.

[14] K. P. Wang to *The New York Times*, February 2, 1919.

for Lu Zhengxiang, foreign minister at the time, and Wang Zhengting, who represented the South and was stationed in the United States when chosen as a delegate to the conference, the others were ministers to European countries or the United States. The Chinese minister to Japan was not a member of the delegation. This omission indicates that China chose to focus on the West and not deal with Japan at the conference.

These were the best diplomats China could offer.[15] Wellington Koo's participation was especially critical owing to his thorough preparation for the conference and his diplomatic skills. Koo, born into a rich merchant's family, had had both Chinese classical training and a Western education. In 1912, immediately after finishing his Ph.D. program at Columbia,[16] he was summoned back to China to serve as a secretary to President Yuan Shikai. Soon he was working for the Foreign Ministry and commencing his brilliant career as a professional diplomat.[17] By 1915 he had become the youngest minister in Washington, representing China at only twenty-seven years of age. Woodrow Wilson was deeply impressed with him, and admitted that Koo spoke English in the way the famous British writer Thomas Macaulay wrote it.[18] Excepting Lu, all four Chinese delegates had been educated in American or European universities.[19]

Along with the formal delegation, influential social elite members also went to Paris in private or semi-official capacities. They included Liang Qichao and his comrades, who left for Paris "dreaming of bringing about justice and humaneness through diplomacy, and believ[ing] that the peace conference would really mean an overhaul of all unjust international relations and establishing a solid foundation for everlasting peace."[20] Wang Jingwei, Li Shizeng, Ye Gongchuo, Chen Youren, among others, traveled to Paris to witness the historical event and push China's causes at a global venue.[21]

---

[15] Chen Sanjing maintained that the choice of Lu was not sound, since he was not qualified as head of the delegation for this important occasion. See Chen Sanjing, "Lu Zhengxiang yu Bali hehui," in *Jindai waijiao shi lunji* (Taibei: Xuehai chubanshe, 1977).

[16] His dissertation, entitled "The Status of Aliens in China," was written under the direction of John Bassett Moore, a leading expert in international law and diplomacy.

[17] Koo had not finished his dissertation when he left for China. His dissertation committee at Columbia University wrote the conclusion for him and got it published as No. 126 of the series Studies in History, Economics and Public Law by Columbia University Press.

[18] S. Bonsal, *Suitors and Supplicants: The Little Nations at Versailles* (New York: Prentice-Hall, 1946), 288.

[19] Wei was minister to Belgium; Shi was minister to Great Britain and a Cornell graduate. Wang graduated from Yale University.

[20] Liang Qichao, "Ou you xinying lu" (Recollections of my journey in Europe), in Liang Qichao, *Yin bing shi he ji*, XXIII: 38.

[21] For Ye Gongchuo's trip to Europe, see Xia'an huigao nianpu bianyinhui, ed., *Ye Xia'an xianshen nianpu* (Shanghai: Xia'an huigao nianpu bianyinhui, 1946), 63–69.

To be sure, the immediate focus for the Chinese was the recovery of Shandong – the single issue that had motivated them to be interested in the postwar conference in the first place. On January 28, 1919, Koo laid out China's case in the first official Chinese presentation at the conference. Koo argued that China had every right to ask for direct restitution of Shandong: China had reserved its right of sovereignty even after Germany took control of the area; the people in Shandong were homogeneously Chinese and met every requirement of the principle of nationality; and Shandong was the cradle of Chinese civilization, a "Holy Land for the Chinese people." As to the agreements China had signed with Japan during the war, Koo argued that they had been signed only under duress and threat; China had signed them only as a temporary arrangement. They were subject to final revision at the postwar peace conference because they dealt primarily with questions that had arisen from the war, and which, therefore, could not be satisfactorily settled except at the final peace talks. And finally, because China had declared war on the side of the Allies, all treaties, agreements, and conventions concluded between itself and Germany had been abrogated.[22]

As mentioned earlier, China had been preparing for the peace conference since 1915 and had collected many supporting documents to bolster its case for the return of Shandong. The delegation's well-prepared materials included a bulky dossier consisting of six volumes of petitions and complaints concerning the crimes committed by Japanese troops in Shandong. Among these cases are the destruction of entire villages and the senseless murder of, for instance, a farmer who was bayoneted in the belly when he produced a donkey instead of the mule requisitioned by an armed Japanese. Another case involved the wholesale slaughter of villagers who failed to supply a certain number of girls to the Japanese soldiers.[23]

At the conference, China argued that because of China's entry into the war Germany had forfeited its leasehold rights and now possessed no rights in Shandong to surrender to another power. In other words, the Chinese considered their declaration of war on Germany an automatic cancellation of the Sino-Japanese treaties of 1915, with respect to Shandong. They further maintained that morally Japan had no right to keep Shandong under the established principles of international law regarding the termination of treaties and agreements, namely that when

---

[22] For an official report on that meeting, see Secretary's Notes of a Conversation held in M. Pichon's room at Quai d'Orsay, Paris, January 28, 1919, Department of State, ed., *FRUS, the Paris Peace Conference, 1919*, III: 749–57.

[23] David Hunter Miller, *My Diary at the Conference of Paris with Documents*, 21 vols. (New York: Printed for the author by the Appeal Printing Company, 1924), XVIII: 154.

a treaty or agreement was concluded upon threat of force, that treaty or agreement was voidable. Thus China demanded the nullification of the Sino-Japanese treaties of 1915 on three grounds: they were made under duress and threat; they impaired China's independence; and they were a menace to the future peace of the world. The Chinese delegation further pointed out that these secret treaties had been concluded in direct contradiction of the principle of "open covenants." If the League of Nations was not to be built on sand, all secret agreements of whatever kind must meet their proper fate. To support its arguments and demonstrate its sincere trust in open diplomacy, the Chinese delegation publicly distributed copies of its secret treaties and agreements with Japan to the conference, along with its written demand for the direct return of Shandong from Germany.[24]

Thanks to Koo's passionate and convincing arguments, especially his speech on January 28, the Chinese delegation made a deep impression on the assembled representatives. American secretary of state Robert Lansing recorded that Koo "simply overwhelmed the Japanese with his argument."[25] David Miller, who served as legal advisor to the American Peace Commission, called Koo "one of the ablest of the debaters" who "made one of the really brilliant speeches of the meetings on the subject of the rights of small states."[26] A Japanese complained that China "seems to have started on a venture to captivate the world by her tongue and pen."[27] For a time, Japanese delegates did not know how to respond to the Chinese presentation. They were extremely unhappy at the publication of their secret treaties and agreements with China by the Chinese delegation. In response, the Japanese government turned to the well-worn tactic of putting pressure on the Chinese government. On February 2, the Japanese minister to China openly threatened the Chinese government and demanded that the Chinese delegates in Paris be instructed to desist from further embarrassing the Japanese. This strategy

---

[24] See "Lu Zhengxiang to Waijiaobu, January 27, 30, February 5,1919," in Zhongguo shehui kexueyuan, Jindai shi yanjiusuo. Jindai shi ziliao bianjishi, and Tianjin shi lishi bowuguan, *Miji lucun* (Collections of secret documents) (Beijing: Zhongguo shehui kexue chubanshe, 1984), 72–78; see also Chinese Delegation to the Peace Conference, "The Claim of China for Direct Restitution to Herself of the Leased Territory of Kiaochow, the Tsingtao–Chinan Railway and Other German Rights in Respect of Shantung Province," Paris, February 1919, in Manuscript Division, Library of Congress: Woodrow Wilson Papers (hereafter cited as Wilson Papers), Series 6: Peace Conference Documents, 6F/China/reel 461.

[25] Robert Lansing, *The Peace Negotiations: A Personal Narrative* (Boston: Houghton Mifflin Company, 1921), 253.

[26] Edward M. House and Charles Seymour, eds., *What Really Happened at Paris* (New York: Charles Scribner's Sons, 1921), 408.

[27] *The New York Times*, February 2, 1919.

backfired. The Chinese delegation was not intimidated and this heavy-handed diplomacy even upset Japan's allies. For instance, in his very confidential letter to Max Muller on February 21, 1919, the senior British diplomat Ronald Macleay wrote that when the Shandong issue was brought up again, the conference should not allow the "extraordinary and, to my mind highly improper, action of the Japanese minister in Peking, [to pass] unnoticed."[28]

But the Paris Peace Conference meant more than lobbying for the direct return of Shandong: the Chinese took every possible measure to push for recovery of its lost sovereignty in broad terms. This aim had been prominent in Chinese minds even before the opening of the conference. Xu Shichang, who was president of China from October 10, 1918 to June 2, 1922, told a correspondent for *The New York Times* in late 1918 that for at least three-quarters of a century China had suffered from crippling "secret treaties," "spheres of influence," and "balances of power." China now expected to be accorded "a complete revision of her relation with the powers."[29] As Wu Tingfang, the former foreign minister, wrote, "We have heard the public pronouncements of the statesmen of the powers, that after the war, justice and equality will rule among the nations. We believe in them and have great hopes of them. We expect that in carrying them out into practice in China, one of the first things that will be done will be a reasonable and equitable revision of our treaties."[30]

Many proposals surfaced in this light from Chinese elite members and from politicians. For instance, Liang Qichao declared that China should achieve two goals at the conference: (1) It should see the spheres of influence system destroyed so that China could avoid being "a catalyst of future war"; (2) "China should win the right of self-development."[31] To achieve these goals, "we come to the new world with an honest and constructive programme," Liang wrote. "We appeal to the just instincts of modern democracy, to the wisdom of responsible statesmen, to the intelligence of leaders of industry and finance; we appeal especially to our strong neighbor, Japan, to see that our interests on the whole and in the long run are also hers."[32] Liang Qichao also argued that the peace conference should grant China the following concrete relief measures: the

---

[28] PRO: FO371/3682/346.   [29] *The New York Times*, January 16, 1919.
[30] Tyau Min-Chien, *Legal Obligations Arising Out of Treaty Relations between China and Other States* (Shanghai: Commercial Press, 1917), Wu's preface.
[31] Liang Qichao, "Li Guoji shuifa pingdenghui yanshuo" (A speech to the Association for International Taxation Law), in Liang Qichao, *Liang Rengong yanshuo ji* (Collection of Liang Qichao's Speeches) (Shanghai: Shanghai guomin shuju, 1925), 57.
[32] Liang Qichao, *China and World Peace* (Paris, without publishing date), Vincennes, 802N/1604/19–20; see also Quai d'Orsay, Série A, Paix (November 1918–April 1919), XXIX: 1001–13.

revision of unequal treaties, total cancellation of the Boxer Indemnity, and tariff autonomy.[33] In January 1919 Liang Shiyi sent a memorandum suggesting that China focus on the following objectives at the Paris Peace Conference:

1. Annulment of all Chinese–Japanese treaties based on the Twenty-one Demands.
2. Return of Qingdao.
3. Guarantee of economic freedom.
4. Make public all secret treaties China was compelled to sign, damaging its national sovereignty and rights.

Understandably Liang Shiyi argued that China should freely resort to Wilson's Fourteen Points as it worked on the above objectives.[34]

In line with various suggestions mentioned above, the official Chinese goals for the conference fell into three major categories:

1. Territorial integrity, or restoration to China of foreign concessions and leased territories.
2. Restoration of national sovereignty, or the abolition of restrictions imposed upon China by the Protocol of 1901; in particular this meant the withdrawal of foreign troops from China and abolition of foreign consular jurisdictions.
3. Economic freedom, or the exercise of complete tariff autonomy.[35]

With the above-mentioned goals in mind, the Chinese delegation submitted several memoranda geared toward helping China establish new and equal relations with the major powers. These memoranda were well prepared, well written, and well argued.[36]

The Chinese had every hope that the Paris Peace Conference would help China "recover from its diplomatic defeats of the last one hundred years." It would recognize China to be "equal with Britain, France, and the United States."[37] One article and declaration after another expressed these hopes. The Chinese expected Wilson and his ideas to have a strong impact at the peace conference; one writer insisted, "China should not only have a seat at the world's conference, but she should have justice

---

[33] Hollington Tong, "What Can President Wilson Do for China," *Millard's Review* 6, no. 11 (November 16, 1918): 431–34.

[34] Feng Chen, ed., *Liang Shiyi shiliao ji* (Beijing: Zhongguo wenshi chubanshe, 1991), 277–79.

[35] Department of State, ed., *FRUS, the Paris Peace Conference*, II: 492, 509–11.

[36] For details on these memoranda, see "Chinese Delegation to the Peace Conference: Questions for Readjustment," Paris, April 1919, Quai d'Orsay, A Paix: XCCIX: 224–41.

[37] *Minguo Ribao*, January 5, 1919. One article declared, "This is a time when might is overcome by right and justice. China has a great reason to hold its head up and tell the world its sufferings." In *Shishi Xinbao* (New Journal of Current Affairs), February 11, 1919.

done to her for the last hundred years of ill treatment" at the hands of the various powers. This was not a favor for China but "her right."[38]

These Chinese ambitions and long-term goals for the postwar peace conference were noted by many foreigners. For instance, John Jordan informed Lord Curzon that the Chinese "are eagerly looking to the Peace Conference to free them from the shackles which have bound them for the last four years to the military party of Japan, and to restore to them some measure of sovereign right on their own territory."[39]

Of course, China was not the only weak country with high expectations for a new world order. For instance, J. G. Latham, a member of the Australian delegation to the conference, declared it to be "an opportunity of taking a greater share in the moulding of her own [Australia's] destiny."[40]

China tries to shape the new world order

Chinese diplomats not only tried to serve China's interest by demanding a revision of its unequal foreign relations, they also took active roles in attempting to shape the world community and assume full membership in it. After all, China's fate depended on a fairer reordering of the world's nations. Since Wilsonianism was the cornerstone of this proposed new world order, the Chinese showed enormous interest in it. Perhaps the best statement of high hopes for the new Wilsonian order was expressed by the Chinese Patriotic Committee in the United States, one of many citizens' societies set up worldwide to champion China's cause at Versailles. One of the many booklets it published during the conference declared,

Four hundred million people are facing a life-or-death sentence at Paris; and upon this sentence the fate of the permanent peace of the world is going to depend. China pleads for nothing but fair play and sound judgment. For the interest of world peace and for the interest of four hundred million people a death sentence should not be tolerated by the enlightened powers, particularly the United States of America, in whom China has deepest confidence and by whom the upright plan for the League of Nations was originated.[41]

One of the major sources of Wilson's appeal to the Chinese was the new world order idea, especially his plan for a League of Nations and

---

[38] J. O. Y, "China Must Receive Full Justice at the Peace Conference!" *Millard's Review* 6, no. 11 (November 16, 1918), 435–36.

[39] Jordan to Curzon, February 11, 1919, PRO, FO371/3682/28360.

[40] J. G. Latham, *The Significance of the Peace Conference from an Australian Point of View* (Sydney: Melville & Mullen, 1920).

[41] Chinese Patriotic Committee, "China's Claims at the Peace Table," New York, March 1919, Quai d'Orsay, A-Paix, microfilm/P1515, XCCVII: 125–56.

national self-determination.[42] China perhaps was the one country that had the strongest faith in and pushed hardest for creating the League of Nations.[43] At home and overseas, Chinese had formed societies to study the issue and support the cause. On January 25, when a resolution for the creation of a commission on the League of Nations was under discussion, China's chief delegate Lu Zhengxiang declared that China supported the establishment of the League of Nations "wholeheartedly."[44] Wellington Koo also told the conference that "just as no people have been more eager to see the formation of a League of Nations than the people of China, so no people are more gratified than we are to note the distinct step of progress made by the commission of the League of Nations."[45]

For the Chinese the League of Nations also resonated with the traditional Chinese ideal of *datong* (great harmony). Jiang Menglin, in the preface to his translation of *Wilson's Wartime Speeches*, praised highly Wilson's proposed creation and argued that with the League of Nations, *datong* would finally find its place in the world.[46] Liang Qichao, who went to Paris to press China's case, wrote a long essay entitled "China and the League of Nations." In it he also referred to the connection of *datong* with the idea of a league of nations.[47] He wrote, "The essence of our sages' teaching is that 'we should govern the country well in order to secure the peace of the whole world' . . . Our political thought had always been based on this kind of universalism." He further argued that when the civilizations of the world have advanced to their furthest extent, *datong* will be reached and "the different peoples of the world will work together for the common good as members of one organization." Liang concluded his stirring argument with the ringing claim that "as far as

---

[42] For a study on China and the League of Nations, see Tang Qihua, *Beijing zhengfu yu guoji lianmeng, 1919–1928* (The Beijing government and the League of Nations) (Taipei: Dongda tushu gongsi, 1998). Zhang Li, *Guoji hezuo zai Zhongguo: Guoji lianmeng jiaose de kaocha, 1919–1946* (China's international cooperation) (Taipei: Zhongyang yanjiuyuan jindai shi yanjiusuo zhuankan, 1999).

[43] The idea of the League of Nations was not Wilson's invention, of course. In 1693–94 William Penn published a famous essay "Toward the Present and Future Peace of Europe," wherein he elaborated the general idea. Shortly after the outbreak of the First World War, some private groups in England and the United States proposed that such a league be formed at the close of the war. In England, the League of Nations Society was founded in 1915, and in the United States the League to Enforce Peace was set up in the same year. The former president of the United States, William Taft, was chosen as the first president of the American body.

[44] Department of State, ed., *FRUS, the Paris Peace Conference, 1919*, I: 186.

[45] Koo et al., *China and the League of Nations* (London: G. Allen & Unwin Ltd., 1919), 3–5.

[46] Woodrow Wilson, *Wei Erxun canzhan yanshuo* (War speeches of Woodrow Wilson), trans. Jiang Menglin (Shanghai: Shangwu yinshuguan, 1921), Preface.

[47] Liang Qichao went to Paris with several experts as an unofficial advisor to the Chinese delegation on December 28, 1918. The Beijing government provided 60,000 yuan for his funds. He received another 40,000 yuan from private sponsorship.

China is concerned, I can say without the slightest hesitation that we are in favour of the formation of a League of Nations also to a man."[48]

Even Kang Youwei, who had strongly opposed China's participation in the war earlier, was now intrigued by the prospect of Wilson's League of Nations, largely because of his familiarity with the idea of *datong*. Indeed, Kang, with high hopes for the Paris Peace Conference, urged the Beijing government to use the opportunity posed by the conference to help establish a new world order. He wrote, "the Americans achieved a great victory [in defeating Germany], and now sponsor a peace conference based on right and justice. [This conference] should support the weak and small countries. China is fortunate to participate in it and so has an opportunity to recover its lost sovereignty and enjoy equality and freedom."[49] Kang told his son-in-law, "I never dreamed I would have the good luck to see the formation of a League of Nations in my own days. The impossible is about to happen. You can't imagine my happiness."[50] To facilitate the coming of *datong* and inject his own ideas into it, Kang was busily revising his previous book on the subject to capitalize on the "Wilson fever" spreading across China. In this revised version, Kang advocated the formation of a League of Nations preliminary to the organization of an international government and the abolition of national boundaries.

Kang even argued that if the League of Nations was created according to his prescription, within ten years it would have less chance of being overthrown and the different nations would become less aggressive and greedy. The people of the League would rapidly increase, and the land coming under its control would likewise increase. All the powerful countries would become less powerful, and the rights of people everywhere would be enhanced. When that state of affairs was reached, the world would be prepared for the organization of an international government.

Kang's ideas were so appealing to some Chinese they became the major part of a bill introduced into the national assembly on December 6, 1918. The bill added to Kang's ideas the establishment of an international court to settle judicial cases, the organization of an international army and navy, the freedom to live in any country, the prohibition of alienation of land without the approval of the League of Nations, the prohibition of

[48] On his way to Paris, Liang Qichao wrote "World Peace and China," and immediately distributed its English and French versions in Paris in February 1919. See Liang Qichao, *China and the League of Nations* (Beijing: The Society for the Study of International Relations, 1918); the article was also published in *Chen Bao* (Morning Post), June 10–17, 1919.

[49] Tang Zhijun, ed., *Kang Youwei zhenglun ji* (Kang Youwei's writings on politics) (Beijing: Zhonghua shuju, 1981), vol. II, 1061–63.

[50] Hollington Tong, "Kang Yu-wei as Chinese Advocate of the League of Nations," *Millard's Review* 7, no. 10 (February 8, 1919): 342–45.

alliances between countries, the approval of all international treaties by the League of Nations, and the abolition of all secret treaties and illegal transactions between nations. The bill was endorsed by the vice-speaker and some twenty members of the Senate. The majority of the members of the House of Representatives did not want to pass it, however, thinking it contained too many radical ideas. At a session held on January 8, the bill was rejected.[51]

Kang's ideas might have been idealistic, impracticable, or even "radical," but his detailed proposal and its consideration by the Chinese Parliament reflected the strong Chinese interest in the idea of a League of Nations. In February 1919, elite Chinese such as Cai Yuanpei, Wang Daxie, Lin Changmin, Xiong Xiling, and others organized a "Society for Supporting the League of Nations." Its main goal was to "advocate the establishment of the League and help develop it." Cai Yuanpei observed that China's past diplomatic failures had resulted from the practice of secret diplomacy. Now with Wilson's Fourteen Points and open diplomacy, China would be in much better shape.[52]

High expectations for a *datong*-type world order were also entertained by members of the Chinese delegation to the peace conference. Wellington Koo, who was to play a crucial role in the conference, again offered the *datong* analogy. In one of his speeches, he even quoted Confucius' injunction "do not do to others what you would not have others do to you" to elaborate on the importance of a League of Nations to China. Koo proclaimed that, "Nurtured in the philosophy of peace based on reason and justice, the spirit of the Chinese people is the spirit of the League of Nations."[53] Wang Zhengting, another member of the peace delegation, reported, "China is in hearty support of the formation of the League of Nations because it is in full harmony with the cherished ideals of her sages and teachers." Wang believed that

The time has come for a new world order. This new order takes the form of a covenant among the Allied and associated powers, who bind themselves to promote international co-operation and to achieve international peace and security by the acceptance of obligations not to resort to war, by the prescription of open, just and honorable relations between nations, by the firm establishment of the understandings of international law as the actual rule of conduct among governments by the maintenance of justice and a scrupulous respect for all treaty obligations in the dealing of organized peoples with one another.[54]

---

[51] Hollington Tong, "Kang Yu-wei as Chinese Advocate of the League of Nations," *Millard's Review* 7, no. 10 (February 8, 1919): 342–45.

[52] *Chen Bao*, March 13, 1919.

[53] Wellington Koo et al., *China and the League of Nations*, 1–2.

[54] Wang Zhengting, *The League of Nations and China: Extracts from Speeches Delivered by Viscount Bryce* (Wang Zhengting, and Others, at Caxton Hall, Westminster, May 15, 1919) (London, 1919), 8–13.

Strong belief in the League of Nations idea motivated the Chinese to take an active role in its creation and make it work for Chinese interests. To achieve this goal, members of the Chinese delegation worked hard. Koo, one of the original committee of fifteen who drafted a covenant for the League, contributed considerably to the drafting of that document. For example, he made a suggestion one American legal advisor called "very interesting" about Article 15, based on Woodrow Wilson's own draft. The Wilson paragraph reads, "If the difference between the Body of Delegates to be a question which by international law is solely within the domestic legislative jurisdiction of one of the parties, it shall so report, and shall make no recommendation as to its settlement."[55] Koo proposed to add the following words: "unless a recommendation is desired by the party within whose exclusive jurisdiction the question lies." The drafting committee accepted the suggestion. Miller understood Koo's proposal to reflect a natural Chinese reaction to past foreign interference with Chinese internal affairs.[56] An American amendment to Article 10 which reads, "Nothing in this Covenant shall be deemed to affect the validity of international engagements such as treaties of arbitration or regional understandings like the Monroe Doctrine for securing the maintenance of peace" caused Koo to protest: "I do not wish to be understood as opposing the introduction of this amendment. I approve of it in principle, but I should like to suggest that the Monroe Doctrine should be named specifically and alone in this article and not made one of the class of 'regional understandings.'" Koo, of course, did not want Japan to use the amendment as precedent for a Japanese Monroe doctrine, and he therefore wanted to cut the words "regional understandings" or at least "regional."[57] Koo persisted in trying to convince the Americans of the necessity of changing this wording.[58] Although the amendment was finally adopted as originally drafted, Koo's suggestion did receive favorable consideration for Article 20 in which the words "or understandings" were adopted. The revised article reads as follows:

The Members of the League severally agree that this Covenant is accepted as abrogating all obligations or understandings *inter se* which are inconsistent with the terms thereof, and solemnly undertake that they will not hereafter enter into any engagements inconsistent with the terms thereof.

Miller wrote that "This satisfied Mr. Koo's doubt as to the language of the Monroe Doctrine Article."[59]

---

[55] David Hunter Miller, *The Drafting of the Covenant* (New York: G. P. Putnam's Sons, 1928), I: 331.
[56] Ibid., 331–32.   [57] Ibid., 442–50.   [58] Ibid., 453.   [59] Ibid., XVII: 460.

China lost no opportunity to push its case for joining the world as a full and equal member. For instance, on March 29, 1919, Lu Zhengxiang, the head of the Chinese delegation, strongly appealed to Georges Clemenceau, the conference president, to allow China full membership in world organizations such as the new Aeronautic Commission. Lu Zhengxiang sent two letters on the same day to Georges Clemenceau arguing for China's membership in such organizations. In one of the letters, he wrote,

I have learned with a great deal of interest of the establishment by the Conference of an Aeronautic Commission, in which the seven Powers with Special Interests (Belgium, Brazil, Cuba, Greece, Portugal, Roumania, and Serbia) are all represented.

Inasmuch as the question of aeronautics will surely have considerable importance in the future for all countries, China, by reason of the extent of her territory and in view of her ardent desires to come in direct contact with the work which the Commission is following, would be happy to be able to take part therein.

I therefore take the liberty of submitting to you the request which my country has formulated regarding its representation on said Commission.[60]

In the second communication, Lu reminded Clemenceau,

As you know, China declared war on Germany the moment she perceived the impossibility of making Germany abandon submarine warfare. During the course of this terrible struggle from which we now at last emerge victorious, a number of Chinese laborers who came to Europe to offer their services to humanity perished at the time of their voyage, victims of this inhuman measure [of German unlimited submarine warfare].

While permitting myself to recall this fact to your mind, I have the honor to ask your support toward granting China an equal share in the distribution of German submarines among the Allied and Associated countries.[61]

To create a fair new world order, China even supported its arch-rival Japan when the latter proposed racial equality at Paris. When Japan first raised this issue on February 13, 1919, Koo expressed his support for this proposal even though China did not want to be distracted from its main focus. On March 26, 1919, Koo asked Miller about the question of racial equality raised by Japan. Koo wanted to know whether Japan meant to bring up the issue again. Koo told him that the Chinese of course "would have to support it but they did not care anything about it really in view of the larger interests which were here for them."[62] On April 11, when Japan made another proposal on the issue, China again supported it, arguing

---

[60] Miller, *My Diary at the Conference of Paris with Documents*, XVII: 360–361.
[61] Ibid., 361.
[62] Entry, March 26th, 1919, ibid., I: 205; see also Miller, *The Drafting of the Covenant*, I: 336.

that the proposal should be incorporated into the official peace treaty.[63] Ironically, it was Woodrow Wilson who as chair of the League of Nations Commission eventually blocked the inclusion of a racial equality clause in the final treaty.

Chinese disappointments at Paris

High Chinese expectations for the peace conference met mainly with deep disappointment. The Chinese had their first taste of this at the very opening of the conference when they were allotted only two seats at the proceedings. When China entered the war, the Great Powers had promised to treat it as an equal partner at the eventual peace talks. But in the end, getting two as opposed to the five seats the major powers held, China immediately felt itself regarded as a third-rate country, with its faith betrayed.[64] Strong Chinese protests to the decision-makers at the conference made no difference. To add insult to injury, China was allowed to participate only three times in meetings held regarding the Shandong issue despite its stake in the matter. Indeed, the invitation to participate in the first meeting on January 27 came only about one hour before that meeting commenced. In its third and last chance to state its case, on April 22, the Chinese delegation again appealed for fair treatment and justice. But Japan had the right to sit in almost all sessions, especially when its interests were concerned. It had the full five seats and was treated as a member of the "Big Five." More importantly, its claims to Shandong were supported by Britain, France, and Italy, thanks to the secret arrangements Japan had concluded with them in early 1917. The Chinese case was

---

[63] Japan first submitted the racial equality proposal on February 13, 1919; it read: "the equality of nations being a basic principle of the League of Nations, the High Contracting Parties agree to an accord as soon as possible to all alien nationals of states, members of the League, equal and just treatment in every respect making no distinction, either in law or in fact, on account of their race or nationality." The proposal was defeated several times. For a detailed study on Japan's proposal, see Naoko Shimazo, "The Racial Equality Proposal at the 1919 Paris Peace Conference: Japanese Motivations and Anglo-American Responses," D.Phil. thesis, Oxford University, 1995; for Koo's support, see "Lu Zhengxiang, telegram to Waijiaobu," February 13, 1919, April 12, 1919, in Zhongguo shehui kexueyuan, Jindai shi yanjiusuo, *Miji lucun*, 82–83, 129.

[64] The attending countries were divided into three categories. The five principal powers (the United States, Britain, France, Italy, and Japan) were entitled to five seats; countries such as Brazil and Belgium, which rendered certain effective aid and assistance in the war were entitled to three seats; and the remaining members of the allied camp, considered as the less important countries, would be entitled to only two seats. China was considered by the major powers to belong to the last category. When China tried to receive the same level of treatment as Brazil, it was told that it had provided little positive war aid while Brazil, by patrolling the south Atlantic with its naval units, had done a great service to the Allied cause. For details on China's seat issue, see Wellington Koo Memoir, Chinese Oral History Project, Columbia University, *Wellington Koo Memoir*, microfilm, reel 1, II.

further compromised by the treaties China had signed with Japan in 1915 and 1918, respectively, regarding Shandong. This explains why Japan was confident that its claims would eventually be satisfied.[65] Baron Nobuaki Makino, a key member of the Japanese delegation, informed the Council of Ten on January 27 that the Japanese government "feels justified" in claiming "the unconditional cession" of Shandong from Germany.[66]

At the April 22 meeting, British prime minister Lloyd George, having admitted that "he had never heard of the Japanese Twenty-one Demands, let alone the ultimatum" that Japan presented to China, pressed Koo to choose either to allow Japan to accede to Germany's right to Shandong, as stated in the treaty between China and Germany, or to recognize Japan's position in Shandong, as stipulated in the Sino-Japanese treaties. British foreign secretary Arthur James Balfour, with respect to the Shandong issue, wrote to Curzon that "we were bound to the Japanese by pledges they had exacted from us when we asked for naval assistance in the Mediterranean"; and that he was "moved by contempt for the Chinese over the way in which they left Japan to fight Germany for Shantung, and then were not content to get Shantung back without fighting for it, but tried to maintain that it was theirs as the legitimate spoils of a war in which they had not lost a man or spent a shilling."[67] Balfour told Curzon that his sympathies regarding Shandong "were entirely with the Japanese." He argued that China should not be allowed to regain that right which "she could never have recovered for herself."[68]

The major excuse the Big Four (Britain, France, Italy, and the United States) used for pressing China to concede was the treaties China had signed with Japan regarding Shandong in 1915 and 1918. Even Wilson, an advocate of open diplomacy in his Fourteen Points, now joined the other powers. At the session of April 22, he told the Chinese that the war "has been fought largely for the purpose of showing that treaties cannot be violated," and advised that "it would be better to live up to a bad treaty than to tear it up."[69] The 77-year-old French prime minister Georges Clemenceau, "short and sturdy, with eyes that glowed like furnaces," seemed to enjoy watching Wilson abandon his high principles

---

[65] For recent studies on Japan and the First World War, See Frederick Dickinson, *War and National Reinvention: Japan in the Great War, 1914–1919* (Harvard University Asia Center monograph series, 1999); Noriko Kawamura, *Turbulence in The Pacific: Japanese–U.S. Relations During World War I* (Westport, CT: Praeger, 2000).

[66] Miller, *My Diary at the Conference of Paris with Documents*, Entry of January 27, 1919.

[67] Balfour to Lord Curzon, September 20, 1919, in Balfour Papers, Department of Manuscript, British Library, 49734/171–72.

[68] Balfour to Curzon, May 8, 1919, PRO, FO405/226/71444.

[69] Wensi Jin, *China at the Paris Peace Conference in 1919* (Jamaica, NY: St. John's University Press, 1961), 14–15.

step by step.[70] The Chinese delegation responded that Wilson's holding China to the treaties and notes of 1915 was not fair. Japan had seriously encroached on China's sovereignty without provocation, and the said treaties had been concluded only under most extreme duress. China also argued that the notes of 1918 had grown out of the treaty and notes of 1915, and were signed by China out of a desire to relieve the tense situation in Shandong. The presence of Japanese troops along the railway and the establishment of Japanese civil administrative offices in the interior of Shandong had evoked such opposition from the people there that the Chinese government had been obliged to take steps to induce Japan to withdraw pending a settlement of the whole question at the postwar conference.

These arguments fell on deaf ears. Even if China had not signed those treaties with Japan, it would have been difficult to get Shandong back. Britain and France had already conceded German interests in Shandong to Japan in their secret treaties of 1917. During the April 25 meeting of the Big Three (Britain, France, and the United States), Wilson asked if France and Britain "were bound to transfer Kiauchau and Shantung to Japan." Lloyd George said that "sooner or later they were" and "Clemenceau agreed."[71] The Chinese delegates could only protest that China had not been consulted when these treaties were made or informed of their content when invited to join the war as a loyal co-belligerent. China warned that if the Great Powers refused to make a just settlement merely because of obligations imposed on China by threat of force or contracted by France and Britain in circumstances which since had entirely changed, they "may be sowing seeds of a grave discord in the years soon to come."

Faced with such obstacles, the Chinese delegation decided to compromise. In a memorandum to Wilson prepared by Koo on April 23, China no longer insisted upon its original demand of the direct restitution of Shandong. Instead, it proposed that Germany relinquish its rights in Shandong to the five powers for restoration to China and that Japan effect such restoration within one year after the signature of the peace treaty. The memorandum included the following points:

1. Germany renounced to the five Allied and associated powers its holdings, rights and privileges in Shandong for restoration to China.
2. Japan, being in possession of said holdings, rights and privileges, engaged to effect the said restoration to China within one year after the signature of the treaty of peace with Germany.

---

[70] Lord Riddell et al., *Treaty of Versailles and After* (Oxford: Oxford University Press, 1935), 12.
[71] Wilson Papers: Series 6: peace conf. Docs. 6A minutes/notes.

3. China agreed to make pecuniary compensation to Japan for the military expenses incurred in the capture of Qingdao, the amount of said compensation to be determined by the Council of Four.
4. China agrees to open the whole of Jiaozhou Bay as a commercial port, and to provide a special quarter, if desired, for the residence of the citizens and subjects of the treaty powers.[72]

Despite its various efforts, China failed to persuade the Council of Four to honor its request. On April 30, the United States, Britain, and France decided to allow Japan to retain former German interests in China, including Shandong. The Chinese delegation was told of this decision on May 1. The Council of Four did not bother to send the Chinese an official communication of the details of the settlement of Shandong until June 5, one month after the fact. Moreover, while the Chinese delegation was kept guessing about its fate, the Japanese were informed of every development by the Big Three. A letter sent by Arthur Balfour to Baron Makino on April 30, 1919 illustrates the vast difference in treatment:

I have just received from the president a statement of his views upon the suggestion of yesterday. I send you a copy of the proposal which he is prepared to accept . . . If, as I hope and believe, these suggested modifications carry with them no alteration in Japanese policy, and no infringement of the rights and dignity of the Japanese people, I hope you may see your way to accept them. If so, I gather that the whole negotiation may be regarded as happily concluded.[73]

Obviously, all Japan's planning had paid off. Before the fate of Shandong was decided on April 30, Japan adopted one further extremely effective strategy: it threatened to refuse to participate in the League of Nations and also pushed once again its proposal for racial equality. The Japanese made their threats very clear to Wilson and the others. As Baron Makino told Balfour, "If Japan received what she claimed in regard to Shantung, her representatives at the Plenary Meeting would content themselves with a survey of the inequality of races and move some abstract resolution which would probably be rejected. Japan would then merely make a protest. If however, she regarded herself ill-treated over Shantung," Makino threatened that he "was unable to say what line the Japanese delegates might take." Under this pressure, Wilson was unable to resist. He agreed that Japan would be allowed to control Shandong

---

[72] Chinese memorandum, April 23, 1919, in Wilson Papers, Series 6 Peace Conference documents, 6A/minutes; see also Jin, *China at the Paris Peace Conference*, 22; see also Chinese Delegation's Memorandum to the Conference, Paris, April 23, 1919, in Quai d'Orsay, A-Paix, xccviii, microfilm no. 1515, 116–18.
[73] Letter from Balfour to Baron Makino, April 30, 1919, in Balfour Papers, 49749.

in "economic terms."[74] American secretary of state Robert Lansing thus observed, for Wilson "the formation of the League in accordance with the provisions of the Covenant to be superior to every other consideration and that to accomplish this object almost any sacrifice would be justifiable."[75] Wilson himself recognized that "I shall be accused of violating my own principles."[76]

When the Chinese delegation got the news on May 1 that the fate of Shandong had been decided in favor of Japan without China's participation, the members were devastated. They realized that "the peace conference is based on might. Right and justice was defeated by might." In his report to Beijing, Lu Zhengxiang advised that if China was not allowed to lodge reservations, it should not sign the treaty.[77] Thus in early May, the Chinese delegation did officially "register a formal protest with the Council of Three against the proposed settlement" of Shandong.[78] Stephen Bonsal, who had first-hand knowledge of the Paris Conference and worked for the American delegation, recorded on May 4, 1919 what was in the minds of the Chinese delegation: "We are betrayed in the house of our only friend." According to Bonsal, the Chinese were particularly furious with Wilson.[79]

After May 1, the Chinese delegation worked extremely hard to revise the peace treaty with Germany. As a first step, it wanted to formulate provisions for insertion into the preliminaries of peace with Germany. The Chinese reasserted their desires to regain the territory, rights, and property originally obtained "either by intimidation or by actual force, and to remove certain restrictions on [China's] freedom of political and economic development." They wanted particularly to include the following provisions:

1. The termination of all treaties between China and Germany and the opening of Qingdao to foreign trade and residence.
2. A new treaty of commercial and general relations, based upon the principles of equality and reciprocity, with Germany relinquishing most-favored nation treatment.

---

[74] "Notes of a Meeting held at Wilson's Residence in Paris with Lloyd George, Clemenceau and Wilson," April 28, 1919 at 11:00 a.m., in Wilson Papers, Series 6, Peace Conference Documents/ 6A/Minutes.

[75] Lansing, *The Peace Negotiations: A Personal Narrative*, 245. For a recent study on Lansing and the Shandong issue, see Stephen G. Graft, "John Bassett Moore, Robert Lansing and the Shandong Question," *Pacific Historical Review* 66, no. 2 (May 1997).

[76] Harold Nicolson, *Peacemaking 1919* (Boston: Houghton Mifflin Company, 1933), 146–47.

[77] "Lu Zhengxiang and other members of Chinese delegation to Waijiaobu," May 3, 1919, in Zhongguo shehui kexueyuan, Jindai shi yanjiusuo, *Miji lucun*, 146–47.

[78] "Chinese delegation to Council of Three," May 4, 1919, PRO: FO405/226/71445; see also ibid., 147–48.

[79] S. Bonsal, *Suitors and Supplicants: The Little Nations at Versailles*, 239.

3. The withdrawal of Germany from the Protocol of September 7, 1901.
4. The cession to China of German public property in Chinese territory.
5. Compensation for the losses suffered by the Chinese government and its nationals.
6. Reservation of the right to claim war indemnities from Germany.
7. Reimbursement of expenses for the internment and maintenance of prisoners of war.
8. Germany's ratification of the International Opium Convention of January 23, 1912.[80]

This proposal was bluntly rejected. With this added failure, China tried to insert reservations on the three articles affecting Shandong. China proposed to write into the treaty over the signatures of the Chinese plenipotentiaries the words "subject to the reservation made at the Plenary Section of May 6, 1919, relative to the questions" of Shandong. But even Wilson did not support China's motion for a reservation. For Wilson, any reservation by the Chinese delegation might set an example that would be eagerly seized upon by other delegations dissatisfied with decisions on questions of special interest to them. Wilson particularly had in mind the Covenant of the League of Nations, which had been objected to in several of its particulars by the Senate of the United States, and which might provoke reservations from other delegations such as the Japanese. After this rebuff, China tried to make its reservation an addendum to the treaty; this too was denied. Next the Chinese delegation requested that it be given an opportunity to make a declaration on the signing of the treaty. China would sign the peace treaty if it were allowed to send to the president of the conference, before the official signing ceremony, a separate declaration to the effect that the Chinese plenipotentiaries would sign the treaty subject to the reservation that after the signing, China would ask for reconsideration of the Shandong question. Clemenceau, the president of the conference, rejected this proposal immediately.[81] Three hours before the signing ceremony, China was still attempting to insert some reservation. In a letter, Lu Zhengxiang notified Clemenceau that having considered as unjust articles 156, 157, and 158 therein, "which purport to transfer German rights" in Shandong to Japan, China, "the rightful

[80] Neither Germany nor Austria-Hungary ratified the International Opium Convention of January 23, 1912, concluded at The Hague. Their refusal to sign or ratify it was largely responsible for the delay in its execution. For the Chinese, their fulfillment of this obligation would mean the removal of one of the obstacles to the implementation of this important international instrument, whose purpose was not only consonant with the highest interests of China but conducive to the common welfare of the world. For details regarding the insertions, see Quai d'Orsay, A-Paix, xxviii, A-Paix, A-1001-13[microfilm] Chine [November 1918 – October 1920, xccviii: 43–47.

[81] Clemenceau to Chinese delegation, May 14, 1919, Zhongguo di er li shi dang an guan, beiyang wai jiao bu dang, 1039-2-374.

sovereign over the territory and a loyal co-partner in war on the side of the Allied and associated powers," might sign the treaty with the understanding that its signing "is not to be understood as precluding China from demanding at a suitable moment the reconsideration of the Shantung question, to the end that the injustice to China may be rectified in the interest of permanent peace" in East Asia.[82] Yet even this request was rejected. Thus the Chinese delegation had been backed into a corner: it could simply sign the peace treaty or not. It had been afforded no alternative.

Given all that had happened to them at the conference – their plea for the direct return of Shandong having fallen on deaf ears, their proposal for revision having been summarily rejected, their request for lodging a reservation being turned down, and now their plea to make a declaration having been brusquely disregarded – the Chinese felt that "the Peace Conference has denied to the Chinese Delegates the privilege of making any suggestions." Thus there was no alternative but to refuse to sign the treaty, which was described by some Chinese as China's "death warrant."[83] Apparently it had never occurred to the Great Powers that a weak China might dare to stand up to them. Balfour for one had not reckoned on China being the only country to refuse the treaty. He had written to Jordan, "I sincerely hope that [the] Chinese government will not do anything foolish and likely to alienate sympathies of Allies such as refusing to sign the treaty."[84] He could not have known that the Chinese delegation had determined not to sign the treaty unless some sort of reservation was allowed. According to Koo, "there was no doubt the consensus of opinion among the delegates that without a reservation we should not sign." On June 28, all members of the Chinese delegation decided not to sign the treaty and absented themselves from the signing ceremony. Koo remembered this day as more than merely sad: "It was a memorable day for me and for the whole delegation and for China. China's absence must have been a surprise if not a shock to the Conference, to the diplomatic world in France and to the entire world beyond."[85]

Koo was right. Many including Wilson were surprised by the Chinese move. Wilson was "greatly disturbed at the absence of Chinese." He

---

[82] Chinese Patriotic Committee, New York, July, 1919, in National Archive, State Department Records Relating to the Political Relations between China and Other States, 7-18-5/m341/roll 28/793.94/963; see also Jin, *China at the Paris Peace Conference*, 30.

[83] The Diplomatic Association, "China at the Peace Conference," *Far Eastern Political Science Review* (Canton, China, August 1919): 141.

[84] FO to Jordan, May 21, 1919, PRO, FO371/3683/16.

[85] Koo Memoir (Columbia University Oral History Project), reel 2, II.

told Lansing, "That is most serious. It will cause grave complications."[86] Wilson should have understood that China's refusal to sign the treaty functioned as "a protest against injustice as well as an appeal for justice." The statement of the Chinese delegation, issued on the evening of June 28, put it clearly: "After failing in all earnest attempts at conciliation, and after seeing every honorable compromise rejected, the Chinese delegation had no course open save to adhere to the path of duty to their country. Rather than accept by their signatures the Shantung articles in the treaty against which their sense of right and justice militated, they refrained from signing the treaty altogether." In its press release of the same day, the Chinese delegation stated, "The peace conference having denied China justice in the settlement of the Shantung question and having today in effect prevented them from signing the treaty without sacrificing their sense of right, justice, and patriotic duty, the Chinese delegates submit their case to the impartial judgment of the world."[87]

Besides the desire to safeguard Chinese national honor and sovereignty, the refusal to sign the treaty, to a great extent, was influenced by more assertive public opinion. On May 14, Lu Zhengxiang, the head of the Chinese delegation, asked President Xu Shichang for instructions regarding whether or not to sign a peace treaty. In his telegram Lu wrote, "I signed the 1915 treaty [with Japan]. Now if I have any conscience, I shall not sign the new [peace] treaty . . . As public opinion in China is now tremendously aroused, I am very reluctant to sign [any new treaty] for fear of future criticism."[88] As Jordan reported, "It is no exaggeration to say that the feeling of the Chinese over the Shantung question has been aroused in a manner that is not to be mistaken. It permeates all classes."[89] Chinese both in China and abroad sent thousands of telegrams to their delegation in Paris to express their strong disappointment with the Great Powers with respect to the Shandong question, denouncing their decision as unjust and an insult to China, and opposing the signing of the treaty. After May 4, the Chinese delegation received about 7,000 such telegrams.[90] One of

---

[86] "Memorandum by the secretary of state, the signing of the treaty of peace with Germany at Versailles on June 28th, 1919," Department of State, ed., *FRUS, the Paris Peace Conference, 1919*, II: 602.

[87] Chinese Patriotic Committee, New York, July, 1919, in National Archive, State Department Records relating to the Political Relations between China and other States, 7-18-5/m341/roll 28/793.94/963; Jin, *China at the Paris Peace Conference*, 30.

[88] Luo Guang, *Lu Zhengxiang zhuan* (Biography of Lu Zhengxian) (Taipei: Shangwu yinshuguan, 1966), 113.

[89] Jordan to Curzon, May 10, 1919, in Kenneth Bourne, ed., *British Documents on Foreign Affairs: Reports and Papers from the Foreign Office Confidential Print, Series E, Asia*, XXIII, *China, January 1919 – December 1920* (Bethesda, MD: University Publications of America, 1994), 63.

[90] Jordan to Curzon, July 7, 1919, ibid., 82.

them exclaimed, "For humanity's sake do not sign. Let 400,000,000 die a quick death instead of a slow one." Another, on May 4, 1919, asserted that the Shandong decision was "unjust, China['s] integrity lost, [the delegation] should withdraw and return to China."[91]

With feelings running so high, the Chinese delegation's refusal to sign received wide Chinese support. The Tianjin Students Union wrote to the delegation, "Refusing peace treaty signature inspires the whole nation with hope. May you persevere. Whole-hearted cooperation is assured to you." The People's Foreign Relations Society wrote, "The nation is exceedingly grateful for your pains and perseverance in reserving room for recovery of Shantung rights by refusing to sign." The Chinese Chamber of Commerce wrote, "We fully support and appreciate your action and activities at the peace conference and pledge our united support in your fight to secure a full measure of justice for your four hundred million countrymen." Even the Korean delegation to the peace conference, which had itself suffered a major setback in its quest for national independence, extended "sincere congratulations on the right stand taken by Chung Hua Ming Kuo [Republic of China]. You have our sympathy and support," their telegram read.[92]

China's overall demands for sovereignty and self-determination were also rejected by the powers as irrelevant to the postwar peace conference; yet the Chinese performance at Paris demonstrates their continued drive toward internationalization and defining a new national identity. As Zhang Yongjin recently argued,

The fact that the Chinese justified their demand for such an overall readjustment by involving principles of equality, justice, and respect for sovereignty showed how much China had advanced towards accepting the common values of the European international society to qualify itself for the membership in that community.[93]

In his official memorandum to the conference, Koo observed that "China is now at the parting of the ways. She has come to the West for justice. If she should fail to get it, the people may perhaps attribute its failure not so much to Japan's insistence on her own claims as to the attitude of the West which declined to lend a helping hand to China merely because some of its leading Powers had privately pledged to support

---

[91] *Telegrams Received by the Chinese Delegation in Regard to the Kiaochow–Shangtung Question* (Paris: Imp. De Vaugirard, 1919), II.

[92] *Telegrams Received by the Chinese Delegation After They Declined to Attach their Signatures to the Treaty of Versailles June 28, 1919*, III.

[93] Zhang Yongjin, *China in the International System, 1918–20: The Middle Kingdom at the Periphery* (New York: St. Martin's Press, 1991), 61.

Japan."[94] Koo's prediction was proved correct. China's failure to regain Shandong led to outrage on the part of influential Chinese against the United States and Wilson. They complained that Wilson's new world order had not come to China. This so-called new order, wrote one Chinese booklet, was "admittedly sound, but to the present all that China has received is the vibration of the sound but not the application of the principles." The writers of the booklet concluded that might remained more important than right.[95] One newspaper article published in Jinan, the capital of Shandong Province, commented that the United States only "pretended to love peace and justice. It actually has a wolf's heart." The same newspaper attacked Wilson in person the next day, calling him a "hypocrite," "useless," and "selfish."[96]

Mao Zedong had once dreamed of a close relationship with the United States during the war, and he had had high hopes for the Paris conference. After the betrayal of Versailles, Mao's expectations for the United States and other Western countries were disappointed. He now concluded that "in foreign affairs all past alliances or Entente were the union of international bullies" and only revolutions could rectify the irrational and unjust international system.[97] In an article on the treaty, Mao wrote that Wilson had behaved in Paris "like an ant on a hot skillet":

He did not know what to do. Surrounded by thieves like Clemenceau, Lloyd George, Makino, and Orlando, he heard nothing but accounts of receiving certain amounts of territory and of reparations worth so much in gold. He did nothing except to attend various kinds of meetings where he could not speak his mind . . . I felt sorry for him for a long time. Poor Wilson.[98]

For Chen Duxiu, Wilson had become an "empty cannon" and his principles were "not worth one penny."[99] Students across China openly expressed their disappointment at the failure of Wilsonianism. At Beijing

---

[94] Chinese memorandum, April 23, 1919, in Wilson Papers, Series 6 Peace Conference documents, 6A/minutes; see also Jin, *China at the Paris Peace Conference*, 22; see also Chinese Delegation's Memorandum to the Conference, Paris, April 23, 1919, in Quai d'Orsay, A-Paix, XCCVIII, microfilm no. 1515, 116–18.

[95] Chinese Patriotic Committee, New York City, May 1918, "Might or Right? The Fourteen Points and the Disposition of Kiao-Chau," National Archive, State Department Records Relating to the Political Relations between China and Other States, 7-18-5/m341/roll 27/743.94/875.

[96] *Jinan Ribao* (Jinan Daily), May 16, 17, 1919, Clippings in National Archive, State Department Records Relating to the Political Relations between China and Other States, 7-18-5/M341/roll 28.

[97] Mao Zedong, "The Great Union of the Popular Masses (1), July 21, 1919," in Stuart R. Schram, ed., *Mao's Road to Power*, I: 378–81.

[98] Mao, "Poor Wilson, July 14, 1919," in ibid., 338.

[99] *Meizhou pinglun* 20 (May 4, 1919).

University they cynically joked that Wilson had discovered a jolting new formula for the idealistic Wilsonian world order: "14 equals 0."[100]

It has to be pointed out that the deep Chinese disappointment arose largely from their high expectations of Wilson and his new world order. Wilson had not wanted to sacrifice China but did what he had to do to save his own cherished plans. Many members of the American delegation to the conference were both friendly and helpful to the Chinese and both sides cooperated informally in many ways. Americans provided much valuable advice to the Chinese delegates, especially when they engaged in their battle to revise the peace treaty once the major powers had awarded Shandong to Japan.[101] According to Ray Stannard Baker, who was Wilson's secretary, Chinese delegate Wei Congzhou "blew into our offices as breezily every day or so as any American and was on familiar terms with everyone." Even before the conference started, Koo contacted David Miller and told him that he would like to consult with Miller informally from time to time in advance of formal communications between the two governments. Miller informed him that would be "entirely agreeable."[102] Many proposals put forward by the Chinese were discussed with the Americans informally before they were submitted. For example, Wang Zhengting had lunch with Americans such as Miller, Stanley Hornbeck, and James T. Shotwell on January 22, 1919, to discuss his proposal for dealing with China's past treaties with Germany and Austria. Shotwell suggested that Wang add an item for restitution to China for the looting of Beijing in 1900. This suggestion eventually resulted in article 131 of the Treaty of Versailles, which restored the famous old astronomical instruments to China.[103] Miller also suggested China "might properly present her whole case rather than simply the part of it which related to Germany and Austria as the matter was bound up with her relations with Japan and the Allies in the West."[104] As indicated earlier, the Chinese took this advice to heart.

Ironically, the failure of China at Paris, to a great extent, contributed to Wilson's eventual defeat at home. Even members of the American delegation to the peace conference disagreed with Wilson on the Shandong issue. Robert Lansing and Henry White supported Tasker Bliss – all were

---

[100] Zhongguo Shehui kexueyuan jindai shi yanjiuso, ed., *Wu si yundong huiyilu* (Recollections of the May Fourth Movement) (Beijing: Zhongguo shehui kexue chubanshe, 1979), I: 222.

[101] For this point, see *Gu Weijun huiyilu*, I: 200.

[102] Miller, *My Diary at the Conference of Paris with Documents*, I: 60.

[103] James T. Shotwell, *At the Paris Peace Conference* (New York: The Macmillan Company, 1937), 136–39.

[104] Miller, *My Diary at the Conference of Paris with Documents*, Entry of January 22, 1919.

members of the American delegation to Paris – when he criticized Wilson by saying it was wrong to sacrifice China: "It can't be right to do wrong even to make peace. Peace is desirable, but there are things dearer than peace – justice and freedom."[105] Paul Reinsch, the American minister to China, eventually resigned in protest against Wilson's compromise in Paris on China.[106] He wrote,

Probably nowhere else in the world had expectations of America's leadership at Paris been raised so high as in China. The Chinese trusted America, they trusted the frequent declarations of principle uttered by President Wilson, whose words had reached China in its remotest parts. The more intense was their disappointment and disillusionment due to the decisions of the old men that controlled the peace conference. It sickened and disheartened me to think how the Chinese people would receive this blow which meant the blasting of their hopes and the destruction of their confidence in the equity of nations.[107]

Understandably American public opinion was also quite critical over the Shandong issue. Headlines in the United States ran as follows: "Japan the Possessor of Stolen Goods," "The Crime of Shantung," "Far-Eastern Alsace-Lorraine," "Sold – 40,000,000 People." The *Boston Transcript* characterized the Shandong deal as "insolent and Hunlike spoliation." *The New York Call* wrote it up as "one of the most shameless deeds in the record of imperialistic diplomacy." *The Franklin (PA) News-Herald* called it a "damnable enterprise" and "inexcusable injustice." *The Pittsburgh Dispatch* portrayed it as a "conspiracy to rob." *The Detroit Free Press* saw the "betrayal of China to Japan as the price of the latter's adherence to the League of Nations." *The San Francisco Chronicle* described it as "an infamy."[108]

Thus, Wilson's compromise on the Shandong issue to save his cherished plan for a new world order became an effective weapon for his opponents in the US Congress and elsewhere to attack the whole peace treaty and eventually defeat it. As Robert Lansing commented, "The chief objections raised against the treaty in the United States have been to those articles comprising the covenant of the League of Nations and to those dealing with Shantung."[109] According to historian Russell H. Fifield,

---

[105] T. H. Bliss to Wilson, April 29, 1919, *The Paper of Bliss*, Folder 247/W. Wilson/April 1919, Library of Congress, Manuscript Division; see also Jin, *China at the Paris Peace Conference*, 26.

[106] See Paul S. Reinsch, *An American Diplomat in China*, 364–82.

[107] Ibid., 359, 361.

[108] "The Uproar over Shantung," *The Literary Digest* 62, no. 5 (1919).

[109] Robert Lansing, *The Big Four and Others of the Peace Conference* (London: Hutchinson & Co., 1922), 75.

The Shantung issue was a favorite subject of Wilson's opposition in the Senate, because it was associated both with the League of Nations and with the growing sentiment against Japan . . . Accordingly, the Shantung clauses in the Treaty of Versailles provided an excellent basis for an effective "tactical maneuver" in the battle against the pact . . . The Shantung decision was becoming one of the important factors that would lead to the eventual rejection of the Treaty of Versailles by the Senate of the United States.[110]

Harsh criticism of Wilson and the peace treaty in the West was not only an American phenomenon. Some Britons felt uneasy with the defects of the treaty as well. In a letter sent to the British prime minister on May 27, 1919, Robert Cecil complained,

I cannot help feeling that in these negotiations our moral prestige has greatly suffered. A friend of mine described the treaty as the moral bankruptcy of the Entente. That seems to me a very exaggerated description, but I am struck with the fact that, whereas throughout the war all impartial neutral opinion was on our side, it is now all against us.[111]

The London *Times* also opposed the British government's position on China at the postwar peace conference, commenting that

No Japanese ships were ever sunk by German U Boats. No Japanese escort destroyer on the Indian Ocean convoys had to fire a shot at a German raider or submarine. Japan took over German assets, but used them for her own ends. In short, Japan contributed very little indeed to the "war effort," yet it received the rewards of a victor and charged China did nothing. For all she had done, China was treated like the defeated. It is unfair. The avowed object of the war was the destruction of Prussianism, but to use the words from the Chinese protest cabled to the American congress: "the treaty of peace transfers to Japan all Germany's iniquitous rights in the Chinese province of Shantung without conditions and free from all charges. This means that whilst Prussianism is to be destroyed in every other part of the world, America and the Allies have decided to perpetuate it in China in the interests of Japan."[112]

Wilson was a big loser at Paris, at least in the short term. He went to Paris with the determination to set out a new world order, yet with his compromise on Shandong and his damaged image in China, his own country refused to take part in the creation of that new order. The old world system that Wilson had wanted to destroy was still alive and kicking, and the story of Wilson at Paris suggests that neither the American people nor the old powers were yet ready for such a new world order.

---

[110] Russell H. Fifield, *Woodrow Wilson and the Far East; the Diplomacy of the Shantung Question* (Hamden, CT: Archon Books, 1965), 339, 40.
[111] British Library, Cecil Papers, Add. MS 51076.
[112] *Times* [London], May 27, 1919.

Significance of the conference for China

If we say that Wilson and his blueprint for a new world order failed at Paris, what then about China? Overwhelmingly, the scholarship on the period maintains that China experienced total defeat at the postwar peace conference. This view was raised even before the meeting had officially closed. Liang Qichao wrote from Paris claiming China suffered a total defeat; he expressed anger at Japan's carefully and skillfully executed plan to gain control of Shandong from the war's very beginning. According to Liang, Japan had "left no stone unturned, took no chances." He went on to criticize the Chinese delegation for their lack of diplomatic skills, but he reserved most of the blame for Beijing's stupidity at signing a treaty with Japan over Shandong in September 1918, a point at which Germany was bound to be defeated any day.[113] A recent book by Bruce A. Elleman seems to agree with Liang's view. But Elleman argues that China's failure to get Shandong back at the conference was due to what he calls the over-riding Chinese concern with "losing face." For Elleman, the main motivation for China trying to recover Shandong directly from Germany rather than indirectly from the Japanese was to avoid a "loss of face." He writes, "Face was of great importance in traditional Chinese diplomacy" and the fear of losing face led to "Chinese inflexibility" at the Paris conference.[114] To prove his point that Wilson did not betray China on Shandong, Elleman claims that Japan had "an almost unassailable legal position at Paris" – the six secret treaties it signed with the Allied powers and China prior to the conference – from which to win Shandong. He declares that the Chinese should blame themselves, not Wilson, the Japanese, or anybody else for what happened to them at Paris regarding the Shandong issue.[115]

Both Liang Qichao and Elleman link China's goals at Paris primarily with the Shandong issue. Liang was disappointed and upset at China's failure to take back Shandong when he wrote the angry article mentioned above, and he forgot that winning Shandong had been part of China's larger program of internationalization objectives. Elleman, obsessed with his assertion that Wilson was not responsible for China's Shandong loss, fails to realize that the Chinese, and indeed the American, outcry at Wilson's betrayal focused more on the betrayal of his own blueprint for a new world order than on his eventual refusal to support China's claims.

[113] Liang Qichao, "Causes of China's Defeat at the Peace Conference," *Millard's Review* 9, no. 7 (July 19, 1919): 262–68.
[114] Bruce A. Elleman, *Wilson and China: A Revised History of The Shandong Question* (M. E. Sharpe, 2002), 49–50, 94–96, 107–08, 149–51, 170–71.
[115] Ibid., 8.

For Elleman, the Chinese chose to blame Wilson for "failing to uphold his Fourteen Points" because they wanted to "save face" at their failure in Paris.[116] Because of his legalist and diplomatic history approach, Elleman has missed the broader Chinese goals: its internationalization and joining the world community, as well as the recovery of overall national sovereignty. He also failed to realize that a new China – primarily motivated by a desire to engage the international community and the prospect of a new world order rather than by "face" – was at work at Paris. Elleman might not know about, or might have chosen to ignore, the efforts China had made to join the war from its very inception. Instead, he claims that because "Japanese troops fought and died in World War I," Japan deserved to be awarded Shandong at Paris, Elleman completely fails to acknowledge the telling fact that Japan did not send a single soldier to Europe, and that all its war deaths took place in its attack on Qingdao.[117]

If we choose a broader perspective, in particular considering China's motivation to internationalize, to evaluate Chinese accomplishments at Paris, we might argue that China scored quite well.[118] Even by simply presenting its position at the conference, China had already partly succeeded in projecting a new image to the world and injecting its own voice into discussions of the new world order. Moreover, even from the narrow view of the Shandong question, by refusing to compromise with Japan and by its refusing to sign the Versailles treaty, the Chinese had forced the whole world to take notice of their situation and so set the stage for the favorable resolution of the Shandong problem that would occur shortly at the Washington Conference of 1921–22. It was from this perspective that Koo later wrote that China's refusal to sign the Versailles treaty was an extremely important step for its national and diplomatic development.[119] Furthermore, although China did not sign this treaty, it did find a way to become an original member of the League of Nations by signing a peace treaty with Austria.[120] China's obsession with its membership in the League of Nations even after its failure to recover Shandong

---

[116] Ibid., 94.   [117] Ibid., 34.

[118] This success story has been only recently emphasized by some scholars. Historian Zhang Zongfu considered that "although it might have been disappointed with what happened at the Paris Peace Conference, China, without any doubt, had achieved quite a bit." Zhang Chunlun, in her recent article on Koo, also concludes that China did not truly fail at the peace conference; on the contrary, it achieved at least "a limited success." See Zhang Zongfu, *Zhonghua minguo waijiao shi* (Taipei: Zhengzhong shuju, 1957), 284. Zhang Chunlun, "Gu Weijun de hehui waijiao: yi shou hui Shangdong zhu quan wenti wei Zhong xin," *Zhongyang yanjiuyuan jindai shi yanjiusuo jikan* 23, no. 2 (1994).

[119] Gu Weijun, "Bali hehui de huiyi," *Zhuanji wenxue* 7, no. 6 (1965).

[120] One immediate result of its refusal to sign the peace treaty with Germany at Paris was that a state of war continued to exist between China and Germany. By a mandate from its president, China declared the end of that state of war later.

further indicates its strong desire and determination for internationalization. Alston, Jordan's successor in China, was correct when he wrote to Earl Curzon in his 1920 annual report, "The rising tide of international esteem began to flow when China refused, weak as she was, to be bullied into signing the Treaty of Versailles. Though the momentary political victory at that time went to Japan, the moral victory remained with China, and has since culminated in her obtaining one of the temporary seats on the Council of the League of Nations."[121] More importantly, by refusing to sign the Versailles treaty, China managed to sign its first equal treaty with a major power since the Opium War. About two years after Paris, on May 20, 1921, Germany and China signed a treaty that promised their relations "must rest on the principles of perfect equality and absolute reciprocity in accordance with the rules of the general law of nations." Germany "agrees to the abrogation of consular jurisdiction in China, relinquishes in favor of China all the rights that the German government possesses."[122] By setting the stage for the signing of such a treaty, China arguably managed to score a diplomatic success.

One of the major implications of the peace conference for the Chinese was that the image and attraction of the West suffered a serious blow. After the Paris Peace Conference, as historian C. P. Fitzgerald has said, some Chinese became at last "completely disillusioned with the false Gods of the West. They turned restlessly to some other solution."[123] A sense of self-reliance and cries for a new direction filled the air. As Liang Qichao concluded, "In international relationships there is the principle of 'might is right.' This principle still holds sway today as ever. We have heard the principles of justice and humanity. But these are the catch phrases of the strong. If the weak nations, by taking these phrases in their literal sense, hope to be shielded by the strong, they will be quickly disillusioned." He told his fellow countrymen that for China, "The only one she could count upon is herself and her own undefeatable spirit and courage . . . Let us rise above our disabilities and be men, and depend upon ourselves for our own salvation. Therein lies our great hope."[124] This call for self-reliance was echoed by many others. One article declared that "the Peace Treaty of Versailles is by no means a document of justice . . . China must work now to save herself."[125] "The betrayal of Versailles"

---

[121] PRO, FO405/229/2.

[122] The Carnegie Endowment for International Peace, ed., *Shantung: Treaties and Agreements* (Washington, DC: The Carnegie Endowment for International Peace, 1921), 116–17.

[123] C. P. Fitzgerald, *The Birth of Communist China* (London: Penguin Books, 1964), 54.

[124] Liang Qichao, "Causes of China's Defeat at the Peace Conference," *Millard's Review* 9, no. 7 (July 19, 1919): 267–68.

[125] *Millard's Review* 11, no. 1 (December 6, 1919): 8.

made many in the Chinese elite doubt the value, and even the possibility, of China's identifying with the West. The moral and practical attraction of Western ideas in China's quest for national identity and internationalization lost weight among many influential Chinese elite members. Yan Fu, the famous scholar and translator of many Western books, declared that the behavior of the West in 1919 showed that "three hundred years of evolutionary progress have all come down to nothing but four words: selfishness, slaughter, shamelessness, and corruption."[126] Some concluded that the Paris peace treaty testified to a "failure of Wilsonianism and the victory of imperialism." The new world system, based on the exploitation of Germany and China, could not last long.[127] Others even warned that the League of Nations could not do China any good. China had to rely on itself.[128]

The humiliation the Chinese suffered in Paris put a damper on China's pursuit of a Western-style national identity. The Paris Peace Conference, to a great extent, alienated Chinese intellectuals, many of whom had been exposed to ideas about the decline of the West generated by the likes of Oswald Spengler. After many months spent in Europe, Liang realized that both Chinese and Western civilizations had their problems. He believed that combining the good parts of both of them to make a new civilization was the best strategy and encouraged the Chinese to use their higher spiritual civilization to salvage the superior Western material civilization.[129]

From the same sense of disappointment, Koo later commented,

> Looking back at China's stand at the Versailles Peace Conference and the developments preceding, it appears [that these events are] . . . a turning point in China's history, both from the domestic and international point of view . . . One could wonder what would be the situation in China either if China had succeeded in settling the Shantung question at Paris to her satisfaction or if she had signed the treaty without the reservation. These are questions which probably can never be fully answered now.[130]

What Koo tried to suggest here is that the Chinese experience at Paris marked the end of their all-out efforts to join the liberal Western system, efforts begun in Chinese attempts to join the First World War. What happened to China at Paris directly led to the May Fourth Movement, which

---

[126] James Pusey, *China and Charles Darwin* (Cambridge, MA: Harvard University Press, 1983), 439.

[127] *Pacific* 2, no. 1: 9.   [128] *Pacific* 2, no. 2: 2–4.

[129] Li Huaxing and Wu Jiayi, eds., *Liang Qichao xuanji* (Shanghai: Shanghai renmin chubanshe, 1984), 731–34.

[130] Koo Memoir (Columbia University Oral History Project), microfilm, reel 2, vol. II.

explicitly tied domestic politics to international affairs and significantly affected the Chinese pursuit of a place and voice in the world commu-nity.[131] The May Fourth Movement conceived of itself as the product of China's double betrayal – first the rejection by the Chinese of their own traditional culture and the West's betrayal of hopes for justice – and clearly exposed a huge identity vacuum. Having first rejected their own traditions and civilization, many Chinese found their aspirations had been thwarted by the West, making China a country without either roots or external supports. According to Zhang Yongjin, the May Fourth Move-ment successfully transferred Chinese "discontent into a national rejec-tion of an international order imposed upon China by the Powers."[132] Feelings of double betrayal compelled the Chinese to confront many chal-lenging questions: What did it now mean to be Chinese? Where was the country heading? What values should the Chinese government adopt? In short, what was the shape China's national identity should take? Thus, one of the most important themes of the May Fourth Movement was that of "recreating civilization."[133]

During the era of the First World War and before its betrayal in Paris, China had experienced national euphoria, stemming from high expec-tations regarding its renewal and the assumption of a place in the new world order. Now disillusionment leading to the May Fourth Movement prompted a Chinese search for a third way, a way between Western ideas and Chinese traditional culture. Zhang Dongsheng (1886–1973)

---

[131] The best studies on the May Fourth Movement include the following books: Chow Tse-Tsung, *The May 4th Movement: Intellectual Revolution in Modern China* (Cambridge, MA: Harvard University Press, 1960); Benjamin Schwartz, ed., *Reflections on the May Fourth Movement: A Symposium* (Cambridge, MA: Harvard University Press, 1972); Lin Yu-sheng, *The Crisis of Chinese Consciousness: Radical Anti-traditionalism in the May Fourth Era* (Madison: University of Wisconsin Press, 1979); Vera Schwarcz, *The Chinese Enlightenment: Intellectuals and the Legacy of the May Fourth Movement of 1919* (Berkeley: University of California Press, 1986); Yeh Wen-Hsin, *Provincial Passages: Culture, Space, and the Origins of Chinese Communism* (Berkeley: University of California Press, 1996); and Chen Mao, *Between Tradition and Change: The Hermeneutics of May Fourth Literature* (Lanham: University Press of America, 1997). Milena Dolezelová-Velingerová, Oldrich Král, and Graham Martin Sanders, *The Appropriation of Cultural Capital: China's May Fourth Movement* (Cambridge, MA: Harvard University Asia Center, 2001).

[132] Zhang Yongjin, *China in the International System*, 76.

[133] Chen Qitian, "Shumo shi xin wenhua de zheng jingsheng"(What Is the Real Spirit of New Culture), in *Shaonian Zhongguo* (Young China) 2, no. 2: 2. Lucian Bianco also argues that "The importance of the May Fourth Movement should by now be apparent. Intellectually, the Chinese revolution originated in the challenging of China's cultural heritage by Western civilization. The May Fourth Movement was the culmination of that challenge, of the brutal, wholesale repudiation of Confucianism, the symbol of Chinese culture and Chinese history." Lucian Bianco, *Origins of the Chinese Revolution, 1915–1949* (Stanford: Stanford University Press, 1971), 28.

declared that the First World War indicated the collapse of the "second civilization" (the Western one).[134] Accordingly, he advocated a "third civilization," the introduction of socialism to China. Li Dazhao agreed. He argued that Russia, geographically and culturally situated at the intersection of Europe and Asia, was the only country which could undertake "the creation of a new civilization in the world that simultaneously retains the special features of eastern and western civilizations and the talents of the European and Asian peoples."[135] For Li, the October Revolution heralded a world in which weak nations would regain their independence.[136] At this point, Mao Zedong, then just another educated youth in China, concluded that Russia was now "the number one civilized country in the world."[137]

This background explains why some Chinese responded enthusiastically to Russian diplomatic initiatives in the wake of their disillusionment with the West. After the heartbreaking experience at the Paris Peace Conference, many Chinese perceived the Bolshevik Revolution as the only successful model for state building and Bolshevik Russia as the only power that appeared sympathetic to its aspirations to a new national identity. The Chinese admired Soviet Russia, not only because it had just announced to China and the world that it had decided to relinquish its unequal rights to China, but more importantly because the Russians had showed a spirit of humanism and internationalism contrary to the power politics of the West.[138] Russia's denunciation of imperialism and secret diplomacy struck a deep chord in China. For many Chinese elite members, Russia's diplomatic initiatives demonstrated more than the empty promises of the West. Soon the Chinese Communist Party was founded under Russian direction in 1921, and Sun Yat-sen's Guomindang also sided with Russia in the early 1920s.[139] As Benjamin Schwartz explains, "Paradoxically, one can actually assert that one of the main appeals of Marxism-Leninism to young Chinese was its appeal to nationalistic resentments. The Leninist theory of nationalism provided a plausible

---

[134] "Xuanyan" (Declaration), "Di san zhong wenmin" (the Third Civilization), "Zhongguo zhi qiantu: De guo hu? Wo guo hu?" (Model for China: Germany or Russia?), in *Jiefang yu gaizao* (Liberation and Reform), no. 1 (1919); 2, no. 14 (July 15, 1920).

[135] Quote from Maurice Meisner, *Li Ta-chao and the Origins of Chinese Marxism* (Cambridge, MA: Harvard University Press, 1967), 46–47, 64.

[136] Hans J. Van de Ven, *From Friend to Comrade: the Founding of the Chinese Communist Party, 1920–1927* (Berkeley: University of California Press, 1991), 27–28.

[137] John King Fairbank and Albert Feuerwerker, eds., *The Cambridge History of China: 1912–1949*, XIII, Part II (Cambridge: Cambridge University Press, 1986), 802.

[138] *Shaonian Zhongguo*, 2, no. 2: 2.

[139] About Sino-Russian relations in the 1920s, see Akira Iriye, *After Imperialism: The Search for a New Order in the Far East 1921–1931* (Chicago: Imprint Publications, Inc., 1990).

explanation for China's failure to achieve its rightful place in the world of nations."[140]

Interestingly enough, even in this search for a new means to define its position in the world, the Chinese still followed the international trends and the West. After all, socialism is a Western idea. Moreover, interest in socialism was a global phenomenon in the wake of the Great War. The American people in 1919 were "eagerly urged into what are called socialistic experiments."[141] Arif Dirlik clearly notices the shared experience China had with the rest of the world. He wrote that for Chinese intellectuals socialism already appeared "as a rising world tide in the aftermath of World War I, as was dramatized in the worldwide proliferation of revolutionary social movements of which the Russian revolution was the most prominent."[142] The emergence of a Communist movement in China, according to Dirlik, "resulted from a conjuncture of internal and external developments. In 1918–19, socialism appeared as a world political tide, nourished by the successful October Revolution in Russia, labor and social revolutionary movements in Europe and North America, and national liberation movements in colonial societies that found inspiration in socialist ideas."[143] In other words, even though China now refused to follow the West wholeheartedly and was determined to discover a new direction for developing its national identity, it remained motivated by a strong sense of internationalization and the expectation of playing a role in larger world affairs.

---

[140] Benjamin I. Schwartz, "Chinese Perception of World Order," in John K. Fairbank, ed., *The Chinese World Order: Traditional China's Foreign Relations* (Cambridge, MA: Harvard University Press, 1968), 286.

[141] Albert W. Atwood, "Our Forgotten Socialism," *The Saturday Evening Post*, 192, no. 4 (1919): 16.

[142] Arif Dirlik, *The Origins of Chinese Communism* (New York: Oxford University Press, 1989), 142.

[143] Ibid., 253.

Conclusion

> They [the French revolutionaries] were fooled, not because the words
> of Danton and Vergniaud, of Robespierre and Saint-Just, and of all the
> others still rang in their ears; they were fooled by history, and they have
> become the fools of history.
>
> Hannah Arendt[1]

After the Great War was long over, John Jordan, who was British minister
to China and the doyen of the diplomatic corps in Beijing owing to his
long tenure in China, wrote the following report to his government:

It must be admitted at the outset that our official records do not give an adequate
impression of what passed between China and the Allies during the first years of
the war, and do not show the full extent to which President Yuan Shih-Kai and
his Cabinet were willing to throw in their lot with us; they would undoubtedly
have done so, especially in the winter of 1915, had it not been for the strenuous
opposition encountered from Japan. China went out of her way to supply us
with arms, and to commit other un-neutral acts, and was quite prepared to go
further had she been dealing with the European Allies alone . . . [By signing secret
treaties with Japan in early 1917] the Allies had to sacrifice principle on the altar
of military necessity. China was perfectly willing – nay, anxious – to throw in her
lot with us in November 1915 . . . In the summer of 1917, when the intervention
of America in the war had rendered the ultimate defeat of Germany an absolute
certainty, and incidentally showed promise of restoring the balance of power in
the Far East, Japan was no longer able to prevent China from definitely joining
the Allies.[2]

Jordan's statement is extremely interesting and important to us. First
of all, it acknowledges the fact the Allied countries during and after the
war chose not to fully appreciate or understand the depth and determination of China's involvement in the war from the very beginning. Second, it
confirms the degree to which China's intention to join the war was consistent. Third, Jordan acknowledges that the Allied Powers did "sacrifice"

---

[1] Hannah Arendt, *On Revolution* (New York: The Viking Press, 1963), 52.
[2] Kenneth Bourne, ed., *British Documents on Foreign Affairs: Reports and Papers from the
Foreign Office Confidential Print, Series E, Asia*, vol. xxiii, *China, January 1919 – December
1920* (University Publications of America, 1994), 59–60.

their principles and China in the secret treaties with Japan. Lastly but most importantly, Jordan implied that from the outset the world got the story of China's part in the Great War all wrong. The aim of this book is to restore China to our studies of the Great War and bring the war back into Chinese history.

As previous chapters show, China's involvement in the First World War is a unique event in both Chinese and world history. It may be argued that the nature of Chinese participation in the Great War made it truly a *world* war and transformed the meaning and implications of the conflict both for China and for the world, and resulted in the Chinese introducing substantially new contents and perspectives to the postwar peace conference and the emerging new world order. Its involvement in the war also brought China back into the larger world history of the twentieth century. No matter how we evaluate China's war contribution and effort, by studying China in the Great War we can at the very least add a new dimension to our collective memory of the war, its human tragedy, and its significance.

This book, by taking an international history approach to analyze the broadly defined period of the First World War, has used China's determination for internationalization as its focus and the Great War as a reference point. China's involvement in the war and its aftermath offers a vital window onto the ongoing enterprise of nation-building and the new Chinese national consciousness. For the Chinese, their participation in the Great War was to serve multiple national purposes, yet the main force behind the new Chinese approach to world affairs was the strong desire to engage with the international community and gain recognition within that community.

Despite the supposed "failure" of China's principal goals at the post-war peace conference, China's war aims, domestic debates, and multiple efforts to join the war reveal the pivotal place of the war in the formation of a new Chinese perception of self and the world. In other words, we will never understand the full history of twentieth-century China or fully appreciate the importance of China's internationalization to its war effort and war policies if we focus only on the so-called Paris "betrayal" or Chinese diplomatic failures. By overemphasizing the Shandong issue or China's failure or success at the conference we have, to a great extent, become fooled by history, rather than explaining or understanding that particular historical moment. Only when we go beyond the "betrayal" complex and even beyond the Paris Peace Conference itself, can we appreciate how significant the war was in modern Chinese history. Only then can we grasp the extent to which Chinese statesmen, opinion-makers, and other elite members looked to the war as an opportunity to fashion a new sense of nation and a new relationship to the world. To be sure, in light of those high hopes and expectations and the tremendous effort expended to realize them, the inability to gain recognition of even Chinese territorial sovereignty despite all efforts at Paris marked a truly great affront and led to psychological shock and immense disappointment for the Chinese. However strong the Chinese response to the results of the conference, it did not undermine China's desire for engagement in the international arena; instead, the response reflected the deep level of Chinese commitment to internationalization.

In other words, this book aims to redirect our attention from primarily focusing on the postwar peace conference or the Shandong issue to the bigger picture: China taking the opportunity the Great War provided to radically readjust its relation with the growing community of nation-states at the turn of the twentieth century. Two books seem to represent a growing scholarly trend in this area: Bruce Elleman's *Wilson and China* and Zhang Yongjin's work on China and the Paris Peace Conference.[3] Both books focus narrowly either on the Shandong question or on the peace conference itself without paying enough attention to China's larger involvement in the Great War and its motivations for that involvement. Nevertheless, it was exactly because of its war effort and its determination to become part of the nation-state community that China managed to gain a seat at the conference. Therefore, bringing China's war policies and war effort into the picture is absolutely key, no matter how we examine the Shandong issue or how we evaluate Chinese efforts at the postwar peace conference. Without even the limited successes of the New Diplomacy during World War I, the situation China faced in the postwar world would have been much worse. What else might Japan have extracted through its Twenty-one Demands? If Chinese laborers had not been sent to Europe and China had not eventually joined the war, how much more difficult would it have been to gain entry to the peace conference and have a chance to present its case before the world audience? Without its seat at the peace conference, where new Chinese voices gripped the world's attention, China would have been hard pressed to recover Shandong as it eventually did at the Washington Conference of 1921–22.

In a sense, this book is about China's unacknowledged successes and its shared experience with the wider world during the First World War. Thanks to China's refusal to sign the Treaty of Versailles at Paris, China and Germany signed a new treaty in 1921 that finally abolished Germany's unequal rights and established a new relationship of equals

---

[3] For details, see Elleman, *Wilson and China: A Revised History of The Shandong Question* and Zhang, *China in the International System*.

among nation-states. This Sino-German treaty was the first equal treaty China signed with a major power after the Opium War. China and Germany, both very disappointed with the Treaty of Versailles and the shape of the new world order, and both having shared a sense of togetherness in their disappointment with the Paris peace conference result, were determined to turn a new page in their mutual relations after 1921. To a great extent, this explains why Germany enjoyed good relations with China through the 1920s and 1930s.[4] "I think no European nation is more popular in China today than is Germany," as Henry T. Hodgkin, who was secretary of the National Christian Council of China and a close observer of China in the 1920s, wrote:

This may seem strange when one remembers German aggression in Shantung and the fact that Germany and China have been on opposite sides in the Great War. It is due in part to the fact that Germany has been treated by her conquerors in a way that makes China feel a deep sympathy, a sort of fellow-feeling. China and Germany were both wronged by the Treaty of Versailles; both are suffering because might has overstepped the bounds of right . . . Germans are now in China on equal terms with the Chinese. Even though the change has not been of Germany's seeking, it has helped greatly in the reaction of feeling.[5]

As a matter of fact, the new Sino-German treaty was not an isolated event but reflected a new trend in China. After the postwar peace conference, attempts to recover national sovereignty and enter into the family of nations as an equal and active member became dual themes in China's broader interaction with other nations.

It seems obvious that China shared with its European counterparts the sacrifices and suffering of the First World War. But China's experiences in the war had parallels elsewhere, too. The motivations for Chinese entry into the war had much in common with those of the United States. The United States also used the Great War as an opportunity to inject its own blueprint for a new world order into the plans of the old powers, introducing a new set of international systems, and diplomatically internationalizing its status. China used the Great War as a springboard for national renewal, for carving out a new national identity, for recovering national sovereignty, and for sorting out a more equitable basis for interacting with other nations. Even when many Chinese decided to turn away from the West and make China a communist power, they were still striving to realize the dream of internationalizing. It only indicates that, in light of

---

[4] For an excellent study on Sino-German relations in this period, see William C. Kirby, *Germany and Republican China* (Stanford: Stanford University Press, 1984).

[5] Henry T. Hodgkin, *China in the Family of Nations* (London: George Allen & Unwin Ltd., 1923), 168.

the disappointments of one approach, the Chinese tried a different way to gain equal membership among the nations of the world and devise for themselves a new, powerful national identity. After all, the communism of the time was a blend of nationalism and internationalism. The same can be said about the United States. Even though the United States failed to join the League of Nations and its congress refused to support the Treaty of Versailles, internationalism was still a clear theme in American economic, cultural, and even diplomatic engagement with the rest of the world in the 1920s.

Most of all, this book reconsiders why and how the First World War became a *great war* for China, even though the Chinese involvement has apparently been purged from our collective war memory. By studying China and the Great War, I hope to fill a substantial gap between 1911 (a year of great promise) and 1919 (a year of reflection and new thinking, a point of departure) in Chinese modern history. Existing scholarship has it that for China the First World War never became a "great" war; rather, it was only a "lost war," an "ignored war," or a "forgotten war" because few people understand its importance, and the significant implications of China's involvement. To risk plagiarism of Paul Fussell's famous title *The Great War and Modern Memory*, this study, to a great extent, aims to restore the Chinese war memory to its rightful place.[6] It argues that the war was a great war, even for China, and China's active involvement makes it a great war for the world. Like Dickinson's recent book on Japan and the First World War, which brilliantly demonstrates the connection between the war and Japan's national reinvention and successfully rebuts the widespread argument that Japan "did not really experience World War I" and did not "join the twentieth century until 1945,"[7] this book will argue that the Chinese twentieth century started with the broadly defined period of the Great War. The part China played in the war and the part the war played in China fully represent the beginning of China's long journey toward internationalization. That the Great War brought China into the world makes it an important moment in Chinese and world history.

---

[6] Paul Fussell, *The Great War and Modern Memory* (New York: Oxford University Press, 1975).

[7] Frederick R. Dickinson, *War and National Reinvention: Japan in the Great War* (Cambridge, MA: The Harvard East Asia Center, 1999), 3.

Appendix 1
Foreign-trained cabinet members in early Republican China[a]

Prime Minister	Year	Numbers[b]	Foreign-trained	% of foreign-trained
Tang Shaoyi	3.13–6.27.1912	30	22	73.3
Lu Zhengxiang	6.29–9.22.1912	39	31	79.5
Zhao Bingjun	9.25.1912–7.16.1913	34	22	64.7
Duan Qirui	7.19–7.31.1913	26	17	65.3
Xiong Xiling	7.13.1913–2.12.1914	46	28	60.8
Sun Baoqi[c]	2.12.1914–5.1.1914	26	20	76.9
Xu Shichang	5.1.1914–4.22.1916	44	25	56.8
Duan Qirui	4.22.1916–6.29.1916	45	29	64.4
Duan Qirui	6.29.1916–5.23.1917 7.2–11.22.1917	60	40	66.6
Wu Tingfang[c]	5.23.1917–5.28.1917	23	14	60.8
Li Jingxi	5.28–7.2.1917	29	18	62
Duan Qirui	3.23–10.10.1918	29	17	58.6
Qian Nengxun	10.10–12.12.1918	22	15	68.1
Qian Nengxun	12.12.1918–6.13.1919	31	17	54.8
Gong Xinzhan	6.13–9.24.1919	25	13	52
Jin Yunpeng[c]	9.24–11.5.1919	23	9	39.1
Jin Yunpeng	11.5.1919–5.14.1920	30	13	43.3
Sa Zhenbing[c]	5.14–8.9.1920	30	15	50
Jin Yunpeng	8.9.1920–12.18.1921	47	22	46.8
Yan Huiqing[c]	12.18–12.24.1921	27	15	55.5

[a] Sources based on Liu Shoulin, ed. *Xin hai yi hou shi qi nian zhi guan nian biao.* Beijing: Zhong hua shu ju, 1966. Liu Shoulin, et al., eds. *Min guo zhi guan nian biao.* Beijing: Zhong hua shu ju, 1995.
[b] Including ministers and vice-ministers
[c] Provisional cabinets

Appendix 2
List of foreign ministers, 1912–1922[a]

Wang Chonghui	January 1 – April 1, 1912
Lu Zhengxiang	March 30 – September 22, 1912
Liang Ruhao	September 16, 1912 – November 15, 1912
Lu Zhengxiang	November 15, 1912 – September 4, 1913
Sun Baoqi	September 11, 1913 – January 27, 1915
Lu Zhengxiang	January 27, 1915 – May 17, 1916
Cao Rulin[b]	May 17 – June 30, 1916
Chen Jintao[b]	June 30 – December 24, 1916
Wu Tingfang	November 13, 1916 – June 12, 1917
Wang Daxie	July 15 – November 30, 1917
Lu Zhengxiang	December 1, 1917 – August 13, 1920
Yan Huiqing	August 11, 1920 – August 5, 1922

[a] Based on Liu Shoulin, ed. *Xin hai yi hou shi qi nian zhi guan nian biao*. Liu Shoulin, et al., eds. *Min guo zhi guan nian biao*.
[b] Acting foreign minister

Select bibliography

UNPUBLISHED SOURCES IN CHINESE

ZHONGGUO DIER LISHI DANGANGUAN (NATIONAL SECOND HISTORICAL ARCHIVE IN NANJING, PEOPLE'S REPUBLIC OF CHINA)
Beiyang zhengfu waijiaobu dangan 1039/1–654.
Beiyang zhengfu can lu bangongchu, 1014/1–535; du ban bian fan (canzhan) shiwuchu, 1016/1–368; du ban bian fan jun (canzhan jun) xunliangchu 1017/1–230; bian fan jun (canzhan jun) disan si 1018/1–76; bian fan jun (canzhan jun) suo shu ji gou dangan huiji 1019/1–71.
Beiyang zhengfu neiwubu dangan, 1001.
Beiyang zhengfu guowuyuan dangan, 1002.
Beiyang zhengfu guohui dangan, 1060.
Beiyang zhengfu zongtongfu junshichu dangan, 1003.
Beiyang zhengfu jiaoyubu dangan, 1057.
Beiyang zhengfu lin shi zhu zhengfu junwuting dangan, 1004.
Beiyang zhengfu lujunbu dangan, 1011.

ZHONGYANG YANJIUYUAN JINDAI SHI YANJIUSUO DANGANGUAN (ARCHIVE OF INSTITUTE OF MODERN HISTORY, ACADEMIA SINICA, TAIPEI, TAIWAN)
Waijiaobu dang
Ju mei shi guan baocun dangan 03-12/1-18.
Geguan huiwu wenda, 03-11/1-18.
Ouzhan dang, 03-36/1-177.
Bali hehui, 03-37/1-34.
Zhong-Ri guanxi, 03-33/1-29.

Peng, Xiangjin. "Duan Qirui tuidong Zhongguo canjia Ouzhan zhi yanjiu." M.A. thesis, National Taiwan University, 1969.
Wang, Fengzhen. "Gu Weijun yu Bali hehui." M.A. thesis, Donghai daxue, 1980.

UNPUBLISHED SOURCES IN ENGLISH

BRITISH LIBRARY, LONDON
Arthur Balfour Papers.
Robert Cecil Papers.

PUBLIC RECORD OFFICE, KEW, SURREY, UK

Miscellaneous Cabinet Office papers collected by Sir James Masterton-Smith.
Minutes of the cabinets from December 1916 to December 1918.
Papers of the Supreme War Council.
John Jordan Papers.
The Papers of the Foreign Office's Political and War Departments.
The Foreign Office Confidential Print, 1914–18.
The War Office: War Diaries, 1914–18.
The War Office: Papers of the Directorate of Military Operations.
The War Office: Military Headquarters papers.
The War Office: The Correspondence and papers of Military Headquarters.

MANUSCRIPT DIVISION, LIBRARY OF CONGRESS, WASHINGTON, DC.

William J. Bryan Papers.
Robert Lansing Papers.
Woodrow Wilson Papers.

NATIONAL ARCHIVE (COLLEGE PARK, MARYLAND)

Records of the War Department, 1910–1929.
Records of the Department of State Relating to Internal Affairs of China, 1910–1929.
Records of the Department of State Relating to Political Relations between China and Other States, 1910–1929.
Records of the Department of State Relating to Political Relations between the United States and China, 1910–1929.
Records of the Department of State Relating to Political Relations between the United States and Japan, 1910–1929.
Records of Military Intelligence Division Regional Files Relating to China.
Correspondence of Secretary of State Bryan with President Wilson, 1911–1915.
Personal and Confidential Letters from Secretary of State Lansing to President Wilson, 1915–1918.

ORAL HISTORY PROJECT, COLUMBIA UNIVERSITY

Wellington Koo Memoir.

UNPUBLISHED SOURCES IN FRENCH

SERVICE HISTORIQUE DE L'ARMÉE DE TERRE, CHÂTEAU DE VINCENNES

4N8/Gragaux/Orient.
4N63/Coopération Chinois.
5N216/Chine/January–December 1918.
6N111/Fonds Clemenceau/divers secrets.
6N130/Rapports de l'attaché militaire.
6N149/Fonds Clemenceau/mission de recrutement des ouvriers Chinois.

6N 155/dossier 3.
6N 257/Chine/Attaché militaire.
7N 398/Chine.
7N 435/Main-d'Oeuvre indigence.
7N 709/Chine.
7N 829/Chine.
7N 1297/Chinois Evacuation.
7N 1689/Attaché militaire.
7N 2289/Affaires Britanniques/Travailleurs Chinois.
16N 2986/Asie.
16N 3012/Chine–Japon.
16N 3189/Chine et Japon.
17N/156.

ARCHIVES DE LA MARINE, VINCENNES

SSEA 76/Chine.
SSEB 119/Transport Personnel.
SSEB 5/travailleurs coloniaux et étrangers/généralités.

ARCHIVE NATIONALE, PARIS

14F/11331/Main-d'Oeuvre Chinois
14F/11332/Main d'Oeuvre
14F/11334/ Procès-Verbaux de la Conférence Interministérielle.

QUAI D'ORSAY, MINISTRE DES AFFAIRES ETRANGÈRES, PARIS

Ministre des Affaires Etrangères, 1918–1929, Chine.
Ministre des Affaires Etrangères, 1918–1929, NS, Chine.

UNPUBLISHED SOURCES IN GERMAN

POLITISCHES ARCHIV DES AUSWÄRTIGEN AMTS, BONN

R 17754/China.
R 17800/China.
R 17805/China.
R 17811/China.
R 17816/China.
R 17847/China.
R 17985/China.
R 18024/China.
Akten betreffend Nachlass Hintze.

BUNDESARCHIV, KOBLENZ

R 85/1231/774/776/714/706.

PERIODICALS, NEWSPAPERS

The China Press.
The China Quarterly.
The Chinese Students' Monthly.
Da Zhonghua.
Dongfang zazhi (Eastern Miscellany).
The Far Eastern Review.
Hong Kong Telegraph.
Jiefang yu gaizao.
Jindai shi ziliao.
Manchester Guardian.
Meizhou pinglun.
Millard's Review of The Far East.
Minguo dangan.
Minguo ribao.
The North China Herald.
Pall Mall Gazette.
Peking Daily News.
The Peking Gazette.
The Saturday Evening Post.
Shaonian Zhongguo.
Shen bao.
Shi bao.
Xin chao (The New Tide).
Xin qingnian (The New Youth).
Xin Zhongguo (The New China).
Zhongguo xinbao.
Zhuanji wenxue.

PUBLISHED SOURCES IN CHINESE

Bai Jiao. *Yuan Shikai yu Zhonghua minguo* (Yuan Shikai and the Republic of China). Shanghai: Renwen yuekanshe, 1936.

Bao Tianxiao, *Chuanyinlou huiyilu* (Memoirs of Bao Tianxiao). Hong Kong: Da Hua chubanshe, 1971.

Beijing daxue. *Beijing daxue jinian Wu-si yundong qishi zhou nian lunwenji* (Peking University's Collected Papers in commemoration of the seventieth anniversary of the May Fourth Movement). Beijing: Beijing daxue chubanshe, 1990.

Beijing shifan daxue xiaoshi ziliao shi. *Wu-si yundong yu Beijing gaoshi* (The May Fourth Movement and Beijing Normal University). Beijing: Beijing shifan daxue chubanshe, 1984.

Cao Rulin. *Yi sheng zhi huiyi* (Memoirs of Cao Rulin). Hong Kong: Chun Qiu chubanshe, 1966.

Chen Daode, Zhang Minfu, and Rao Geping, eds. *Zhonghua minguo waijiao shi ziliao xuanbian (1911–1919)* (Selected original materials relating to the diplomatic history of Republican China). Beijing: Beijing daxue chubanshe, 1988.

Chen Duxiu. *Chen Duxiu shuxinji* (Collection of Chen Duxiu's letters). Hong Kong, 1988.

Duxiu wencun (Surviving Writings of Chen Duxiu). Hefei: Anhui renmin chubanshe, 1987.

Chen Duxiu zizhuan (Autobiography of Chen Duxiu). Hong Kong: Xiandai chubanshe, 1969.

Chen Duxiu wenzhang xuanbian (Selected articles by Chen Duxiu). Beijing: Sanlian shudian, 1984.

Chen Duxiu zhuzuo xuan (Selected writings of Chen Duxiu). Shanghai: Shanghai renmin chubanshe, 1984.

Chen Feng, ed. *Liang Shiyi shiliaoji* (Collection of original materials about Liang Shiyi). Beijing: Zhongguo wenshi chubanshe, 1991.

Chen Ruifang and Wang Huijuan. *Tianjin shi lishi bowuguan guancang Beiyang junfa shiliao* (Materials about Beiyang warlords collected by the Tianjin Historical Museum). Tianjin: Tianjin guji chubanshe, 1992.

Chen Sanjing. *Huagong yu Ouzhan* (Chinese laborers and the European War). Taipei: Monograph Series, Institute of Modern History, Academia Sinica, 1986.

"Jidu qingnianhui yu Ouzhan Huagong" (the YMCA and Chinese laborers in Europe during the First World War). *Zhongyang yanjiuyuan jindai shi yanjiusuo jikan* 1, no. 17 (1988): 53–70.

"Lu Zhengxiang yu Bali hehui" (Lu Zhengxiang and the Paris Peace Conference). In *Jindai waijiao shi lunji*. Taipei: Xuehai chubanshe, 1977.

"Zhongguo pai bing canjia Ouzhan zhi jiaoshe" (The negotiations regarding China's decision to send military forces to Europe during the First World War). In *Zhonghua minguo lishi yu wenhua taolunji*, 97–117. Taipei, 1984.

Chen Sanjing, Lu Fangshang, and Yang Cuihua, eds. *Ouzhan Huagong shiliao* (Original materials about Chinese laborers in Europe during the First World War). Taipei: Zhongyang yanjiuyuan jindai shi yanjiusuo, 1997.

Chen Wanxiong. *Wu-si xin wenhua de yuanliu* (The origins of the May Fourth New Culture Movement). Beijing: Sanlian shudian, 1992.

Chen Xulu, Xu Mao, and Li Huaxing. *Wu-si hou sanshi nian* (The thirty years after the May Fourth Movement). Shanghai: Shanghai renmin chubanshe, 1989.

Chen Zhiqi, ed. *Zhonghua minguo waijiao shiliao huibian* (Selected materials about the diplomatic history of Republican China). Taipei: Bohai tan wenhua gongshi, 1996.

Cui Shuqing. *Sun Zhongshan yu gongchan zhuyi* (Sun Yat-Sen and Communism). Hong Kong: Yazhou chubanshe, 1954.

Di Jie. *Long zheng hudou: Beiyang junfa milu* (Untold stories of Beiyang warlords). Beijing: Tuanjie chubanshe, 1994.

Deng Ye. "Bali hehui juyue wenti yanjiu" (Study of China's refusal to sign the Versailles Peace Treaty). *Zhongguo shehui kexue* (Chinese Social Sciences Quarterly) 2 (1984).

"Cong Gu Weijun huiyilu kan Gu Shi qi ren" (Koo seen from his memoir). *Jindai shi yanjiu* (Beijing: Study of modern history), no. 6 (1996).

Di Ji. "Feng Guozhang wanglai han dian" (Telegrams and letters from and for Feng Guozhang). *Jindai ziliao* (Materials of Modern History) 40 (1979).

Ding Wenjiang, ed. *Liang Rengong xiansheng nianpu changbian chugao* (Life chronology of Mr. Liang Qichao). Taipei: Shijie shuju, 1959.

Ding Xianjun, and Yu Zuofeng, eds. *Wu Tingfang ji* (Collection of Wu Tingfang's Writings). Beijing: Zhonghua shuju, 1993.

Ding Xiaoqiang, and Zi Xu. *Wu-si yu xiandai Zhongguo: Wu-si xin lun* (The May Fourth Movement and modern China). Taiyuan: Shanxi renmin chubanshe, 1989.

Ding Zhongjiang. *Beiyang junfa shi hua* (Stories of Beiyang warlords). Beijing: Zhongguo youyi chuban gongsi, 1992.

Dong Yao. *Beiyang junfa Wu Peifu* (Biography of warlord Wu Peifu). Beijing: Tuanjie chubanshe, 1995.

Du Chunhe, Lin Binsheng, and Qiu Quanzheng, eds. *Beiyang junfa shiliao xuanji* (Selected materials on Beiyang warlords). Beijing: Zhongguo shehui kexue chubanshe, 1981.

Fang Hanqi, ed. *Zhongguo xinwen shiye tongshi* (A general history of Chinese journalism). Beijing: renmin daxue chubanshe, 1992.

Fei Jingzhong. *Duan Qirui* (Biography of Duan Qirui). Shanghai: Shijie shuju, 1921.

Feng Dali. *Wo de fuqin Feng Yuxiang* (My father, General Feng Yuxiang). Chengdu: Sichuan renmin chubanshe, 1985.

Feng Gang et al., eds. *Minguo Liang Yansun xiansheng shiyi nianpu* (Life Chronology of Mr. Liang Shiyi). Taipei: Commercial Press, 1978.

Gao Pingshu, ed. *Cai Yuanpei quanji* (Complete Collection of Cai Yuanpei's Writings). Beijing: Zhonghua shuju, 1984.

Ge Gongzhen, *Zhongguo baoxue shi* (History of Chinese journalism). Taipei: Xuesheng shuju, 1960.

Gu Weijun. "Bali hehui de huiyi" (Recollections about the Paris Peace Conference). *Zhuanji wenxue* 7, no. 6 (1965).

   Gu Weijun huiyilu (Memoir of Wellington Koo). Beijing: Zhonghua shuju, vol. 1, 1983.

Gu Xingqing. *Ouzhan gongzuo huiyilu* (Memoirs of Working for the European War). Shanghai: Shangwu yinshuguan, 1937.

Guan Meirong. *Wu Jingliang yu Minchu guohui* (Wu Jingliang and the Parliament in Early Republican China). Taipei: Guoshi guan, 1995.

Guo Tingyi, and Shen Yunlong. *Zhong Boyi xiangsheng fangwen jilu* (Record of interviews with Zhong Boyi by Guo Tingyi and Sheng Yunlong). Taipei: Zhongyang yanjiuyuan jindai shisuo, Academia Sinica, 1992.

Guo Tingyi, ed. *Zhonghua minguo shi shi rizhi* (Daily records of historical events in Republican China). Taipei: Zhongyang yanjiuyuan jindai shisuo, Academia Sinica, 1979.

Han Bo. *Yuan Shikai biezhuan* (Biography of Yuan Shikai). Shanghai: Shanghai renmin chubanshe, 1998.

Han Zuo. *Yuan Shikai pingzhuan* (Biography of Yuan Shikai), Hong Kong: Dong-Xi wenhua shiye chuban gongsi, 1988.

   Yuan Shikai. Taipei: Tianyuan chubanshe, 1987.

Hou Yijie. *Yuan Shikai pingzhuan* (Biography of Yuan Shikai). Zhengzhou: Henan jiaoyu chubanshe, 1986.

Yuan Shikai quanzhuan (Complete biography of Yuan Shikai). Beijing: Dangdai Zhongguo chubanshe, 1994.

Yuan Shikai yi sheng (The life of Yuan Shikai). Zhengzhou: Henan renmin chubanshe, 1984.

Hu Hanmin. ed. *Zongli quanji* (Complete writings of Sun Yat-Sen). Shanghai, 1930.

Hu Shi, ed. *Zhongguo xin wenxue daxi: jianshe lilun ji* (Collections of Chinese New Literature: volume on theory building). Shanghai: Liangyou tushu gongsi, 1935.

Shi Hua. "Zhang Xun cang zha" (Letters collected by Zhang Xun). *Jindai shi ziliao* (Materials on modern history) 35 (1965).

Huang Fu. *Ouzhan zhi jiaoxun yu Zhongguo zhi weilai* (Lessons of the European war and China's future). Shanghai: Zhonghua shuju chubanshe, 1918.

Huang Jiamu. "Zhongguo dui Ouzhan de chubu fanying" (China's initial response to the European war). *Zhongyang yanjiuyuan jindai shi yanjiusuo jikan*, no. 1 (1969): 3–18.

Huang Jinlin. "Lishi de yishi xiju: Ouzhan zai Zhongguo" (History and ritual: the European war in China). *Xin shi xue*, vol. 7, no.3 (September 1996).

Huang Zheng, Chen Changhe, and Ma Lie. *Duan Qirui yu Wanxi junfa* (Duan Qirui and the Anhui warlords). Henan renmin chubanshe, 1990.

Ji Yu. *Duan Qirui zhuan* (Biography of Duan Qirui). Hefei: Anhui renmin chubanshe, 1992.

Jia Shucun. *Beiyang junfa shiqi de jiaotongxi* (The communication clique during the Beiyang warlord period). Henan renmin chubanshe, 1993.

Jiang Kefu. *Beiyang junfa he Guomin geming jun* (Beiyang warlords and the nationalist revolutionary army). Beijing: Zhonghua shuju, 1987.

Minguo junshi shi lungao (The military history of Republican China). Beijing: Zhonghua shuju, 1987.

Jiang Tingfu. *Jiang Tingfu huiyilu* (Memoirs of Jiang Tingfu). Taipei: Zhuanji wenxue chubanshe, 1979.

Jin Wensi. *Cong Bali hehui dao Guolian* (From the Paris Peace Conference to the League of Nations). Taipei: Zhuanji wenxue chubanshe, 1983.

Jing Guangyao, ed. *Gu Weijun yu Zhongguo waijiao* (Gu Weijun and China's foreign relations). Shanghai: Shanghai Guji chubanshe, 2001.

Lai Xinxia, Guo Jianlin, and Jiao Jingyi. *Beiyang junfa shigao* (History of the Beiyang warlords). Hubei renmin chubanshe, 1983.

Lai Xinxia, ed. *Beiyang junfa* (Documents on the Beiyang warlords). Shanghai: Shanghai renmin chubanshe, 1988.

Li Ciming. *Yuemantang Riji* (Li Ciming diary). Taipei: Wenhai chubanshe, 1963.

Li Dazhao. *Li Dazhao wenji* (Li Dazhao's collected writings). Beijing: Renmin chubanshe, 1984.

Li Guoqi. *Minguo shilunji* (Collections of papers on the history of Republican China). Taipei: Nantian shuju, 1990.

Li Huang. *Xue dun shi Huiyilu* (Memoirs of Li Huang). Taipei: Zhuanji wenxue chubanshe, 1973.

Li Huaxing, and Wu Jiayi, eds. *Liang Qichao xuanji* (Selected writings of Liang Qichao). Shanghai: Shanghai renmin chubanshe, 1984.

Li Longmu. *Wu-si shiqi sixiang shilun* (On political thought of the May Fourth period). Shanghai: Fudan daxue chubanshe, 1990.

Li Shizeng. *Li Shizeng xiansheng wenji* (Li Shizeng's collected writings). Taipei: Zhongguo Guomindang zhongyang weiyuanhui, 1980.

Shi seng biji (Notebooks of Li Shizeng). Taipei: zhong guo guo ji wen xue xue kan she, 1961.

Li Shuyuan. *Ruoan zongtong Li Yuanhong* (Weak President Li Yuanhong). Changchun: Jilin wenshi chubanshe, 1995.

Li Xin, and Li Zongyi, eds. *Zhonghua ninguo shi* (History of Republican China). 2 vols. Beijing: Zhonghua shuju, 1987.

Li Xisuo, and Yuan Qing. *Liang Qichao zhuan* (Biography of Liang Qichao). Beijing: Renmin chubanshe, 1993.

Li Yuanhong. *Li fuzongtong shu du huibian* (Selections from Vice-president Li Yuanhong's letters and documents). Taipei: Wenhai chubanshe, 1988.

Li Yushu, *Zhong-Ri ershiyi tiao jiaoshe* (Sino-Japanese negotiations over the Twenty-one Demands). Taipei: Zhongyang yanjiuyuan jindai shi yanjiusuo, Academia sinica, vol. I, 1966.

Li Zongtong. "Bali Zhongguo liu xuesheng ji gongren fandui dui De heyue qiangzi de jingguo" (The story of how Chinese students and workers in Paris opposed the Chinese delegation's signing of the Treaty of Versailles). *Zhuanji wenxue* 6, no. 6 (1965): 41–43.

Li Zongyi. *Yuan Shikai zhuan* (Biography of Yuan Shikai). Beijing: Zhonghua shuju, 1980.

Liang Jingchun. "Wo suo zhidao de Wu-si yundong" (What I knew about the May Fourth Movement). *Zhuanji wenxue* 8, no. 5 (1966): 4–8.

Liang Qichao. *Yin bing shi heji* (Collected writings of Liang Qichao). Beijing: Zhonghua shuju, 1989.

Xin min shuo (On New Citizenship). Taipei: Zhonghua shuju, 1959.

"Ouzhan hou sixiang bianqian zhi yanshuo" (Speech on intellectual changes in the post-European War). *Shen bao*, November 11, 1914, 6.

Liang Rengong yanshuoji (Liang Qichao's collected speeches). Shanghai guomin shuju, 1925.

Liaoning sheng danganguan lishibu. "You guan Zhong-De duanjiao de yizu zi liao" (Several documents relating to China's breaking relations with Germany). *Minguo dangan* 1 (1991).

Liao Yizhong. *Yidai xiao xiong Yuan Shikai* (Biography of Yuan Shikai). Beijing tushuguan chubanshe, 1997.

Liao Yizhong, Luo Zhenrong, Tianjin tushuguan, and Tianjin shehui kexueyuan lishi yanjiusuo. *Yuan Shikai zou yi* (Yuan Shikai's memorials to the court). Tianjin guji chubanshe, 1987.

Liu Guang, and Fan Zhou. *Guan chang bai chou tu: Beiyang junfa milu* (Secret stories of Beiyang warlords). Hunan chubanshe, 1992.

Liu Ou zazhi she, and Chen Sanjing, eds. *Liu Ou jiao-yu yundong* (China's work-study movent in Europe). Taipei: Zhongyang yanjiuyuan jindai shi yanjiusuo, Academia Sinica, 1996.

Liu Shoulin, ed. *Xinhai yihou shiqi nian zhi guan nianbiao* (Chronological tables of high office holders for the period from 1912 to 1928). Beijing: Zhonghua shuju, 1966.

Liu Shoulin et al. eds. *Minguo zhi guan nianbiao* (Chronological tables of high office holders in Republican China). Beijing: Zhonghua shuju, 1995.

Liu Yan. *Zhongguo Waijiao shi* (Diplomatic history of China). Taipei: Sanmin shuju, 1962.

Liu Zhenlan, and Zhang Shuyong. *Kuilei zongtong Li Yuanhong* (Puppet President Li Yuanhong). Henan renmin chubanshe, 1990.

Lu Xun. *Lu Xun quanji* (Complete writings of Lu Xun). Beijing: Renmin wenxie chubanshe, 1982.

Lu Zengyu, *Wushi zi shu* (Memoir of the fifty-year-old man). (n.p., n.d.).

Luo Guang. *Lu Zhengxiang zhuan* (Biography of Lu Zhengxian). Taipei: Shangwu yinshuguan, 1966.

Peng Ming. *Wu-si yundong shi* (History of the May Fourth Movement). Beijing: Renmin chubanshe, 1984.

Qi Qizhang, and Wang Yuhui, eds. *Jia Wu zhanzheng yu jindai Zhongguo he shijie* (The impact of the Sino-Japanese War of 1895 on modern China and its relations with the world). Beijing: Renmin chubanshe, 1995.

Ren Guangchun. *Wu-si hongbo qu* (The May Fourth Movement). Beijing: Shidai wenyi chubanshe, 1991.

Rong Mengyuan, and Zhang Bofeng, eds. *Jindai bihai* (Materials on modern China). Chengdu: Sichuan renmin chubanshe, 1985.

Shen Yunlong, ed. *Xiandai zhengzhi renwu shuping* (Critical biographies of modern political figures). Taipei: Wenhai chubanshe, 1966.

Sima Qian. "Qinshihuang benji" (The annals of the First Emperor of Qin). In *Shiji* (Records of the Grand Historian). Hong Kong: Zhonghua shuju, 1969.

Su Wenzhuo, ed. *Liang Tan Yuying ju shi suo cang shu han tu zhao ying cun* (Collections of letters and photographs collected by Liang Tanyu). Hong Kong, 1986.

Sun Yao, ed. *Zhonghua minguo shiliao* (Historical records of Republican China). Taipei: Wenhai chubanshe, 1966.

Sun Yat-sen. *Sun Zhongshan xuanji* (Selected writings of Sun Yat-sen). Beijing: Renmin chubanshe, 1981.

Sun Zhongshan quanji (Complete writings of Sun Zhongshan). Beijing: Zhonghua shuju, 1985.

Zhongguo cunwang wenti (Questions of China's survival). Shanghai: Mingzhi shuju, 1928.

Tang Qihua. *Beijing zhengfu yu Guoji lianmeng, 1919–1928* (Beijing government and the League of Nations). Taipei: Dongda tushu gongsi: 1998.

Tang Yijie. *Lun chuantong yu fan chuantong: Wu-si 70 zhou nian jinian wenxuan* (Selected papers in commemoration of the 70th anniversary of the May Fourth Movement). Taipei: Lianjing chuban shiye gongsi, 1989.

Tang Zhengchan. *Cai Yuanpei zhuan* (Biography of Cai Yuanpei). Shanghai: Shanghai renmin chubanshe, 1985.

Tang Zhijun, ed. *Kang Youwei zhenglunji* (Collection of Kang Youwei's writings on politics). Beijing: Zhonghua shuju, 1981.

Tao Jin-Shen. *Two Sons of Heaven: Studies in Sung-Liao Relations*. Tucson: The University of Arizona Press, 1988.

Tao Juyin. *Beiyang junfa tongzhi shiqi shihua* (History of the period of Warlord governments). Beijing: Shenghuo dushu xinzhi sanlian shudian, 1983.

Dujun tuan zhuan (Biographies of the corps of military governors). Taipei: Wenhai chubanshe, 1971.

Tianjin shi danganguan, ed. *Yuan Shikai Tianjin dangan shiliao xuanbian* (Selections of archival materials on Yuan Shikai found in Tianjin). Tianjin guji chubanshe, 1990.

Tong Te-kong. *Wan Qing qishi nian* (The last seventy years of the Qing). Taipei: Yuanliu chuban shiye gufen youxian gongsi, 1998.

Wan Renyuan, and Zhongguo dier lishi danganguan. *Yuan Shikai yu Beiyang junfa* (Yuan Shikai and the Beiyang warlords). Hong Kong: Shangwu yinshuguan, 1994.

Wang Gangling. *Ouzhan shiqi de Meiguo dui Hua zhengce* (America's China policy during the First World War). Taipei: Xuesheng shuju, 1988.

Wang Kaiyun. *Xiangyilou riji* (Wang Kaiyun's Diary). Taipei: Xuesheng shuju, 1964.

Wang Qisheng. *Zhongguo liuxuesheng de lishi guiji* (A history of Chinese returned students). Wu Han: Hubei jiaoyu chubanshe, 1992.

Wang Shi, ed. *Yan Fu ji* (Collected writings of Yan Fu). 3 vols. Beijing: Zhonghua shuju, 1986.

Wang Yigong. *Tianjin shi lishi bowuguan guancang Beiyang junfa shiliao* (Archival materials about Beiyang warlords collected in the Tianjin museum). Tianjin guji chubanshe, 1996.

Wang Yuanhua. *Chuantong yu fan chuantong* (Tradition and anti-tradition). Shanghai wenyi chubanshe, 1990.

Wang Yunsheng. *Liushi nian lai Zhongguo yu Riben* (China and Japan over the last sixty years). Beijing: Sanlian shudian, 1980.

Weng Tonghe. *Weng Tonghe riji* (Weng Tonghe's Diary). Beijing: Zhonghua shuju, 1989.

Wo Qiu zhongzi (Fei Jingzhong). *Duan Qirui* (A biography of Duan Qirui). Shanghai: Shijie shuju, 1921.

Wu Changyi. *83 tian huang di meng* (Yuan Shikai's 83-day dream of becoming emperor). Beijing: Wenshi ziliao chubanshe, 1983.

Wu Dongzhi, ed. *Zhong Guo Wai Jiao Shi* (Diplomatic History of China, 1911–1949). Kaifeng: Henan renmin chubanshe, 1990.

Wu Xiangxiang. *Yan Yangchu zhuan* (Biography of Yan Yangchu). Taipei: Shibao wenhua shiye gongsi, 1981.

Xia'an hui gao nianpu bianyinhui, ed. *Ye Xia'an xianshen nianpu* (A chronological life of Ye Xiaan). Shanghai: Xia'an hui gao nianpu bianyinhui, 1946.

Xiao Chaoran. *Beijing daxue yu Wu-si yundong* (Peking University and the May Fourth Movement). Beijing daxue chubanshe, 1995.

Xie Benshu. *Yuan Shikai yu Beiyang junfa* (Yuan Shikai and the Beiyang warlords). Shanghai: Shanghai renmin chubanshe, 1984.

Xu Daoling, ed. *Xu Shuzheng xiansheng wenji nianpu hekan* (Xu Shuzheng's writings and chronology). Taipei: Shangwu yinshuguan, 1962.

Xu Dingxin, and Qiang Xiaomin. *Shanghai zong shanghui shi* (History of the Shanghai general chamber of commerce). Shanghai: Shanghai shehui kexueyuan chubanshe, 1991.

Xu Gang. *Feng yu Qionglou: Yuan Shikai chenfu* (The rise and fall of Yuan Shikai). Beijing: Zhongguo qingnian chubanshe, 1994.

Xu Guoqi. "Zhongguo canzhan Huagong yanjiu" (Laborers as soldiers: China's contribution to the First World War). *Ershi yishiji* (The twenty-first century, Hong Kong) 62 (2000): 53–62.

"Zhongguo zhishi fenzi dui Wudeluo Weierxun de fangyin, 1917–1919" (Chinese intellectuals' response to Woodrow Wilson), *Lishi jiaoxue* 10 (1989).

Xu, Guoqi et al. *Meiguo waijiao zhengce shi, 1775–1989* (A history of American foreign policy). Beijing: Renmin chubanshe, 1991.

Xu Qing, Liu Hong, and Wu Shaoquan. *Beiyang sanjie: Wang Shizhen, Duan Qirui, Feng Guozhang hezhuan* (Combined biography of Wang Shizhen, Duan Qirui, and Feng Guozhang). Beijing: Guangming ribao chubanshe, 1993.

Xu Shichang. *Ouzhan hou zhi Zhongguo* (China after the European war). Taipei: Wenhai chubanshe, 1966.

Xu Tian (Zhang Guogan). "Dui De-Ou canzhan" (China's declaration of war on Germany and Austria). *Jindai shi ziliao* (Materials on modern history) 2 (1954).

Yang Du. *Yang Du ji* (Yang Du's collected writings). Changsha: Hunan renmin chubanshe, 1986.

Yang Du riji, 1896–1900 (Diary of Yang Du). Beijing: Beijing dananguan, 2001.

Yang Kailing, ed. *Minguo Li Shizeng xiansheng nianpu* (Chronology of Li Shizeng). Taipei: Taiwan shangwu yinshuguan, 1980.

Yong Dingcheng. "Junhuo mai ban Yong Jianqiu de yi sheng" (Life of arms and munitions merchant Yong Jianqiu). In *Wenshi ziliao xuanji* (Selected Materials on Literature and History). Beijing: Wenshi ziliao chubanshe, 1981.

Yu Baotang. "Jiang Jieshi yu Sun Zhongshan" (Jiang Jieshi and Sun Yat-sen). *Minguo dangan* 4 (1990).

Yuan Daofen. *Gu Weijun zhuanji* (Biography of Wellington Koo). Taipei: Shangwu chubanshe, 1987.

Yuan Jingxue, and Yuan Keqi. *Yuan Shikai mixin* (Secret letters of Yuan Shikai). Taipei: Dong-Xi wenhua shiye gongsi, 1986.

Yuan Shikai. *Yuan Shikai weikan shuxin shougao* (Unpublished handwritten letters of Yuan Shikai). Beijing: Zhonghua quanguo tushuguan wenxian suowei fuzhi zhongxin, 1998.

Zeng Leshan. *Wu-si shiqi Chen Duxiu sixiang yanjiu* (A study of Chen Duxiu's political thinking during the May Fourth Movement). Fuzhou: Fujian renmin chubanshe, 1983.

Zeng Shubai. *Zhongguo xinwen shi* (History of Chinese journalism). Taipei: Taiwan Shangwu yinshuguan, 1966.

Zhang Bofeng. "Shilun 1917 nian suowei 'canzhan wenti' de shizhi" (A preliminary study of China's so-called entry into the war in 1917), in *Shixue yuekan*, March 1965.

Zhang Bofeng, Li Zhongyi, Wen Liming, Li Xuetong, and Wang Shanzhong. *Beiyang junfa, 1912–1928* (Archival materials on Beiyang warlords). Wuhan: Wuhan chubanshe, 1990.

Zhang Chunlun. "Gu Weijun de hehui waijiao: Yi shouhui Shangdong zhuquan wenti wei zhongxin" (Wellington Koo at the peace conference: Focus on the return of the Shandong sovereignty). *Zhongyang yanjiuyuan jindai shi yanjiusuo jikan* 23, no. 2 (1994).

Zhang Guogan. "Jin Dai Shi Pian Duan De Ji Lu" (Random memory of a certain portion of modern history). In *Jindai shi ziliao* (Materials on modern history). Beijing: Zhonghua shuju, 1978.

Zhang Guogan wenji (Zhang Guogan's collected writings). Beijing: Beijing yanshan chubanshe, 2000.

Zhang Hongxiang, Wang Yongxiang, and Gao Defu. *Wu-si yundong yu Zhongguo Gongchandang de dan sheng* (The May Fourth Movement and the birth of the Chinese Communist Party). Tianjin shehui kexueyuan chubanshe, 1991.

Zhang Junmai. *Zhong Xi Yin zhexue wenji* (Collected works on the philosophy of China, the West, and India). Edited by Chen Wenxi. Taipei: Xuesheng shuju, 1981.

Zhang Li. *Guoji hezuo zai Zhongguo: Guoji Lianmeng jiaose de kaocha, 1919–1946* (International cooperation and China: a study of the League of Nations). Taipei: Zhongyang yanjiuyuan jindai shi yanjiusuo, 1999.

Zhang Nan, and Wang Rongzhi, eds. *Xinhai geming qian shi nian jian shilun xuanji* (A collection of discussions of issues in the ten years before the 1911 Revolution). Beijing: Sanlian shudian, 1960.

Zhang Pinxing, ed. *Liang Qichao jiashu* (Family letters of Liang Qichao). Beijing: Zhongguo wenlian chubanshe, 2000.

Zhang Shizhao. "Jiaru Ouzhan zhi yijian" (Suggestions on [China's] Participation in the European War, February 10, 1917). In *Jia Yin zazhi cungao* (Existing manuscripts of the Tiger Magazine). Taipei: Wenhai chubanshe, 1977.

Zhang Weihan, and Yuan Zhongshu, eds., *Yuan Shikai shiliao huikan* (Selected archival materials on Yuan Shikai). Taipei: Wenhai chubanshe, 1967.

Zhang Xia, Sun Baoming, and Chen Changhe. *Beiyang lujun shiliao, 1912–1916* (Archival materials on the Beiyang army). Tianjin renmin chubanshe, 1987.

Zhang Yilin. *Xin Taiping (shi ji)* (Zhang Yilin's collected writings). Taipei: Wenhai chubanshe, 1966.

Zhang Yufa. "Xin wenhua yundong shiqi de xinwen yu yanlun, 1915–1923" (News reporting and public opinion during the period of the New Cultural Movement). *Zhongyang yanjiuyuan jindai shi yanjiusuo jikan* 23 (1993): 285–329.

Zhonghua minguo shigao (Draft history of Republican China). Taipei: Lianjin chuban shiye gong si, 1998.

Minguo chunian de zhengdang (Political parties in early Republican China). Taipei: Zhongyang yanjiuyuan jindai shi yanjiusuo, 1985.

Zhang Yunqiao. *Wu Tingfang yu Qing mo zhengzhi gaige* (Wu Tingfang and the late Qing's political reforms). Taipei: Lianjing chuban shiye gongsi, 1987.

Zhang, Zhongfu. *Zhonghua minguo waijiao shi* (Diplomatic history of Republican China). Shanghai: Shanghai renmin chubanshe, 1983.

Zhang Zongxiang. "Dongjing zhi san nian" (My three years in Tokyo). *Jindai shi ziliao (Materials on modern history)* 38 (1979).

Zheng Xiaoxu. "Zheng Xiaoxu Bing Ding Riji" (Diary of Zheng Xiaoxu). *Jindai shi ziliao (Materials on modern history)* 35.

Zhongguo renmin zhengzhi xieshang huiyi quanguo weiyuanhui, Wenshi ziliao weiyuanhui. *Minguo da zongtong Li Yuanhong* (President Li Yuanhong). Beijing: Zhongguo wenshi chubanshe, 1991.

Wu-si Yundong qin liji (Witness to the May Fourth Movement). Beijing: Zhongguo wenshi chubanshe, 1999.

Zhongguo shixuehui, ed. *Xinhai geming* (The 1911 Revolution). Shanghai renmin chubanshe, 1961.

Zhongguo dier lishi danganguan, ed. "1916 Nian Zhengjiatun Zhong-Ri jundui shijian jiaoshe wenjianxuan" (Selected documents regarding the Zhengjiatun Incident). *Minguo dangan* (Archives of Republican China), 1992.

Zhonghua minguo shi ziliao huibian: Disanji, waijiao (Collections of archival materials on Republican China: Vol. III, Foreign Relations). Nanjing: Jiangsu guji chubanshe, 1991.

Zhonghua minguo shi dangan ziliao huibian: Disanji, zhengzhi (Collections of archival materials on Republican China: Vol. III, Politics). Nanjing: Jiangsu guji chubanshe, 1991.

Beiyang junfa tongzhi shi qi de bingbian (Mutinies in the era of the Beiyang warlords). Nanjing: Jiangsu renmin chubanshe, 1982.

Zhongguo shehui kexueyuan jindai shi yanjiusuo, ed. *Wu-si yundong huiyilu* (Recollections of the May Fourth Movement). Beijing: Zhongguo shehui kexue chubanshe, 1979.

Zhongguo shehui kexueyuan jindai shi yanjiusuo, Jindai shi ziliao bianjishi, and Tianjin shi lishi bowuguan, ed. *Miji lucun* (Collections of secret documents). Beijing: Zhongguo shehui kexue chubanshe, 1984.

Zhongyang yanjiuyuan jindai shi yanjiusuo, ed., *Yuan Shikai jiashu* (Yuan Shikai's family letters). Taipei: Zhongyang yanjiuyuan jindai shi yanjiusuo, 1990.

Zhong-Ri guanxi shiliao: Ershiyi tiao jiaoshe (Archival materials on Sino-Japanese negotiations: the Twenty-one Demands), 2 vols., Taipei: Zhongyang yanjiuyuan jindai shi yanjiusuo, 1985.

Zhong-Ri guanxi shiliao: Dongbei wenti (Archival materials on Sino-Japanese negotiations: the Manchuria question). Taipei: Zhongyang yanjiuyuan jindai shi yanjiusuo, 1989.

Zhong-Ri guanxi shiliao: Junshi waijiao jiaoshe (Archival materials on Sino-Japanese negotiations: military and diplomatic issues). Zhongyang yanjiuyuan jindai shi yanjiusuo, 1996.

Zhong-Ri guanxi shiliao: Yiban jiaoshe (Archival materials on Sino-Japanese negotiations: general issues). Zhongyang yanjiuyuan jindai shi yanjiusuo, 1986.

Zhong-Ri guanxi shiliao: Ouzhan yu Shandong wenti (Archival materials on Sino-Japanese negotiations: the European war and the Shandong question). Zhongyang yanjiuyuan jindai shi yanjiusuo, 1974.

Zhou Jianchao. Gu Weijun yu Bali hehui (Wellington Koo and the Paris Peace Conference), *Minguo dang an* 1 (1997).

Zhu Laichang, and Nie Wanhui. *Beiyang junfa he Minguo jianli* (Beiyang warlords and the founding of the Republican China). Hefei: Anhui renmin chubanshe, 1981.

Zhu Ying, "Qing mo xinxing shangren ji minjian shehui (The new type of business people and civil society in the late Qing)," *Ershi yishiji* (The twenty-first century, Hong Kong, 1991), 3: 37–44.

PUBLISHED SOURCES IN ENGLISH

Almond, G. A. *The American People and Foreign Policy*. New York: Frederick Praeger, 1960.

Anderson, Benedict. *Imagined Communities: Reflections on the Origin and Spread of Nationalism*. New York: Verso, 1991.

Arendt, Hannah. *On Revolution*. New York: The Viking Press, 1963.

Armstrong, J. D. *Revolution and World Order: The Revolutionary State in International Society*. New York: Oxford University Press, 1993.

Atwood, Albert W. "Our Forgotten Socialism." *The Saturday Evening Post* 192, no. 4 (1919).

Bailey, Paul. "The Chinese Work-Study Movement in France." *The China Quarterly* 115 (1988).

Bailey, Thomas. *The Man in the Street*. New York: Macmillan Company, 1948.

Baker, Keith Michael. *Inventing the French Revolution*. Cambridge: Cambridge University Press, 1990.

Baker, Ray Stannard. *What Wilson Did at Paris*. Garden City: Doubleday, Page, & Company, 1919.

Bastid-Bruguière, Marianne. "France and the 1915–1916 National Protection Movement," paper presented to Centennial Symposium on Sun Yat-sen's Foundation of the Kuomintang for Revolution, Taipei: November 19–23, 1994.

Beers, Burton F. *Vain Endeavor: Robert Lansing's Attempts to End the American-Japanese Rivalry*. Durham, NC: Duke University Press, 1962.

Bergère, Marie-Claire. *Sun Yat-Sen*. Translated by Janet Lloyd. Stanford: Stanford University Press, 1998.

The Golden Age of the Chinese Bourgeoisie, 1911–1937. Cambridge: Cambridge University Press, 1989.

Bianco, Lucian. *Origins of the Chinese Revolution, 1915–1949*. Stanford: Stanford University Press, 1971.

Billig, Michael. *Banal Nationalism*. London: Sage Publications, 1995.

Blick, Judith. "The Chinese Labor Corps in World War I." *Papers on China (from Harvard East Asia Regional Studies Seminar)* 9 (1955): 111–45.

Bloom, William. *Personal Identity, National Identity and International Relations.* Cambridge: Cambridge University Press, 1990.

Blythe, Samuel G. "Banzai and Then What?" *The Saturday Evening Post* 187, no. 47 (1915).

——— "The Chinese Puzzle: A Talk on Policies and Conditions with the President of China." *The Saturday Evening Post* 187, no. 46 (1915).

——— "The First Time in Five Thousand Years." *The Saturday Evening Post* 189, no. 44 (1917).

——— "A Talk with the Japanese Premier." *The Saturday Evening Post* 187, no. 45 (1915).

Boerner, Peter, ed. *Concepts of National Identity: An Interdisciplinary Dialogue.* Baden-Baden: Nomos, 1986.

Bonsal, S. *Suitors and Supplicants: The Little Nations at Versailles.* New York: Prentice-Hall, 1946.

Bourne, Kenneth, and Ann Trotter, eds. *British Documents on Foreign Affairs: Reports and Papers from the Foreign Office Confidential Print: Part II, From the First to the Second World War, Series E, Asia, 1914–1939,* vols. XXII, XXIII. Bethesda, MD: University Publications of America, 1994.

Breuilly, John. *Nationalism and the State.* Chicago: University of Chicago Press, 1994.

Britton, Roswell S. *The Chinese Periodical Press, 1800–1912.* Kelly & Walsh Limited., 1933.

Brødsgaard, Kjeld Erik, and David Strand. *Reconstructing Twentieth-Century China: State Control, Civil Society, and National Identity.* New York: Oxford University Press, 1998.

Burdick, Charles B. *The Japanese Siege of Tsingtau.* Hamden, CT: Shoe String Press, Inc., 1976.

Chand, Mool. *Nationalism and Internationalism of Gandhi, Nehru and Tagore.* New Delhi: M.N. Publishers and distributors, 1989.

Chang, Carsun. "Inside History of China's Declaration of War." *Millard's Review* 5, no. 12 (1918).

Chang, Hao. *Liang Chi-Ch'ao and Intellectual Transition in China, 1890–1907.* Cambridge, MA: Harvard University Press, 1971.

Chartier, Roger. *The Cultural Origins of the French Revolution.* Durham, NC: Duke University Press, 1991.

Chen, Jerome. *Yuan Shih-Kai.* Stanford: Stanford University Press, 1972.

Chen, Jiang. "Western Learning and Social Transformation in the Late Qing." In *China's Quest for Modernization: A Historical Perspective,* ed. Frederic Wakeman and Wang Xi. Berkeley, California: University of California Press, 1997.

Chen, Ta. *Chinese Migrations, with Special Reference to Labor Conditions, 1919–1927.* Washington, DC: Government Printing Office, 1923.

Chesneaux, Jean. *The Chinese Labor Movement: 1919–1927.* Translated from the French by H. M. Wright. Stanford: Stanford University Press, 1968.

Chi, Madeleine. *China Diplomacy, 1914–1918.* Cambridge, MA: East Asian monographs, distributed by Harvard University Press, 1970.

Chinese foreign ministry (Waichiaopu), ed. *Official Documents Relating to the War.* Beijing: Printed by the "Peking Leader" Press, 1918.

Diplomatic Documents: Sino-Japanese Agreements for Common Defense. Beijing: The Waichiopu Press, 1921.

"Chinese Labour Corps Bravery, a Very Gallant Act." *The North China Herald* 132 (1919): 631.

Chinese National Welfare Society in America, ed. *The Shantung Question: A Statement of China's Claim Together with Important Documents Submitted to the Peace Conference in Paris.* San Francisco: Press of Ramsey Oppenheim Co., 1919.

Chou, Tse-tsung. *The May Fourth Movement: Intellectual Revolution in Modern China.* Cambridge, MA: Harvard University Press, 1960.

Chu, Pao-chin. *V. K. Wellington Koo: A Case Study of China's Diplomat and Diplomacy of Nationalism, 1912–1966.* Hong Kong: Chinese University Press, 1981.

Ci, Jiwei. *Dialectic of the Chinese Revolution: From Utopianism to Hedonism.* Stanford: Stanford University Press, 1994.

Clemenceau, Georges. "The Cause of France." *The Saturday Evening Post* 187, no. 17 (1914).

Cohen, Bernard C. *The Press and Foreign Policy.* Princeton: Princeton University Press, 1963.

Cohen, Paul A. "Remembering and Forgetting: National Humiliation in Twentieth-Century China." *Twentieth-Century China* 27, no. 2 (2002): 1–39.

Craft, Stephen G. "Angling for an Invitation to Paris: China's Entry into the First World War." *The International History Review* 16, no. 1 (1994).

"John Bassett Moore, Robert Lansing, and the Shandong Question." *Pacific Historical Review* 16, no. 2 (1997).

Cross, Gary S. "Toward Social Peace and Prosperity: The Politics of Immigration in France During the Era of World War I." *French Historical Studies* 11, no. 4 (1980): 610–32.

Crossley, Pamela. *A Translucent Mirror: History and Identity in Qing Imperial Ideology.* Berkeley: University of California Press, 1999.

Darroch, John. "The China Labourer's Reading." *The North China Herald,* August 3, 1918, 286.

Daruvala, Susan. *Zhou Zuoren and an Alternative Chinese Response to Modernity.* Cambridge, MA: Harvard University Asia Center, 2000.

DeFrancis, John. *Nationalism and Language Reform in China.* New York: Octagon Books, 1972.

Dickens, Charles. *A Tale of Two Cities.* Oxford: Oxford University Press, 1989.

Dickinson, Frederick R. *War and National Reinvention: Japan in the Great War, 1914–1919.* Cambridge, MA: The Harvard East Asia Center, 1999.

Dikötter, Frank. *The Discourse of Race in Modern China.* London: Hurst & Company, 1992.

Dillon, E. J. *The Inside Story of the Peace Conference.* New York: Harper & Brothers Publishers, 1920.

Dirlik, Arif. *Anarchism in the Chinese Revolution.* Berkeley: University of California Press, 1991.

The Origins of Chinese Communism. Oxford: Oxford University Press, 1989.

Dittmer, Lowell, and Samuel S. Kim, eds. *China's Quest for National Identity.* Ithaca: Cornell University Press, 1993.

Dolezelová-Velingerová, Milena, Oldrich Král, and Graham Martin Sanders. *The Appropriation of Cultural Capital: China's May Fourth Movement.* Cambridge, MA: Harvard University Asia Center, 2001.

Duara, Prasenjit. *Rescuing History from the Nation, Questioning Narratives of Modern China.* Chicago: University of Chicago Press, 1995.

Eisenstein, Elizabeth L. *The Printing Press as an Agent of Change: Communications and Cultural Transformations in Early Modern Europe.* Cambridge: Cambridge University Press, 1979.

Eliot, Charles William. *Some Roads Towards Peace; A Report to the Trustees of the Endowment on Observations Made in China and Japan in 1912.* Washington, DC: The Endowment, 1914.

Elleman, Bruce A. *Wilson and China: A Revised History of the Shandong Question*: M. E. Sharpe, 2002.

Erikson, Erik. *Identity: Youth and Crisis.* New York: W. W. Norton & Company, 1968.

Childhood and Society. New York: Norton, 1963.

Esherick, Joseph. *Remaking the Chinese City: Modernity and National Identity, 1900–1950.* Honolulu: University of Hawaii Press, 2000.

Fairbank, John King. "A Preliminary Framework." In *Chinese World Order: Traditional China's Foreign Relations.* Cambridge, MA: Harvard University Press, 1968.

Ferguson, Niall. *The Pity of War.* London: The Penguin Group, 1999.

Fifield, Russell H. *Woodrow Wilson and the Far East: the Diplomacy of the Shantung Question.* Hamden, CT: Archon Books, 1965.

Finer, S. E. *The Man on Horseback: The Role of the Military in Politics.* Boulder, CO: Westview Press, 1988.

Fitzgerald, C. P. *The Birth of Communist China.* London: Penguin Books, 1964.

Fitzgerald, John. *Awakening China: Politics, Culture, and Class in the Nationalist Revolution.* Stanford: Stanford University Press, 1996.

Franke, Wolfgang. *China and the West.* Columbia: University of South Carolina Press, 1967.

The Reform and Abolition of the Traditional Chinese Examination System. Cambridge, MA: Harvard University Press, 1963.

Friedman, Edward. *Backwards toward Revolution: The Chinese Revolutionary Party.* Berkeley: University of California Press, 1974.

Frodsham, J. D. (translator and annotator), ed. *The First Chinese Embassy to the West: The Journals of Kuo Sung-T'ao, Liu Hsi-Hung and Chang Tê-Yi*: Oxford: Clarendon Press, 1974.

Fussell, Paul. *The Great War and Modern Memory.* New York: Oxford University Press, 1975.

Gasster, Michael. *Chinese Intellectuals and the Revolution of 1911: The Birth of Modern Chinese Radicalism.* Seattle: University of Washington Press, 1969.

Gibbs, Mark J. "Recombination in the Hemagglutinin Gene of 1918 'Spanish Flu.' " *Science* 293, no. 5536 (2001): 1842–45.

Gilbert, Martin. *The First World War: A Complete History*. New York: Henry Holt and Company, 1994.

Gillis, John R. *Commemorations: The Politics of National Identity*. Princeton: Princeton University Press, 1994.

Goodman, Bryna. *Native Place, City, and Nation: Regional Networks and Identities in Shanghai, 1853–1937*. Berkeley: University of California Press, 1995.

Grey, Edward. *Twenty-Five Years, 1892–1916*. New York: Frederick A. Stokes Company, 1925.

Gull, B. Manico. "The Story of the Chinese Labor Corps." *The Far Eastern Review* 15, no. 4 (1918): 125–35.

Harrell, Paula. *Sowing the Seeds of Change: Chinese Students, Japanese Teachers, 1895–1905*. Stanford: Stanford University Press, 1992.

Harrison, Henrietta. *China*. London: Arnold Publishers, 2001.

The Making of the Republican Citizen: Political Ceremonies and Symbols in China, 1911–1929. Oxford: Oxford University Press, 2000.

Hayford, Charles Wishart. *To the People: James Yen and Village China*. New York: Columbia University Press, 1990.

Hevia, James L. *Cherishing Men from Afar: Qing Guest Ritual and the McCartney Embassy of 1793*, Durham, NC: Duke University Press, 1995.

Hodgkin, Henry T. *China in the Family of Nations*. London: George Allen & Unwin Ltd., 1923.

Horne, John. "Immigrant Workers in France During World War I." *French Historical Studies* 14, no. 1 (1985): 57–88.

Hoston, G. *The State, Identity, and the National Question in China and Japan*. Princeton: Princeton University Press, 1994.

House, Edward M., and Charles Seymour, eds. *What Really Happened at Paris*. New York: Charles Scribner's Sons, 1921.

Howard, Michael. "The Great War: Mystery or Error?" *The National Interest* 64 (2001): 78–84.

Hoyt, Edward P. *The Fall of Tsingtao*. London: Arthur Barker Limited, 1975.

Hsu, Immanuel C. Y. *China's Entrance into the Family of Nations: The Diplomatic Phase, 1858–1880*. Cambridge, MA: Harvard University Press, 1960.

Huntington, Samuel P. *Political Order in Changing Societies*. New Haven: Yale University Press, 1968.

The Soldier and the State. Cambridge, MA: Harvard University Press, 1957.

Iriye, Akira. *Cultural Internationalism and World Order*. Baltimore: Johns Hopkins University Press, 1997.

"Culture and International History." In *Explaining the History of American Foreign Relations*, ed. Michael J. Hogan and Thomas G. Paterson, 214–25. Cambridge: Cambridge University Press, 1991.

"Culture and Power: International Relations as Intercultural Relations." *Diplomatic History* 3, no. 3 (1979).

Global Community: The Role of International Organizations in the Making of the Contemporary World. Berkeley: University of California Press, 2002.

"The Internationalization of History." *American Historical Review* 94, no. 1 (1989): 1–10.

Japan and the Wider World: From the Mid-Nineteenth Century to the Present. London: Longman, 1997.

Janowita, Morris. *The Military in the Political Development of Nations: An Essay in Comparative Analysis.* Chicago: University of Chicago Press, 1964.

Jin, Wensi. *Woodrow Wilson, Wellington Koo, and the China Question at the Paris Peace Conference.* Leiden: A. W. Sythoff, 1959.

China and the League of Nations. New York: St. John's University Press, 1965.

China at the Paris Peace Conference in 1919. New York: St. John's University Press, 1961.

Johnson, David G., Andrew J. Nathan, Evelyn Sakakida Rawski, and Judith A. Berling, eds. *Popular Culture in Late Imperial China.* Berkeley: University of California Press, 1985.

Joll, James. *The Origins of the First World War.* London: Longman Group UK Limited, 1984.

Jones, A. Philip. *Britain's Search for Chinese Cooperation in the First World War.* London: Garland Publishing, Inc., 1986.

Judge, Joan. *Print and Politics: "Shibao" and the Culture of Reform in Late Qing China.* Stanford: Stanford University Press, 1996.

"Talent, Virtue, and the Nation: Chinese Nationalism and Female Subjectivities in the Early Twentieth Century." *The American Historical Review* 106, no. 3 (2001).

Karl, Rebecca E. *Staging the World: Chinese Nationalism at the Turn of the Twentieth Century.* Durham, NC: Duke University Press, 2002.

Kawamura, Noriko. *Turbulence in the Pacific: Japanese–U.S. Relations During World War I.* Westport, CT: Praeger Publishers, 2000.

Keegan, John. *The First World War.* New York: Alfred A. Knopf, Inc., 1999.

Kelly, John S. *A Forgotten Conference: the Negotiations at Peking, 1900–1901.* Geneva: Librarie E. Droz, 1963.

Kennedy, David. *Over Here.* New York: Oxford University Press, 1980.

Kennedy, Paul. "The First World War and the International Power System." *International Security* 9, no. 1 (1984): 23–24.

Kirby, William C. *Germany and Republican China.* Stanford: Stanford University Press, 1984.

"The Internationalization of China: Foreign Relations at Home and Abroad in the Republican Era." *The China Quarterly* 150, no. 2 (1997).

"Traditions of Centrality, Authority, and Management in Modern China's Foreign Relations." In *Chinese Foreign Policy: Theory and Practice,* ed. Thomas W. Robinson and David L. Shambaugh. Oxford: Oxford University Press, 1994.

Kissinger, Henry. *A World Restored.* New York: Grosset and Dunlop, 1964.

Klein, Daryl. *With the Chinks.* London: John Lane at the Bodley Head, 1918.

Kohn, Hans. *The Idea of Nationalism, a Study in Its Origins and Background.* New York: The Macmillan Company, 1944.

Koo, Vi Kyuin Wellington, and Ching-Ting Thomas Wang. *China and the League of Nations.* London: G. Allen & Unwin Ltd., 1919.

Kuhn, Philip A. *Origins of the Modern Chinese State.* Stanford: Stanford University Press, 2002.

La Fargue, Thomas Edward. *China and the World War*. Stanford: Stanford University Press, 1937.

La Motte, Ellen Newbold. *Peking Dust*. New York: The Century Co., 1919.

Lansing, Robert. *The Big Four and Others of the Peace Conference*. London: Hutchinson & Co., 1922.

   The Peace Negotiations: A Personal Narrative. Boston: Houghton Mifflin Company, 1921.

   War Memoirs of Robert Lansing. New York: The Bobbs-Merrill Company, 1935.

Latham, J. G. *The Significance of the Peace Conference from an Australian Point of View*. Sydney: Melville & Mullen, 1920.

Lee, Feigon. *Chen Duxiu: Founder of the Chinese Communist Party*. Princeton: Princeton University Press, 1983.

Levenson, Joseph Richmond. *Confucian China and Its Modern Fate: A Trilogy*. Berkeley: University of California Press, 1968.

Levine, Marilyn A. *The Found Generation: Chinese Communists in Europe During the Twenties*. Seattle: University of Washington Press, 1993.

Li, Jiannun. *The Political History of China*. Trans. and ed. Ssu-yu Teng and Jeremy Ingalls. Princeton: Princeton University Press, 1956.

Liang, Qichao. *China and the League of Nations*. Beijing: Society for the Study of International Relations, 1918.

Lin, Yü-sheng. *The Crisis of Chinese Consciousness: Radical Anti-traditionalism in the May Fourth Era*. Madison: University of Wisconsin Press, 1979.

Lin, Yutang, *A History of the Press and Public Opinion in China*. New York: Greenwood Press, 1968.

Link, Arthur, ed. *The Papers of Woodrow Wilson*. Princeton: Princeton University Press, 1966–94.

Liu, Lydia H. *Translingual Practice: Literature, National Culture, and Translated Modernity – China, 1900–1937*. Stanford: Stanford University Press, 1995.

Liu, Zehua, and Liu Jianqing. "Civic Associations, Political Parties, and the Cultivation of Citizenship Consciousness in Modern China." In *Imagining the People: Chinese Intellectuals and the Concept of Citizenship, 1890–1920*, ed. Joshua A. Fogel and Peter Gue Zarrow. Armonk, NY: M. E. Sharpe, 1997.

Lloyd George, David. *War Memoirs of David Lloyd George* (Boston: Little, Brown, and Company), 1933–1937.

Lo, Hui-min, ed. *The Correspondence of G. E. Morrison*. Cambridge: Cambridge University Press, 1976.

Lodwick, Kathleen L. *Crusaders against Opium: Protestant Missionaries in China, 1874–1917*. Lexington, KY: University Press of Kentucky, 1996.

Longman, Jere. "Delegates Hope China Spurs Openness." *The New York Times*, July 14, 2001, B16.

Luo, Zhitian. "National Humiliation and National Assertion: The Chinese Response to the Twenty-one Demands," *Modern Asian Studies* 27, no. 2 (1993): 297–319.

MacNair, Harley Farnsworth. *The Chinese Abroad, Their Position and Protection; a Study in International Law and Relations*. Shanghai: The Commercial Press Limited, 1924.

May, Ernest R. *The World War and American Isolation, 1914–1917*. Cambridge, MA: Harvard University Press, 1966.

May, Henry F. *The End of American Innocence: A Study of the First Years of Our Own Time, 1912–1917*. New York: Columbia University Press, 1992.

McCord, Edward A. *The Power of the Gun: The Emergence of Modern Chinese Warlordism*. Berkeley: University of California Press, 1993.

"Warlords against Warlordism: The Politics of Anti-Militarism in Early Twentieth-Century China." *Modern Asian Studies* 30, no. 4 (1996).

Meisner, Maurice. *Li Ta-chao and the Origins of Chinese Marxism*. Cambridge, MA: Harvard University Press, 1967.

Millard, Thomas. *The Great War in the Far East, with Special Consideration of the Rights and Interests of China and the United States of America*. Shanghai: Printed by the Mercantile Printing Co. Ltd., 1915.

Miller, David Hunter. *The Drafting of the Covenant*. New York: G. P. Putnam's Sons, 1928.

My Diary at the Conference of Paris with Documents. 21 vols. New York: Printed for the author by the Appeal Printing Company, 1924.

Moberly, F. J. *The Campaign in Mesopotamia: 1914–1918*. London: H.M. Stationery Office, 1923–27.

Mowat, Charles L., ed. *The New Cambridge Modern History: Vol. XII, the Shifting Balance of World Forces, 1898–1945*. Cambridge: Cambridge University Press, 1968.

Nakanishi, Hiroshi, and Naoko Shimazu. *Japan and The First World War* (Discussion paper). London School of Economics and Political Science, September 1995.

Nathan, Andrew J. *Chinese Democracy*. New York: Knopf: Distributed by Random House, 1985.

Nicolson, Harold. *Peacemaking 1919*. Boston: Houghton Mifflin Company, 1933.

Paine, S. C. M. *The Sino-Japanese War of 1894–1895: Perceptions, Power, and Primacy*. Cambridge: Cambridge University Press, 2003.

Pan, Lynn. *Sons of the Yellow Emperor, the Story of the Overseas Chinese*. London: Secker & Warburg, 1990.

Pan, Lynn, ed. *The Encyclopedia of the Chinese Overseas*. Singapore: Archipelago Press, 1998.

Pastor, Robert A., ed. *A Century's Journey: How the Great Powers Shape the World*. New York: Basic Books, 1999.

Pearl, Cyril. *Morrison of Peking*. Sydney: Angus and Robertson, 1967.

Peyrefitte, Alain. *Immobile Empire*, trans. J. Rothschild. New York: Alfred A. Knopf, 1992.

Pfaff, William. *The Wrath of Nations: Civilization and the Furies of Nationalism*. New York: Simon & Schuster, 1993.

Pickrell, John. "The 1918 Pandemic: Killer Flu with a Human-Pig Pedigree?" *Science* 292, no. 5519 (2001): 1041.

Pope, Stephen, and Elizabeth-Anne Wheale, eds. *Dictionary of the First World War*. New York: St. Martin's Press, 1995.

Pugach, Noel H. *Paul S. Reinsch, Open Door Diplomat in Action*. Millwood, NY: KTO Press, 1979.

"Embarrassed Monarchist: Frank J. Goodnow and Constitutional Development in China, 1913–1915." *Pacific Historical Review* 42, no. 4 (November 1973).

Pusey, James Reeve. *China and Charles Darwin*. Cambridge, MA: Harvard University Press, 1983.

Pye, Lucian. "Identity and the Political Culture." In *Crises and Sequences in Political Development*, ed. Leonard Binder. Princeton: Princeton University Press, 1971.

Ramsey, S. Robert. *The Languages of China*. Princeton: Princeton University Press, 1987.

Reinsch, Paul Samuel. *An American Diplomat in China*. Garden City, NY: Doubleday Page & Company, 1922.

Lord Riddell et al., *Treaty of Versailles and After*. Oxford: Oxford University Press, 1935.

Robinson, Thomas W., and David L. Shambaugh, *Chinese Foreign Policy: Theory and Practice*. Oxford: Oxford University Press, 1994.

Romero Salvado, Francisco J. *Spain 1914–1918: Between War and Revolution*. London: Routledge, 1999.

Rossabi, Morris. *China among Equals: The Middle Kingdom and Its Neighbors, 10th–14th Centuries*. Berkeley: University of California Press, 1983.

Russell, Bertrand. *The Problem of China*. New York: Century Co., 1922.

Saari, Jon L. *Legacies of Childhood: Growing up Chinese in a Time of Crisis, 1890–1920*. Cambridge, MA: Harvard University Press, 1990.

Salter, Sir James Arthur. *Personality in Politics: Studies of Contemporary Statesmen*. London: Faber and Faber, 1947.

Allied Shipping Control: An Experiment in International Administration. Oxford: Oxford University Press, 1921.

Schacter, Daniel L. *The Seven Sins of Memory: How the Mind Forgets and Remembers*. Boston: Houghton Mifflin Company, 2001.

Schram, Stuart R., ed. *Mao's Road to Power, Revolutionary Writings*. Armonk, NY: M. E. Sharp, 1992.

Schwarcz, Vera. *The Chinese Enlightenment: Intellectuals and the Legacy of the May Fourth Movement of 1919*. Berkeley: University of California Press, 1986.

Schwartz, Benjamin. *In Search of Wealth and Power: Yen Fu and the West*. Cambridge, MA: Harvard University Press, 1964.

Scott, Peter T. "Chinese in France in WW I." *War Monthly* 8, no. 76 (1980): 8–11.

Sheridan, James E. *Chinese Warlord: The Career of Feng Yu-hsiang*. Stanford: Stanford University Press, 1966.

Shimazu, Naoko. *Japan, Race, and Equality: The Racial Equality Propoposal of 1919*. London: Routledge, 1998.

Shotwell, James T. *At the Paris Peace Conference*. New York: The Macmillan Company, 1937.

Simpson, Bertram Lenox. *The Re-Shaping of the Far East*. New York: The Macmillan Company, 1905.

Smith, Anthony D. *National Identity*. Reno: University of Nevada Press, 1991.

Smith, Craig S. "Joyous Vindication and a Sleepless Night." *The New York Times*, July 14, 2001, A 1, B 16.

Smith, Richard J. "Divination in Ch'ing Dynasty China." In *Cosmology, Ontology, and Human Efficacy: Essays in Chinese Thought*, ed. Richard J. Smith and D. W. Y. Kwok. Honolulu: University of Hawaii Press, 1993.

Southall, Robert. *Take Me Back to Dear Old Blighty: The First World War through the Eyes of the Heraldic China Manufacturers*. Horndean, Hants: Milestone Publications, 1982.

Steenbergen, Bart van. "The Condition of Citizenship: An Introduction." In *The Condition of Citizenship*, ed. Bart van Steenbergen. Thousand Oaks, CA: Sage, 1994.

Stone, Lawence. *The Causes of the English Revolution 1529–1642*. New York: Harper Torchbook, 1972.

Summers, C. F. "The Chinese Labour Corps: What They Learned in France." *The North China Herald* 132 (1919): 186–87.

Summerskill, Michael. *China on the Western Front: Britain's Chinese Worker Force in the First World War*. London: n.p., 1982.

Sun, Yat-sen, and Frank W. Price. *San Min Chu I (The Three Principles of the People)*. New York: Da Capo Press, 1975.

Tang, Xiaobing. *Global Space and the Nationalist Discourse of Modernity: The Historical Thinking of Liang Qichao*. Stanford: Stanford University Press, 1996.

Telegrams Received by the Chinese Delegation in Support of Their Stand on the Shantung Question. Paris: Imp. de Vaugirard, 1919.

Teng, Ssu-Yü, and John King Fairbank, eds. *China's Response to the West: A Documentary Survey, 1839–1923*. Cambridge, MA: Harvard University Press, 1954.

The Carnegie Endowment for International Peace, ed. *Shantung: Treaties and Agreements*. Washington, DC: The Carnegie Endowment for International Peace, 1921.

Thompson, Roger R. *China's Local Councils in the Age of Constitutional Reform, 1898–1911*. Cambridge, MA: Harvard University Press, 1995.

Tocqueville, Alexis de. *The Old Regime and the French Revolution*. New York: Doubleday, 1955.

Tory, Douglas. *Tomorrow in the East*. London: Chapman & Hall, 1907.

Tsang, Chiu-sam. *Nationalism in School Education in China*. Hong Kong: Progressive Education Publishers, 1967.

"Nationalism in School Education in China since the Opening of the Twentieth Century." Printed by the South China Morning Post Ltd., 1933.

Tso, S. K. Sheldon. *The Labor Movement in China*. Shanghai: n.p., 1928.

Tung, William L. *V. K. Wellington Koo and China's Wartime Diplomacy*. New York: Center of Asian Studies, St. John's University, 1977.

Tyau, Min-Chien. *Legal Obligations Arising out of Treaty Relations between China and Other States*. Shanghai: Commercial Press, 1917.

China Awakened. New York: The Macmillan Company, 1922.

Unger, Jonathan, and Geremie Barmé, eds. *Chinese Nationalism.* Armonk, NY: M. E. Sharpe, 1996.

US Department of State, ed. *Papers Relating to the Foreign Relations of the United States: 1914–1917 Supplements: The World War.*

The Paris Peace Conference.

The Lansing Papers, 1914–1920.

United States Congress. *Congressional Record,* vols. LIII–LX.

"The Uproar over Shantung." *The Literary Digest* 62, no. 5 (1919): 28–30.

Van de Ven, Hans J. *From Friend to Comrade: the Founding of the Chinese Communist Party, 1920–1927.* Berkeley: University of California Press, 1991.

"Public Finance and the Rise of Warlordism." *Modern Asian Studies* 30, no. 4 (1996): 829–68.

War and Nationalism in China: 1925–1945. London: Routledge Curzon, 2003.

"The Military in the Republic." In *Reappraising Republican China,* ed. Frederic Wakeman, Jr., and Richard Louis Edmonds. Oxford: Oxford University Press, 2000.

Van Ness, Peter. *China as a Third World State: Foreign Policy and Official National Identity.* Canberra: Research School of Pacific Studies, Australian National University, 1991.

Verba, Sidney. "Sequences and Development." In *Crises and Sequences in Political Development,* ed. Leonard Binder, 282–361. Princeton: Princeton University Press, 1971.

Waldron, Arthur. *From War to Nationalism.* Cambridge: Cambridge University Press, 1995.

"The Warlord: Twentieth-Century Chinese Understandings of Violence, Militarism, and Imperialism." *The American Historical Review* 96, no. 4 (1991).

Wallerstein, Immanuel. "The Construction of Peoplehood: Racism, Nationalism, Ethnicity." In *Race, Nation, Class: Ambiguous Identities,* ed. Etienne Balibar and Immanuel Wallerstein. London: Verso Press, 1991.

Wang, Guanhua, *In Search of Justice: The 1905–1906 Chinese Anti-American Boycott.* Cambridge, MA: Harvard University Asia Center, 2001.

Wang, Gunwu. *Chinese Overseas.* Cambridge, MA: Harvard University Press, 2000.

Wang, Q. Edward. *Inventing China through History.* Albany, NY: State University of New York Press, 2001.

Wang, Zhengting. *The League of Nations and China: Extracts from Speeches Delivered by Viscount Bryce* (Wang Zhengting, and Others, at the Caxton Hall, Westminster, May 15, 1919). London, 1919.

War Office, British Government. *Statistics of the Military Efforts of the British Empire During the Great War, 1914–1920.* London: H.M. Stationery Office, 1922.

Wei, Julie Lee, et al., eds. *Prescriptions for Saving China, Selected Writings of Sun Yat-Sen.* Stanford: Hoover Institution Press, 1994.

Wells, H. G. *Mr. Britling Sees It Through.* New York: The Macmillan Company, 1916.

"What the Chinese Learned in the War." *The Literary Digest* 62, no. 11 (1919).

Wheeler, W. Reginald. *China and the World-War.* New York: The Macmillan Company, 1919.

"Why China Did Not Sign." *The Literary Digest* 62, no. 3 (1919).

Wilbur, C. Martin, and Julie Lien-ying How. *Documents on Communism, Nationalism, and Soviet Advisers in China, 1918–1927; Papers Seized in the 1927 Peking Raid*. New York: Columbia University Press, 1956.

Wilmer, Harry B. "Chinese Coolies in France." *The North China Herald*, September 21, 1918, 711–13.

Wilson, Woodrow. *Wei Erxun Canzhan Yanshuo* (War speeches of Woodrow Wilson). Trans. Jiang Menglin. Shanghai: Shangwu yishu guan, 1921.

Winter, J. M. *The Great War and the British People*. London: Macmillan Publishers Ltd., 1986.

Wohl, Robert. *The Generation of 1914*. Cambridge, MA: Harvard University Press, 1979.

Wong, Young-tsu. *Search for Modern Nationalism: Zhang Binglin and Revolutionary China, 1869–1936*. Hong Kong: Oxford University Press, 1989.

Woodward, E. L., et al., eds. *Documents on British Foreign Policy, 1919–1939*. London: H.M. Stationery Office, 1946–85.

Wou, Pen-chung, *Travailleurs Chinois et La Grande Guerre*. Paris: Editions A. Pedone, 1939.

Wright, Mary. *China in Revolution: The First Phase, 1900–1913*. New Haven: Yale University Press, 1968.

Wu, Tingfang. *America and the Americans from a Chinese Point of View*. London: Duckworth, 1914.

Xu, Guoqi: "Internationalism as Nationalism: China During 1895 and 1919." In *Chinese Nationalism in Perspective: Historical and Recent Cases*, ed. George Wei and Xiaoyuan Liu. Westport, CT: Greenwood Publishing Group, 2001.
   "China's Quest for National Identity: A Speculative Essay." In *Harvard Vision: Student Essays on Our Collective Future*, ed. Peter Tse et al. Cambridge, MA: The Dipylon Press, 1996.

Yahuda, Michael. "The Changing Faces of Chinese Nationalism: The Dimensions of Statehood." In *Asian Nationalism*, ed. Michael Leifer. London: Routledge, 2000.

Yan, Huiqing. *East–West Kaleidoscope: 1877–1944: An Autobiography*. New York: St. John's University Press, 1974.

Yeh, Wen-hsin. *Provincial Passages: Culture, Space, and the Origins of Chinese Communism*. Berkeley: University of California Press, 1996.

Yen, Ching-Hwang. *Coolies and Mandarins: China's Protection of Overseas Chinese During the Late Ch'ing Period, 1851–1911*, Singapore University Press, 1985.

Young, Ernest. *The Presidency of Yuan Shih-K'ai: Liberalism and Dictatorship in Early Republican China*. Ann Arbor: The University of Michigan Press, 1977.

Yujiro, Murata. "Dynasty, State, and Society: The Case of Modern China." In *Imagining the People: Chinese Intellectuals and the Concept of Citizenship, 1890–1929*, ed. Joshua A. Fogel and Peter G. Zarrow. Armonk, NY: M. E. Sharpe, 1997.

Zhang, Pengyuan. "Provincial Assemblies: The Emergence of Political Participation." *Zhong yang yan jiu yuan jin dai shi yan jiu suo ji kan* 22 (1983).

Zhang, Yongjin. *China in the International System, 1918–20: The Middle Kingdom at the Periphery*. New York: St. Martin's Press, 1991.

Zhao, Suisheng. "Chinese Nationalism and Its International Orientations." *Political Science Quarterly* 115, no. 1 (Spring 2000): 1–33.

Zheng, Yongnian. *Discovering Chinese Nationalism in China: Modernization, Identity, and International Relations*. Cambridge: Cambridge University Press, 1999.

Zhou, Yongming. *Anti-Drug Crusades in Twentieth-Century China: Nationalism, History, and State Building*. Lanham, MD: Rowman & Littlefield, 1999.

Index

Studies in the Social and Cultural History of Modern Warfare

Titles in the series: